Accounting Classics Series

Editor

ROBERT R. STERLING

University of Kansas

Publication of this Classic was made possible
by a grant from Arthur Andersen & Co.

Suggestions of titles to be included
in the Series are solicited and should
be addressed to the Editor.

ACCOUNTING PUBLICATIONS OF SCHOLARS BOOK CO

Sidney S. Alexander, et al., *Five Monographs on Business Income*
F. Sewell Bray, *The Accounting Mission*
Henry Rand Hatfield, *Accounting: Its Principles and Problems*
Bishop Carlton Hunt (Editor), *George Oliver May: Twenty-Fve Years of Accounting Responsibility*
Kenneth MacNeal, *Truth in Accounting*
George O. May, *Financial Accounting: A Distillation of Experience*
William A. Paton, *Accounting Theory*
William Z. Ripley, *Main Street and Wall Street*
DR Scott, *The Cultural Significance of Accounts*
Charles E. Sprague, *The Philosophy of Accounts*
George Staubus, *A Theory of Accounting to Investors*
Robert R. Sterling (Editor), *Asset Valuation and Income Determination: A Consideration of the Alternatives*
Robert R. Sterling (Editor), *Institutional Issues in Public Accounting*
Robert R. Sterling (Editor), *Research Methodology in Accounting*

ACCOUNTING THEORY

With Special Reference
to the Corporate Enterprise

by

WILLIAM ANDREW PATON, PH.D.
Professor of Accounting, University of Michigan

Scholars Book Co.
Box 3344
Lawrence, Kansas 66044

Copyright © 1962
A.S.P. Accounting Studies Press, Ltd.

Reprinted 1973 by

Scholars Book Co.
with special permission of
Accounting Studies Press, Ltd.

Library of Congress Card Catalog Number: 73-84526
Manufactured in the United States of America

FOREWORD TO THE REISSUE

In 1922 a young (33), red-headed professor, of Scotch ancestry and decidedly conservative economic and political beliefs, published a pioneering and even radical book, which he called *Accounting Theory*. That it was pioneering is scarcely subject to question, even though it was preceded by such landmarks as Cole's *Accounts: Their Construction and Interpretation* (1908); Esquerre's *Applied Theory of Accounts* (1914); Sprague's *Philosophy of Accounts,* which achieved its fifth edition in 1922, having begun as a series of articles in *The Journal of Accountancy* in 1907-08; and Hatfield's *Modern Accounting,* first published in 1909. There had also been general accounting textbooks for many years, though many of the older ones were not much more than treatises on double-entry bookkeeping, notable mainly for rules of thumb which would enable the well-bred young lady to keep simple accounts. A cluster of the more modern type of accounting texts had appeared within a half-dozen years prior to *Accounting Theory,* notably books by Gilman (1916), Kester (1917), G. E. Bennett (1920), Wildman (1914), Saliers (1920), and others — not to forget Paton and Stevenson, *Principles of Accounting,* first published in 1916.

Some of the writers on theory, notably Sprague and Hatfield, not satisfied merely to describe practice, had earnestly addressed themselves to exposition of pure theory; but the textbook writers, for the most part, had quite naturally concerned themselves primarily with practice and with not much more than an occasional nod toward theory, where it seemed to bolster practice. Paton's *Accounting Theory* is concerned only with theory; it touches on practice only for illustration or contrast; and it is quite the opposite of an apologia for practice.

Further light on the pioneering aspect of this book is afforded by calling to mind that the American Accounting Association did not commence its publications in this area until 1936, fourteen years after *Accounting Theory* appeared, and that the

American Institute's Committee on Accounting Procedure was not organized to begin its fragmentary series of publications on theoretical questions until 1939. It was not, indeed, until 38 years after *Accounting Theory* appeared that the Institute began organizing itself for a really comprehensive attack on these problems.

That this book is radical scarcely needs illustration for anyone who has followed Paton's writing and career through the years. Much of what the author says is still radical, even after forty years, though some of his 1922 radicalism is today's commonplace. A few selected quotations well illustrate the author's unawed attitude toward practice and precedent and his impatience with sacred cows:

"Unfortunately it is often true that the purpose actuating those having authority over the preparation of the financial statements is to obscure rather than to disclose."

". . . certain long-standing theories and policies of accountants must . . . undergo modification . . ."

"As a matter of conservatism this position is reasonable enough; although its logic is weak as is the case with all accounting views based largely on conservatism."

"The accountant who in one breath insists on the importance of the sale as the only trustworthy evidence of income, and in the next contends that current assets should be priced at cost or market, whichever is lower, is throwing reason to the winds."

". . . it is precisely at this point that accounting practice is most irrational."

Perhaps the evidence of radicalism in this 1922 publication of greatest interest in 1962 is the following flat statement: "The consistent valuation of standard materials . . . on the basis of replacement cost is a thoroughly sound procedure." Compare this with Sprouse and Moonitz's statement in *A Tentative Set of Broad Accounting Principles for Business Enterprises:*

> Since the use of a future exchange price is ruled out as inapplicable . . . and a past exchange price as defective, we are left logically with the possibility of using a current exchange price, or replacement cost.

The obvious shock with which this proposition is commented on

FOREWORD TO THE REISSUE vii

by most members of the Project Advisory Committee is sufficient demonstration that this Patonian doctrine is still radical.

One of the questions uppermost in the mind of one rereading *Acconting Theory* forty years later is, would the author say the same things today that he did then? In fact, if he would not, the whole project of republication becomes somewhat questionable. The book is not an antique, like *Summa de Arithmetica*, and the author is altogether too much alive and able to express his own views for even the boldest of publishers to take a chance on misrepresenting his current philosophy by excavating something from the better-forgotten past. As one who is familiar with the author's current views leafs through the pages of this forty-year-old opus, he is bound to be struck far more by the similarities between the author's former and current views than by any differences.

The differences, such as they are, are nevertheless of some interest. Matters of terminology are particularly apparent. He talks about "surplus," "balance sheet," and "accountancy" — terms which he has eschewed in more recent years. He uses the terms "income" and "revenue" interchangeably, and what he would now call "net income," he designated then as "net revenue." He talks in the book about the "purchase" of treasury stock, an expression which he now uses only to condemn it. He exhibits a multi-step income statement, whereas he would now strongly favor the single-step variety. He accepts unpaid stock subscriptions as assets, while in *Corporation Accounts and Statements* (1955) he seriously questions their asset character. He emphasizes the importance of the balance sheet and belittles the income statement in language which he would probably not use today:

> In a study of the theory of accounts, the income statement is of little importance, showing, as it does an elaboration of an element finally incorporated in the balance sheet. The balance sheet, . . . on the other hand, is of the utmost consequence for our purpose.

In spite of these words, three of the twenty chapters and parts of several others are devoted to income-statement considerations.

While even as long ago as 1922 Paton was concerned with changes in the value of the measuring unit and their effect on capital maintenance, his treatment was then by no means as thorough or as sophisticated as are, for example, Chapters 14 and 15 of *Asset Accounting* (1952). Evidence of a somewhat less aggressive approach to this problem can be seen in the following quotation: ". . . fixed asset costs which have never appeared on the books as asset charges can scarcely be loaded into depreciation expense." The author would hardly be so timid today.

One thing which the Paton afficionado misses in *Accounting Theory* is his more recently developed fondness for effective figures of speech, many of them drawn from his farm-boy background. In *Corporation Accounts and Statements*, for example, we are regaled by a mangled metaphor in which "Hired managers" are said to "get the bit in their teeth and act as if they could run the show as they see fit," whereupon "management needs to be brought up with a jerk . . ." The 1922 Paton was a more matter-of-fact writer, and seldom indulged in picturesque language.

Not the least interesting chapter in this book, in view of recent developments in the American Institute's research program, is the final chapter, entitled "The Postulates of Accounting." As a definition of "postulates" Paton adopts language very close to that of Webster's second and fourth definitions of the term — definitions which have been roundly rejected in a recent publication on the subject. Postulates are equated by Paton with "general assumptions . . . few if any of which are capable of complete demonstration." "Indeed, some of them can be disproved from the standpoint of literal accuracy." "They are largely assumptions of expediency, without which it would be impossible for the accountant to proceed." In view of the last remark one is inclined to wonder whether the author was enumerating the postulates as he thought they ought to be, or merely reporting the postulates which he found to underlie accountants' actual procedures. The chapter is not entirely clear on this point. The author's avowed object in writing it is to provide accountants with a checklist of their own assumptions, in order that they might not delude themselves into believing that accounts set forth absolute truths.

> . . . accountants are sometimes in danger of forgetting their own premises and, therefore, the limitations of their work. If the ac-

FOREWORD TO THE REISSUE

countant sees clearly the foundation upon which he is standing, with all its implications, he is less likely to fall into the mire of improper applications and erroneous general conclusions.

Enumeration of the postulates reflects the flavor of the entire book. The accountant assumes:

1. "... the existence of a distinct business entity..."
2. "... the continuity of this entity..."
3. "... an equation ... between the total of the properties and the total of the representations of ownership..."
4. "... that a statement of assets and liabilities [surely a slip of the Patonian pen] in dollars and cents is a complete representation of the financial condition of the enterprise..."
5. "... that the value or significance of the measuring unit remains unchanged..." [This is one of the demonstrably false assumptions.]
6. "... that cost gives actual value for purposes of initial statement."
7. "... that the value of any commodity, service, or condition, utilized in production, passes over into the object or product for which the original item was expended and attaches to the result, giving it its value."
8. "... that costs accrue..."
9. "... that a loss in asset value falls upon or extinguishes the most recently accumulated proprietorship."
10. "... that all disbursements to shareholders absorb earnings before tapping investment..."
11. "Another assumption ... widely adopted by the accountant is that units of raw material or merchandise consumed or sold are always taken from the oldest in stock..." [Needless to say, this postulate had far more nearly universal acceptance in 1922 than it has had since the advent of lifo.]

One is tempted to try to evaluate this book in terms of its influence on other writers, students, and practitioners. The trouble is that it is impossible to separate the book from the man, his other writings, and especially his long years of teaching at the University of Michigan and elsewhere. Generations of students, many of whom have become eminent in the practice and teaching of accounting, have been exposed to the logical fire which has mercilessly exposed unreason and inconsistency in certain widely held accounting views and in even more widely followed accounting practices.

That progress has been made in transforming accounting from an arbitrary set of rules of thumb to an orderly body of reasoned principles is obvious to the informed observer. While the progress which has been made can certainly not be credited to any one man, it is surely due, to no small extent, to the sincere, persistent, penetrating efforts of those who, like the author of *Accounting Theory*, have insisted that accounting is not merely a trade, whose sole interest is in practice and expediency, but instead is, or should be, founded on logic and a full appreciation of its responsibility as a guide to economic conduct.

There are those who profess to be unable to understand the role of sound accounting theory as divorced from practice. This point of view is sometimes expressed in terms like these: With respect to a particular type of transaction, if tax considerations, clerical expense, or other practical aspects dictate a certain method of recording and reporting, what is the good of a theory, no matter how logical, which advocates different treatment? A theory can't be much good if, in view of practical considerations, it can't be followed. The answer is simply that theory supplies the standard, the zero milestone, from which deviations may be measured and evaluated. Without the guidance of theory, accounting would be aimless wandering in the forest of constantly changing "practical" considerations. What would be deemed satisfactory accounting on one day or for one particular entity would be wholly inappropriate or inadequate on another day or for a different enterprise. With a solid body of theory, which does not change with each tax decision or each new development in the art of data processing (or which changes slowly and for reasons founded on logic), the nature and extent of deviations from sound accounting which may be suggested by practical circumstances can be evaluated, and their significance and effects weighed against their practical advantages.

Accounting is not the only art or science (*Accounting Theory* calls it an art) in which this phenomenon exists. Law and medicine, for example, have their bodies of recognized and accepted theories, but neither lawyer nor doctor would be so doctrinaire in the practice of his profession as to refuse to bow to the exigen-

FOREWORD TO THE REISSUE

cies of particular circumstances and to apply procedures which are adapted to the needs of the moment. The surgeon does not refuse to operate with the hog-sticking knife on the kitchen table merely because he knows that the proper place to operate is an aseptic room in a modern hospital with all the latest in instruments, anesthesia, and assistants. He operates, however, from a background of established theory and he is therefore able to formulate judgments as to the significance of his deviations and their probable impact on the patient's chances. The fact that he ignores his theory to the extent required by circumstances, casts no doubt on the validity of his theory. Instead, his theory enables him to deviate intelligently, to evaluate his deviations adequately, and to carry them no further than necessary to save the life of the patient.

Accounting, too, needs its standards. Accountants need to be aware of how far from the ideal the arbitrary rules of taxing authorities or the need for economy in the employment of clerical procedures are taking them. They need to know when to stand and fight (as in the case of *Schlude v. Commissioner*) and when to bow to the inevitable. Just as the original publication of *Accounting Theory* in 1922 helped to provide accountants of that day with adequate standards for the exercise of their art, so now its republication may serve to reinforce the efforts of the many practitioners and teachers who, with an appreciation of the part which theory can play in advancing accounting toward the goals we all strive for, endeavor to further the progress of accounting toward that professional status so eagerly sought and so widely proclaimed.

Herbert F. Taggart
Ann Arbor
May, 1962

PREFACE

As commonly presented in current textbooks and other writings, the theory of accounting is saturated with the "proprietorship" concept. In fact, since the adoption of this expression by Sprague in his admirable "Philosophy of Accounts" most American writers have couched their explanations of the system of double entry largely in proprietary terms. In the usual treatment of the subject the structure of the accounts is described from the point of view of the proprietor; as far as possible transactions are explained and rules governing entries are formulated with reference to the effect upon proprietorship; and the other important classes of accounting data—assets, liabilities, expenses and revenues—are defined as mere accessories of proprietorship. Indeed, the prevailing accounting theory might well be described as "proprietary accounting."

It is the opinion of the writer that these doctrines of proprietorship, as propounded by Sprague, Hatfield, and others, are not an entirely adequate statement of the theory of accounts under the conditions of modern business organization. The technique of accounting has developed rapidly to meet the conditions of the large-scale enterprise, but theory—as is so often the case—has lagged far behind practice. In the case of the "single-proprietorship," so-called, or the simple partnership, the proprietary is a fairly satisfactory pivotal category around which to construct the necessary accounting framework, but as an explanation of the accounting system of the *corporation*, the present dominant form of business organization, such an arrangement of accounting principles is seriously defective.

In this book, accordingly, an attempt has been made to present a restatement of the theory of accounting consistent with the conditions and needs of the business enterprise *par excellence,* the large corporation, as well as applicable to the simpler, more primitive forms of organization. The conception of the business enterprise as in all cases a distinct entity or personality—an extension of the fiction of the corporate entity—is adopted, although not without important qualifications. This view, so much deplored by some writers, is nevertheless very useful, indeed well-nigh indispensable, to the accountant. The business enterprise is a *reality,* an important economic institution, and is certainly of the utmost significance in the field of accounting. In its main outlines the conventional corporate balance sheet is held to be a thoroughly rational scheme for the presentation of the financial condition of any business enterprise, the division of its data into two numerically equal groups being considered to be a matter of logical cleavage and not of mere custom or convenience. In other words, the view that the balance sheet is composed of *three* distinct categories, *assets, liabilities,* and *proprietorship,* and that the first two of these classes are of importance primarily in that their difference discloses the last, is abandoned, and the theory of the accounting system is presented in terms of the *two* fundamental dimensions, *properties* and *equities.*

The emphasis of this treatise, as has just been indicated, lies in a revision of the broad outlines of the proprietary theory of accounts. In addition, however, it is believed that it will throw light upon quite a number of the dark crannies in theory and procedure. There are many aspects of accounting which have always been inaccurately or superficially explained, or have been evaded entirely, by writers on the subject. In this book an attempt has been made to meet every difficulty squarely, to explore carefully every segment and connection in the accounting framework, to state in a rational and consistent manner the essential nature of all important accounting situations. For example, the analysis of the expense and revenue classes, the explanation of the valuation account, and the classification of transactions, here presented, are, it is believed, more satisfactory than other statements of these matters.

Further, in the later chapters, a careful study is made of certain important topics closely related to the theory of the double-entry system on the one hand and to practical accounting problems on the other. From time to time the accountant is inevitably brought face to face with such questions as the treatment of interest prior to operation, the significance and treatment of goodwill, the determination of a criterion of revenue, etc.; and if his work is to be placed upon the highest possible plane of usefulness he must formulate specific judgments and conclusions in connection with such matters on the basis of rational doctrines covering all of these difficult problems. Some of these subjects are no doubt worn rather threadbare as a result of much discussion; others have been seriously neglected. In every case, so it appears, the questions involved have been left unsettled and the whole topic is in need of precise restatement. It is hoped that the treatment here given will contribute something to the solution of the difficulties involved and will stimulate further study and inquiry along these lines.

Incidentally the relations between certain accounting concepts and fundamental classes of economic theory are noted in this study. It is hoped that this discussion may help to unravel the confusion of accounting and economic ideas and terminology in which many accountants (and perhaps some economists) appear to have lost themselves. The accountant naturally looks upon the business world through the eyes of the individual enterprise; the economist views the situation primarily from the standpoint of an entire industrial community, a whole market situation. Consequently concepts and terms entirely valid in one field cannot be transferred to the other without, at any rate, very careful qualification. Yet, in discussing such subjects as the relation of interest on investment to manufacturing cost, for example, the accountant has often made unwarranted use of certain concepts of the economist. Similarly some economists [1] have attempted to make dubious applications of the point of view of the business enterprise to the problems of economic theory.

The accountant, although he may well note with satisfaction that his field is coming to be rated as a branch of economic analysis, must recognize that accounting concepts and principles are measurably distinct from those of economic theory, and that, while a thorough grounding in fundamentals may be of genuine advantage to him, a smattering of economics —a mere superficial familiarity with certain stock phrases and definitions of the economist—may serve to confuse rather than assist him in his attempt to place accounting procedures upon a rational footing.

Certain omissions of material which one might perhaps expect to find under the title chosen for this study should be mentioned in the foreword. In the first place it is noticeable that clerical details are entirely neglected. There is no description of original documents, journals, books of account, working papers, or financial statements. Even the use of the terms "debit" and "credit" is avoided entirely in the early chapters. This procedure implies that the theory of accounting consists in a body of doctrine which can best be developed without reference to any system of clerical routine. The concern of this treatise is with inherent, underlying concepts and principles, not with the details of bookkeeping procedure.

A discussion of valuation for purposes of accounting would not be altogether out of place under the caption "theory of accounting." The nature and treatment in the accounts of depreciation of plant and equipment, depletion of natural re-

---

[1] Fisher, Davenport, *et al.*

PREFACE

sources, and amortization of patents and other intangibles; the proper methods of pricing inventories of merchandise and supplies under various conditions; the relation of selling price to book value; the effect of price movements upon the values of units in hand—these and other questions of valuation are generally recognized as a part of the field of accounting. In fact, the determination of proper *bases* of valuation for purposes of preparing financial statements under the various conditions of business organization and operation is perhaps the most important question now facing the accounting profession, a problem rendered acute by the advent of income and profits taxes.

In this book, however, no attempt has been made to discuss the problems of valuation except in so far as the explanation of the structure of the accounts here developed has a bearing upon these matters.[2] Incidental references to bases of valuation, of course, are frequently made throughout. The liberal view that, ideally, all bona fide value changes in either direction, from whatever cause, should be reflected in the accounts has been adopted without argument. To show that all possible types of situations and transactions can be handled in a rational manner in accordance with the principles enunciated is a chief reason for this attitude. At the same time the writer believes that this logical position is the proper one for the professional accountant, at least as a starting point.

Perhaps, since this is a theoretical study, no apology need be offered for the fact that the terminology employed does not conform closely, at many points, to current academic or professional usage. The nomenclature of practice is unfortunately full of ambiguities, and consistency is essential in a statement of theory. The phraseology of the Interstate Commerce Commission's prescribed classifications has been drawn upon

---

[2] In Part II, for example, are considered interest during construction, the nature of goodwill, and certain other problems of valuation closely related to the theory of accounts.

to some extent. It is not intended to suggest that the language here adopted is in general any great improvement over other usages. It is believed that the term "equities," as a designation to cover all the items on the so-called "liabilities" side of the corporate balance sheet, is a suitable one, and might well be employed in practice. The use of the expression "properties," to denote the other side of the balance sheet, on the other hand, is of doubtful advantage here, and for general use is probably a less satisfactory term than the more technical "assets."

Part I covers the theory of the accounting system *per se*. In Part II certain special topics relating to points of view adopted in Part I, but inadequately considered in the earlier chapters, are elaborated.

The indebtedness of the writer to Sprague and Hatfield will be evident to any reader familiar with the literature of accounting. "The Philosophy of Accounts" and "Modern Accounting" contain the first elaborate statements of the essential nature of the double-entry system in English which exhibit a rational method of approach. The present effort, as suggested above, takes these writings as a starting point.

WILLIAM ANDREW PATON

Ann Arbor, Michigan,
   September 10, 1922.

CONTENTS

Part I—The Accounting Structure

CHAPTER   PAGE

I   INTRODUCTION 3
     A Definition of Accounting
     The Rôle of Accounting
     The Present Emphasis Upon Accounting
     Accounting and the Business Enterprise
     Other Situations Requiring Accounts

II   FUNDAMENTAL CLASSES 28
     Properties
     Equities
     The Equation

III   PROPRIETORSHIP AND LIABILITIES 50
     The Proprietorship Equation
     The Significance of Ownership
     Equities in Sole-Proprietorships and Partnerships
     Types of Corporate Equities
     Corporate "Proprietor" and "Creditor"
     A "Residual" Equity

IV   PROPERTY AND EQUITY ACCOUNTS 90
     Fundamental Effects of Operation
     Fundamental Requirements of the Account
     The Parallel Column Account
     Current Resource and Equity Accounts

V   TYPES OF TRANSACTIONS 113
     The Accounting Transaction
     Property Transactions
     Equity Transactions
     Property-Equity Transactions
     Combination Transactions
     Summary—Double and Single Entry

VI   EXPENSE AND REVENUE ACCOUNTS 142
     The Need for Supplementary Accounts

Chapter		Page
	The Revenue Division	
	The Expense Division	
	Expense, Expenditure, and Cost Incurred	
	An Illustration	
	Expense and Revenue, and Proprietorship	
VII	OTHER TYPES OF SUPPLEMENTARY ACCOUNTS	171
	The Net Revenue Classification	
	Net Gains, Losses, and Taxes	
	The Surplus Classification	
	Special Surplus Situations	
	Valuation or Contra Accounts	
	Graphic Summary	
VIII	ACCOUNT CLASSIFICATION	205
	The Overlapping of Account Classes	
	Functional Classification	
	Statement Classification	
IX	PERIODIC ANALYSIS AND SPECIAL CASES	218
	Closing Current Asset Accounts	
	Closing the Labor Account	
	The Mixed Merchandise Account	
	Closing the Rent Account	
	Some Miscellaneous Cases	
X	DEBIT AND CREDIT	240
	The Debtor-Creditor Explanation	
	The Responsibility Rules	
	Debit and Credit, and Proprietorship	
	Conclusion	

Part II—Special Problems

XI	NET REVENUE	253
	Operating Net Revenue	
	Current Liabilities and Net Revenue	
	Net Revenue and Proprietary Profit	
	Proprietary Salaries	
	Proprietary Interest and Rent	

CONTENTS

Chapter		Page
XII	INCOME PRIOR TO OPERATION	283
	In the Unincorporated Competitive Enterprise	
	Actual Cost versus Selling Value	
	In the Incorporated Enterprise	
	In the Public Utility or Railway	
XIII	GOODWILL AND GOING VALUE	307
	A Definition of Intangibles	
	An Analysis of Goodwill	
	The Treatment of Non-Purchased Goodwill	
	The Treatment of Purchased Goodwill	
	Going Value	
XIV	PRELIMINARY VALUATION PROBLEMS	333
	General Initial Costs	
	Preliminary Depreciation	
	Preliminary Losses	
	Property Valuation and Securities	
XV	RELATIONS BETWEEN OWNER AND BUSINESS	354
	Owners' Borrowings	
	Adjustments for Interest	
	New Investment and Revaluation	
	Investors' Salaries and Other Compensation	
XVI	PHASES OF CAPITAL STOCK	372
	Stock Discounts	
	Treasury Stock	
	Stock Dividends	
XVII	SOME VALUATION ACCOUNTS	400
	Sales Discounts and Allowances	
	Discounts and Allowances on Purchases	
	Discounts on Contractual Securities	
XVIII	REVALUATION AND MAINTENANCE CAPITAL	424
	Book Values, Capital, and Price Movements	
	Appreciation and Depreciation	
	Special Objections and Considerations	

CHAPTER	PAGE
XIX CRITERIA OF REVENUE	443

    The Receipt of Cash
    The Credit Sale
    Physical Completion
    Percentage of Completion
    Appreciation and Revenue

XX THE POSTULATES OF ACCOUNTING	471

    The Business Entity
    The "Going Concern"
    The Balance-Sheet Equation
    Financial Condition and the Balance Sheet
    Cost and Book Value
    Cost Accrual and Income
    Sequences

ACCOUNTING THEORY

PART I

THE ACCOUNTING STRUCTURE

CHAPTER I

INTRODUCTION

Although perhaps not strictly necessary to a technical presentation of the theory of accounting, an introductory statement dealing with the nature and scope of accounting will serve to call attention to underlying points of view and relationships, and furnish a convenient background or setting. After such a preliminary statement it should be possible to proceed directly with an analysis of the structure of the accounting system without frequent explanatory discursions. This first chapter, accordingly, will be devoted to a statement of general definitions, and to a brief consideration of the general significance of accounting in the economic process, the factors contributing to the present emphasis upon accounting analysis, the relation of accounting to the business enterprise, and the situations outside the enterprise proper which require something in the way of accounts.

A DEFINITION OF ACCOUNTING

It is always difficult to frame a useful definition for a broad subject. Precise definitions are likely to be inadequate at best, and are often positively misleading. It is doubtless often better to permit the entire exposition to build what definition it may in the reader's mind than to attempt to formulate the essence of the matter in a few words. Accordingly no effort will be made to present a satisfactory characterization of accounting in a single statement. It is believed, however, that a few inquiries and suggestions in the direction of a definition, and from several points of view, will shed some light upon our subject and especially aid in the development of a proper perspective.

In the first place, how does the subject of accounting appear to the practitioner? In what does the art of accounting, the actual practice or profession of accounting, consist? A three-sided answer is fairly satisfactory. First, there is what might be called "constructive" accounting. Every business enterprise requires a system of accounts and accounting titles, a "set of books" and underlying documents and forms, and a scheme of clerical procedures. That is, someone must organize, plan, arrange the actual accounting mechanism suited to the needs of the particular situation.[1] Accounting analyses and conclusions would only be possible in the presence of some concrete arrangement or set of technical devices. This work of "system construction" is sufficiently distinct to be viewed as a more or less separate branch of accountancy; and there are many accountants who professedly specialize in such work. And it should be evident that the planning of accounting forms and procedures on a rational basis can only be accomplished by one who, in addition to being fully acquainted with the details of the particular case, is thoroughly appreciative of all the fundamental relationships in the accounting structure.

Second, a systematic record of all explicit happenings affecting the particular business must be made. A diary of business events must be kept and the data thereof classified and recorded. This part of accounting is commonly referred to as "bookkeeping"; and it is of course largely a routine orderly process of analyzing and booking business transactions. On the whole the attempt to differentiate sharply between bookkeeping and accounting is entirely fruitless. If

---

[1] The particular system may, of course, pass through a process of "evolution," and in this case could hardly be said to represent the product of definite planning on the part of any one person.

bookkeeping be defined in the broadest possible manner the terms become virtually synonymous. In view of common usage, however, the word "accounting" is probably the better designation for the general field, "bookkeeping" being viewed as an important integral part thereof.

The third phase involves the periodic interpretation and analysis of the records of the business enterprise in the light of various valuations and inventories, and the preparation of the important financial statements for the use of managers, investors, *et al.*, based upon this analysis. Here we have the crux of accounting, the difficult and interesting part of professional practice. There may be some doubt as to just how far the work of actual valuation is a part of the accountant's legitimate sphere, but at any rate he must interpret and pass judgment upon valuation data and incorporate these data in his fundamental financial exhibits. Further, the accountant is certainly expected to compute accruals and gauge intangibles, and to formulate depreciation policies and work out rules of valuation in connection with merchandise and other assets even if the actual work of appraisal and taking inventory is left to others.

This third branch of accounting involves the presentation of periodic income and balance sheets, and all other exhibits and reports designed to show periodic expense and revenue, or any phase thereof, and asset balances, liabilities, or other aspects of momentary financial status. Even the preparation of a tax return might well be comprehended in this division.

Detail auditing, or the checking of clerical work, might perhaps be said to constitute a fourth phase of professional accounting practice. But while this is no doubt often considered to be a branch of accounting, and an important branch, the writer feels that mere checking as such does not deserve emphasis as a significant part of the accountant's work. A conception of accounting in terms of an endless succession of red or blue check marks is all too common, and is certainly grounded on a misapprehension of its true purposes.

From the standpoint of student or teacher, on the other hand, accounting consists in that body of doctrines, principles, important generalizations, which underly the technical double-entry system, the valuation of assets attaching to the particular enterprise, and all phases of the art of accountancy. The accounting textbook, for example, seeks to explain the essence of the accounting structure, to set forth the important rules and general procedures involved in dealing with particular groups of accounts, to indicate the fundamental types of transactions, to expose the essentials of the work of preparing financial statements, to analyze existing rules and principles of valuation and to formulate additional principles in this direction, etc., etc. It is only from this standpoint that it is in any way proper to speak of accounting as a science.

More specifically, to put the matter in terms of the fundamental classes of data, accounting attempts to follow and exhibit periodically, in rationally classified form, the assets and the equities of the business enterprise, and the important subsidiary phases of these classes. It is the function of accounting to register all values coming into the particular business, to follow their course within the enterprise, and to note their final disappearance from the business, and at the same time to record the effect of all of these processes upon the various elements of ownership. Or, again, to put the matter definitely in terms of the leading financial statements, the essence of the accountant's task consists in the periodic determination of the net revenue and the financial status of the business enterprise.

THE RÔLE OF ACCOUNTING

A further point of view from which the subject might be defined is the social. What is the function of accounting from

INTRODUCTION

the standpoint of the community, of the entire industrial situation? What part does accounting play in the economic process? Of what significance is accounting from the standpoint of general industrial welfare? To emphasize this commonly neglected aspect of the matter it will be convenient to consider it as a special topic.

We commonly think of accounting as a mere tool of trade, a mechanism with which the business man, for his own immediate purposes, counts profits and losses. While this is true enough, a somewhat different perspective is discovered if a fundamental point of view is adopted. Let us ask what, in the broadest terms, is the function of accounting? Further, what relation, if any, does the theory of accounts bear to general economic analysis?

An incidental statement of Mitchell's is stimulating in this connection. In speaking of the function of the price system he says that "prices render possible the rational direction of economic activity by accounting, for accounting is based upon the principle of representing all the heterogeneous commodities, services, and rights with which a business enterprise is concerned in terms of money price." [2] This suggests a significant rôle of accounting. Accounting, by making price data available in a systematic and intelligible manner, is perhaps the principal instrument by which the directors of business are enabled to conduct their affairs rationally. Accounting is a means by which the complex data of the market, as they attach to the particular business, are translated into effective managerial criteria. It is the function of accounting to record values, classify values, and to organize and present value data in such a fashion that the owners and their representatives may utilize wisely the capital at their disposal.

It would of course be indulging in hyperbole to say that

---

[2] *Business Cycles*, pp. 31-32.

accounting is the *sole* mechanism by which business conduct in its various ramifications is directed. Dealing only (or at least largely) with price statistics, value facts, from the point of view of the specific enterprise, accounting has a relatively narrow scope. By no means all the facts with which the entrepreneur is concerned are disclosed by a system of financial accounts, however complete. The business manager is interested in many aspects of personnel, properties, production methods, physical product, and other data with respect to his own particular establishment, and in the statistics of foreign and domestic commerce, the volume of agricultural and mineral production, the intensity of manufacturing activity, the condition of bank reserves, and all other general information which can possibly be of assistance to him in his attempts to forecast market conditions and conduct his business efficiently. Nevertheless there is much truth in the commonplace of the economist that the system of market prices exerts a dominant influence in the direction of business activity. The data of prices, particularly price trends, are undoubtedly of great immediate importance in controlling business policies. Prices are signs which are read by the enterpriser and which markedly affect his actions with respect to direction and volume of production. It is especially as the manifold influences of the economic situation come to a focus in value figures that managerial judgments are passed. And, as suggested above, accounting has a part to play here. If the tendencies of the economic process as evidenced in market prices are to be reflected rationally in the decisions of business managers, efficient machinery for the recording and interpreting of such statistics must be available; and a sound accounting scheme represents an essential part of such a mechanism.

To put the matter in very general terms, accounting, in so far as it contributes to render effective the control of the price system in its direction of economic activity, contributes to general productive efficiency, and has a clear-cut social significance, a value to the industrial community as a whole.

Just a word may be said at this point to suggest more concretely the rôle of accounting, the function of the accountant, in transmuting price data into terms essential for certain purposes of the individual producer. It is the task of the accountant to follow market prices as, attached to *specific property items*, they become affected by the business process. Guided by the facts of the market, the manufacturer, for example, acquires land, buildings, equipment, tools, materials, and services of various types, and, combining these elements with his own peculiar contribution, has for sale a product. It is the function of accounting to record these costs, properly classified, as they are incurred, to follow their subsequent history as they lose their identity and reappear in new forms as a result of manufacturing operations and the passage of time, and to indicate their final disappearance from the business as costs of product.

Further, it should be emphasized that the history of a particular item may cover a considerable period. Some of the assets acquired are not only not immediately consumed but are highly permanent in character. Land is physically nearly imperishable, at least as far as its site character is concerned; modern buildings are very durable; substantial units of equipment may remain as economic factors in the particular business for years. What becomes of the values attached to such items? This record it is peculiarly the function of accounting to show. Present market prices give the values of new units as they pass from buyer to seller; but it is only by means of accounting that the economic history of the items in use is preserved. Without accounting the rational utilization of the durable items that make up a large part of the capital of the industrial community at any time would, under modern conditions, be well-nigh impossible.

It is in this connection that accounting may be said to deal with the determination of values. The laws of the market, the principles of demand and supply, are matters with which the accountant is only indirectly concerned, but it is his business to redetermine, in a manner not inconsistent with current market processes and from the point of view of the individual enterprise, the values of specific items that have disappeared from the market and constitute a part of the capital of the particular enterprise.

THE PRESENT EMPHASIS UPON ACCOUNTING

Before going further with a statement of the relation of accounting to the private business enterprise brief consideration will be given to the principal factors contributing to the current interest in and importance of accounting. In the first place the inherent characteristics of modern industry—to which attention is being called with perhaps undue frequency nowadays—make imperative the need for accounting and other forms of statistical analysis. The large size of the typical modern enterprise, and the variety of properties which it requires to carry on its operations, are general conditions which in themselves complicate the problems of valuation referred to above and render necessary an elaborate accounting structure.

Less than a century ago the large business organization was the marked exception, the small sole-proprietorship or partnership being the typical form of enterprise. The amount of capital involved was small; relatively few kinds of equipment were used in production; goods were produced for a limited market area. The utmost simplicity in operating and marketing organization was the rule. In such a situation the need for accounting as we now know it was not urgent. The owner could readily keep in mind much of the detail of his business, and could be personally cognizant of the status of each important property item without elaborate records. A more or less systematic diary of explicit business transactions was usually the extent of his accounting, little in the way of managerial analysis or valuation being attempted.

But today, while small enterprises are still the more numerous, the simple sole-proprietorship or partnership is hardly the dominant type of enterprise in the industrial order. We are familiar now with the large-scale enterprise, usually organized under the corporate form, which requires a vast aggregate of capital, employs a numerous personnel, utilizes scores or even hundreds of types of property, operates perhaps several distinct plants, and sells goods in a world market. In the case of these large and complex enterprises there is evidently need for an extensive system of accounts.

Another general feature of current industry which emphasizes the importance of accounting is the frequency and severity of price movements. If prices were comparatively stable, as was the case over fairly long periods of early English industrial history, the problem of ascertaining the status of properties would be essentially a matter of physical measurement and appraisal and hence would be relatively simple; physical units could be converted directly into value terms. But prices are now but little controlled by custom and tradition; the modern market is subject to serious disturbances, distinctly pecuniary in character. These price fluctuations, constituting as they do a change in the significance of the money unit itself, complicate the task of the accountant and at the same time render his work more essential.

In recent years the change in the value of the dollar—the accountant's yardstick in this country—has been especially serious. This situation emphasizes sharply the need for accounts and financial statements which shall show as nearly as possible the actual economic situation in each case. It is coming to be recognized that accounting systems must become more sensitive and accurate gauges of values if the purposes of the various interests involved are to be adequately served. Satisfactory technical methods by which changes in the value of money may be reflected rationally in the accounts have yet to be developed, however.[3]

In connection with the relation of accounting to price movements the general importance of adequate financial statistics as a means of allaying the severity of the so-called "business cycle" should be noted. A never-ending series of booms and depressions, rather than a prosaic steadiness, seems to characterize the industrial process under modern conditions. The graveness of these disturbances in the past half-century has no doubt been due in a measure to unsound banking and credit institutions, but it should be recognized that reforms in this direction can never be more than palliatives. An essential cause of the business cycle is the difficulty experienced by business men in becoming really acquainted with the current situation and in accurately forecasting future market conditions. It is coming to be recognized that the ascertaining and dissemination of complete and reliable information concerning the entire industrial process is the most promising remedy for alleviating the situation. And the data concerning the financial condition of the various business enterprises furnished by accounting forms an important part of the information necessary for the construction of a satisfactory trade barometer.

Much emphasis is being placed at present upon the necessity for efficiency of operation in industrial enterprises. Internal efficiency rather than external expansion has become the shibboleth of business managements. Sound organization of personnel and economical utilization of plant and materials are the factors receiving especial attention. And efficient manage-

---

[3] See Chapter XVIII for some further discussion of this matter.

INTRODUCTION 13

ment, it is beginning to be seen, depends upon the availability of extensive statistical information, an important part of which must be presented by the accountant.

Stated broadly, the problem of management is the problem of improving the utilization of our economic resources, a matter which was referred to in the preceding section; and the current stressing of managerial efficiency is a natural concomitant of fundamental industrial conditions and tendencies. The opportunities to increase revenues through the exploitation of undeveloped natural resources are diminishing, and hence the eyes of business managers are not turned in this direction to the extent they were. In addition, the technique of industry, after undergoing a complete transformation in the past century, is becoming more dependable, and consequently the opportunities to promote enterprises to develop new inventions are more restricted than formerly. The country is growing older; population is increasing; competition (in one sense at least) is becoming keener. Under these circumstances the current interest in managerial statistics need not be unexpected.

The striking development of "cost accounting," so-called, evidences this interest in management. The business man is beset on all sides these days by a host of cost "experts" and "systematizers." Scores of manufacturing associations have prepared or are preparing standard systems of accounts, and are urging their adoption by their individual members. Even retail and wholesale associations have been studying cost systems and advocating cost analysis, despite the very doubtful value of intensive cost accounting in the trading field. Leading trade journals are constantly stressing the importance of elaborate accounting along managerial lines. Everywhere one hears of the need for "system" and "efficiency." [4]

---

[4] In fact this movement, while doubtless soundly grounded, has become a furor, and needs an occasional dash of cold water.

An immediate factor which has probably contributed more to the present emphasis upon accounting than the efforts of generations of accountants is the advent of income and profits taxes. The levying of high rates of tax upon the net returns of business enterprises has made it imperative from the standpoint of both the taxpayer and the government that net income be rationally determined, that the integrity of the profit figure be protected by adequate accounting principles and devices. As a single example of the influence of the income tax program upon the development of accounting policies, the situation with respect to the treatment of accrued depreciation may be cited. Before the days of income taxation it was very difficult for the accountant to convince the business man, especially the owner of the small enterprise, that it was important that the value expiration of his fixed assets be accrued upon his books. Now he appears to appreciate the significance of accrued depreciation very clearly, and no urging is required to induce him to book a liberal allowance.

The Income Tax Unit of the Bureau of Internal Revenue has really become a great *accounting* organization, engaged in the examination of accounting data and the formulation of rules of procedure, many of which are essentially rules of accounting. The influence of this organization upon the theory and technique of accounting has already been of consequence; and while accounting for the ordinary purposes of the commercial enterprise and accounting as a basis for tax returns can never be expected to become completely consistent with respect to either theory or procedure, it must be recognized that governmental authority and influence in tax matters will tend to affect the detail practices and policies of accounting to a marked degree.

The activities of other departments of the government, especially during the recent war, should be noted in this connection. The Food Administration, Federal Trade Commission, Fuel Administration, and other governmental branches, have stressed the importance of accounting in certain fields and have exercised considerable influence upon the character of accounting procedures. The system of accounts for flour millers worked out by the Food Administration and the system for retail coal dealers prepared by the Fuel Administration, for example, have had wide adoption.

The influence of the prescribed classifications of the Interstate Commerce Commission upon accounting is a commonplace to any accountant. The Hepburn Act of 1906, which gave to the Commission the authority to prescribe uniform accounting methods for transportation agencies engaged in interstate traffic, recognized the fact that public regulation of industry could be made more effective through the control of the accounts. Since these classifications were promulgated they have not only become the standard accounting manual for the enterprises under the Commission's jurisdiction and have been followed more or less closely by public utilities everywhere, but they have had a profound effect in encouraging and shaping the development of scientific accounting in other fields.

Put in general terms, it may be said that the present tendency in the direction of governmental control of industry contributes vitally to the need for accounting analysis, affects the development of accounting principle and technique, and complicates considerably the task of the accountant. The public is fully aroused to the need of controlling the activities of the private enterprise when the interests of the enterprise conflict with those of society. The setting of "fair" prices in monopolistic or quasi-monopolistic industries, the adjudication of disputes between capital and labor, the preservation of the rights of the many classes of security-holders possible in the modern business organization—these are some of the important current tasks of the state and its agencies which require data from the accounts for their efficient performance.

ACCOUNTING AND THE BUSINESS ENTERPRISE

It has been pointed out that from the social standpoint accounting can be conceived as a part of the mechanism which makes possible the effective utilization of value data in directing economic action, particularly in the field of production. It has also been indicated that the important unit of organization with which accounting deals is the *private business enterprise*. In other words, the broad purposes accounting might be said to serve are accomplished only through the accounting systems of a host of specific business entities. Production of commodities and services for the market is carried on under modern conditions largely by business enterprises. It is the "management" of the private business that takes cognizance of price statistics and acts accordingly in purchasing raw materials and other productive factors and in disposing of the finished product. Further, the accounts are kept by the employees of the business enterprise and consequently primarily from the standpoint and in the interests of the private owners.

Hence the function of accounting and explanations of accounting principles and procedure must be stated immediately in terms of the needs and purposes of the owners of the individual business.[5] Each transaction, account, principle, procedure, has concrete significance for the accountant only as it relates to the specific business entity. It is the function of accounting to follow the investment of the particular private enterprise as it takes shape in various commodities and services, and to report to the management and owners the amount and rate of net income and other related facts.

This matter should be emphasized roundly. The distinctive unit upon which accounting is based is the private business

---

[5] As was stated in the preface, the idea of the business entity will be stressed through this study. The usefulness of this concept has its limitations, however, and these will not be neglected. In the next section, and at various points in later chapters, attention will be called to situations in which the accountant is interested but to which the distinctive attributes of the business enterprise attach in small degree, if at all.

INTRODUCTION 17

entity. The accountant looks upon business operations essentially through the eyes of the particular group of managers and owners. Accounting classifications and procedures are significant only as they are related to the conditions of the specific business organization. Here we have the underlying conception of the accountant, a conception which conditions the entire accounting structure.[6] It is a point of view in marked contrast to that of the economist, who focuses attention largely upon markets, communities, general industrial situations; and in this contrast lies the chief explanation of the difference between accounting and economic categories.

Just what is the business enterprise for purposes of accounting? To put the matter broadly, a business enterprise is any commercial undertaking involving the investment of capital funds and constituting an essential unit from the standpoint of management and ownership. In the United States three main types are usually distinguished: the sole-proprietorship, the copartnership, and the corporation. The sole-proprietorship is a business enterprise conducted by a single individual. Actual ownership of the property used commonly resides primarily in the hands of the "proprietor," so-called. The proprietor is usually the active manager of the business and may also furnish a considerable part of the ordinary labor services required.

In a strict sense any capitalist, however humble, who is utilizing his resources in an independent commercial venture, is a proprietor and his business a single-proprietorship. The majority of retail stores are of this type, many wholesale and manufacturing businesses are sole-proprietorships, and agricultural establishments are almost always in this class. Such enterprises range in importance from the fruit stand on the street corner to the private banking house or other large busi-

---

[6] In Chapter XX the reality and importance of the accountant's "business-entity" assumption is further considered.

ness having an investment of many thousands, or even millions. Very large aggregates of capital, however, are seldom brought together under the sole-proprietorship form.

Although the sole-proprietorship has no legal existence as an entity, and no formal steps are required for its initiation, it is nevertheless useful for the accountant to view such a business as a distinct unit for his purpose. This conception of the sole-proprietorship in its relation to the theory of accounts will be elaborated in Chapter III, and its qualifications will be carefully noted.

Many single proprietors make but an imperfect use of accounts; but something in the way of statistical records is essential in nearly all such cases, and efficiency in the management of even the small concern would generally be much advanced by an extension of the use of systematic accounting methods. It is sometimes a little hard to draw the line between personal affairs and business affairs in such cases. This matter will be briefly considered in the next section.

The partnership is a business undertaking conducted by two or more persons associated by means of a contractual agreement. Although in practice there are usually but two, three, or four partners, there may, in theory, be any number of firm members. The partnership association is commonly based upon a written agreement called the "articles of copartnership." This agreement usually contains stipulations in regard to investments, withdrawals of principal or income, management, division of income, dissolution, etc. There are many kinds of partners and partnerships. In several states "special" partnerships, so-called, can be created which are endowed with the essential privileges of the corporate form of enterprise.

The corporation, the third type of enterprise mentioned above, is in many respects the most important form of business organization. In point of aggregate capital controlled, number of employees, quantity of output, financial influence,

INTRODUCTION 19

etc., the corporation easily leads in many important lines of industry; and the development of this form of organization does not yet appear to have reached its limit. The corporation is marvelously well adapted to the exigencies of large-scale production. By this device the capital of the investor, great and small, is brought together and welded into a unit for purposes of carrying on economic production. By means of a great variety of securities the corporate form permits of the division of the important elements of ownership in such a way as to attract all classes of investors. It is the corporation, as was stated in the preface, to which particular attention will be paid in the statement of the theory of accounts in this study. It is in the case of the corporation that an actual legal existence puts substance in the accountant's assumption of a business entity. The state endows the corporation with a being which is separate and distinct from its membership. Limited liability and other important consequences result. Thus the corporation is the business enterprise *par excellence*.

In Chapter III particular attention will be devoted to an analysis of the essential nature of the corporation and the main classes of securities from the standpoint of accounting. The meaning of the corporate entity, with reference to its accounting applications and limitations, will be carefully considered; and especially the significance of the balance sheet, the fundamental accounting statement, will be discussed from the point of view of the corporation.

In all these forms of business organization the interests of the private owners are uppermost. It is the private investors and their managers that control operations. It is the representatives or employees of the enterprise that keep the accounts. Consequently, as was stated above, the influence of the private equities upon accounting principle and technique is predominating. It is hardly possible to overemphasize the importance of this fact.

Specifically, from the standpoint of the business enterprise, it is the function of accounting to furnish two kinds of statements: (1) a periodic showing of the financial status of the business enterprise, its assets and equities; (2) a report of income, its origin, amount, and distribution.[7] These statements, the balance sheet and the income sheet, respectively, present the results of the entire accounting process. In a study of the theory of accounts, the income statement is of little importance, showing as it does an elaboration of an element finally incorporated in the balance sheet. The balance sheet, the financial summary, on the other hand, is of the utmost consequence for our purpose. The balance sheet presents a statement of all the property items at a given moment, and shows the concurrent distribution of ownership in the same.[8] A record of properties is obviously essential to sound management, to fix responsibilities, show the residence of the capital of the enterprise, and control policies of replacement and extension. Similarly, the status of each interest in the business must be shown periodically to insure that each owner receive equitable treatment. Especially in the case of the corporation, with its constantly changing membership, is it important that the integrity of the net income figure *in each period* be preserved. The income statement, in so far as it shows the revenue and costs of a particular period, is, of course, of consequence for detail managerial purposes; but its most vital significance for the theory of accounting arises in that it exhibits net income, the change in the status of the equities.

It is not intended here to state in detail the importance of accounting to the business enterprise. It is an essential preliminary in our study, however, that the conception of accounting as a mechanism operating essentially through the sys-

---

[7] *Cf.* Hatfield, *Modern Accounting*, p. v.
[8] The significance of the fundamental classes of the balance sheet is discussed in Chapter II.

tems of financial accounts for specific business entities be fully grasped.

OTHER SITUATIONS REQUIRING ACCOUNTS

Although, as has just been emphasized, accounting is primarily concerned with and functions through the business enterprise, there are other situations which may require accounts and yet which do not present the characteristics of the typical enterprise. A brief consideration of these situations will serve to qualify properly the preceding discussion, and will also throw some light on underlying views and concepts.

First may be mentioned those spheres of the individual's personal economy which offer some analogies to business operations and may require financial records. A considerable part of the community's wealth at any one time consists in more or less durable "consumption" goods. Residence sites, houses, automobiles, furniture, clothing, jewels, paintings, and books are important examples. To know the amount and disposition of his wealth and to control administration and replacement in a rational manner, the millionaire owner may not only desire a record of expenditures for such assets, properly classified, but also an analysis of utilization and depreciation—"operating" records.

Further, although such assets from the general point of view do not represent productive capital, it is quite possible for the particular individual to effect direct conversion of consumptive property into business capital to a considerable extent, as well as to use his private wealth as a basis for capital borrowings. Somewhat indirectly, then, the business man's consumption goods are related to his business capital, and a systematic accounting for such items is not only possible but it often desirable. A special reason for such accounting in

DENNIS KNUTSON

these days lies in the fact that items of income (and "allowable deductions" as well), for purposes of federal taxation, may arise in connection with consumption goods. For purposes of the tax return the government makes no fundamental distinction between the profits on the sole-proprietor's business and those that arise on the sale, for example, of his residence.

Little in the way of systematic accounting, however, is ordinarily attempted by the individual with respect to such properties. In most cases his private affairs are not so complex but that he can keep the situation in mind without extensive accounts. There are no business operations *per se* and no net income in the usual sense. Problems of distribution (except in the settlement of estates) seldom arise. In other words, the personal economy of the individual does not present the characteristic problems of accounting.

From the standpoint of good management there is also something to be said in favor of "household" accounts. The sound administration of family finances may conceivably require a budget and an accounting scheme. Household operation presents problems of management as does factory operation. There are the regular operations of cooking, washing, cleaning, etc., and the more elaborate special processes of canning, sewing, repairing, and so on. Considerable equipment is found in the modern household. We have vacuum sweepers, electric washing machines, furnaces, etc., as well as the numerous kitchen utensils and other paraphernalia. Here we find, by analogy, the problems of valuation and cost accounting. To determine rationally the cost of a specific household operation(such as broiling and serving a steak, for example) would be as difficult a problem of statistical analysis as can be found in the factory or elsewhere in the business enterprise.

Here too, beyond those of the occasional enthusiast, we find few efforts in the direction of elaborate accounting. The housewife, no doubt, needs accounts, but not a complete system analogous to that of the typical business enterprise. Common sense and good judgment, with little in the way of systematic records, are usually adequate. At any rate these situations likewise do not furnish characteristic accounting data.

Again, the individual may have assets and income of a semibusiness character accompanied or unaccompanied by actual business affairs. Thus he may own government bonds, or a tract of land. He may receive royalties on some publication or invention, or income from occasional services furnished. Such an individual—in these connections—is not a business proprietor in the ordinary sense, but still may make use of accounts.

The professional man, who invests little or no capital but who derives an income from services furnished, requires in some cases a fairly elaborate accounting system. He must, of course, keep something in the way of a customers' ledger. As the profession of such an individual comes to require some little capital in the shape of office furniture, car, and current funds, it approaches the condition of the genuine sole-proprietorship. A personal-service sole-proprietorship or partnership may rate for the accountant as a true business enterprise.

Just where the line may be drawn between the enterprise and the "non-enterprise" in such cases can hardly be stated in set terms. At one extreme we have the ordinary laborer furnishing services but investing nothing in the way of capital (except in so far as his waiting for his pay check and furnishing a few small tools may perhaps be said to constitute the furnishing of capital); at the other is the firm of accountants or lawyers having a definite place of business, thousands in capital, and a considerable staff of employees. The productive operations of the typical laborer or professional man cannot be said to constitute the conditions of the business enterprise which the accountant must have in mind, as such cases do not furnish characteristic accounting data or problems.[9] The organized firm, on the other hand, usually represents a distinct accounting unit.

For practical accounting purposes it is very necessary to distinguish between the genuine business affairs of the sole-proprietor or partner and his semibusiness or private affairs. This is one reason for the necessity of insisting upon the business-enterprise view of accounting. If the statistics of a business enterprise are mixed with those covering the owners' private loans, personal expenditures, and other outside transactions, any real accounting analysis is well-nigh impossible.[10]

It is not always easy to draw the line between business and personal operation, however, no matter how emphatically the integrity of the business enterprise be stressed. Costs of obtaining income and objects for which income are utilized are classes of data often hard to distinguish. This is illustrated by the extensive rulings of the Income Tax Unit on this subject. The difficulty of dividing the cost of operating the semibusiness car between business and living expenses is the "classic" illustration. In so far as possible the distinction must be carefully observed, however, if the accounts are to serve satisfactorily the essential purposes lying back of their use.

It should be admitted that, as the law in general does not segregate the "business" assets of the sole-proprietorship or the partnership from the personal estates of the proprietors, from some points of view the line between these spheres is

---

[9] A complete double-entry system would be entirely unnecessary or even well-nigh impossible in such a case.

[10] The "books" of a family in a little country town furnished a striking case of this. The various brothers, sisters, uncles, etc., between them owned and operated the "Little Gem Theatre," the "O. K. Barber Shop," the "Palace House," and other business ventures. In so far as any accounts were kept they were all included in a single "set" of books. Not only were the affairs of the various businesses hopelessly entangled, but many personal transactions were recorded in the accounts. Uncle Charles' loan to Aunt Jemima, the purchase of son Willie's new velocipede, Tom's advance to brother Jim to enable him to pay his poker losses—all were thrown in together. The resulting confusion can be imagined.

artificial. As far as the satisfaction of creditors in the event of liquidation is concerned, the personal property of the proprietor (with certain statutory limitations) is as fully available as are his business assets. However, the accounts cannot well be constructed purely from the standpoint of the creditors at time of liquidation. Other and more consequential purposes are involved. This matter will be discussed somewhat further in Chapter III.

An important type of situation outside the business enterprise proper which requires extensive accounting is the governmental unit—federal, state, and municipal. The United States government, for example, owns a great aggregate of properties, carries on extensive commercial and non-commercial operations, handles large sums of cash, is obligated to pay enormous debts. Evidently elaborate schemes of accounts are necessary if these affairs are to be handled properly. Similarly the state and municipal units require accounts. The municipality often carries on genuine commercial activities, such as owning and operating water, light, and gas plants. The problems of property accounting and cost accounting in such cases are closely analogous to those faced by the typical private enterprise.

On the other hand, explicit "proprietorship" [11] as such does not exist as an accounting fact in any of these cases. Definite liabilities are involved but no specific proprietary items. The citizens of the unit involved might be said to constitute the proprietary, however; and there is nothing to prevent the use of the complete double-entry system in such cases. The difference between properties and liabilities can conveniently be labeled "surplus." [12] The "balance sheet" of any govern-

---

[11] The significance of this term will be fully discussed in later chapters.
[12] The accounting significance of "balance sheet," "surplus," "liabilities," "assets," and other expressions used here will be dealt with at length a little later.

mental unit however, is a somewhat conventional thing, and does not have the same significance as that of the private concern. The financial strength of the state or any of its subdivisions depends essentially upon the power to tax the citizens thereof rather than upon any specific list of properties to which it may have title at a given moment. The state or municipality may consequently have liabilities greatly exceeding its properties without being in any way insolvent.

In this connection it will be desirable to consider briefly the largely theoretic question of the character and scope of accounting in the communistic society or socialistic state. How would accounting be affected if private enterprises were eliminated and a genuinely socialistic régime substituted? In answer it may be safely said that accounting in a broad sense would not be done away with if such a revolution in economic organization occurred. Indeed, accounting or bookkeeping of a kind would doubtless be greatly emphasized. Elaborate bookkeeping would be needed if the more or less automatic control of industry now effectuated through the price system were supplanted by a collectivist program under the direction of the state. The apportionment of resources and products in a rational manner could not possibly be accomplished in a large and complex society without extensive accounting and other statistical analysis.

Accounting for socialistic units would be significantly different from accounting for the private business enterprise, however. Private property interests, now a controlling consideration in production, would have disappeared. Ownership and net income, the disclosure of which in the last analysis is now the problem of accounting, would be extinct elements, or at least would be very much modified. The profit margin would not be the all-important guide that it now is. Further, the whole property category would alter at important points, particularly in that intangibles such as goodwill and patents

INTRODUCTION 27

would probably entirely disappear as definite accounting data.[13]

However, as was stated above, the accountant has only a theoretic interest in these matters. Despite the extension of governmental control already referred to there are no actual developments, and apparently none impending, which strike at the heart of the private business enterprise. Surely no elaborate argument need be advanced to justify the stating of the theory of accounting essentially in terms of the needs and purposes of the private business enterprise rather than of those of the socialistic unit.

Finally, there are many quasi-commercial institutions and enterprises, border-line cases, ranging from social organizations such as the college fraternity to the nearly commercial building and loan association. Philanthropic societies, "improvement" associations, agricultural organizations, chambers of commerce, mutual insurance companies—these and other similar enterprises require accounting systems somewhat analogous to those necessary for the typical business enterprise.[14]

In attempting to state the theory of accounts, however, none of these situations will be considered as typical. Rather the private business enterprise, engaged in transportation, trading, extraction, manufacturing, banking, etc., utilizing appreciable capital, producing some service or commodity to be sold on the market, and operated primarily in the interests of the private owners, viz., for net profit, will be kept in mind.

---
[13] This matter is further considered in the next chapter.
[14] Estates, trusts, etc., constitute still another kind of situation which may furnish many of the conditions of the typical business enterprise.

CHAPTER II

FUNDAMENTAL CLASSES

The first step in a study of the theory of accounts should be an attempt to establish an underlying point of view, to isolate and focus attention upon that element, phase, or unit of the economic world which is peculiarly the realm of the accountant. In the preceding chapter this step has been taken. It has been pointed out that the fundamental organization with which the accountant is concerned is the private enterprise, the profit-questing business entity; that particular accounting captions, procedures, and principles have significance only as they are attached to the specific business situation; that accounting theory must be stated in terms of the needs and purposes of the individual group of managers and investors. The second logical step consists in the determination of the basic categories, within the business enterprise, over which the accountant has authority. What are the *fundamental classes* of data with which the accountant deals? What primary divisions can be discovered? What are the lowest terms to which the financial statistics of the enterprise can be reduced?

In trying to answer these questions either of two highly divergent methods might be followed. On the one hand an attempt could be made to proceed from details to fundamentals. An isolated transaction, an individual account, or other minute fragment might be seized upon as a nucleus, and an effort made to add thereto, bit by bit, the entire structure, properly arranged and with fundamental relationships disclosed. The opposite method involves the immediate deduction and isolation of underlying elements, and the gradual addition to this

FUNDAMENTAL CLASSES

foundation, in a logical manner, of all subsidiary divisions. The first plan might be the more desirable if one were exploring absolutely virgin territory; but the second seems much the better method of approach in dealing with ground already fairly well charted.

In presenting a statement of these fundamental classes it will naturally be necessary to gather the exposition around the specific enterprise; and for this purpose a hypothetical business, the X Co.,[1] will be referred to from time to time. To begin with, this enterprise, it will be assumed, is organized and is just ready to start operations.[2] The plant is completed; equipment has been acquired and installed; materials are in stock; operatives have been secured; the organization of managerial personnel has been perfected. Now what, at this time, are the underlying classes of data which should appear in the accounts?

It has already been emphasized that accounting is concerned primarily with economic facts—with values. Consequently a great many factors may be excluded from consideration at the outset. For example, the accountant is not directly interested in the weight, shape, volume, color, chemical constitution, or other material characteristic, of any land, buildings, merchandise, etc., which may be in the Company's possession; in technical methods of production and other engineering data; in the number, age, race, or religion of actual or prospective employees; in the geographic location of the plant or the probable markets for product; or in the social or moral aspects of the Company's product and policies. Many interesting and

---

[1] The corporate form will be used in this illustrative case since, as was stated in the preface, it is a primary purpose of this study to state the philosophy of accounts in terms of the conditions and needs of the corporation, the dominant type of business organization. No attempt will be made, however, to adhere closely to the conditions of any one actual situation; rather the emphasis will be placed upon conditions and elements common to virtually all companies.

[2] The preliminary period of promotion and construction requires accounting records and, if of considerable length, presents some peculiarly difficult accounting problems. In Chapters XII and XIV some of the questions arising during this initial period will be considered.

important questions with respect to the nature of this enterprise and its relation to the economic community readily suggest themselves. But with most of these matters the accountant is only indirectly concerned, if at all; his sphere of interest and influence covers only certain especial aspects of the *financial* situation.[3] Accordingly the question may be put more specifically, what are the fundamental classes of *value* facts which the accounts of the *X* Co. should show? What basic groups of *price* data can be discovered? What facts must (or can) be presented to show the *economic* or financial condition of this enterprise?

PROPERTIES

At least a partial answer immediately suggests itself. Clearly one important category consists in all the resources, assets, or *properties* to which the *X* Co. has any title. Obviously if we are to know anything about the financial status of this company we must have a complete statement of its property. A natural first query of the accountant is, what are the assets?

What is meant by the term "properties"? In brief, a property is any consideration, material or otherwise, owned by a specific business enterprise and of value to that enterprise. Materiality is no test as to what is or what is not an asset, a fact commonly recognized by business practice. Thus the properties of an enterprise may consist not only of many different kinds of tangible *structures* and *goods*, such as land, buildings, machinery, tools, supplies, merchandise, cash, etc., but also of a wide variety of *rights*. One class of rights

---

[3] This needs emphasis as there seems to be a tendency in some quarters to ignore the inherent limitations of accounting. The accountant has a specialized and relatively narrow field, and nothing is to be gained by trespassing beyond its natural boundaries. The attempt sometimes made by some accountants to express all kinds of hypothetical cost analyses in explicit accounting entries illustrates this misapprehension with respect to the true scope of accounting.

consists in claims against individuals, firms, corporations, and governmental units, for services, money, or commodities. Monopolistic privileges and conditions of various kinds likewise give rise to assets. Examples of immaterial assets are ordinary book accounts, promissory notes, mortgages, stocks, bonds, and other securities, leaseholds, patents, trade-marks, prepaid insurance, etc. Under the complex conditions of modern business operation the accountant meets with almost innumerable kinds of property; but each kind of asset, however dissimilar it may be in many respects to other items, has one characteristic in common with all other assets; viz., it must be of value to some specific business enterprise or entity.

The properties attaching to a particular business may be listed under a few heads or they may be classified very minutely, the degree to which such classification should be extended being largely a matter of expediency. The purpose in hand and the character and size of the business are the controlling considerations. We will suppose the property of the X Co. to consist of the following items: land, $100,000; buildings, $200,000; equipment, $100,000; patents, $100,000; organization costs, $25,000; materials, $100,000; cash, $75,000. Then a statement showing the financial condition of the X Co. must exhibit this list of properties, although the items may be grouped in any convenient way. It is a conventional procedure to list them in a vertical column, thus:

Properties

Land	$100,000
Buildings	200,000
Equipment	100,000
Patents	100,000
Organization Costs	25,000
Materials	100,000
Cash	75,000
Total	$700,000

Before raising the question of further classes it will be of advantage to examine more thoroughly this concept of properties and its significance in accounting. In the first place it should be noted that the immediate fact for the accountant is not a property in its entire objective state, but only the *value-representation* of such property; i.e., it is not the X Co.'s land which will be recorded in the accounts, but a statement of the value of that land in dollars and cents. Strictly speaking, then, "properties," as accounting data, consist of two principal elements: (1) an appropriate name or title, and (2) a statement of value in terms of some money unit.

Next, the question should be considered further as to just what this concept covers or includes. As was stated above, two main types of assets are involved: (1) structures, equipment, commodities, and all other tangible things possessed by business enterprises and having value, and (2) all recognized securities, privileges, and claims which give the holder definite right to money, valuable services, or commodities, and all valuable considerations arising from monopolistic conditions.

It seems scarcely necessary to add, in view of the emphasis already placed upon this matter, that no structure, commodity, right, condition, or service, which has no economic significance to the company possessing it, can be considered a property. The X Co., for example, may find a supply of water a necessity in certain operations, but if an abundance of water is available without cost from an adjacent river the water supply would not enter into its statement of financial condition.[4] To have economic significance as far as the accounts are concerned, however, an object or condition need not have price in the ordinary sense; it need have value only to the particular enterprise possessing it. Thus if the X Co. had

---

[4] In so far as this water supply were a factor in the determination of the value of the Company's site it would, of course, find indirect expression in the accounting data.

secured essential water rights at a nominal figure because there happened to be no competing buyers, such rights might still have a high economic value to this particular company. If these rights were not replaceable, the price the Company would set upon them if contemplating their sale would, in such a case, reflect real value more accurately than the nominal cost.

Similarly properties may be secured by donation, coercion, and other non-commercial means; but this makes them none the less properties to those coming into their undisputed possession and use. For example, an interested municipality may donate a tract of land to the promoters of a manufacturing enterprise; the large corporation may force the small firm to dispose of its patent rights for a "song"; a railroad company may secure the property of the small feeder line which has become insolvent at a bargain simply because it has no value to other lines. In all these cases important property values may be involved.

A consideration of the relation of the class, "properties," to the economist's concept, "wealth," will serve to throw some light upon the fundamental nature of this accounting category. In general it may be said that anything which can constitute wealth may, under certain circumstances, become an asset to the accountant. It has been already emphasized, however, that accounting has to do primarily with enterprises engaged in producing a commodity or service for the market. Thus consumers' goods, goods actually in the hands of those who will utilize them for personal use, do not ordinarily enter into the accountant's reckoning. Residences, cars, furniture, clothes, books, etc., are property, of course, in the legal sense; but such items—in the possession of the ultimate user—do not furnish characteristic accounting data. Such objects in the hands of manufacturer, agent, merchant, or dealer, on the other hand, rate as producers' goods and become a matter of concern to the accountant.

But there are many things which can be assets which do not constitute any part of the community's wealth. A business enterprise may invest a considerable sum in prepaid services. Insurance is perhaps the best example. A company pays in advance for protection from fire and other hazards. This payment gives rise to an asset, a property, which might be said to consist of the right the company making the payment has against the insurance company. The insurance company is obligated to furnish the service of protection for a certain period; and this constitutes a bona fide property to the insured. But the economist would doubtless not include this prepaid service—this benefit which will accrue in the future to a particular enterprise—in a computation of the community's wealth. Similarly a company may invest funds in hire paid in advance, setting the amount up as an asset under such a caption as "prepaid rent," or "leases." It is not difficult to find cases where the property of a company consists largely of leaseholds. Even in the case of ordinary labor services payments are sometimes made in advance, and thus give rise to a transitory property item.

Rights to future payment of money and goods are also considered assets by the accountant, although they do not constitute a part of the community's wealth. "Accounts receivable" are an important example. Such items originate largely through sales on account, and as a result of deposits with and advance payments to actual or prospective creditors.

Stocks, bonds, mortgages, notes, etc., are properties of the individuals, firms, and companies owning such securities. Again, such rights are not a part of the total wealth. In this respect accounting, from the viewpoint of the industrial community, clearly involves duplication. Thus, if every individual, firm, and company in the United States prepared a list of all its properties, the sum of such lists would greatly exceed the wealth of the nation. It would be necessary to eliminate all inter-enterprise relationships to arrive at even an approximate figure for total wealth.

In still another important particular may the properties of the private enterprise differ from wealth from the social standpoint. Monopolistic advantages of various kinds give rise to properties under certain conditions as already noted. These are the so-called "intangible" assets. Such advantages may be due to governmental grants—e.g., patents, copyrights, trademarks, franchises—or to control of natural agents, financial control, various "unfair" methods, secret processes, more efficient management, etc. An intangible asset item arising from any of these conditions may be just as truly property to the private concern as any other valuable consideration,[5] but obviously should not be viewed as wealth from the standpoint of the community. Indeed such properties in a sense express a distinct disadvantage from the standpoint of the consuming public.

Evidently the accountant's class, properties, is somewhat akin to the economist's "capital," especially as conceived by those who make no distinction between land and produced goods. Natural resources and plant and equipment are important properties in the case of a great many enterprises; and commonly the accountant makes no fundamental distinction between "natural" and "produced" factors.[6] Certainly from the point of view of the business enterprise any necessary factor for which a price must be paid is clearly an asset, regardless of its physical character.[7] But while all natural

---

[5] According to the accountant such properties should not be given definite recognition in the accounts unless purchased in a bona fide manner, and should never appear above cost. For a discussion of this matter see Chapter XIII.

[6] Although distinct rules of valuation are usually applied to each type of property.

[7] This does not mean, however, that those theorists are right who insist that therefore land should be placed in the same category with produced goods for purposes of economic reasoning. The central problem of economics is the analysis of value and price; and in the processes of price determination very different laws apply in the case of natural agents from those which hold with respect to producible goods. Further, in dealing with questions concerning general economic welfare and progress it is necessary to distinguish, for example, between increase in land value and the growth of wealth due to an increase in the number of units of produced capital goods. Hence the economist has need of other classifications.

agents and produced capital goods may become assets, by no means all assets could be included in the capital category, even by those economists who profess the point of view of the business enterprise. Prepaid services, current receivables, securities, and general intangibles all constitute bona fide assets as has already been pointed out, but such items no more represent a part of the community's capital than a part of its total wealth.

A further consideration should be stressed before we leave this discussion of the general characteristics of the property class. Although this category may include a great variety of items, it has definite limitations—limitations not always clearly recognized in accounting theory and practice. Not all the conditions, circumstances, factors, and tendencies affecting the financial position of a company can be given definite statistical recognition in dollars and cents. A case in point are the so-called "contingent" assets. Possible compensation under guaranties, assessments callable on outstanding stock, possible damages from pending legal contests, etc., are examples. Such conditions should not be confused with actual properties.

Further, a company's general credit, the possibility it has of raising funds, may be "worth" more than any or even all of the specific assets it happens to possess. But, again, the mere possibility of securing funds can hardly be rated, in advance, as an actual asset.[8] Still further, as was noted above, the monopolistic advantages possessed by a particular company may be of marked value in that such advantages may contribute greatly to earning power; but the capitalization of excess earning power to obtain such an asset (in the absence of a genuine purchase and sale transaction) is not recognized as proper accounting. Again, the loyalty and efficiency of the labor organization may be a matter of more moment than,

---

[8] To consider treasury stock an asset involves a mistake of this kind. See Chapter XVI.

for example, $100,000 worth of merchandise; yet this fact can hardly be given explicit recognition in the accounts in value terms. Only under special circumstances can the "imponderables" of business be given definite statistical expression. Here is one of the serious limitations of accounting. A list of properties as of a given date is a very imperfect representation of the true economic strength of a business enterprise. The term "properties" connotes not valuable and advantageous conditions and circumstances in any broad sense but rather definite structures, commodities, and rights capable—according to recognized business practice—of explicit value expression.

In view of the fact that the phrase "possession" has been used frequently in the above discussion it might be well to add that mere physical possession does not, of course, make an item a property. Thus a bank which holds securities as collateral for loans, or which holds in its vaults valuables of various kinds for safe-keeping, cannot count such items among its own assets. The legal right of private property must be involved. In Chapter III the significance of property rights in relation to accounting theory will be further considered.

EQUITIES

But does a list of properties or assets as such give a satisfactory statement of the financial condition of the X Co.? Is the work of the accountant restricted, in its lowest terms, to a presentation of resources? Is there no other underlying class of data which it is his business to disclose? The answer is fairly evident. A bare statement of assets would be clearly inadequate, either from the standpoint of the interests of the business itself, a probable purchaser of the business, the employees, the public, or any other interest concerned. As implied in the last paragraph of the preceding section the *situs of the title* to these properties must be determined. What are the claims against or rights in this property? Where is the distribution of ownership? Or, more concisely, what are the *equities* in this property? The equities, like the properties, may have a variety of forms, especially in the large corporation. The particular interest which has immediate control of operation may own all the assets outright, or it may, at the opposite extreme, have only a relatively small equity in the property, while the greater part of the ownership is vested in other parties whose rights and claims are represented by various kinds of bonds, mortgages, promissory notes, current accounts, etc. For an illustration it will be assumed that the equities of the X Co. consist of the following items: capital stock—common, $200,000; capital stock—preferred, $200,000; mortgage bonds, $100,000; debenture bonds, $100,000; notes payable, $100,000. These equity facts may be listed in a column as was done in the case of the property items, thus:

Equities

Capital Stock—Common	$200,000
Capital Stock—Preferred	200,000
Mortgage Bonds	100,000
Debenture Bonds	100,000
Notes Payable	100,000
Total	$700,000

An equity, as an immediate datum of accounting, is then a value representation of a *right in property,* and consists in an appropriate title or name coupled with a statement of dollars and cents. Thus an equity fact, as a mere statistical statement, is entirely independent of any property fact. On the other hand, without the coexistence of properties there could be, of course, no equities. Properties connote equities and equities connote properties; and associated with both classes must be the conception of a business entity of some sort. A property item cannot exist suspended apart from private interests; neither can an equity or interest mean anything without a more or less objective property residence. The accountant must constantly keep in mind both the independence and interdependence of these fundamental classes. On the one hand he must recognize two distinct divisions upon the basis of which the entire technical structure of the accounts is organized; on the other hand he must perceive that both underlying classes are but aspects of a single business situation. This matter will be elaborated a little later.

As in the case of the property items the equities do not cover all actual and possible rights, claims, and privileges which may be directly or indirectly associated with a given group of properties. They represent merely the *equitable dispersion* of a specific body of asset values—the starting point —among the various interests concerned. Definite statistical expression can only be given to rights fulfilling certain conditions. Not all conditions contributing to the financial strength of an enterprise can be listed among the properties; neither can all rights and privileges in the properties be given explicit recognition in value terms.

The so-called "contingent" liabilities are a case in point. A contingent liability represents a possible or probable equity in properties, not an actual one. Thus a parent company may guarantee principal or income in the case of a security of a subsidiary. The parent company becomes "contingently liable." If an enterprise endorses notes for another we have a similar case. Other examples are furnished by guaranties in connection with the sale of product, endorsement of customers' notes discounted, claims in litigation, etc. None of these contingent liabilities are equities *per se,* but may become bona fide equities if certain eventualities materialize.

All private property rights are limited by the tax power of the state and its subdivisions and the right of eminent domain. And according to the experience of recent years the state has the right or power in times of emergency to apportion raw materials, supplies, and transportation service, to prescribe the character of output, to regulate accounting procedures, financial policies, and prices. Private property rights are limited by and subordinate to the residual and active powers of government. The state, then, might be said to have an interest in, a most important interest in and control of, the affairs of the private enterprise. The state's authority, however, gives rise to an expressible value equity in property only in connection with the tax power. In so far as the state can coerce payments from income or principal as taxes, it clearly has an accounting equity. Accordingly, as taxes "accrue" it is the business of the accountant to recognize this claim in dollars and cents.[9]

As was stated in the introductory chapter, the laborer unquestionably has rights in the business enterprise. The precise extent of his influence in management is, in general, a matter of dispute; but without doubt the control exercised by the employees, especially in certain lines, is coming to be very considerable. Only as such influence comes to involve definite value rights do we have an accounting equity under this head, however. The laborer contributes valuable services to the process of production and until payment is made for such services he clearly has an enforceable right, an equity that rates legally as a "preferred claim," and commonly ranks next to accrued taxes. The laborer might be said to sell valuable services "on account." The economist expresses this situation by saying that the laborer, in so far as he waits for his compensation, virtually furnishes a part of the capital required to carry on production. Further, it may be noted

---

[9] At the end of a particular period it is usually not possible to do more than estimate roughly the amount of income and profits taxes which will be finally levied on the business of that period. In other words the equity of the government, while known to exist, is relatively indeterminate. This is especially true in the case of a complex tax system, subject to continuous statutory and administrative revision. The liability is a fact, but its amount cannot be stated with absolute precision.

FUNDAMENTAL CLASSES

that the laborer has contingent rights under the various employers' liability and workmen's compensation acts.

The accounting treatment of the equities of state and employee involves many difficult questions and will be further discussed later in this study.

How is one to determine the amount to be attached to a given equity? In the next section it will be reiterated that the starting point for equity valuation is property valuation; that fundamentally the amount of the properties determines the amount of the equities. The parceling out of this amount among different equities is a matter depending upon the legal rights and privileges of each particular interest. For purposes of initial statement the amount invested is the best statistical measure of the equity. Thus the amounts given above in the statement of the X Co.'s equities may be presumed to represent in each case the amount of funds invested by the persons or interests represented by the title involved.

It should be emphasized, however, that neither the figure of original investment nor any amount derived from asset values gives a thoroughly complete and adequate expression of the rights and obligations attaching to a particular interest. A certain bond contract, for example, may call for the payment of a series of semiannual amounts during thirty years and the par sum at the date of maturity. What is the proper representation in value terms, on a given date, of such a combination of rights?[10] In practice either par or an adjusted investment figure is usually exhibited as a correct statement of such an equity. Or take the case of the common stockholder. He has residual rights to assets in case of dissolution, and he is entitled to such part of the residual earnings as the directors shall see fit to appropriate as dividends. What sum expresses these rights on a specific date? Evidently such

---

[10] This question will be briefly discussed in Chapter XVII.

questions cannot be fully answered by reference to a definite value figure; and such answer as the accountant may be able to give is quite likely to be proved thoroughly inaccurate by subsequent events.

Equities, as a practical matter, must be stated in terms of properties *as of a given date*. The present interests may be such as to have a right to all the future earnings of the business; but it is only as such earnings are realized, that is, *reach a condition where they are capable of definite statistical expression in terms of current properties,* that they can be reflected in the equities.

The types of properties, the terms used to designate them, and the procedures connected with the asset accounts, do not depend primarily upon the form of business organization; but the nature of the equities varies noticeably between the principal types. Indeed, the chief intrinsic peculiarities in sole-proprietorship, partnership, and corporation accounting lie in the equities and the procedures associated therewith. In the partnership, for example, the equities of the partners are represented by the partners' "capital" accounts, the name of the partner with the term "capital" or "proprietor" being the usual designation. The holders of promissory notes, mortgages, and open accounts constitute the other common interests. In the corporation formal securities represent the bulk of the equities; and the procedures and accounts relating thereto are necessarily much more elaborate. Various kinds of stocks, bonds, and long-term notes are met with. In the next chapter, which attempts a study of proprietorship and liabilities, these peculiarities of the equities under different forms of organization will be further discussed and illustrated.

In this connection may be emphasized the importance of the equities as an independent accounting category. The list of equities, alone, is a more illuminating statement than the list of assets, alone. As has just been stated, it is the character of the equities rather than that of the properties which indicates the type of business organization involved. Further, the *distribution* of the total capital among the different classes of investors can be determined from a statement of equities and constitutes a most significant basis for judging the financial condition of the enterprise. In other words, if one knows the total of a company's capital and the dispersion thereof between classes of equities he has information of possibly more vital significance than would be represented by a statement of the distribution of the capital among specific kinds of objective structures, commodities, and rights. Both classes are of course necessary for any adequate expression of the financial condition of an enterprise.

THE EQUATION

The property and equity columns given above, which represent the financial condition of the newly organized X Co. may be juxtaposed in various ways. A tabulation in parallel-column form is convenient.

The X Co.

Properties		*Equities*	
Land	$100,000	Capital Stock—Common	$200,000
Buildings	200,000	Capital Stock—Preferred	200,000
Equipment	100,000	Mortgage Bonds	100,000
Patents	100,000	Debenture Bonds	100,000
Organization Costs	25,000	Notes Payable	100,000
Materials	100,000		
Cash	75,000		
Total	$700,000	Total	$700,000

Such a parallel-column arrangement, it should be emphasized, is a purely arbitrary procedure. A great many methods of designating and separating these groups by symbols, colors, spatial arrangement, etc., could readily be suggested. The essential thing is to have all the property and equity facts presented in the fundamental statement; and from every point of view it appears to be desirable to separate in some way the two distinct classes. The above arrangement follows the form of the conventional balance sheet.[11] It is a lucid and concise way of exhibiting the necessary facts; and it is especially useful here in that it is consistent with the account construction and transaction analysis developed in later chapters. The definition of the balance sheet need not be dependent upon this arrangement, however. In a broad sense the balance sheet is a *complete statement of the properties and equities pertaining to a particular enterprise, regardless of the form of arrangement adopted.* It is in this sense that the balance sheet is truly what Sprague said of it, the "groundwork of all accountancy, the origin and terminus of every account." [12] The balance sheet, conceived as just stated above, represents a classification of facts which is the basis of the whole structure of financial accounts.

It is apparent that these two classes, properties and equities, will always be numerically equal, for in a sense they are merely different aspects of the same thing. In one case we are listing the facts of objective property; in the other case we are looking at the same property, but indirectly, through the eyes of the various individuals and interests having claims therein.[13] In one instance attention is being focused upon the objects for which funds have been expended; in the other, upon the sources of these funds. The assets constitute a *direct* statement of the value of the properties of the enterprise; the equities are an *indirect* expression of this same value total. On one side we have a statement of values in terms of *ob-*

---

[11] Other more elaborate balance forms are, of course, in wide use; but in the published summarized balance sheets of corporations the old parallel-column device is still followed in a large majority of cases.
[12] *The Philosophy of Accounts* (3d Ed., 1910), p. 26.
[13] *Cf.* A. G. Belding, *Accounts and Accounting Practice*, p. 2.

FUNDAMENTAL CLASSES 45

jective and specific residences; on the other is listed the *capital distribution*. The total of properties is also the total of the capital of the enterprise, and the equities express the *equitable dispersion* of this total—the legal relationships connecting this wealth and certain individuals or interests, the division of ownership. And since the same measuring unit, the dollar, is being used in stating both classes of facts, we have numerically equal totals.

The point may be emphasized by noting again that the *total* of the equities at a given date is essentially determined by the *total* of the properties on the same date. To put the matter in its logical sequence it might be said that the accountant first determines the kind and amount of each asset, and takes the total of properties; he then apportions *this same total* among the various individuals and interests involved in accordance with what appears to be the legal rights and privileges of each equity. The two lists taken together constitute a balance-sheet statement of financial condition.

Under two heads, then, may be listed the data representing a statement of a company's financial status at its inception; [14] and the sum of the properties is always equal to the sum of the rights-in-properties, or equities. Further, as will be shown fully in later chapters, this classification and its inevitable equality is the foundation of the double-entry system of accounts. Here is the origin of the equality between left-hand balances and right-hand balances.

The reality of this equation can be more readily and clearly appreciated in the case of the corporation, the business enterprise *par excellence*. But the equation exists, nevertheless, in

---

[14] Are there more than two classes? Can others be discovered? It is hardly necessary to argue that the balance sheet as defined above covers all facts measuring the initial financial standing of the enterprise in so far as it is possible to express this financial status in definite value terms. The data of the balance sheet, however, are often stated in three, rather than two, divisions. This matter of balance sheet classification will be carefully considered in Chapter III.
The question as to whether or not all operating classifications can be reduced to balance-sheet terms will be dealt with a little later.

the partnership, sole-proprietorship, or other business situation, however simple or complex. An illustration drawn from a very small-scale "business" may be useful at this point. Suppose that A, a newsboy, has $2 in cash in his pocket, a stock of papers which cost $3, and no other assets of any description. It might seem at first thought that the following was a complete statement of A's financial condition:

Cash	$2
Merchandise	3
Total	$5

A little reflection should make it clear, however, that this is not the whole story. The question then arises, what is A's actual equity? Does he own this property outright or are there other interests? Further data must be discovered. Let us suppose that B, A's brother, acting as a kind of silent partner, has invested $2 in the venture and that there are no other equities. Then a complete statement of the status of the business would be as follows:

Properties		*Equities*	
Cash	$2	A, Capital	$3
Merchandise	3	B, Capital	2
Total	$5	Total	$5

It is quite likely that if A owned all the assets outright he would, if setting up a statement of his financial condition, list only the properties. But this would not mean that the equity facts did not exist. A would simply be taking his ownership for granted; the facts of ownership would be implicit in the statement of properties, and would not require formal expression.

In very simple situations incomplete accounting is often successfully practiced, one or more elements being ignored as far as explicit statement is concerned. "Single entry" is the

FUNDAMENTAL CLASSES

name commonly used to designate a system of accounting which is incomplete in some respects; and it is usually some element of the equities which is omitted. But it should be emphasized that if all the facts are presented the fundamental equation appears.

There are, however, apparent exceptions to this equation in accounting practice. Whenever the assets of a business have been seriously impaired and the *current* property situation is compared with an *earlier* equity situation, the two classes as stated will, of course, be unequal. Thus the insolvent company may have claims against its properties which at face or original value are greatly in excess of assets. But this is evidently only a specious exception. When the assets of the bankrupt enterprise are distributed the amounts received by the various interests concerned cannot exceed the sum realized from these assets. The insolvent business pays less than "100 cents on the dollar." While it may be convenient for purposes of distributing the assets equitably to present original and face values of equities in the liquidation statements, it is surely evident that they will not give a correct current figure for the total of properties.[15]

A feature of the structure of accounts which will be dealt with at length a little later is the separation of positive and negative items. This procedure has advantages from the standpoint of clerical efficiency; and there are in many cases special reasons for maintaining original figures. For example, it is customary to keep capital stock or other securities on the

---

[15] In reorganization more weight may sometimes be given to a particular security issue than the original investment would seem to warrant; but the *total* of real outstanding equities after reorganization is completed obviously cannot exceed the *total* of the properties of the new enterprise.
In *The Philosophy of Accounts*, 4th Ed., p. 54, Sprague expresses insolvency by the equation, assets plus insolvency equals liabilities. As a matter of fact, effective assets equal effective equities. To define insolvency as "negative wealth" is to make use of an entirely unnecessary figure of speech. Properties and equities are interdependent classes of facts, and are coincident in amount. When properties decrease the equities automatically decline to a corresponding level. The use of historical figures for the equities when property values have in part disappeared gives rise to merely an apparent exception to the underlying equation.

books at *par,* so-called. If, then, a company is financed through the issue of securities at a discount, and the par values are recorded instead of the actual amount of the equities, an offset item must be set up equivalent to the amount of the discount. Such an offset is often listed among the assets although it should be shown as a deduction from overstated capital.[16] Similarly property items are sometimes left at original figures for various purposes, and suspended deductions are listed among the equities. It will be sufficient at this point to emphasize the fact that the substitution of addition to the opposite side for actual subtraction, or, as it is sometimes put, the use of *valuation* items,[17] explains all these apparent exceptions to the equation, properties equals equities.

In the private affairs of the individual a situation sometimes appears which gives a real exception to the equation. Suppose, for example, that A borrows funds from friends without furnishing conventional security. These funds he invests, not in property but in a college training. The accounts of such an individual, as far as this transaction is concerned, would show equities but not assets. And yet these equities might be as certain of payment as though supported by definite properties. The imponderables in the borrower's situation, his integrity, health, prospective earning power, etc., might, from the standpoint of the lenders, furnish adequate security.

Here is a case where equities are capable of definite statistical expression while "properties" cannot be so recognized. Even the business man will occasionally take the "moral risk"

---

[16] Par value as we know it in American corporation finance, at least as far as stock issues are concerned, might well be dispensed with altogether. Certainly the investor is often misled by par value, the nominal capitalization. Stocks might well be listed in the balance sheet at the bona fide value of property paid in. Changes from this level could be recorded in the surplus or deficit account. Dividends can easily be paid in terms of dollars per share, or percentages of actual, rather than fictitious, capital. Certainly dividend rates stated in terms of par percentages are often positively confusing to the stockholder. With par value eliminated the temptation to treat discount as property would be gone, and most of the other difficulties of accounting for capital stock would disappear. In this connection the recent development of "no-par" stock is encouraging. In Chapter XVI certain phases of capital stock from an accounting standpoint are discussed in some detail.

[17] See Chapter VII.

into account and loan money to a borrower who has no immediate properties whatever. If some reliable test for assaying and gauging these imponderables could be developed, more significance might be attached to such factors in the business world. In intrinsic importance these elements often outweigh formal properties many times. Until an appropriate index and method of measurement can be found, however, such matters cannot enter definitely into the accountant's realm. Further, cases such as the above, in which there are claims although no conventional assets, do not constitute true business enterprises and need not disturb the validity of the equation as a representation of the status of the genuine commercial entity.

Similarly, the "balance sheets" of governmental units are often more or less invalid as an expression of financial condition. As was noted in Chapter I, the tax power of the state, municipality, or other unit is the principal fact upon which its financial standing rests. Any specific list of properties which the state may own measures its condition very inadequately. And it is quite possible for the definite equities to exceed the properties, as a normal, rational condition. Thus the state may have bonds and other securities outstanding greatly in excess of the properties to which it has title at a particular moment of time. In such a case there is no equation in the ordinary sense. The tax power—the right to levy upon the properties of the citizens and others under its jurisdiction—is an incommensurate asset; it cannot be given definite statistical expression in dollars and cents. The outstanding bonds, etc., on the other hand, are explicitly expressible in values. But here again we are not dealing with the conditions typical of the private business enterprise.

There are other possible ways of expressing the equation than the scheme adopted in this chapter. In the discussion of proprietorship and liabilities in the next chapter certain alternative forms will be considered.

CHAPTER III

PROPRIETORSHIP AND LIABILITIES

Before proceeding further with a statement of the essentials of the accounting structure it will be necessary to consider more carefully the form and significance of the equation developed in the last chapter, especially with reference to its right-hand member. The presentation of the financial status of the enterprise in two terms or dimensions, properties and equities, is somewhat at variance with the orthodox treatment of the subject. In this chapter the more common arrangement will be stated and a careful examination of the content of its terms attempted, in order to determine its validity, as compared with the scheme adopted in Chapter II, under the various conditions of business organization.

THE PROPRIETORSHIP EQUATION

According to the usual view, the financial condition of a business should be expressed in three dimensions. The left-hand side of the conventional balance sheet is conceded to cover a single homogeneous class, commonly called "assets" or "resources." The right-hand side, however, is held to include two fundamentally distinct classifications, "proprietorship" and "liabilities." Furthermore, the attempt is usually made to state the theory of account construction and to present the principles of transaction analysis primarily in terms of relation to and effect upon proprietorship, the other classes, resources and liabilities, being conceived as subsidiary, for accounting purposes, to the proprietary.

Sprague, for example, considered the essence of the balance sheet to be most naturally expressed in the equation, assets minus debts equals "net worth," or, phrased more conventionally, assets less liabilities equals proprietorship. According to this view the essence of the accounting process is the disclosure of proprietorship; the ascertainment, periodically, of the amount of proprietorship is the goal of the accountant. Sprague pointed out that in balance-sheet form the equation is usually written, assets equal liabilities plus proprietorship; but he implied that this is a conventional rather than a logical arrangement, and is indeed not the best form to follow in published financial statements.[1] On the other hand he admitted at one point (although his explanation of the accounts was in nowise modified thereby) that "the right-hand side of the balance sheet is entirely composed of claims against or rights over the left-hand side." [2]

Proprietorship is elevated to a still more important and independent position by Hatfield.[3] According to this writer the underlying equation of the business enterprise can be reduced to "goods equals proprietorship." This is a two-term equation, proprietorship being rated as one of the fundamental categories, economic goods as the other. But, for convenience, the "goods" class is divided into positive and negative groups. Liabilities then are disposed of as "negative goods." In other words, liabilities are conceived as representing an aspect of goods and in nowise directly related to proprietorship. Net goods (positive goods less negative goods) equals proprietorship. The arrangement of the conventional balance sheet, according to this view, is only algebraically correct, negative goods being transposable to the proprietary side by changing

---

[1] *The Philosophy of Accounts* (4th Ed.), p. 17 (pars. 46 and 47); p. 20 (par. 52); p. 33 (par. 92); p. 36 (par. 100).
[2] *The Philosophy of Accounts* (4th Ed.), p. 46 (par. 125).
[3] See *Modern Accounting*, Chaps. I and II.

the sign. Similarly Hatfield places all accounts in this twofold classification. That is, each individual heading represents either a good, positive or negative, or an aspect of proprietorship.

This position, with slight modifications, has been very generally adopted by recent writers.[4] Proprietorship is not only treated as an independent category, but is conceived to be the accounting classification preëminent. The end of the entire accounting process is held to be the determination of proprietorship, and consequently accounts are classified and procedures formulated largely in terms of proprietorship.

With this brief statement of the underlying doctrines of proprietorship as a preliminary, the question at issue may now be put. Can we insist that the conventional two-dimensional balance sheet exhibits a logical arrangement of business data, proprietorship and liabilities being simply more or less distinct subdivisions of a single category—ownership, capital, or equities? Or is it more rational to classify the financial status of the enterprise into three divisions, two of which, resources and liabilities, are especially significant because their difference discloses the third, proprietorship? In other words, *shall the proprietary or the managerial point of view be adopted in stating the theory of accounts?* Shall accounts and transactions be classified and analyzed from the standpoint of the entire business enterprise as an operating unit, or shall accounting principles be presented in terms of a single interest, the proprietary?

This is not a matter of tweedledum and tweedledee. If proprietorship is the fundamental and pivotal concept for the accountant in dealing with modern business transactions, the interpretation of expense and revenue (or "profit and loss") items and accounts as direct accessories of proprietorship

---

[4] See, for example, Kester, *Accounting, Theory and Practice*, vol. I (1st Ed.), Chap. II.

naturally follows. The expiration of labor and materials purchased by the enterprise and consumed in putting out its product becomes a charge of the same general significance as the net return on all capital invested by other interests than the proprietary. It is at this point, the writer believes, that the doctrines of proprietorship have led to serious error. The commonly accepted conceptions of the operating accounts advanced by the proponents of proprietary accounting have tended to shut the door to all discriminating analysis of the income sheet. As a result the average income sheet is a hodge-podge of illogical, non-illuminating classifications. The importance of revision of accounting theory at this point is acute. The income sheet of the large corporation, certainly, is not an adjunct of any single interest or equity in the balance sheet, to be defined in terms of that interest; and any attempt to view it so results in distortion of so serious a character as largely to destroy the utility of the statement.[5]

In the remaining sections of this chapter it will be our task particularly to attempt to show that the classes, proprietorship and liabilities, are actually sections of a larger division, equities, and that the equation, properties equals equities, is the most logical expression of the financial condition of the business enterprise.[6] In other words, it will be contended that the balance sheet, as a statement of two independent and equal classes of data, is not a merely conventional arrangement, but is founded in the immanent nature of the business situation. We will attempt to show that practice has been more rational

---

[5] This matter will be elaborated in later chapters. It should be noted that in the preparation of the income sheet, practice is not always as irrational as theory. The income sheet prescribed by the Interstate Commerce Commission does not adhere to the proprietary doctrines and is on the whole a well-arranged statement. Likewise the accountants for many large companies organize their accounts and prepare their statements in a manner showing a grasp of the real situation.

[6] "Accounting is concerned primarily with two broad classifications. The first of these is called assets. . . . The second class consists of the various rights of persons to these assets. This class again divides into two groups, the rights of creditors, known as liabilities, and the rights of proprietors." (C. B. Couchman, "Classification of Surplus," *Journal of Accountancy*, vol. XXXII, p. 265.) This statement is an illustration of essentially the point of view adopted here.

than theory;[7] that the fundamental statement of the accountant is thoroughly reasonable, but that the theory of accounts, couched in terms of a more or less distinct subdivision which has been mistaken for an independent class, is not sound, especially when applied to the conditions of corporate organization. It will be insisted that the equities constitute a logical class on a level with the property or asset division, and that it is not an artificial combination of fundamentally dissimilar things.

Sharp distinctions, of course, may exist between equities as between assets. An element of the proprietary interest in a given case may differ markedly from some contractual equity; an asset such as notes receivable, for example, is quite distinct from that represented by a material object such as buildings. The accountant could make little headway without drawing many distinctions, making use of many classifications. But the underlying division, the starting point for all subsequent classification, is expressed by the equation, properties equals equities.[8]

THE SIGNIFICANCE OF OWNERSHIP

In Chapter II the equity category was conceived as the representation of the properties of the business enterprise in

---

[7] In practice the right-hand side of the balance sheet is usually denominated "liabilities." The proprietary element, upon which so much stress has been laid in accounting theory, is seldom given explicit recognition in balance-sheet headings. In other words, the general practice of grouping all equities as a single class under a single heading has persisted despite the efforts of accountants to break this class into two fundamental parts, or to attach such captions as "liabilities and capital," "liabilities and net worth," etc. According to the view held throughout this study, practice is more rational than prevailing theory in this matter. The use of the term "liabilities" to cover the entire equity side is somewhat unfortunate, however, since this expression is also commonly used in practice to denote contractual interests as opposed to residual proprietary interests. If the term "equities" were adopted for the general heading, the subsidiary terms "proprietorship" and "liabilities" could be used without confusion. There is, of course, little hope of changing usage that is so well established; and no great harm need result from the conventional nomenclature if the content of the classes involved be understood. Indeed, in the case of the large corporation, where a distinct legal entity must be recognized, to label all the equities "liabilities" is not as far-fetched a procedure as it has often been assumed to be.

[8] The full statement would be, "the *total* of the properties equals the *total* of the equities." This accounts for the use of the singular verb throughout.

terms of economic ownership. That is, the equities were said to consist in the amount of properties parceled and diffused appropriately among the various interests having rights in the situation. It will now be desirable, before turning specifically to an examination of equities in the different types of enterprises, to discuss the general significance of property ownership in both legal and economic terms.

What is the content of the concept, *ownership?* What is the significance of ownership? In what does the right to private property consist? What are the conditions, privileges, and obligations connected with title to assets? Where is the situs of title? In whom is title vested? Is the proprietor, so-called, the owner, and is the creditor in a fundamentally different position? Or are these terms merely expressions for different aspects of ownership in a broad sense?

It seems scarcely necessary to repeat that physical possession does not constitute property ownership and is not necessary to ownership. The furniture of the householder is not the property of the storage company having possession; the proprietor of the garage is not the owner of the cars committed to his care; canned goods purchased by the X Co., the wholesaler, may be left temporarily in the warehouse of the Y Co., the manufacturer; transportation companies do not acquire ownership in goods which they handle. Nevertheless one of the elements of ownership is the right to *control;* ultimate management is a prerogative and responsibility of the owner. We usually think of the owner of a property, whatever its form, as having the power to direct the method of its use, to hire or lease it as he sees fit, to dispose of it by sale, to destroy it, or withhold it from use if he desires. In the case of a manufacturing enterprise, for example, the determination of the extent and character of output, employment, financing, etc., ultimately devolves upon the owners.

But the right of the private owner to control his property

is by no means unrestricted under modern conditions. The most complete ownership does not carry unlimited authority. In the first place, as has been already noted, the scope of private interest is always subject to the general rights of the state as well as to specific statutory limitations. The ownership of certain kinds of property and the production of certain products may be specifically prohibited. The recent sweeping interference with the so-called property rights of the liquor interests is a striking example of the power of the state to limit the private owner's control. Further, the state, through its power of eminent domain, can on occasion completely nullify the individual's control of his properties. It can also, under certain conditions, levy upon and confiscate property for taxes. To a marked degree it can dictate methods of production, control character and extent of output, regulate prices, and assume other managerial functions. During the recent war the state, legally or illegally, assumed almost complete control of many industries. The amount, character, and source of raw material, the length of the working day, the amount and kind of output, the personnel of customers—these and other matters were in many cases controlled by the federal government.

Further, public opinion, although unexpressed by definite statutes, ordinances, and regulations, can and does exercise a powerful influence upon business methods, and hence upon the control of properties.

Indeed, the control of the so-called private owner is very far from absolute (aside from the inherent limitations surrounding any human agency), being restricted at many essential points by the public and the state in its various forms. The supposed right "to do with mine own as I will" has little existence.

Again, the control of the so-called owner is frequently limited by powers vested in or obligations assumed in connection with other private interests. One who inherits an estate is commonly thought of as the owner of the properties involved, although the control of the legatee may be very much restricted and hedged about by the terms of the will. It is also common, in the case of land purchases, for example, for the new owner to buy subject to the rights of other specific interests. Thus the buyer may be bound to give some person or persons a right of way on a part of his tract; he may be obliged to construct certain kinds of buildings, if any, so as not, for example, to obstruct the view of some adjacent land owner. Restrictions of this kind are common in the case of the sale of residence sites and other real estate.

Still further, by means of a long-term lease the nominal owner may delegate virtually all control to the lessee. The lessor in such a case is still commonly viewed as the owner, but for all practical purposes ownership, in so far as control is an essential, has passed to the lessee. Thus it is not unreasonable to view the long-term lease as in some respects the equivalent of an outright sale.

The proprietor, in accounting phraseology, is often spoken of as the "owner." The liabilities are said to represent the "debts" of the proprietor. From this standpoint the only way in which the creditors are related to the properties is through proprietorship. The proprietor *owns* the assets and *owes* the creditors.

Is this a correct interpretation of the situation from the standpoint of control, control being viewed as an aspect of ownership? Does the limited control of the private owner inhere exclusively in the proprietor? A negative answer must be given. While the large element of control is commonly vested in the proprietary it would certainly be an exaggeration to say that the creditors have no control, especially when the term "creditor" be considered to include the contractual investors in the corporation. The creditor always has contingent control (in the case of insolvency supplanting the proprietor), and in many cases considerable direct control. In later sections of this chapter this matter will be further considered with reference to the various types of business organization. At this point it will be sufficient to point out, first, that private ownership under modern conditions seldom if ever connotes complete and absolute control of properties; and, second, that such control as does reside in private ownership is not exclusively vested in proprietorship, as this concept is ordinarily understood in accounting.

A strictly legal criterion of ownership is *title*. To own property, we say, means to have the title thereto. What is meant by "title"? This is a highly technical matter to examine which in detail is entirely beyond the scope of this study and of little relation to our purpose. A brief statement will suffice. In the first place title does not constitute any one obligation, responsibility, or privilege, and it does not arise in any single standard set of circumstances and conditions. Aside from the limitations on the control of the owner such as were mentioned above, title does not indicate any particular complete status. An individual may be said to have title under a great variety of circumstances. And yet the owner, so-called, does not always have title. For example, an individual buys land on a contract, paying 10 per cent of the purchase price down. Such an individual would usually think of himself as the owner of the property involved, and we are in the habit of so viewing him. And, subject to the terms of the contract and so long as its conditions are fulfilled, the purchaser in these circumstances has as much control of the property as any private interest could have. Yet he would not, as a rule, be said to have title under these conditions.

Again, where there are mortgages or other liens in connection with properties the situs of title is hard to determine exactly, and is, in general, divided. According to one legal view, a mortgage gives actual title to the mortgagee. At any rate the ordinary mortgage is virtually a suspended deed, a deed which does not become effective as to control, however, unless the mortgagor fails to fulfill the terms involved. Still, we are accustomed to think of a farmer, for example, as the "owner," even though his farm is heavily mortgaged, and his net interest but a "shoe-string."

The difficulty of determining the passing of title in merchandising transactions illustrates the technical character of title. A dealer orders a lot of goods from a manufacturer; the goods are shipped, freight to be paid by consignee; the shipment is received and checked; receipt of goods is acknowledged; the freight bill is paid by consignee; a check on account is mailed to the consignor; and so on. When, in such a series of circumstances, does title pass to the buyer? As an occasion for accounting entry receipt of goods is usually followed. But receipt of goods is by no means always the occasion of title passing. In some situations even complete payment may not give the buyer title. Instances could be cited where raw materials have been received, manufactured, and the product sold, although title had not passed.

With respect to title, how do proprietorship and liabilities compare? The proprietary is usually defined as the interest which has exclusive legal right or title to a property. As a matter of fact the proprietor, so-called, does not have exclusive title. As stated above, the mortgage-holder, a creditor, has title according to one theory. And it is certainly true that the mortgage bondholder comes nearer to having title to *specific corporate assets* than the common stockholder. This matter will be discussed further in a later section.

On the basis of legal title, accordingly, it is not possible to draw a clear-cut distinction between proprietorship and liabilities as these terms are used in accounting. Vestiges of title may appear under either form, may attach to the creditor's equity as well as to the proprietor's.

In economics the property-holder, investor, is commonly thought of as furnishing two principal conditions or functions in production: (1) risk and responsibility-taking, and (2) "waiting power"—pure capital service. The agents corresponding to these elements are the entrepreneur and "capitalist proper," respectively.[9] The line drawn in accounting between proprietorship and liabilities roughly corresponds to this economic division of functions. The specialization of securities in the corporation has this distinction as a general starting point. But, from the point of view of economics, the argument that proprietorship and liabilities are simply more or less distinct subdivisions of a larger class, equities or ownership, is easily made. Even if it were peculiarly the function of the proprietor to take risk, and that of the creditor to furnish capital, we could still insist that both functions were aspects of ownership. As a matter of fact these aspects of ownership are always inseparable; i.e., there can be no risk of loss in the ordinary sense without the furnishing of capital. As is the case with many economic concepts, the terms "entrepreneur" and "capitalist" indicate functional divisions which can never be found exactly in the specific personalities of the business world. *All economic characteristics found in connection with any equity attach in some degree to every other equity.* And, since the accountant is concerned primarily with values, the economic point of view must receive recognition as well as the legal.

We are dealing here not with fundamental distinctions but merely with differences in degree. The individual or interest that assumes the *larger* element of risk in a business enterprise, and takes the major share of responsibility and control, approximates the economist's "entrepreneur" and the accountant's "proprietor"; the individual or interest that furnishes capital but takes comparatively little risk, and has

---

[9] *Cf.* Taylor, *Principles of Economics* (1921), pp. 82-84.

but slight or indirect control of ordinary operations, approaches the economist's "capitalist proper" and the accountant's "creditor." But it cannot be stated too emphatically that every equity, proprietary or otherwise, furnishes capital (money, commodities, or services); [10] every equity involves risk of loss; virtually all equities have some privileges and responsibilities with respect to management; and all long-term equities have rights in income and capital.

To sum up: property ownership connotes such attributes as control, title, risk-taking, and capital furnishing. No one of these elements attaches exclusively to what the accountant labels "proprietorship" as opposed to liabilities. Consequently we can conclude that ownership or equities constitutes a class rationally comprehending both of these divisions.

We have still to examine proprietorship and liabilities in detail under the various types of business enterprise mentioned in Chapter I, in order to substantiate this conclusion completely. What is meant by the proprietor and the creditor in the sole-proprietorship, the partnership, and the corporation? And are the purposes of accounting in these various cases best served and the accounting structure most rationally put together by treating the right-hand side of the balance sheet as a single logical class?

EQUITIES IN SOLE-PROPRIETORSHIPS AND PARTNERSHIPS

As a starting point in coming to an appreciation of the nature of proprietorship and liabilities in the case of unincorporated businesses it is necessary to recognize that from a legal point of view there is no such thing as a "business entity" in such cases. In other words, the accountant, in conceiving of the affairs of a proprietor engaged in business—or of

---

[10] With, perhaps, the single exception of what we may call the state's equity.

two or more partners so engaged—as a distinct business entity, is making use of a conception which has no legal reality; to speak of such situation as "business enterprises," to personify sole-proprietorships and partnerships, involves the adoption of a more or less questionable figure of speech. The law does not segregate the business affairs of Jones, the groceryman, from his other economic activities and interests. Similarly the partnership is viewed as merely a contractual relationship between two or more individuals;[11] and the properties and affairs of the business undertaken by the partners are not legally endowed with any special character or privileges as compared with their outside affairs and interests. Thus we have the unlimited liability feature of the typical partnership; the partners are jointly and severally liable for all obligations contracted by the firm, and no immunity is granted with respect to any other business or private assets of a partner (except such statutory personal property exemption as may happen to be allowed to a bankrupt).

Yet, as was stated in Chapter I, it is very convenient for the accountant to view every business endeavor as an undertaking, an enterprise, having a distinctive existence. And this view has its popular reality. The terms "firm," "house," "company," "establishment," "concern," "business," are used as freely in connection with unincorporated businesses as in the case of the corporation. Further, from the standpoint of economic character and of operation, formal organization does not alter the situation. It is hard to see how scientific accounting could be applied to such situations without the business-enterprise conception. At the same time the limitations of this view must also be kept in mind if mistaken judgments are to be avoided.[12]

---

[11] Commonly none but an individual (a natural person) can be a partner; i.e., a partnership, corporation, or other association cannot be a partner.

[12] Certain situations in which the accountant must firmly brush aside the fictitious personality of the enterprise to get at the realities of the case will be discussed in Chapter XV.

At least three possible viewpoints which the accountant might adopt as a basis for his work accordingly suggest themselves. The accounts and procedures may be constructed and planned from the standpoint of the proprietor, so-called, as an economic individual, embracing all his economic activities, business and personal. Thus the books of Jones, the grocer, might be organized in such a way as to show all the assets and liabilities connected with or arising in the grocery business, as well as all other properties of Jones and obligations relating to these properties or to his personal credit. Based on this view the financial statement of Jones would show on the left side all properties, both business and private, in which he had any equitable right; the opposite column would present Jones' net interest in these properties, together with all outside obligations and liens.

This statement would represent pretty accurately the legal conception of Jones as an economic entity. Further, it would express the creditor's position with respect to Jones. In general, as was noted above, a creditor in the case of a sole-proprietorship has an equity in the assets outside of the business as fully as in the business properties.

A second possible view for the accountant is that of Jones, the proprietor, in his strictly business capacity. The accounts may be constructed purely from the standpoint of "business" proprietorship. The general heading for the summary financial statement in this case would not be "Jones, the Economic Citizen," but "Jones, the Grocery Proprietor." It is this view in general which is adopted by accountants; and it is on the whole highly rational. As was noted above, little headway can be made with scientific accounting unless business and private affairs are carefully distinguished. A common source of confusion in sole-proprietary accounting systems is the failure to keep outside transactions out of the books of the business.

A third slightly different position assumes an actual business entity regardless of the fact that no such entity legally exists. According to this view the sole-proprietorship is a genuine *business enterprise,* involving a more or less complex list of properties and various equities, proprietary and otherwise. This might be called the "managerial" view. It is the most convenient conception from the standpoint, in particular, of the hired manager, to whom are entrusted various properties for which he will later be called to account by the owners, and who naturally desires to present a record of successful administration. To the operating manager Jones' grocery business constitutes a distinct economic unit.

The use of the equation, properties equals equities, as a presentation of the underlying financial status of the sole-proprietorship, would be especially justified if this last position were adopted. Such a point of view undoubtedly has distinct advantages, and is perhaps the most sound on the economic side; but it has limitations from the legal standpoint.

Similarly, in the case of the partnership, there are the three possible bases for the presentation of financial status and the construction of the accounts. From the standpoint of the creditors all of the personal and outside properties and liabilities of the partners, together with the business assets, liabilities, and capital, might well be shown in their financial statement.[13] On the other hand, it is generally agreed that for most accounting purposes it is well to conceive of the partnership as an entity, and to restrict the accounts of the partnership to a presentation of business data.

This brief statement gives the background the accountant must bear in mind in constructing and interpreting accounts for the sole-proprietorship and copartnership. To return to the

---

[13] Indeed, a two-section partnership balance sheet would not be an unreasonable device in some cases. One section could be devoted to the business assets and equities, the other to outside properties and liabilities.

specific question in hand, how can the equation of the financial position of such an enterprise best be expressed? Is the expression, properties equals equities, a logical statement in such cases, or have we three independent classes, assets, liabilities, and proprietorship?

It must be admitted that the conventional proprietary theory of accounts receives its strongest support from the nature of these situations. As an expression of accounting theory for the simple sole-proprietorship or partnership the statements by Sprague, Hatfield, and others are fairly satisfactory. The proprietor of the small establishment is commonly thought of as the owner. He frequently furnishes a large percentage of the capital involved. The essential accounting facts, properties, costs, etc., naturally center around proprietorship. The proprietor is usually in active control.

Further, the liabilities are commonly represented largely by trade creditors whose accounts run from thirty to ninety days. These creditors in nowise view themselves as owners and ordinarily are not thought of as having title to or an interest in the assets; rather their claims might be said to represent the personal obligations of the sole-proprietor or, as the case may be, the joint obligations of the partners. In other words, it is perhaps more accurate to conceive of the liabilities in these cases as claims against the proprietor rather than as rights or equities in assets. From this standpoint there appear to be three classes involved: (1) properties, (2) "ownership" of these properties, and (3) obligations of the owners; and thus the proprietary equation, and the use of the proprietary as a pivotal category for all accounts and transactions, would seem to be justified.

On the other hand, the two-dimensional equation as a means of representing the financial condition of the sole-proprietorship and partnership is not without its validity. In the first place the proprietor, so-called, does not always furnish even the larger amount of the capital. Many proprietors are operating on a "narrow margin," the necessary funds being largely secured from other interests. And if part of the capital is furnished by a mortgage-holder, for example, the proprietor can hardly be said to have title, as was noted in the last section. The mortgagor in such a case may be essentially a kind of "silent" partner, having little voice in routine matters but coming into active control in case of financial embarrassment or bankruptcy.

Similarly merchandise creditors may, on occasion, be the power behind the throne. The small retail establishment is sometimes largely financed by the interested wholesaler. Special elements of control are usually reserved by such creditors, and direct liens upon goods are often involved. In such cases it is surely not fantastic to say that the proprietor's status is represented by a certain interest, share, or equity in the properties; while the partner-creditor likewise has an equity.

In the case of actual insolvency the creditor's interest becomes paramount. And to what does his claim attach? Not (since the days for debt imprisonment are largely gone) to the body or person of the proprietor, or to his future earnings or properties, but to the *currently available properties*. Take the case of a current claim such as payroll accrued. Is it unreasonable to say, even aside from the case of insolvency, that this constitutes an equity in current assets? It is certainly an enforceable claim, and its settlement depends upon existing property values.

Further, as was stated above, from the economic or managerial points of view we have in any sole-proprietorship and partnership essentially a mass of capital taking shape in various properties, and a list of persons or interests representing the ownership, the *equities* in this property. From these points of view—and they are of far-reaching significance for the accountant—the equation, assets equals equities. is thoroughly rational. Especially in the large unincorporated enterprise—of which there are still numerous examples—is this interpretation of consequence. And, while the very large sole-proprietorship or partnership is not typical, the business in which the accountant is usually interested is an enterprise of some importance, not that of the newsboy or pop vender. It would seem that the reality of this form of equation, for the accountant, is at least comparable with that which recognizes three distinct members.

Property suggests ownership, presupposes ownership. Each item of property must be owned by some person, interest, or group. Then, since the proprietor's equity is not commonly equal to the total value of the properties involved, is he the *owner* of the *entire* amount of the properties in the most significant sense of the term? Where the proprietor has an interest of from 90 to 100 per cent of the assets under his control, proprietorship and equities are practically identical. But, in general, is it reasonable to say that a *residual* interest, merely, embraces all elements of ownership?

In conclusion, it is submitted that while the distinction between proprietor and creditor is in general clear-cut in the unincorporated business, there is sufficient relationship between the two to justify placing the amount of their interests, for balance-sheet purposes, under the one head, equities. The equation, assets equals proprietorship plus liabilities, is of course thoroughly reasonable for such cases, as the relationship between proprietor and creditor is indicated by the placing of both types of equities on the right-hand side. The equation, assets less liabilities equals proprietorship, on the other hand, is not logical or rational, unless it be used for some special purpose. It evidences a too great stress upon proprietorship, an over-emphasis which is likely to lead to serious error in the interpretation of operating accounts.

But it is in the case of the corporation that the form of

equation adopted in this study finds its especial justification. We will now turn to an examination of corporate equities.

TYPES OF CORPORATE EQUITIES

As was noted in Chapter I, the present dominant form of business organization in the mining, transportation, manufacturing, and financial fields is the corporation. Further, it is doubtful if the corporation has reached the limit of its development; the continued improvement of this scheme of organization and its more complete utilization in all important lines of business is to be expected. Hence, to couch the theory of accounts particularly in terms of the conditions, needs, and purposes of the corporation, rather than those of the simpler business situations, is a procedure not without justification.

As has already been suggested, the need for elaborate statistical analysis is commonly more urgent under the conditions of corporate organization than elsewhere. Indeed, the development of the corporation has been synchronous with the rise of modern accounting. Certainly, in view of this situation, an explanation of the structure of modern accounts with virtually no reference to the corporation, such as is usually given, is entirely inadequate. Accounting practice has been greatly modified and extended to keep pace with the development of the corporation; accounting theory requires restatement in terms of this development.

The corporation, it may be reiterated, is the business enterprise *par excellence*. In this case we have a genuine business entity. The state endows the corporation with attributes which give it an independent personality, an existence apart and distinct from that of its individual members. Limited liability and other significant consequences follow. Hence, for the accountant to view the corporation as a distinct institution, as having a real business identity, is thoroughly sound. No apology whatever need be offered for this standpoint.

How is ownership represented in the corporation? Is the term "equities" applicable in this case? What is corporate proprietorship? What are corporate liabilities? Are these fundamentally distinct classes, or can they both be logically placed under the single category, equities. In what respects is the corporate creditor distinct from the corporate proprietor?

The capital funds of the corporation are secured primarily through the issue of two main classes of securities, stocks and bonds; and this division indicates, it should be emphasized, the most important distinction found on the right-hand side of the corporate balance sheet. It will be necessary, then, to consider the important characteristics of each of these types of securities as a first step in attempting to decide as to whether or not the caption "equities" is a satisfactory designation for one member of the fundamental equation. No attempt will be made to describe corporate securities in detail. Stress will be laid solely on those features which have a distinct bearing on the problem in hand.

In the first place it should be noted that the line drawn between entrepreneur and capitalist proper, already referred to, corresponds in a rough way to the distinction between stockholder and bondholder. The stockholder assumes the larger element of risk in that he has residual rights to assets as either income or principal. The stockholder profits most if the enterprise is very successful; he suffers first if the venture proves to be disastrous. That is, the stockholder's equity is a buffer for the bondholder's equity in the enterprise. Likewise the stockholder commonly has the larger share in immediate management; it is his influence which has the most marked effect upon immediate financial and production policies.

The specialization of securities, however, goes much further than this. There are, on the one hand, many kinds of capital stock. The most important distinction here is between *preferred* and *common* issues. This subdividing of stocks carries the specialization of the economic and legal elements of ownership one step farther. The common stock is in general the more speculative, carrying the heavier risk. It frequently involves the greater direct control of operation. Common stock is often issued as a bonus with preferred stock or with bonds, and in such a case its value is small and depends primarily upon the voting power attached and the attraction of possible future earnings. The preferred stock may have prior rights to assets as income or principal, or both. Usually the preferred stock carries a definite dividend rate.

But, again, there is an almost indefinite variety of preferred stocks. Many issues are "callable" or "redeemable" under certain conditions; in some cases this amounts to virtually a definite repayment date. Some issues are "convertible" into other securities. In some cases the conversion privilege may be exercised at the option of the investor; in other instances conversion is required of the shareholder at a specified date. Preferred stocks occasionally carry "participating" rights in excess income above a certain percentage amount, as well as a right to a regular fixed rate. Dividends on preferred stock are often "cumulative." In the matter of voting power and other aspects of control a host of different provisions are possible. Some corporations have preferred stocks outstanding which rank very nearly on a level with the common stock, which, in other words, are preferred principally in name. In other cases the gap between the common stock and the preferred is very wide.

In recent years, the advance in interest rates having made the issue of long-time bonds unwise, a marked development in the direction of preferred stocks has occurred.[14] Corporations already in existence have resorted almost universally to pre-

---

[14] The fact that capital secured from bond issues has not been rated as a part of invested capital for excess-profits tax purposes, may also have had something to do with this development.

ferred stocks and notes as a means of increasing capital; and new corporations have also adopted the same plan in a majority of cases. In general highly conservative types of stock have been issued, in the endeavor, on the part of corporate financiers, to tap that part of the community's capital accumulation which would ordinarily flow into bond issues. Current issues of preferred stocks are loaded with all sorts of special provisions to make them appeal to the conservative investor.

There seems to be no limit to the way in which the preferred stockholder, so-called, can be safeguarded and endowed with rights and privileges ordinarily conferred upon none but a bondholder.[15] A certain corporation, for example, has outstanding an issue of $250,000 in "preferred stock," secured by a first mortgage on the principal corporate properties! The fixed return to the stockholders in this case is called "interest" rather than dividends. These preferred stockholders have no general voting power, but are endowed with veto power with respect to specified fundamental matters of operating and financial policy. An administrative branch of the federal government was called upon to pass upon the question as to whether or not such a security represented "borrowed" capital. Any number of other dubious cases might be cited.

Similarly there are a great variety of bond issues. We have "income" bonds, "debenture" bonds, "collateral trust" bonds, etc., and innumerable types of "mortgage" bonds. The ingenuity of the corporate financier seems to know no limit in this regard; and almost any kind of contractual security may be legally labeled "bond." In fact, virtually every specific issue has its peculiar features in regard to income, safety of principal, and control of operation. Many issues are divided between "coupon" and "registered" blocks. A coupon bond is essen-

---

[15] See "Recent Tendencies in Corporation Finance," by A. S. Keister, *Journal of Political Economy*, vol. XXX, pp. 257-273. This study of current corporate securities substantiates emphatically this statement and the general point of view which is stressed throughout this chapter.

tially a security with respect to which income and principal are payable to bearer; while a registered bond is made out to a particular holder, whose account is kept on the corporate books (or on the books of its agent), in much the same manner as is the individual stockholder's account.

Mortgage bonds are based upon some sort of mortgage contract. It may be a first, second, third, or other mortgage, however. The term "mortgage bond" is often used when relatively little security is given by the mortgage instrument on which the issue is based. A bond issue on a first mortgage covering but a small part of a company's property and, for example, a fourth mortgage on the balance, is not highly secured as far as the mortgage itself is concerned. The earning power and general position of the corporation are the factors in such a case upon which the bondholders are really depending. These factors in a great many instances outweigh the significance of the specific safeguards. The point to be emphasized is that even among mortgage bonds, so-called, the widest kind of variation in regard to security of principal and income obtains.

Bonds such as debentures,[16] which are not based upon specific liens and encumbrances but entirely upon the general credit of the corporation, are also issued subject to a great variety of conditions. In some cases such securities are highly speculative, being much less secure than conservative preferred stock issues. A certain corporation, for example, has outstanding a large issue of debenture "bonds" which carries an interest rate—according to the provisions—of 1 to 5 per cent, actually pays nothing, and is non-cumulative.

To sum up, if all existing corporate stocks and bonds were to be arranged in a series according to degree of risk attaching

---

[16] "The term 'debenture,' in this country, indicates that the investment assumes in part both the proprietorship and the creditorship relation, the latter dominating." (Milton Rindler, "Relation of Capital Stock to Invested Capital," *Administration*, vol. I, p. 39.)

to each, beginning with the most speculative types of common stock at one extreme, followed by the better grade common issues, the less conservative preferred stocks, the highly safeguarded preferred issues, and all the various grades of bonds grouped according to security, it would be impossible to draw any hard and fast line of division which followed security types and corresponded to the proprietor-creditor grouping of the sole-proprietorship or the entrepreneur-capitalist classification. And if control or any other aspect of ownership were followed in making the arrangement there would again be no clear-cut line of cleavage.

The differentiation of ownership elements in practice goes far beyond the underlying legal and economic distinctions. What we have is a marvelous diffusion of all aspects of ownership—control, income, risk, etc.—among a host of investors. *Each* security issue carries certain privileges and obligations with reference to *all* of the elements of ownership. The modern financier has developed the specialization of securities to such a point that the pocketbook of the investor of every degree of whim and inclination—the outright speculator at one extreme, the savings-bank depositor at the other—can be tapped. By means of this specialization of securities the corporation has become a device by which the capital of hundreds and thousands of individual investors, and of many different types of investors, can be drawn into a single undertaking, welded into a huge economic unit.

Other kinds of securities than stocks and bonds are of course found in corporation finance. Large sums of capital are frequently raised by note issues. Such securities commonly run from two to ten years and represent, consequently, a more or less temporary group of investors in each case. They constitute essentially, for our purposes, a short-term bond of the debenture class. Annuities, perpetuities, and other special types of contractual securities are also occasionally encountered. In small corporations mortgages, without a security issue, are sometimes used directly as a means of securing capital. No serious complications with respect to the theory of accounts are presented by these cases. These all represent means of raising the necessary funds just as do the more important classes of securities—stocks and bonds. The whole situation may be summed up by saying that the corporation secures its capital from a wide variety of sources, and that each security or lien, whatever its individual peculiarities, represents an equity in the corporate assets.

The principal part of a corporation's capital is usually secured through stock, bond, and note issues. As in the case of the sole-proprietorship or partnership, however, the corporate balance sheet commonly shows a considerable amount of current or "floating" liabilities. Short-term notes, creditors' accounts, accrued wages, taxes, and other current items, arise in the case of the corporation as elsewhere. It may seem at first glance that such current items can hardly be included in the class, equities. It is true that the individuals and interests represented in such cases are not members of the corporation even in a remote sense. They are not typical "investors" and do not view themselves as such. Nevertheless it is not unreasonable for the accountant to consider all these current claims as equities.[17] The individuals involved, while making no long-term commitments of capital, do in general concede values to the corporation in the form of goods, services, and cash for which payment is not immediately made. In other words, the assets under the control of the corporation at a particular moment have been acquired in part from current creditors. The amount of these claims measures the excess of asset values over the equities of the long-term investors. Ex-

---

[17] A recent advertisement of an income tax service includes this statement, "Uncle Sam is the first preferred partner in your business, whether you are incorporated or not." The state's "equity" is, of course, the most doubtful case of all.

plicit income seldom accrues on such current equities (except in the case of notes drawing interest). Little or no control commonly rests with these interests. But here again we have a difference of degree and not a new category. Current liabilities deserve a place in the same *general* classification as the long-term capital interests; and the construction of the conventional balance sheet recognizes the propriety of this view.

Further, while the personnel of the trade creditors and other current claimants, and the identity of the individual account items involved, are constantly changing, the *total* of the floating debt may be continuously a considerable sum.[18] That is, the current equities, *en masse,* may explain the origin, continuously, of 10 per cent or more of the total of properties in the hands of the corporation. And in the case of insolvency or reorganization the trade creditors may be of sufficient importance to assume the position of a highly significant interest.[19]

CORPORATE "PROPRIETOR" AND "CREDITOR"

Under these circumstances, who is the corporate "proprietor" and who is the "creditor"? According to the usual view the body of stockholders represents the corporate proprietary; all others are creditors. The total equity of the stockholders is the accountant's corporate proprietorship. The bondholders, noteholders, and all other parties having contractual claims are the creditors of the corporation, and the amount of their claims represents the corporate liabilities.

Of just what significance and validity is this view for the accountant? Is the underlying equation of the corporate balance sheet most logically expressed, properties less liabilities equals proprietorship (stockholders' capital)? Or is it more

---

[18] "A firm that perpetually has at least $10,000 of commercial loans outstanding is to all intents and purposes obtaining $10,000 of permanent capital from commercial banks." (M. A. Copeland, "Problems in Financial Administration," *Journal of Political Economy,* vol. XXVIII, p. 797.)

[19] For an example, see Dewing, *Corporate Promotions and Reorganizations,* p. 195.

reasonable for the accountant to view the regular two-class balance sheet as a rational expression of the equation, corporate properties equals corporate equities or investments? Does the right-hand side of the conventional corporate balance sheet represent, fundamentally, a homogeneous class of facts, or are the corporate liabilities, for accounting purposes, merely negative aspects of corporate assets, while the stockholders' interest measures the underlying accounting category? Is there a fundamental line of cleavage for accounting purposes between the stockholder and all other investors? Or, to go still further, in the case of the corporation can the proprietor-creditor grouping be maintained as a useful classification for the accountant, even if both classes be considered as subdivisions of a more general heading, equities?

In the first place it should be admitted that the legal view supports, in a measure, the line of differentiation commonly adopted by the accountant.[20] In law the membership of the corporation is conceived to reside peculiarly in the body of stockholders. A shareholder of a corporation is a member; a bondholder is a creditor, virtually an outsider. We by no means have here, however, the precise analogue of the owner-creditor classification of the sole-proprietorship. The corporation itself, an entity apart and distinct, legally, from any investor or class of investors, is the owner in about the same sense that the sole-proprietor in an unincorporated business is the owner.[21] In

---

[20] It should be emphasized, however, that although the accountant should be cognizant of legal viewpoints, he need not, in fact should not, always organize his principles and procedures *solely* in terms of legal positions. A view legitimate for the accountant may not always be the strict legal interpretation. In the case of a bond sold at a discount for example, the accountant is inclined to consider the net amount invested as the original effective liability, a liability which gradually accrues to par as the discount is accumulated. The lawyer, on the other hand, would probably consider the par of the bond as the true liability throughout the duration of the contract.

[21] "But, looking through the form, we cannot disregard the essential truth disclosed; ignore the substantial difference between corporation and stockholder; treat the entire organization as unreal; look upon stockholders as partners, when they are not such. . . . We must treat the corporation as a substantial entity separate from the stockholder. . . ." (From the opinion of the United States Supreme Court in *Eisner v. Macomber*, decided March 8, 1920; 252 U. S. 189, 214.)

PROPRIETORSHIP AND LIABILITIES 77

so far as there is any such thing, specifically, as corporate ownership, it resides in the corporate entity itself. The *corporation* "owns" the corporate properties.[22] As has been pointed out many times by various writers on corporate finance, no individual stockholder has any title whatever to any corporate asset! The stockholder has no claim to or rights in any specific corporate property. All that can be said of his interest, strictly, is that he has an "equity" in the *total* of corporate assets. Clearly the term "equity" and not "owner" is applicable here.

Indeed, the bondholder in many cases may be said to approach the status of an owner much more closely than the stockholder. In so far as the bond investor's interest rests on a mortgage or other lien covering specific properties his right may approximate title; for, as was noted in a preceding section, from the standpoint of one widely accepted legal interpretation of the case, title resides in the mortgage-holder rather than in the residual equity. But in general, the bondholder, like the stockholder, is not an owner *per se*. His interest constitutes precisely an equity, as does the stockholder's. In other words, the expression "equities" exactly designates (as far as bonds and stocks are concerned) the interests appearing in the right-hand side of the corporate balance sheet. In a sense, indeed, the legal point of view really supports this classification more closely than the theory that the stockholder is the owner or proprietor and that the liabilities (represented by bondholders, etc.) are mere deductions from total assets for the purpose of determining net proprietorship.

In certain circumstances even the equity of the stockholder may be said to embrace both proprietary and liability elements. When a dividend is appropriated from undivided income the

---

[22] In a sense there are three classes in the corporate balance sheet: (1) the properties, (2) the corporate owner and (3) the investors. That is, the rights of the actual investors focus upon the corporate properties only through and in terms of the corporation itself.

amount thereof—between declaration and payment dates—is usually rated as a liability. According to this view a stockholder may be at once a member of the corporation and a corporate creditor. By the mere action of the board of directors a section of his equity passes into the liability group. This emphasizes the uncertainty of the proprietor-creditor classification in the corporation as a fundamental distinction.

The discussion must be carried still further, however, as there are several objections to our tentative conclusion which might be advanced. It might be urged, for example, that the fact that bonds [23] have definite repayment dates places such securities in an altogether distinct category as compared with stocks. This is most certainly a distinction, but not, for our purposes, on a fundamental level. As was stated above, preferred stocks are often callable under specific conditions and at specific dates and are liquidated with cash or exchanged for other securities. Again, perpetuities, which have all the characteristics of bonds—and may be labeled "bonds"—except repayment dates, are common in England, and have been used in this country.[24] Undoubtedly the use of such instruments will increase as the country becomes older and opportunities for speculative investment decrease. Further, bonds are commonly paid by "refunding," and this means that, although the entire list of bondholders may change and be replaced by a new list holding a somewhat different form of security, from the standpoint of the corporation the issue is in a sense continuous. In other words, a corporation may *permanently* secure a large part of its capital by emitting contractual securities which are replaced from time to time by new issues. While particular bondholders are retired, bondholders as a class may be continuous. The contractual capitalization of American railways,

---

[23] The bondholder's equity will be referred to throughout this section as the prototype of the corporate liability.
[24] Largely by governmental units.

for example, is, broadly speaking, as permanent a part of the total capitalization as is the stock capital.

Still further, it is quite possible to finance an entire *terminable* project with stock issues. A company may be organized to operate a mine until exhaustion, cut a timber tract, develop a parcel of urban property, exploit a terminable franchise, etc., with the understanding that the enterprise is to be wound up, and the stock canceled, at the conclusion of the undertaking. A definite date may even be set in advance for this consummation. Incorporated societies and associations sometimes terminate after a definite or indefinite number of years; and the capital stock is then retired in accordance with a prearranged plan.

Again, it would be quite conceivable (aside from legal complications) for an economic project to be financed entirely by bond issues (or at least by "borrowings" of some sort), either continuous or terminable. Such securities, it is true, would have no residual or buffer equity standing back of them, but they might rest on first mortgages covering all the properties and thus be more conservative than many actual bond issues which have stockholders' capital as a buffer. Municipalities and other governmental units commonly make use of bonds and notes exclusively in raising capital.[25] A partnership is occasionally met with which is operating entirely, or almost entirely, on borrowed funds.

A general distinction between stocks and bonds which is of considerable practical significance lies in the fact that if bond interest or principal is defaulted outright, insolvency, or at least a receivership, commonly ensues, whereas a failure to pay dividends on stocks would ordinarily bring no immediate legal complication. A court will usually appoint a re-

---

[25] The "stocks" issued by some municipalities are really a sort of bond. These debenture stocks are now little used in the United States but are common in England and some of the British possessions. In modern British usage the term "stock" is often applied to a security which draws a specified rate of interest in perpetuity.

ceiver more readily on petition of creditors, so-called, than on that of stockholders. In general the "fixed" charges must be paid or serious consequences result.

This situation, however, has its qualifications. In the matter of forcing insolvency income bondholders, for example, are in a position quite different from that of first mortgage bondholders. The annual return to the income bondholder has about the same status as the preferred stockholder's dividend. Its payment depends upon the success of the company as an operating enterprise, and if the corporation is unsuccessful there is no legal recourse.[26] Indeed, in the case of many conservative American issues, a failure to pay the regular fixed dividend on the preferred stock would be considered as almost as serious a matter as a default with respect to bond interest.

Further, it should be remembered that any *stockholder* has definite legal rights, and can proceed against the corporation if these rights are infringed in any way. Witness the hundreds of actions brought by both common and preferred stockholders against the corporations in which they hold equities! Suits for the most part covering disputes with regard to matters of income and control. In some cases virtual insolvency and reorganization have been brought about by the preferred stockholders.[27]

It was noted in the preceding section that in general stocks carry more control of business operation and financial policies than bonds. But it should be re-emphasized that not all control resides in the body of stockholders. This is another general distinction of consequence but it is not on a sufficiently fundamental level to overthrow the legitimacy of the class, equities. Further, like other general distinctions, it becomes

---

[26] See a discussion of the "participating" bond by C. O. Hardy in "Some Recent Financial Devices," *Journal of Political Economy*, vol. XXIX, pp. 249-250.

[27] For a case in point, see Dewing, *Corporate Promotions and Reorganizations*, Chap. II.

obscure when specific cases are examined. The bondholder frequently has considerable direct and indirect control. Specifications in regard to sinking fund appropriations, capitalization, general financial policies, etc., are of common occurrence in the bond contract. The bondholder often has voting and veto power in connection with important measures. Further, there is an evident tendency in corporate finance to endow the bondholder with more and more direct control. The prospective bondholder is awake to the fact that large sums of capital cannot safely be committed to modern business enterprise if control be entirely relinquished to other interests, regardless of the original security. The looting of large corporations by unscrupulous stockholders operating on a narrow margin is a too familiar fact.

Still further, the typical shareholder as a matter of fact commonly exercises little or no direct influence upon operating and financial policies. He may possibly send in a proxy once a year, as directed by the "insiders," but evidently exerts thereby a very slight control. A relatively small coterie of stockholders often constitutes the real power behind the throne. It is a familiar fact that where stock ownership is highly diffused, a compact 25 per cent of the total stock outstanding may constitute, for practical purposes, a majority interest. And, again, the controlling group commonly delegates its authority in part to a board of directors and a group of officers who, in turn, entrust actual direction in large measure to hired subordinates.

Another point of importance in this connection is the fact that the bondholder comes into practically complete control in the case of receiverships and reorganizations. Thus the bondholder has contingent direct control. And it is hard to say that this is an unimportant matter or relates to a wholly exceptional situation. Bankruptcies, receiverships, and reorganizations are always with us. A considerable percentage of the total railway mileage of this country, for example, has been in receivers' hands at various times.

Reorganizations furnish additional evidence of the instability of the stockholder (owner)-bondholder (creditor) classification. In such cases we often have wholesale exchanges of bonds for stocks and stocks for bonds.[28] Former stockholders may pass into the bondholder class, and bondholders sometimes become stockholders. The exchange of securities is also a common financial operation outside of reorganization. Many issues of bonds give the holder the privilege of converting his security into stock under certain conditions. This is often true of bond issues put out by copper mining companies, for example. This conversion privilege has on occasion meant that the real controlling interest resided, for a time, in the convertible bonds.

In connection with reorganization should be noted the attitude commonly taken by the courts in such cases. The tendency is to take just the view we are trying to establish as the proper standpoint for the accountant. One group of security-holders is not looked upon as absolute owners, while all other groups are viewed as rank outsiders. Instead all interests are viewed as having "equities," rights and obligations, in the enterprise. All are considered to be investors who have committed their capital to a joint undertaking. And each class is expected to make sacrifices, concessions, and adjustments in accordance with its particular privileges and duties.

It should be stated emphatically at this point that it is not the writer's intention to attempt to overthrow or distort legitimate distinctions; just the reverse is the case. The corporate equities are markedly varied in character as are the corporate properties. It is this very fact which gives rise to some of the

---

[28] Dewing, *Corporate Promotions and Reorganizations*, p. 608, tables Ia and Ic.

most important questions of accounting. The general distinction between stocks and bonds is of real significance for the accountant. But distinctions should be observed for certain purposes, similarities for others. It may safely be urged that such differences as exist in this case do not overthrow the legitimacy of the property-equity classification set forth in the preceding chapter as the fundamental expression of the financial condition of the corporate enterprise. The equation, properties equals equities, expresses the underlying line of cleavage in accounting data. Further classification breaks both equities and properties into new groups. There may be many kinds of assets, differing sharply with respect to physical character, permanence, liquidity, etc. Similarly the rights and privileges of the various equities with respect to income, control, risk-bearing, etc., are admittedly very diverse. All of these further distinctions, however, are merely of degree, and do not give rise to fundamental categories.

In concluding this section it may be noted that continental European usages strongly support the view that the corporation balance sheet (or any other, for that matter) consists in two main classes of facts, properties and equities. Thus the German and French balance sheets are commonly designated "active" on the left side and "passive" on the right. This usage is particularly happy in that it suggests the interdependent character of the two classes. The "active" class, representing a sum of values in the hands of the enterprise, is the objective starting point. The "passive" list represents the manifestations of ownership, the dispersion of this sum of asset values among the various interests concerned.

Further, the subheadings on the right-hand side of the corporate balance sheet as frequently found in financial statements denote very clearly the view that the stockholders' or members' equity is a division of the same main heading as is the bondholders'. In the Belgian statistical year-book for

1913,[29] for example, we find the balance sheet of a Belgian colonial enterprise organized under the two main headings, *"Actif"* and *"Passif,"* and under the latter the two principal subheadings, *"Dettes de la Société envers elle-même"* and *"Dettes de la Société envers des Tiers."*

In view of the remarkable development of the corporate form of organization in the United States, it is somewhat surprising to find that American accountants have been more backward in applying this development to accounting theory and usage than have European accountants.

A "RESIDUAL" EQUITY

On the basis of the above discussion it may be concluded that while in the sole-proprietorship and partnership the accountant may with some reason couch his explanations of the accounting structure and organize procedures entirely in terms of proprietorship and from the standpoint of the proprietors, the view implicit in this cannot rationally be established in the case of the corporation. Here there is no element corresponding closely to the sole-proprietor or partner. The stockholder is not the owner; he has merely an equity. The same can be said of the other investors. The managerial view, a conception of the corporation as a legal and economic entity operating a mass of properties in the interest of a whole body of investors of various classes, is the proper starting point.

It is not intended, however, to deny the peculiar importance of the stockholders' equity for the accountant. The liabilities are in general fixed [30] and contractual. The stockholder's equity is elastic and residual. The stockholder furnishes a buffer for all other interests. And a residual equity is of

---

[29] In the *Annexe ou Bulletin Officiel du Congo belge,* pp. 474-475.
[30] Except for interest accruals or definite accumulation and amortization.

particular importance to the accountant because it is in such an equity that much of his work comes to a focus.[31] The analytical work of the accountant, his judgments, estimates, valuations, bear upon and are of especial importance to the residual interest. The concluding figure of the income sheet relates to this equity. The surplus account, the final result in the accounting process of all operating and income accounts, expresses a section of this equity. It is here that the special estimates, calculations, and interpretations of the accountant finally come home to roost.

But, strictly speaking, it is not the entire body of stockholders of all classes upon which the accountant must fix his attention. The residual interest in the case of the corporation is represented by the equity of the *common* stockholder. In the organization of the accounts and the preparation of statements the preferred stockholders can best be classed, for most purposes, with the bondholder and other contractual security-holders. In general the preferred stockholder draws a fixed rate of return, has no equity in surplus, has relatively slight direct control. The analytical work of the accountant has no more relation to the preferred stockholder's equity than to that of the bondholder.

This is especially true where the preferred stock is a relatively small issue, highly secured and safeguarded, owned by a body of investors of conservative inclinations entirely outside the group of common shareholders, and not represented in active control. Such an issue should certainly be classed with the fixed, contractual equities for purposes of accounting analysis. On the other hand, cases may be found where the preferred stock is closely allied to the common, is of about the same amount, has participating rights in income and sur-

---

[31] The equity of the sole-proprietor or partner is also of especial importance to the accountant because it is *residual*, not because it is supposed to represent exclusive ownership.

plus, and has equal voting power. In such instances the preferred stock may with some justification be viewed as a part of the residual equity.

It is interesting to note that there are some recent cases in corporate accounting practice where explicit recognition has been given in the balance sheet to this distinction between the "fixed" equities on the one hand and the residual interest on the other. A recent balance sheet of a large publishing company, for example, shows the common shareholders' equity as a final, concluding figure on the right-hand side of the statement, thus, "Equity for Common Stock, $4,638,952." On the same balance sheet the preferred stock is listed among the liabilities at the even fixed sum, $2,500,000. This usage reveals an interpretation of corporate accounts in practice which is exactly in line with the foregoing discussion. A clear-cut showing of the residual balancing equity in the financial statement is a practice to be commended. It is still better usage, of course, to exhibit all the ledger balances (capital stock, surplus, etc.) which go to make up the common shareholder's interest, with the algebraic sum thereof definitely set forth in the outside column of the balance sheet.

Accountants have, of course, often stressed the advantages of the "net worth" statement, i.e., a three-class balance sheet showing assets, liabilities, and the difference between the two, as net worth or proprietorship. The desirability of such arrangements under special circumstances is not to be denied. Where it is desired to focus attention upon the buffer protecting a particular equity, for example, such a statement may be used to advantage. In general, however, in corporate statements, such a "net worth" can best be restricted to the common stockholders' interest. As has been just stated, it is this equity which expresses the residual equity. To amalgamate common and preferred equities in a single figure is to lose, in part at least, such advantages as inhere in this sort of statement.

It must be admitted that the conception of "net worth" as a conglomerate of the interests of all stockholders, however dissimilar the various issues outstanding may be, has received strong support in recent years from the definitions of "invested capital" adopted by Congress in its recent excess-profits tax legislation. Aside from numerous statutory exceptions, "invested capital" for tax purposes and the accountant's conventional "net worth" are very closely related. That is, the several revenue acts have defined the invested capital of the corporation as embracing only the equities of the various classes of shareholders, adjusted with respect to certain phases of asset valuation. It would be a mistake to conclude from this fact, however, that herein lies any ultimate justification of this "net worth" conception, either as a basis for invested capital for tax purposes or as a view of fundamental consequence for general accounting purposes.[32] This feature of the excess-profits tax program has been roundly criticized from all sides. It has been pointed out repeatedly that plans of capitalization, mere methods of financing, furnish a wholly unsatisfactory basis for the measurement of comparative financial success. In general the only reasonable definition of invested capital must be based upon the bona fide total of asset values devoted to the operations of the particular business enterprise, regardless of the particular distribution of security issues adopted.

But, again, the importance of even this modified conception of corporate proprietorship must not be overemphasized. An insistence upon the common shareholder's interest as a pivotal and entirely independent category would lead to improper analysis. It would mean the organization of all operating and income accounts as direct adjuncts of the shareholder's interest; for it is clear that, from the standpoint of the common stockholder, interest and dividends accruing in

---

[32] An article by Stuart Chase. "What Is a Reasonable Profit?" (*Journal of Accountancy*, vol. XXIX, pp. 416-434) contains some interesting discussion of this subject.

favor of all prior equities are deductions, charges, which must be taken care of before the residual return can be ascertained. The same is true of a genuine operating expense. Thus, on this basis, would be developed the doctrine that returns to contractual equities are in the same category as operating expenses, offsets to what would otherwise be increase in the net worth or corporate proprietorship. This sort of analysis entirely loses sight of the point of view of the manager, the point of view of the enterprise as an economic entity. The only rational definition for corporate net revenue must be based upon the equities in their entirety. Net operating revenue measures the net increase (allowance being made for withdrawals and new investments) in *all the equities*. A rational cleavage is thus developed between *deductions* from *gross* revenue, and *distributions* of *net* revenue.[33]

An error has been made in viewing corporate accounts entirely from the standpoint of a more or less arbitrary legal proprietorship, an error which has led to serious confusion in accounting analysis; and to transfer the same kind of allegiance to the conception of a residual equity would not greatly improve matters. Consider this statement from Sprague: "the whole purpose of the business struggle is increase of wealth, that is, increase of proprietorship." [34] This would do very well for an establishment where a 100 per cent equity were vested in a single individual or homogeneous interest. But how seldom do we find but one equity even in the sole-proprietorship, so-called! And when we come to the corporation, where proprietorship is made synonymous by Sprague with the total equity of all stockholders, we certainly cannot reasonably say that the whole purpose of the business struggle is the increase of proprietorship. Such a view does not at all agree with the facts of corporate organization. In the United

---

[33] This will be elaborated in later chapters.
[34] *The Philosophy of Accounts* (4th Ed.), p. 59.

States a large percentage of the total corporate capitalization is represented by bonds and other contractual equities. In the case of the railroad companies the liabilities, so-called, exceed stock equities, even when all preferred stocks are included in the latter class. The return to *all* equities constitutes the increase in wealth which, from the accounting standpoint, motivates the business enterprise. The success of an enterprise as an operating unit cannot be directly determined and measured by the return to the stockholders. The proportion in which operating net revenue is divided between contractual return and residual return is a mere matter of financial organization, and it in nowise reflects operating success. The importance of this matter in the analysis of the concepts of expense, revenue, and income will be developed in detail in later chapters.

To sum up, the equation, properties equals equities, is a satisfactory expression for the financial condition of any enterprise; although in the sole-proprietorship there is a sense in which three classes are present, the proprietor's interest, "his" properties, and "his" obligations. The corporate balance sheet clearly represents the two homogeneous classes. In the corporation the residual equity is represented most accurately by the common stockholders' interest, the preferred stock equity, if any, falling naturally into the contractual group.

The explanation of the construction of the system of accounts from the underlying equation will now be undertaken.

CHAPTER IV

PROPERTY AND EQUITY ACCOUNTS

It has been shown that the financial status of any business enterprise can be expressed in two numerically equal classes, properties and equities.[1] These are the fundamental divisions of accounting data, the essence of any complete system of financial accounts. It will now be our task to demonstrate, in terms of this equation, the construction of the various types of accounts required in the modern business. It will be shown that a highly rational and convenient system of classifying and presenting the facts necessary to an exhibit of the periodic financial history and status of the business enterprise can be built upon this foundation; that every possible account can be constructed and explained directly with reference to a logical relationship to these underlying classes. The present chapter will be confined to a consideration of the structure of the balance-sheet accounts, i.e., those accounts designed to show pure asset and equity elements.[2] Later, careful attention will be directed to the important types of supplementary accounts.

FUNDAMENTAL EFFECTS OF OPERATION

It will first be necessary to consider what the operation of a business, and all of the changes attendant upon lapse of time,

---

[1] That is, in so far as this financial status can be reduced to a definite statement of dollars and cents, it can be presented under these two headings. As was noted in Chapter II, many factors and circumstances having immediate and potential bearing upon the financial condition of a business enterprise cannot be translated into definite value terms.

[2] As will be explained a little later few accounts in practice show either a distinct asset or equity element *continuously*. There are certain processes of change going on in every business situation which it is commonly not feasible to reflect concurrently in the accounts. In this chapter, however, it will be assumed that there *are* groups of accounts in practice corresponding exactly to the fundamental classes.

must mean in terms of the underlying classes of data already developed. How are the properties and equities of an enterprise affected by business transactions? How shall the accountant conceive of the fundamental value processes of the business enterprise?

To begin with let us look at the asset side. A manufacturing enterprise, for example, acquires land and constructs or otherwise obtains buildings and equipment. Tools, supplies, and materials are purchased. A personnel is built up; in other words, managerial services and ordinary labor services are provided for. Provision is also made for insurance, advertising, and many other types of services. The properly co-ordinated use of all these essential structures, commodities, and services (in combination with the peculiar elements furnished by the investors themselves) results in a flow of product, either goods or services, which is offered for sale on the market. In the nature of the case, however, continuous operation will be accompanied by a process of gradual deterioration, consumption, and lapse of value with respect to the necessary physical assets involved, and can only be maintained if the required structures and goods are replaced and replenished from time to time. Further, a more or less steady stream of the essential services must be forthcoming. In other words, there will always be a fairly continuous process of change going on among the properties of the enterprise. Individual items will more or less quickly lose their identity and disappear; new constituents will promptly replace them. The funds of the enterprise, its *capital,* may be maintained intact or may even be increased, but the specific structures, commodities, services, rights, and conditions in which this capital inheres and to which it attaches, will not remain unchanged for any significant period. The concept of a fund of capital, inhering in a mass of commodities and services but in a sense independent of the variations in the character and identity of the concrete units making up the mass, is thus a particularly convenient idea for the accountant.

The changes which take place with reference to the assets are of three main types. First, shifts occur due to purchase or sale; certain assets are exchanged for other properties. For example, merchandise is purchased with cash. Second, particular assets are utilized in operation and lose their identity without thereby causing a reduction in the total of the properties within the business. Thus, raw materials are expended upon manufacturing operations. The materials as such disappear, but the values involved are not lost; they are presumed to inhere in the work in progress, the inchoate goods in the production of which they were utilized.[3] Third, the values of particular structures, commodities, and services are finally consumed through the sale of the completed product, and thus disappear from the business (although presumably being replaced from the proceeds of the sale). A variation of this case arises when asset values are lost or destroyed without any return, direct or indirect. All three of these cases will be more fully considered a little later.

The *rate* of value change, of course, varies noticeably with the type of asset. Some costs—such as those covering a fire-proof building, for example—may retain their asset character with relatively slight change over a long period. The values of items such as postage stamps, on the other hand, are likely to pass soon into expense or cost of sales. We commonly express this distinction by saying that some assets are durable, *fixed,* while others are transitory, *current.*

The whole problem of revaluation, as well as the task of recording definite changes due to purchase, construction, etc., arises here. Valuation is the crux of accountancy. It is comparatively easy to record in dollars and cents the amount

---

[3] It is a fundamental assumption of accounting that the values of all essential commodities and services consumed in acquiring another good or service pass over into the resulting product and constitute its value. See Chapter XX, pages 490-493.

of the costs incurred by a business enterprise for commodities, services, and rights, classified according to original kind. To exhibit the subsequent history of such values in terms of definite accounting periods, on the other hand, is a problem which taxes every resource of the accountant to the utmost.

Admitting that it is the business of the accountant to record the investment of an owner or group of owners in a specific business situation, and to follow this investment as it takes shape in manifold structures, commodities, services, rights, and conditions, it then appears that any adequate system of accounts must be so constructed as to facilitate a presentation of all possible fluctuations and transpositions with respect to asset values.

Concurrent with this process of acquisition, fluctuation, expiration, replacement, etc., with respect to the properties, we find a similar and, to some extent, a resulting process of transposition, shrinkage, and expansion among the equities. First, one equity may be directly replaced by another. Certain noteholders, for example, may be induced to accept capital stock in a company in exchange for their notes. Further, particular equities may be retired through payment and new investment may be secured. Again, equities may be increased or decreased as a result of successful or unsuccessful operation, respectively.

Evidently the changes in the equities in a given period may be in large part explained as a reflection of changes in asset values. Indeed, the *net* variation in assets, the periodic change in the asset total, expresses exactly, in amount, the net variation in equities. As has already been pointed out, the equities in one sense constitute a restatement of the total of the properties from another point of view, legal and economic ownership. Shrinkage or expansion of the asset *total*, from whatever cause, must consequently be accompanied by a corresponding diminution or increase in the *total* of the equities. Net losses or net gains are the result of processes which have affected both assets and equities. New investments and withdrawals of investment likewise disturb both sides of the equation.

Nevertheless the two processes, changes in properties on the one hand and changes in equities on the other, are independent in fact to a degree and should be kept quite distinct as accounting conceptions. As long as the *total* of properties is not affected, innumerable changes and transpositions may occur without in any way affecting the statement of equities. As has been noted, one asset may be exchanged for another of equal value significance. Similarly one type of ownership may be retired and replaced by another kind of equity without a concomitant disturbance among the properties. All transpositions of equities, all changes which do not affect the *total* of equities, are independent of asset fluctuations.[4]

It may be worth while to emphasize again at this point the fact that the only inevitable relationship existing between assets and equities is the equality of totals. All that we can say for certain about the universal balance sheet is that the total of the properties must equal the total of the equities. Mistakes and misunderstandings are constantly arising in accounting and business practice due to a failure to appreciate fully this fundamental fact. Cash, a specific asset, and surplus, a specific equity heading, are often confused, for example. The truth of the matter is that no specific equity is inevitably associated with any specific property; and no individual asset —as a matter of accounting processes—is reflected in a particular equity.[5]

Usually there is not even a numerical identity between the specific asset and the specific equity. But if subsidiary equa-

---

[4] In the next chapter illustrations of all these fundamental situations, and explanations of their accounting treatment, will be given.

[5] This is an overstatement. Certain equities may be based upon liens applying to particular properties. That is, an equity may sometimes be said to express a right in or to a specific asset as well as (or perhaps, occasionally, instead of) a right in the total of assets.

tions were found in a particular case they would not, necessarily, represent more than accidental situations. Suppose, to take a most extreme example, that the balance sheet of the Y Co., shortly after organization, stood as follows:

Assets		Equities	
Real Estate	$ 40,000	A, Partner	$ 40,000
Plant and Machinery	60,000	B, Partner	60,000
Supplies	20,000	C, Noteholder	20,000
Cash	10,000	D, Noteholder	10,000
	$130,000		$130,000

It might appear from this statement that A had invested the real estate; B, the plant and machinery; C, the supplies; and D, the cash. And such, in fact, might have been the case. But it evidently would be *possible* to assume an almost indefinite number of series of transactions which might logically account for the above conditions. And, still further, even if each specific equity did relate originally to a particular property item of the same figure, such coincidence would seldom be long maintained and in any case would have little real significance. Strictly speaking, the real estate is represented by B's equity quite as much as by A's; the cash is measured by C's equity quite as fully as by D's or any other; and so on.

Properties and equities are interdependent in that one category cannot exist without the other. Further, it is quite possible, especially if a chronological series of balance sheets is available, to guess shrewdly as to the character of the transactions which have brought about each important change.[6] Nevertheless the two classes, and the accompanying processes which we have been discussing, must be thought of as quite distinct. Once the underlying classification is made it constitutes a fundamental line of cleavage for accounting purposes and must be rigidly adhered to.

---

[6] To take a very simple example, it is almost certain that a marked reduction of current liabilites will be accompanied by a corresponding decrease in current assets.

To sum up, business operation and all the conditions incident thereto, have their fundamental expression from the accounting standpoint in the transposition, expiration, ebb and flow, increase and decrease, of assets and equities. Evidently, then, the accounts of the business enterprise must be so constructed as to make it possible to follow these changes in a convenient manner and to facilitate the process of drawing periodic conclusions therefrom.

FUNDAMENTAL REQUIREMENTS OF THE ACCOUNT

How are these purposes to be accomplished? What is the most efficient clerical arrangement? What device should be selected as the essential integer of the technical structure of accounting? How shall we fashion the individual account?

It should be evident that, from a theoretic standpoint, the most direct and clear-cut method of accounting would be to use the balance sheet itself as the main clerical unit, a single, all-inclusive account. All changes in original items that occurred would then be recorded by altering in the proper direction and in the proper amount the property and equity items as they appeared on a tabular financial statement such as was exhibited for the *X* Co. in Chapter II. And when new kinds of property were secured, and when new equities appeared, appropriate headings and amounts could be added directly to the original lists. Thus, if materials were purchased for cash to the amount of $5,000 the original figures for both cash and materials could be erased and the corrected amounts substituted therefor. Or, if an outstanding promissory note matured and were retired with cash, $1,000, the amounts attached to the cash and notes payable headings could be appropriately rewritten.

But accounting by means of direct alterations of the

balance sheet would obviously be very inconvenient, even in the simplest situations; more space would be required for an orderly and adequate record. At the very least it would be necessary to extend or stretch out the underlying financial statement so that space would be available in which to exhibit the effects upon the original amounts of the various processes and transactions. This would virtually mean the opening of an independent account for each important kind of property and for each equity.

If the balance sheet of the X Co., given in Chapter II, were extended in such a way as still to exhibit the fundamental relationship and yet give space for a separate account under each specific property and equity heading, it might appear somewhat as follows:

Properties	*Equities*
LAND	CAPITAL STOCK—COMMON
$100,000	$200,000
BUILDINGS	CAPITAL STOCK—PREFERRED
$200,000	$200,000
EQUIPMENT	MORTGAGE BONDS
$100,000	$100,000
PATENTS	DEBENTURE BONDS
$100,000	$100,000
ORGANIZATION COSTS	NOTES PAYABLE
$ 25,000	$100,000
MATERIALS	
$100,000	
CASH	
$ 75,000	

Before going further it should be interpolated that there are other fundamental objections to any method of accounting designed to present the facts of business operation directly in a summary financial sheet. Accounting by this system would be seriously defective in that it would throw little light upon the business process; and it is evident that the data of the historical as well as the synoptic situation are necessary to meet the needs of the various interests involved. Causes as well as results must be indicated. Further, many business transactions are of such a character that it is not always feasible or even possible to state the literal effect thereof upon assets and equities immediately. In other words, the data of the individual happening cannot always be resolved at once into its underlying balance-sheet elements. Instead it is usually found to be necessary to permit certain kinds of information to accumulate for a time in intermediate and supplementary classifications and accounts; and no attempt is made to reduce these temporary divisions to their lowest terms except at regular intervals. This matter will be fully considered in a subsequent chapter.

Additional practical reasons for a more elaborate accounting technique likewise readily suggest themselves. Subdivision of the accounts and records is necessary in the case of the large enterprise so that a staff may be utilized which is sufficiently numerous to take care of the great flow of transactions. Further, a certain amount of systematic routine procedure and an extension and specialization of accounting devices is essential to the development of adequate means for testing responsibilities and a proper system of "internal check." Again, accuracy, speed, neatness, and other important attributes of good bookkeeping are undoubtedly fostered by a reasonable use of technical expedients. These considerations, of course, reach far beyond the simple question of the advisability of restricting the accounting structure to the parallel-column

PROPERTY AND EQUITY ACCOUNTS 99

balance sheet, and apply to matters of technique which are entirely outside the scope of this study.

The first step in the construction of the individual accounts, then, can be conceived as the stretching out or extension of the summary balance sheet so that space will be available under each heading in which to record the data which may affect the status of the particular kind of asset or equity involved in any case. The second step consists in the division of the space under each heading into two compartments or sections. To demonstrate the inherent necessity for this second feature it will be necessary to show more definitely the *numerical* effect of all possible transactions upon an existing balance.

First, with respect to the properties. As regards *amount,* property balances can clearly be affected in but two ways; an asset may be either increased or decreased. Accretion, enhancement, improvement, replacement, extension, etc., and expiration, decay, shrinkage, abandonment, withdrawal, etc., all simmer down in their value aspects to mere *addition* and *subtraction,* respectively. Since properties are always expressed numerically, in terms of some value unit, all possible changes are essentially matters of increase and decrease, plus and minus.

Similarly, since equities are likewise represented by amounts, all transactions effecting the same result in either increases or decreases. The numerical effect upon the equities of additional investment, borrowings, gains, etc., is in every case an addition; payments, income distributions, losses, etc., result in subtractions from equities. The accountant expresses the equities with value numbers; hence there are no other numerical possibilities.

Accordingly, every individual property or equity account has need of two sections, parts or divisions, one for additions, the other for subtractions. Or, at any rate, some device for dealing with these opposing tendencies, if they are not to be physically separated, must be worked out. A scheme might be evolved, of course, which would make it possible to carry out an actual arithmetical process on the occasion of every entry, the account then showing only the balance or algebraic sum of all positives and negatives. Other means of designation than spatial arrangement might also be adopted. Plus and minus signs could be used to indicate the opposing elements, or colored inks. It would not be difficult to suggest many devices along this line.

As a matter of fact the plan adopted in modern accounting involves the physical separation of positives and negatives for a period. Additions and subtractions are allowed to accumulate separately and a balance is struck only at regular intervals. This plan, while appearing to be somewhat arbitrary, is in fact founded in the immanent necessities of the situation. In the first place arithmetical processes (with respect to the data of the accounts proper at any rate) are thus avoided as far as individual transactions are concerned. This not only saves clerical effort but minimizes the possibility of error. Further, the segregation and preservation of the positives and negatives applicable to a particular heading results in a more complete and satisfactory accounting record. Subtractions from a particular property and additions to the same property may each constitute facts of intrinsic importance for managerial purposes. The cash account, for example, should evidently be so constructed that cash receipts and cash disbursements for a given period are both clearly presented. A cash record which exhibited only the net balance would be inadequate; it should show all positive and negative items as, temporarily, distinct classes of data. And the two kinds of facts should be separated in such a way that the net balance may be conveniently taken at the end of the accounting period.

Let us sum up the statements in this section. First, the summary balance sheet is not in itself a satisfactory account-

PROPERTY AND EQUITY ACCOUNTS 101

ing unit. To secure the necessary space, to present an adequate historical record, and to avoid the necessity of reducing certain complex kinds of transactions immediately to their lowest terms, the balance sheet must be extended into a system of individual accounts. Second, since the numerical effect of all transactions may be reduced to mere addition and subtraction each account has need of two divisions or designations. Third, the separation and temporary preservation of positives and negatives under each heading is necessary as a matter of clerical convenience and because the periodic amounts of the opposing tendencies in the individual account may each constitute a fact of intrinsic importance to the management.

THE PARALLEL-COLUMN ACCOUNT

The skeleton of the balance sheet, the *master* account, consists essentially in two parallel vertical columns.[7] As it happens this device exactly meets the requirements for the individual property or equity account. As has just been explained, two divisions or compartments are needed in connection with each account heading, one for additions, the other for subtractions; and the parallel vertical column or "T" account adequately supplies this need. Here we have, then, the fundamental accounting device, an individual heading followed by two vertical columns.[8] Each subsidiary account, in form, may be conceived as a miniature replica of the fundamental

---

[7] As was emphasized in Chapter II, the essence of the balance sheet is a statement of the two fundamental classes, properties and equities, the arrangement adopted in presenting these classes in the statement being a matter of clerical convenience only. The parallel-column form is still in very general use; although there is some tendency nowadays to exhibit the two divisions in sequence, the resources or assets being stated first, the equities following. Especially where an elaborate statement is desired the parallel-column device has its disadvantages. The balance sheet as a report of financial condition may well consist in a comprehensive statement of the assets, perhaps covering several pages, followed by a complete statement of the equities. This procedure permits the showing of certain computations and adjustments of importance directly in the balance sheet. It also tends to dispel the technical aspect of the statement, so confusing to the layman.

[8] Each side of an actual account in practice, of course, usually consists of columns for dates, explanations, journal folio numbers, etc., as well as various money columns. For our purposes, however, it is sufficient to emphasize the two main divisions.

financial statement. The balance sheet itself constitutes the initial account, an account which shows all the properties and equities of the business. To record the facts of business operation the accountant finds it necessary to extend this parent account into a system of subsidiary accounts, each of which, however, retains the form of the summary. Periodically, also, he must undertake the reverse operation, the concentration of all data appearing in the subsidiaries and their return to the master account.

The next question is the arrangement of columns in the individual account. In the case of the property accounts, to begin with, shall the positive items be placed in the left column and the negatives in the right, or vice versa? This question should be answered purely on the basis of expediency. As a matter of principle either arrangement will serve as well as the other. However, in the tabular statements of properties and equities thus far presented the property items were placed in the left column and the equity balances in the right. This is the arrangement followed in practice almost universally.[9] Accordingly, if it is decided to have "left" stand for the property balances and "right" for equities in the summary or master account, it follows, if the accounting scheme is to be consistent throughout, that the left-hand column under each individual asset heading should be used for positive items and the right-hand column for subtractions; for only thus can the positive property balances be preserved at the left.

In the case of the equity accounts how shall the positive and negative columns be arranged? Again the answer is that the arrangement is a matter of expediency, the only essentials to be observed in constructing these accounts being the preservation of the fundamental equation, and the segregation

---

[9] The English usage is the only important exception. Peculiarly, the English accountants adhere to the universal practice with respect to the organization of the individual account, but reverse this scheme in their financial summary. Such inconsistency is, to say the least, unfortunate.

PROPERTY AND EQUITY ACCOUNTS   103

of pluses and minuses. But, again, to keep positive property balances at the left and equity balances at the right, it will be necessary, if the accounting structure is to be consistent throughout, to use the left-hand column under each equity heading for subtractions and the right for additions.

The scheme of the X Co.'s [10] balance-sheet accounts, in their relation to the fundamental equation and master account, can now be expressed graphically, thus:

THE X CO.

Properties		*Equities*	
Additions	Subtractions	Subtractions	Additions
LAND		CAPITAL STOCK—COMMON	
$100,000			$200,000
BUILDINGS		CAPITAL STOCK—PREFERRED	
$200,000			$200,000
EQUIPMENT		MORTGAGE BONDS	
$100,000			$100,000
PATENTS		DEBENTURE BONDS	
$100,000			$100,000

[10] To return to the illustration of Chapter II.

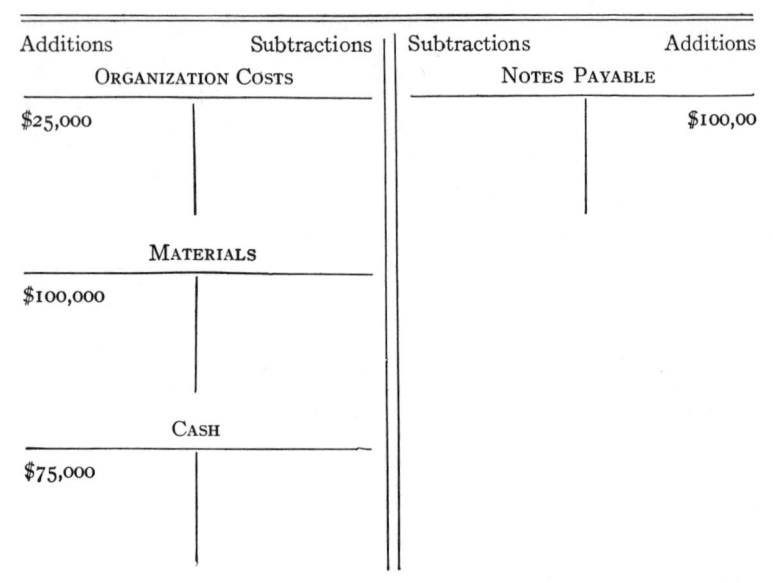

ACCOUNTING THEORY

Properties		Equities	
Additions	Subtractions	Subtractions	Additions
ORGANIZATION COSTS		NOTES PAYABLE	
$25,000			$100,00
	MATERIALS		
$100,000			
	CASH		
$75,000			

In the above diagram, it should be noticed, the lines representing each skeleton account are not in contact with those of any other account or with the central rulings. This emphasizes the point that each account should be considered a distinct unit. It should be noted further that there is no intention to suggest that this scheme would be desirable in actual practice. An alphabetical arrangement in a bound or loose-leaf volume or volumes, one or more pages being given to each account and with little or no attention paid to grouping by logical classes, is of course to be preferred from the standpoint of efficient bookkeeping. The outline given is simply intended to emphasize sharply the logical relations between the individual property and equity accounts and the underlying balance-sheet equation.

As has already been pointed out, the "T" form is not the only possible device for the individual account; yet it would be hard to suggest a more efficient scheme. It conforms nicely to the fundamental requirements of the account outlined in the preceding section. That is, it enables the bookkeeper to segregate positive and negative items for a time, thus eliminating all computation except a single balancing operation and reducing the likelihood of error; and it preserves the opposing elements—additions and subtractions—intact throughout the accounting period, thereby making these classes of data—which may each be of intrinsic importance—available to the management. Further, it is safe to say that no other plan will ever be discovered which will be as convenient as the vertical-column device. This scheme makes it possible to write *particular numbers* in horizontal lines and *take totals* by adding vertical columns. Comparison with any other method will readily disclose the fact that this is, intrinsically, the most advantageous procedure.

CURRENT RESOURCE AND EQUITY ACCOUNTS

It was stated above that the accountant should conceive of the operation of a business enterprise as consisting in the utilization of a more or less considerable variety of commodities and services for the purpose of producing some commodity or service for sale. Now it is fairly obvious that even in a very simple situation other kinds of commodities and services than those given above as representing the properties of the X Co. just prior to operation would be necessary. A manufacturing enterprise, for example, requires services from various classes of employees, such as managers, operatives, clerks, etc. Virtually every business enterprise of any consequence must purchase a fairly consistent flow of such services. Successful operation also usually demands payments for insurance, advertising, lighting, etc. It is necessary to buy fuel, stationery, and other current supplies. The number of types of such transitory commodities and services required in any case will, of course, depend upon the character of the business involved.

The question arises, how will accounts with current items, such as office supplies, fuel, insurance, labor services, etc., fit into the scheme of accounts thus far outlined? Accounts with these items are variously labeled in the accounting texts as "force," "nominal," "fictitious," "economic," "interior," or "loss" accounts. Just what is the nature of these items and how shall the accountant conceive of the procedures affecting them and the accounts in which they are recorded? As there is serious confusion concerning these matters in accounting theory and practice, it is desirable that these questions be carefully examined.

As was stated in an earlier chapter, all valuable considerations, commodities, services, rights, and conditions, contribute to the total of properties as they come into the hands of the business enterprise. According to this conception current services and supplies represent assets, or add value to other assets, and the recognition of their acquirement requires entries in the left-hand column of asset accounts. This seems fairly obvious in the case of such tangible items as fuel and supplies. Coal in the bin is evidently just as fully an asset as show-cases and other more durable properties. Further, it has been sufficiently emphasized that values in the business enterprise may inhere in more or less intangible conditions, rights, and services, that the property concept covers both material and immaterial assets. Hence labor, insurance, and advertising services may all add to the amount of properties, and may even exist independent of particular physical assets. All represent services essential to business operation; and all are considered valuable by the business man.

Any element, material or otherwise, for which the owners freely invest their funds, gives rise, at the outset, to an asset value. When the entrepreneur pays for insurance, advertising,

PROPERTY AND EQUITY ACCOUNTS 107

or other services he expects to receive a value equivalent for his expenditure, just as in the case of the purchase of a building, a machine, or any other item of physical property. Valuable services contribute just as surely to the sum total of the properties of an enterprise as do valuable material objects. In fact, any unit of "tangible" property, so-called, is usually valuable largely because services of various kinds have so changed the location and character of the original raw material (which, in the natural state, would usually have but a trifling economic significance) that it is fitted to furnish a series of services contributing in turn toward the production of some other commodity or service.[11]

The average business man recognizes the facts of the case very well. If one approached the owner of some retail establishment with the intention of purchase, for example, what would the prospective seller include in a statement of his properties? Certainly coal or other current supplies on hand, as well as merchandise, fixtures, etc., would appear in that statement. Further, if any insurance service, advertising service, transportation service, or other valuable services or rights had been purchased by him but were not yet consumed in the sense that the benefits therefrom were not exhausted, such items would surely be included in a statement of the total assets of the business.[12]

It is not intended for a moment to suggest that there are not very important distinctions between durable physical assets and valuable current commodities and services. There are, in fact, very sharp differences of theoretic and practical importance. It should be emphasized roundly, however, that the

---

[11] For practical accounting purposes, "commodities" and "services" should undoubtedly be distinguished; although it is of course true that in the last analysis the cost of a so-called "material" asset is largely a composite of the various services necessary to put it in usable form, and it is valuable, from the standpoint of the user, because it can furnish services which he requires.

[12] Prepaid insurance and advertising are really a type of account receivable, not services. As the insurance and advertising companies liquidate these accounts they become services, and add to the value of the properties in another form.

difference between buildings and fuel, for example, is not that the former is a property and the other a loss; and nothing but confusion can result from using terminology that suggests that there is such a difference even if the writer is entirely clear as to the nature of these assets and the manner in which accounting procedures must vary as between the two cases. The only fundamental way in which such assets differ is as regards permanence.[13] The coal in the bin may be largely consumed in a month; the building may last fifty years. The coal is a current, transitory asset, soon losing its identity; the building is of a more durable character, its value disappearing and passing on into other forms only very gradually. The line drawn in economic theory between "fixed" and "circulating" capital is much the same distinction.

The fact that these current assets soon disappear as such must not lead the accountant to conclude that the values involved have completely disappeared from the business. The use of current commodities and services is, as has been pointed out, an essential condition for the completion of the product of the enterprise. It is not unreasonable to assume, therefore, that until this product is sold all these values expended are still in the business, in the form of work in progress and finished stock. Here we have one of the underlying assumptions of all factory accounting. The cost accountant ordinarily assumes that the value of any commodity or service expended upon a given result passes over into the object for which the service or commodity involved is utilized.[14] From this standpoint virtually all costs incurred by a business enterprise for commodities or services necessary to successful operation, converge first upon goods in process, later reappear as finished goods, and finally leave the enterprise only as these goods are

---

[13] The distinction between fixed and current assets is elaborated in Chapter VIII.
[14] This assumption is similar to Marx's doctrine that the value of labor expended upon a product attaches itself thereto, giving it its value.

sold. Indeed this is as true of fixed as of current assets, the difference being, however, that the fixed asset very gradually gives up its value to productive operations, whereas the current asset is transitory, loses its identity very soon after purchase. In fact the current *service* might be said to inhere immediately in the object for which or upon which it is expended.

However, the fact that all valuable commodities and services, however short-lived, are assets as purchased, and contribute to the sum total of the properties of an enterprise acquiring the same, does not mean that we are justified, as a practical matter, in designating the accounts in which the costs of such items are initially recorded as *property* accounts. Coal burned is no longer coal; labor expended upon factory operations is no longer inchoate service. And it is not always feasible to preserve a continuous record of coal consumed and labor utilized. Thus an account may come to have a character quite different from the original nature of the items entered therein.

At the instant of acquisition it seems clear that all current commodities and services are assets, and the accounts in which their values are entered, if defined in terms of the character of the items as acquired, are asset accounts. But from the standpoint of the normal condition of the account, of its predominating element under ordinary bookkeeping conditions, it may represent something quite different. This question of account classification will be further considered a little later.

For the time being we will define accounts in which are recorded current commodities and services from the standpoint of the nature of such items as received; in other words they will be considered as *current asset* accounts. For illustration, it will be assumed that the X Co. has need of four such accounts, one each for labor, fuel, insurance, and miscellaneous commodities and services. There would be others in almost any business situation, but these will be sufficient for illustrative purposes. According to the explanation of property account construction given in the preceding sections, the accounts for these items would be opened in exactly the same manner as other property accounts, the left-hand column being used for additions, acquisitions, the right-hand for subtractions, expirations, thus:

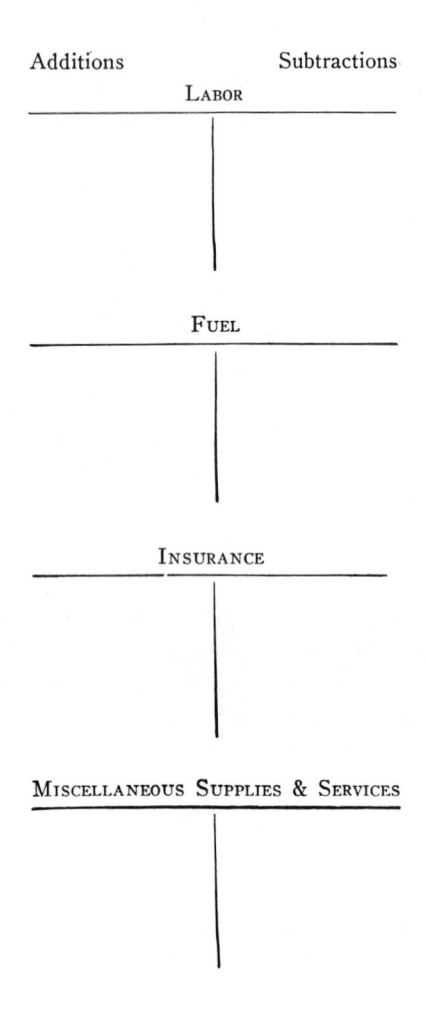

Additions	Subtractions
LABOR	

FUEL	

INSURANCE	

MISCELLANEOUS SUPPLIES & SERVICES	

Another type of current asset common to virtually all businesses is the ordinary account receivable, the "book" claim against a customer to whom goods have been shipped but who has not yet completed payment. It is a well-known characteristic of American business that goods and services produced by the enterprise are often sold "on account"; i.e., payment is not made until some time after the good or service involved is furnished. This situation gives rise to the recognition of the right against the customer on the books of the seller as an asset, a *receivable*. These rights are transitory in that they are shortly converted into cash (if paid); they are not used in business operation, however, and hence do not give rise to the complications involved in the cases just discussed above. The accounts receivable account is constructed in the same way as the other asset accounts, thus:

Additions	Subtractions
ACCOUNTS	RECEIVABLE

So-called "accrued" assets, such as interest and rent receivable, are simply a kind of account receivable. The enterprise has furnished some service in advance of payment and hence has a claim against the recipient. Prepaid insurance, as mentioned above, is also a right, a receivable; it is a receivable, however, that is normally liquidated by the furnishing of service rather than the payment of cash. Cash itself is usually rated as a current asset, because it is the most liquid form of property. The different classes of assets will be further discussed in a later chapter.

Similarly, current equity items, quite different from any of those listed above for the X Co., will appear as the operation of a business proceeds. Merchandise, supplies, and services are frequently purchased on account; i.e., payment is made not as these current commodities and services are secured but later. An accounts payable account [15] is constructed in the same way as is any other equity account, the left-hand column being used for subtractions, the right-hand for additions, thus:

Subtractions	Additions
ACCOUNTS PAYABLE	

"Accrued" liabilities, such as rent and interest payable, are at least periodically recognized in a modern system of accounts. The necessity for such accounts arises out of the acquiring of the various services represented prior to payment therefor. The accounts with such items are likewise constructed in accordance with the rules governing the more important equity accounts.

No attempt will be made here to enumerate any complete list of the current assets and liabilities arising in the case of the representative business enterprise. The illustrations given will be sufficient for the present to suggest the manner in which accounts designed to exhibit the ebb and flow of current resources and equities may be incorporated into the initial group of balance-sheet accounts.

---

[15] In practice, of course, both accounts receivable and payable are subdivided into detailed customers' and creditors' accounts, respectively. No additional principle of account construction is thereby introduced, however.

CHAPTER V

TYPES OF TRANSACTIONS

Before taking up a study of the various classes of intermediate and supplementary accounts required in a complete system of records for a modern business enterprise, it will be desirable to complete the foregoing analysis of the construction of property and equity accounts by indicating very definitely the way in which all possible types of business transactions may be recorded in such accounts. It will be shown in this chapter that all occurrences, happenings, processes, and circumstances affecting the financial status of a business enterprise can be expressed at once (provided the information required is available) in pure balance-sheet accounts. In other words, it will be demonstrated that every accounting transaction can be defined with direct reference to the underlying equation, can be stated, if analyzed into its fundamental elements, in terms of the two dimensions, properties and equities.

This discussion should serve to show clearly that all further accounting classifications are distinctly subordinate to the main divisions of the balance sheet, and that the supplementary accounts which are required in business practice do not represent intrinsically new elements but exhibit instead temporary *phases* or aspects of the fundamental equation which cannot, conveniently, be resolved at once into their primary factors.

THE ACCOUNTING TRANSACTION

Reference has been made at various points in the preceding chapters to business operation and to the accounting *trans-*

action. It will now be necessary to state more fully and carefully what is meant by the transaction, and to indicate the principal types. In the broadest sense the transaction may be defined as *any happening, occurrence, process, condition, or policy which brings about a change in the status of individual asset or equity items* in a business enterprise. Any circumstance or situation which sooner or later requires entries in the accounts is a transaction. According to this view the accounting transaction is by no means confined to definite financial operations and occurrences. Any process of value change within the business must also be treated as a transaction.

With this definition as a basis all transactions may be grouped under three heads. First should be mentioned all *explicit* business happenings involving the particular enterprise and some other business, person, or interest. Purchases of plant, materials, services, or other assets fall into this class. Sales furnish another example. Collections and payments, proprietary investments, dividend payments or other income withdrawals, the incurring and retirement of liabilities—all these constitute explicit business occurrences. It is universally agreed that it is the function of accounting to make and preserve a history of these transactions. An accurate, systematic, intelligible record of purchases, sales, payments, collections, etc., must be made available. To maintain the rights of customers, creditors, laborers, and investors in the complex enterprise, to fix the responsibilities of managers and other employees, indeed to make it possible to carry on a business in any fashion, such data must be carefully compiled. This is accounting at a minimum.

But anyone who is at all familiar with the status of modern accounting must realize that this is only a beginning. A bare record of the so-called "actual" transactions occurring usually reflects the economic history of an enterprise only in a very imperfect manner. Without further analysis and entry no accurate conclusions with respect to the fundamental facts of income and financial condition could be drawn from a mere diary of business events, however well arranged. A second class of transactions, the *implicit* or internal transactions, those exhibiting the value changes due to internal operating processes and the lapse of time, must be dealt with. The precise status of commodities and services as purchased is only momentarily maintained (even if cost be assumed to be correct for purposes of initial statement). The values of all assets evaporate more or less rapidly, and pass on into other forms. As was stated before, a record of these changes is the crux of accounting. The depreciation of fixed assets, the utilization of labor and materials in production, the consumption of other current commodities and services, the disappearance of asset values embodied in finished product—these and all other processes of change which affect the character and amount of the properties of the business must be recorded.

To make appropriate entries from time to time covering the important movements of asset values within the business, and the ebb of values from the enterprise as product, is as definitely a part of the accountant's task as the recognition of explicit transactions. And because of the peculiar difficulties involved this phase of accounting is of the first importance.

A third class is represented by all *formal book entries* which do not indicate transactions with the outside and which are not accompanied by objective process of change among the assets. The "closing" entries, so called, furnish many examples. To summarize and draw conclusions at the end of the accounting period the bookkeeper may find it necessary to transfer particular balances from account to account, to combine several account balances, perhaps, under a single head. Thus, in a particular instance, it may be desirable to draw together "salesmen's salaries," "salesmen's traveling costs," and "salesmen's entertainment account" under a more general caption, "selling cost." Such a process of concentration would require accounting entries but would not be accompanied by actual value changes. The subdivision or appropriation of net earnings or surplus to indicate the policies and intentions of the management also furnishes many illustrations of *book* transactions. This class of entries will be illustrated and discussed more fully in later chapters.

We may now superimpose upon this preliminary outline of transactions another classification. All possible accounting transactions may be grouped in terms of effects upon balance-sheet classes, as follows:

1. Transactions which affect only properties.
2. Interequity occurrences.
3. Transactions which affect both of the underlying classes.
4. Combinations of cases (1), (2), and (3).

Each of these divisions incudes explicit business transactions and formal book entries, and, with the exception of case (2), illustrations of implicit transactions may also be found under each heading. It is this technical classification which we will now follow in analyzing transactions and explaining their effects upon the accounts.

PROPERTY TRANSACTIONS

From the standpoint of the balance sheet one important class of transactions consists in exchanges of properties. In the representative enterprise a large number of financial occurrences are of this type. Money, commodities, and services are exchanged for other commodities and services of equal value. These might be called "interproperty" transactions. Entries covering this class may represent actual exchanges between the enterprise and outsiders or they may simply express the recognition of processes of value fluctuation going on within the business, internal transpositions of asset values. In either case the effect upon the accounts is the same; one kind of property is paid out or undergoes expiration or transfer, a subtraction from an asset, and another type of property is received or recognized in exchange, an equal addition to an asset.

The effects of this type of transaction upon the accounts can best be brought out by the consideration of a number of definite illustrative situations. As a first example let us assume that the X Co. pays cash to the amount of $300 for fuel. Here we have a subtraction from one asset, cash, and an equal addition to another, fuel.[1] According to the accounting scheme outlined in the preceding chapter, then, this transaction would be recognized by an entry of $300 in the left-hand column of the fuel account and an equal entry in the right-hand column of the cash account. Evidently these entries register the entire effect of the transaction; and, since we have equal entries in opposite columns, the underlying equation is not disturbed.

The X Co. loans $500 in cash to Smith Bros., the latter giving in exchange their 60-day promissory note for $500 at 6 per cent. Here we have another illustration. The X Co. has exchanged cash for another kind of asset, a right or claim which is customarily labeled a "note receivable." What would be the entries in this case? There has been a reduction in one asset and an equal addition to another. Consequently the transaction would be recorded by a left-hand entry of $500 in the notes receivable account, to reflect the increase in this asset, and an equal right-hand entry in the cash account, to register the decrease in cash. Again we have equal entries in opposite columns.

---

[1] As has been noted, it is a universal assumption of accounting that cost determines value for purposes of initial statement. This assumption doubtless holds in the case of a fair commercial transaction, based on normal competitive conditions. Of course, if the X Co. is not proceeding rationally, and in some way suffers loss, the transaction would not involve an equal exchange. We will adhere, however, to the usual assumption of the economist and accountant, viz., that in a voluntary transaction no undue advantage is gained by either side.

For a third illustration let us assume that an open book account of $500 in favor of the X Co. and against Smith Bros. is settled with a note. That is, the customer gives the Company a written promise to pay to replace a book account. From the standpoint of the X Co. this transaction involves the exchange of one kind of right against Smith Bros. for another type of right of equivalent amount; a formal evidence of indebtedness has been substituted for a more or less informal understanding. This involves a subtraction from outstanding accounts receivable and an equal addition to notes receivable. One claim has been replaced by another of a somewhat different legal status, although the claim is still directed against the same parties. The transaction would then be reflected in the accounts by an entry of $500 in the positive column of the notes receivable account and an equal entry in the negative column of the accounts receivable account.

The Company's buildings and equipment are insured for one year, the insurance premium of $800 being paid in cash. Protection from certain possible losses is secured for one year, and payment is made in advance. The asset consists of the Company's right against the insurance company; and this right will gradually disappear or be liquidated with the lapse of time. The transaction would be recorded by an entry of $800 in the left-hand column of the insurance account (an addition to one asset), and an entry for a similar amount in the right-hand side of the cash account (an equal subtraction from another asset).

In the case of the corporation special funds of cash or other liquid assets are sometimes set up to provide for replacements, retirement of liabilities, and other purposes. The directors of the X Co., for example, appropriate $5,000 in cash to be placed in the hands of a trustee as a sinking fund for purposes of retiring certain bonds as they mature. This involves virtually a division of the cash account; a fund is segregated for a special purpose and accounting recognition is given to this fact. Let us assume that the caption "sinking-fund assets" is used to designate this special fund. This action of the directors would then be recognized in the accounts by a left-hand entry of $5,000 in the sinking-fund assets account and a right-hand entry for the same sum in the general cash account.

For an illustration of the "internal" transpositions of assets brought about by the conditions of operation let us assume that raw materials to the amount of $700 have been requisitioned from the X Co.'s storeroom and have been put in process, that is, have been placed in manufacturing operations. In this case no relationship with any outside firm or individual is involved. Here there is simply a shifting within the business. The total of assets is not affected but individual items are changed. The residence of $700 in value has been transferred from raw materials to inchoate goods, work in various stages of completion. There has been a subtraction from one kind of property, raw materials, and—supposedly—an equal addition to another type of asset, goods in process. The transition would be reflected in the accounts by an entry of $700 in the left-hand column of the "work in process" account and an equal right-hand entry in the materials account.

Three accounts—or groups of accounts—corresponding to the important stages in the manufacturing process are usually introduced, separate accounting recognition being given to materials, work in process, and finished goods. At intervals the changes in form which some of the assets are undergoing, the shifting with respect to physical location and form of the various costs the enterprise has incurred, are recognized in the accounts. Ideally such recognition should immediately accompany the actual process of production; but it is not always feasible to carry out such a continuous accounting procedure.

The transfer of values from work in progress to finished

goods is an illustration of the same type of transaction as the case given and would be recorded according to the same rules.

Material cost is not the only cost which is undergoing transformation. Other current items, such as ordinary labor, supervision, supplies, etc., and the more permanent assets, such as buildings and equipment, are, in theory at least, following the same route. In fact the value of each and every item necessary to the manufacturing operations of the business might with some reason be said to converge upon goods in process. In the more complete cost systems in practice virtually all costs (except strictly selling costs and certain administrative and highly general items) are considered to inhere successively in work in process and finished stock. We need not be concerned here with the methods and principles of allocation involved, nor with the almost insurmountable technical difficulties in the way of following in the accounts, accurately and concurrently, this process of value-shifting.[2] For our purposes it is only important to emphasize the nature of this process and its effect upon the accounts, assuming that the facts in any case can be ascertained.

One illustration involving labor cost will be given. The X Co. acquires labor services to the amount of $1,000. Assuming that these services are paid for and booked as acquired, this transaction can be viewed as an exchange of assets.[3] The record, then, would be made by a left-hand entry in the labor account and a right-hand entry in the cash account. But, assuming that this labor has been utilized in manufacturing operations, another transaction may be immediately recognized, namely, the transfer of the value of $1,000 from the labor

---

[2] It is ordinarily assumed that during this entire process of internal transformation, values remain unchanged. Such an assumption, of course, does not always square with the facts. Pronounced movements in prices on the market can with reason be held to affect the value of materials in process, for example. We have in mind as illustrations of pure property transactions only those cases where a cost, when passed on to a new stage, can reasonably be held to remain fixed.

[3] The accounting treatment for purchases of labor services on account will be discussed in the next section.

account, representing an intangible, ephemeral asset, to the goods in process account, representing a tangible property. This last would be recognized by a left-hand entry of $1,000 in the work in process account and a corresponding entry in the right-hand column of the labor account.

One more illustration of the internal transformation of values and the corresponding transfer of appropriate items from account to account may be given. The X Co. buys a unit of equipment, at a price f.o.b. of $6,000, and pays the transportation and installation charges as follows: freight, $200; labor, $50; supplies, $10. If all of these expenditures were first set up in the freight, labor, and supplies accounts, respectively, it would later be necessary to transfer the amounts involved to the equipment account; as it requires no elaborate argument to show that expenditures for carriage and installation are just as fully cost of the fixed asset, equipment, as any part of the invoice price itself. The recognition of this transfer in the accounts would be accomplished by a left-hand entry of $260 in the equipment account and right-hand entries in the freight, labor, and supplies accounts totaling the same sum.

Formal interproperty entries, unaccompanied by any objective operations or value processes, would be required only where it were necessary for statistical or other purposes to subdivide an already existing property balance. Suppose, for example, that the management of the X Co. should decide to give definite accounting recognition to an especially important kind of raw materials. To inaugurate this plan it would be necessary to make a left-hand entry in the special materials account for the appropriate amount and an equal right-hand entry in the general materials account.

The above illustrations should be sufficient to show the nature of the principal situations in which interproperty transactions arise, and to bring out clearly the effects of the recognition of such transactions upon the system of accounts and the underlying equation. The point should be emphasized that in each of these occurrences we have numerically *equal* entries in *opposite* columns, an addition to an asset always being indicated by a left-hand entry in the appropriate account and a subtraction by a right-hand entry. Hence the original equality between property balances and equity balances is undisturbed. These transactions affect only one of the fundamental classes, properties, and do not disturb the *total* of that class. They consist merely in transpositions of property values from one account to another, and accordingly only affect the financial status of the enterprise in that the character and amounts of particular assets are thereby changed.

All of these transactions involve the exchange of commodities or services for other commodities and services of equal value. In the case of purchases from the outside it is noticeable that cash is usually affected. This is to be expected, since cash is the only legal tender and barter transactions are very uncommon in the modern business enterprise. Transactions representing definite purchases are usually recorded as they occur.[4] In the case of the acquisition of services, however, the accounting does not always conform, concurrently, to the actual process of value accretion. Labor services, for example, are often allowed to accrue for some time before payment is made and before they are recognized in the accounts. Insurance services, on the other hand, are commonly prepaid, and are registered in the accounts at time of payment. With respect to the internal transformation of assets due to operation it is not feasible, as was stated above, to recognize such

---

[4] The so-called cash purchase may, of course, involve some little time and not until payment is made could the transaction be said to be complete and ready for entry. The giving of the order, the receipt of the goods, the payment—all these incidents are important elements in establishing the relationship between buyer and seller. If the goods are received for an appreciable period prior to payment, the transaction is not strictly an exchange of assets. Instead we have virtually two transactions: (1) the acquisition of a good and the incurrence of a liability, (2) the liquidation of the liability with cash.

occurrences except at intervals. Thus it appears that in the case of interproperty transactions there is not always an actual coincidence in time between transactions as recognized by the bookkeeper and actual processes of acquisition and transformation.

Evidently the method of entering interproperty transactions in a parallel-column system of accounts is in itself very simple and could be mastered almost immediately by anyone. The difficulty in practice is that of interpretation. It is not always easy to see, in a complex of data, just what has happened to the assets. Once it is recognized which assets have been increased and which have decreased, the entries follow almost as a matter of course.

EQUITY TRANSACTIONS

The second class of transactions mentioned above includes all those occurrences, transpositions, and exchanges which affect only the equities. Transactions may occur in which one equity is increased and another decreased by a like amount, without any accompanying effect upon properties. Accordingly, such happenings may be labeled "interequity" transactions. These are especially common in corporate procedure; and certain cases are very frequently misunderstood. The conversion of securities, the appropriation of surplus, the issue of a stock dividend, the accumulation of discounts, the declaration of a cash dividend, the issue of securities to fund floating obligations, the giving of a promissory note to replace an open creditor's account—all of these operations involve the exchange of equities and do not directly disturb the property accounts. Further, the third type of transaction discussed in the first section of this chapter, the book entries which do not represent any actual happening or process affecting the properties or any transaction with the outside, comes under this head almost entirely.

The exchange of notes and accounts payable gives a simple example. The X Co., let us suppose, gives its 60-day promissory note for $3,000 to cover an open account in favor of the Y Co. for that amount. This is analogous to the exchange of accounts and notes receivable discussed in the preceding section. The X Co. does not *pay* the Y Co. Instead, a formal written evidence of indebtedness is substituted for a more or less informal claim. One kind of liability is replaced by another. An equity, accounts payable, is decreased by $3,000 and another equity, notes payable, is increased by a like amount. Proceeding in accordance with the method of constructing parallel-column equity accounts explained in Chapter IV, this transaction would then be recorded by an entry of $3,000 in the left-hand column of the accounts payable account (a subtraction from an equity) and an entry of $3,000 in the right-hand column of the notes payable account (an equal addition to another equity). Evidently the transaction results in equal entries in opposite columns, and the equality of property and equity totals is maintained.

It was noted in the last chapter that in practice "accounts receivable" and "accounts payable" are usually controlling accounts.[5] The same thing may be said of "notes payable," the notes payable register being virtually a subsidiary ledger. In this event the above transaction (and all similar transactions) would be recorded in duplicate, i.e., in both a subsidiary and in controlling accounts. In the case of certain occurrences (e.g., the payment of an account receivable) it is evident that only one side of the transaction would require entry in duplicate. This gives, of course, no real exception to the numerical equality of opposite entries which we are now stressing.

The exchange of stocks for bonds and vice versa are fa-

---

[5] The "controlling" account might be defined as *an account which shows in summary form information which is shown elsewhere, concurrently, in detail duplicate.*

miliar financial operations in corporation accounting. Or a particular kind of stock may be exchanged for stock of a different type. As was noted in Chapter III, a situation in which such transactions often occur on a large scale is reorganization. At such times whole issues of bonds are frequently exchanged for stocks. For an example of this kind of a transaction let us suppose that in the reorganization of the Y Co. an issue of bonds amounting to $100,000 is retired by the emission of the Company's preferred stock to the bondholders for the same amount.[6] This transaction would be recorded by an entry of $100,000 in the left-hand column of the bonds account (denoting the decrease in an equity) and an equal entry in the right-hand column of the preferred stock account (indicating the increase in an equity). Here again the equality of classes is not affected.

The various appropriations of net revenue and surplus represent simply transpositions of equity balances. Many of the entries necessary at the time of the periodic closing of the books also fall into this class. These situations will be somewhat further discussed and illustrated in Chapter VII and elsewhere.

The cases given will be sufficient for the time being to illustrate the interequity transactions. It should be emphasized that in every instance the recognition of such a transaction involves equal entries in opposite columns, and the equality of left-hand and right-hand balances is consequently maintained. Further, only individual equity items are affected, the equity

---

[6] In such exchanges the various equities are seldom treated as on an equal footing as far as nominal or par values are concerned, and consequently much more complicated transactions than the above often arise. The bondholders in the above case might receive, for example, $125,000 par in stock in exchange for their bonds totaling only $100,000. This would still be a pure equity transaction, in no way affecting the property accounts. The additional $25,000 might measure simply a fictitious par value and hence be properly offset by discount on stock. If the preferred stock had an actual significance of $125,000, the difference between this sum and the original claim of the bondholders would constitute a deduction from some residual equity, probably the common stockholders'.

total remaining unchanged. That is, such transactions do not affect either the individual properties, the total of the properties, or the equity total; they involve simply a shifting among the equities. Just as any number of pure property transactions may take place without disturbing the total of properties and, accordingly, the equities, so in equity transactions an indefinite number of exchanges among the equities may occur without in any way disturbing the equity total and, hence the properties.

In practice, interequity transactions are usually registered on the books concurrently with the actual happening. In fact, in such cases as the appropriation of a section of surplus in a special account it might be said that the transaction consists in the authorizing resolution of the board of directors coupled with the formal recognition of this resolution in the accounts. It is only in this type of transaction that it is feasible to present continuously the current situation in the accounts. This is due to the fact that none of the gradual processes of transformation which affect the assets, and which are so hard to discern and follow, are involved in pure equity transactions. That is, the problems of valuation are not directly involved in interequity occurrences.

Because of the somewhat formal character of many of these equity transfers, however, and because no inevitable processes are connected therewith, it must not be concluded that they are not *real*. They constitute actual accounting transactions, reflecting, in a measure, the financial history and status of the business, the intents and established policies of the management in certain connections; and they are accordingly of importance to all concerned in the accounts. The *distribution* of the total of the equities among the different types is in itself a matter of first importance in the determination of the current and long-run financial condition of any business enterprise.

PROPERTY-EQUITY TRANSACTIONS

The third main type of transaction includes all those occurrences and processes which bring about concomitant changes in both of the fundamental balance-sheet classes. Certain transactions result in an increase or decrease in properties and an equal increase or decrease in equities. These transactions deserve a special emphasis. If all happenings connected with business operation were reflected only in the two types of occurrences already discussed, the *totals* of the balance sheet would evidently always remain unchanged. Accounting in this event would consist merely of two independent processes, the record of the shifting of property items and of transpositions among equities. Evidently such transactions would never alter the financial status of a business enterprise in the broad sense, since the totals of properties and equities would remain fixed.

This third class of transactions, however, affects both sides, an increase or decrease in properties being accompanied by a corresponding increase or decrease in equities. Transactions in the present group always affect the totals of both balance-sheet classes and in the *same amount and direction*. These property-equity occurrences, accordingly, are the most significant group of all possible transactions. Further, this class presents peculiarly difficult cases. It includes the reduction of certain complex business situations and processes to their lowest terms, assets and equities. The facts, in this underlying sense, are often hard to ascertain; and their translation into accounting entries, even when determined, is a matter offering some difficulties.

For the first illustration we will take an explicit business occurrence. The X Co. retires notes payable to the amount of $5,000 with cash. Here an equity, notes payable, is reduced, and there is a corresponding decrease in a liquid property, cash. Proceeding in accordance with the analysis of the structure of accounts developed in the preceding chapter this transaction would be reflected in the accounts by a left-hand entry of $5,000 in the notes payable account (indicating a decrease in an equity) and an equal entry in the right-hand column of the cash account (indicating an equal decrease in an asset). The result is equal entries in opposite columns. Thus the equality of fundamental classes, and of left-hand and right-hand balances, is not disturbed; but the total of each class has been reduced by the amount of $5,000.

The X Co. buys merchandise to the amount of $3,000 on account. This transaction involves an increase in a property item, merchandise, and an equity, accounts payable, is expanded by a like amount. It would then be recorded by an entry of $3,000 in the left-hand column of the materials account, and an entry for an equal amount in the right-hand column of the accounts payable account.

The bringing in of additional capital will serve as a third illustration. The X Co., for example, issues new common stock (at par) for cash to the amount of $25,000. Evidently this transaction would require a left-hand entry of $25,000 in the cash account and an equal right-hand entry in the capital stock—common account.[7] This procedure maintains the equality of classes, as the total of each is increased by the same amount.

A net earning furnishes a case of direct increase in both classes. A, for example, clips the coupons from some municipal bonds which he owns, and cashes the same, receiving $300. Here we have an increase in an asset, cash, of $300, with no accompanying decrease in property and no incurrence of liabilities. Consequently this property increase means a corre-

---

[7] Organization entries are much more elaborate than this in practice. It is customary to recognize the taking of subscriptions, the payment of subscriptions, and the issuing of the stock as independent occurrences. However, the entries given here represent the summary of the whole series.

TYPES OF TRANSACTIONS

sponding expansion in A's ownership or equity. The transaction would then be recorded by an entry of $300 in the left-hand column of the cash account (indicating an increase in assets) and a right-hand entry of the same amount in A's capital (or earnings) account (indicating an increase in equities).

The receipt of a bequest or donation affects the accounts in much the same way. For example, let us assume that A is planning to erect a factory in a certain city and that the site, worth $5,000, is donated to him by the municipality. An asset is received amounting to $5,000; no assets are concurrently consumed or liabilities incurred; the proprietary equity is consequently increased. The record of the transaction would then be made by a left-hand entry of $5,000 in the land account and an equal right-hand entry in A's capital account. Again we have equal entries in opposite columns, and the fundamental equation is accordingly maintained.

The opposite of the donation or net gain is the case of property lost or given away. Suppose, for example, that a tornado totally destroys a semicompleted factory building (uninsured) which A is erecting, which had cost $10,000. This is a loss in assets without any compensating advantages; and since A's equity is residual, the reduction in ownership is at the expense of his interest. The procedure necessary to give effect to this misfortune in the accounts would be an entry of $10,000 in the left-hand column of A's capital account and an equal entry in the right-hand column of the building account.[8]

One of the fundamental assumptions of accounting, already referred to several times in this study, is that *cost gives true value for purpose of initial statement.* That is, it is assumed

---

[8] The accountant usually assumes that any losses in asset values bring about an impairment of the most recently accumulated proprietorship. But there would surely be good reason for viewing the loss of semifinished capital assets as occasioning a reduction in original ownership.

that when the business man acquires a property the purchase price is the proper test of value for purposes of entry in the accounts. On the whole this is a thoroughly reasonable assumption for the accountant, although, strictly speaking, there is no such rationality with respect to purchases as is implied thereby. Payment is doubtless frequently made for an asset greatly in excess of its reasonable value. Both during the period of organization and construction and the period of operation funds are often carelessly handled, if not deliberately misused. In extreme cases the accountant should probably refuse to follow ostensible or even actual costs as a basis for asset values, and should enter the difference between real values parted with and values received as a deduction from equities, a loss. This aspect of valuation, as it arises during organization and construction, will be considered more fully in Chapter XIV.

An additional assessment of federal income and profits taxes some time after the year in which the tax should have been paid gives another illustration of an enforced reduction in proprietary capital. Let us suppose that A has filed an incorrect return in 1919 and that in 1922 he is required to pay an additional assessment of $2,000. The transaction would be properly reflected in the accounts by a left-hand entry in A's capital account of $2,000, and an equal right-hand entry in cash.

The significance and treatment of net gains and losses, withdrawals of earnings in the form of dividends or otherwise, and similar cases of property-equity transactions will be considered in Chapter VII.

Credit transactions are characteristic of modern business, at least in America. Purchases and sales in many lines are largely on a credit basis. The enterprise buys commodities and services, acquires title thereto, but postpones final settlement for some time. Original plant and equipment and, in part, initial working assets are quite likely to be secured, in the final sense, from funds furnished by long-term investors, in the case of the corporation the stockholders and bondholders. (Short-term liabilities, of course, may be temporarily incurred in connection with property construction.) Subsequent acquisitions of all types of commodities and services, however, are likely to be secured on a credit basis, current liabilities being incurred thereby. Thus a machine or a shipment of merchandise is purchased on account. Assets are increased and liabilities are correspondingly expanded. Later the liabilities so created are retired with cash. Properties are diminished; current equities are similarly reduced.

These two processes of equal increase in properties and equities and subsequent equal decrease in properties and equities are constantly going on in the typical business enterprise. Commodities and services are acquired, are made up into finished goods, are sold on account, and the funds thereby made available are used in part to liquidate the liabilities incurred in the acquirement of the original commodities and services or other similar units. One process is likely to just about offset the other, no serious increase or decrease in the amount of current claims against the enterprise resulting. In fact any considerable expansion of current obligations is likely to be dangerous from the standpoint of immediate solvency. All of these transactions are property-equity occurrences and all can be recorded in the manner just outlined without disturbing the equality of left-hand and right-hand balances.

As was noted in a preceding section, the acquisition of labor services is not always (not commonly in fact) given current recognition in the accounts. Laborers may furnish services for two weeks or more without pay, in this way, as the economist has pointed out, often carrying a small part of the true capital cost of production. Literally this means, from the accounting standpoint, that the business enterprise buys these services on account, i.e., acquires the service in advance of payment just as in the case of merchandise purchased "on time." If the true situation were correctly followed we would have two distinct accounting transactions. First would come the recognition of the acquisition of the services. Suppose, for example, that the X Co. acquires labor services on a certain day having a cost value of $3,000. The transaction would be recorded by a left-hand entry of $3,000 in the labor services account (an addition to assets) and an equal entry in the wages payable account. This last would represent a true liability and would measure the claim or equity the employees had in the properties of the Company.[9] Second, the retirement of this current liability with cash would occur, another property-equity transaction. This occurrence would be registered in the accounts by a left-hand entry in the wages payable account (a subtraction from a liability) and an equal right-hand entry in the cash account (a subtraction from an asset).

The acquisition by lease of the services represented by the use of any property, such as a building, machine, etc., payment being delayed, would be similarly handled according to the ideal accounting procedure. As acquired the services would be periodically entered in the left-hand column of a "building services" account, for example, the concurrent right-hand entries being made in the rents payable account. Later the equity, rents payable, would be retired with cash, and the proper entries made to recognize this occurrence.

In concluding this discussion of property-equity transactions the point should be again emphasized that in every possible case we have equal entries in opposite columns, the equation of left and right balances thus being preserved. In

---

[9] Wages payable are indeed usually considered to constitute a "preferred claim" in bankruptcy cases. That is, the laborer has an equity which the courts, in general, view as ranking above all others except accrued taxes. The wages payable account is closely analogous to the merchandise accounts payable. The time cards and other payroll records would virtually constitute a subsidiary ledger, controlled by the wages payable account.

each case, however, the total of each fundamental class is changed. Some transactions bring about an equal decrease in both properties and equities; others result in an equal increase in both classes. In all instances the change in each division is in the same direction and amount.

COMBINATION TRANSACTIONS

A final group of transactions includes those occurrences and processes representing combinations of two or more of the other types. No new principles of analysis are here introduced; hence this group cannot be thought of as a fundamental case. But what is commonly called the "transaction" in practice sometimes covers a combination of two, or even all three, of the kinds discussed in the preceding sections.

The most complex case of the "mixed" transaction is the *sale*. When the commodity or service produced by the enterprise is sold, how does this situation affect the fundamental balance-sheet elements? It will be necessary to answer this question with some care, as the rational explanation of the sale transaction is one of the most difficult problems in accounting theory.

From one standpoint the sale transaction might be viewed as exactly analogous to the cash purchase, an exchange of assets. Some commodity or service produced by the enterprise is exchanged for other goods, money, or rights (usually cash or accounts receivable). And, as was stated in connection with the discussion of purchases in the preceding section, the only reasonable assumption for purposes of analyzing such situations and setting forth the accounting principles involved is that all such transactions involve fair and equal exchanges between equally intelligent and rational individuals. However, it was also noted above that accounting valuation is in general based upon cost prices, buying prices, rather than selling prices.

In consistence with this plan the finished product of the enterprise must be considered to be worth, for purposes of accounting, not selling price but cost.[10] In other words, accounting is based upon a scheme which is designed to show earnings or losses as a residuum, a difference, positive or negative as the case may be, between cost and selling price. In the competitive enterprise this difference may be conceived as roughly expressing the price of the services of the investors, the value of the functions of ownership—management, capital service, risk-taking, etc.; and it is accounted for as an increase in equities, not as a cost. To put the matter still differently, it is a fundamental view of the accountant, and on the whole a rational one, that it is only the *purchased* commodities and services, not those services which are performed by the owners themselves, which should be represented in the accounts by asset values.[11] And if this view is adopted the normal sale transaction must be conceived as an exchange of properties (commodities or services) for other properties of *greater value*, the difference measuring the gain to the enterprise.

From this standpoint a sale is a combination of inter-property and property-equity transactions. An illustration will serve to indicate this clearly. The X Co., for example, sells finished goods with an effective cost (including selling and administration expenses) of $500 for $600 in cash. Here we have an addition to one asset, cash, of $600, and a subtraction from another asset, finished goods, of only $500. In what does the difference consist? Clearly the excess $100 expresses an increase in equities. Instead of owning goods valued at $500, the enterprise now owns goods valued at $600. Consequently there must be $600 of capital and surplus as

---

[10] This need not exclude the use of effective *cost of replacement*. Ideally, in the going concern, the figure which it is most rational for the accountant to adopt as a basis for all valuations, is current buying price. The study of the proper basis for valuation, however, forms a subject in itself, and, as was stated elsewhere, will not be attempted in this book.

[11] This matter will be dealt with at length in later chapters.

compared with a former amount of but $500. The transaction would accordingly be recorded by a left-hand entry of $600 in the cash account, a right-hand entry of $500 in the finished goods account (and in cash or other accounts covering selling and administrative costs not collected previously under the caption "finished goods") and a right-hand entry of $100 in some appropriate equity account.[12] Evidently the entire situation can be recorded directly in terms of balance-sheet accounts; and the entries required do not disturb the equality of opposing columns.

This analysis of the sale transaction, as was stated above, follows the conventional theory of valuation; viz., that finished stock ready to ship is for accounting purposes a property only to the amount of the costs actually incurred by the enterprise in producing this stock. If finished goods prior to sale were valued at selling price less marketing costs yet unincurred, on the other hand, the sale itself would constitute essentially an exchange of assets.[13] Finished goods, plus cash and other properties expiring in shipping and other marketing operations, would just equal the cash or accounts receivable arising from the sale. The sale would then represent merely a special case of the interproperty transaction.

Preliminary entries would of course be necessary to bring the increase in value above cost into the accounts, to capitalize, in other words, the services and functions of the enterprise itself, in so far as the net earnings might be said to be a payment for such services and functions. The accretion might

---

[12] "Net revenue" will be the heading used in this study to register the net earnings of the business as a whole from the standpoint of the long-term equities. See Chapter VII.
As pointed out in a previous section of this chapter, the building up of the finished goods account involves the transfer of asset values from original accounts such as equipment, materials, labor, etc. (a much more gradual process in the case of equipment than in the case of materials, and a practically immediate process in the case of labor), to goods in process and then finally to finished goods.
[13] The policy of valuing goods on hand at selling price less costs to market is not without its justification from the standpoint of established accounting practice. See Chapter XIX for further consideration of this matter.

be gradually recognized by a series of entries as goods approached the completion stage, or the increment covering all completed goods on hand might be brought in in a lump sum periodically. In any case the amount of the enhancement would be reflected in the accounts by a left-hand entry in the finished goods account (or first in the various goods in process accounts and then finally in the finished goods account), and an equal right-hand entry in some equity account.

If the productive process were instantaneous (as the typical conventional accounting procedures for the trading enterprise assume) the entries covering a sale would be much more elaborate than has been indicated. There would then be no occasion for the recognition of inchoate or finished goods. The cash received could be considered as being exchanged directly for the original commodities and services acquired by the enterprise. The left-hand entry would be made, as above, in the cash account, but the right-hand entries covering the $500 of costs would be made to the sundry property and current accounts recording the original costs incurred. Entries in the accounts with building, equipment, materials, labor, supplies, insurance, advertising, etc., would be made for appropriate amounts, the total being $500.

It will be shown in the next chapter that it is not expedient in practice to reduce sale transactions immediately to the original two dimensions, properties and equities. Accounts showing temporary, intermediate classifications are required. Special *phases* of the assets and equities are set up, provisionally, and are later, periodically, resolved into their lowest terms. It will be shown further that the services and commodities required in the selling process (the costs of which it is not usually considered reasonable to treat as part of the value of finished goods) require temporary accounting recognition apart from their real balance-sheet character. The point to be emphasized here is that the sale and all other possible

TYPES OF TRANSACTIONS 137

transactions in the realm of business *can* be stated directly and definitely in terms of the two balance-sheet classes, and recorded directly in pure property and equity accounts in accordance with the simple rules of procedure explained in Chapter IV, *provided the correct information is available, or can be ascertained, concurrently with the actual happening or the actual process.*

The above discussed situation, the sale, is a combination of the interproperty and property-equity cases in what might be termed a "chemical" sense.[14] There are many so-called transactions in practice, however, which are merely "mechanical" combinations of the fundamental cases. For example, the X Co. buys supplies from the Y Co. amounting to $500. In making payment the Company transfers to the seller an account which it holds against Z amounting to $100, gives its 30-day note at 6 per cent for $200, and pays the balance, $200, in cash. Viewing this whole operation as a single transaction we have therein an increase in one asset, supplies, of $500, a decrease in accounts receivable (claims against Z) of $100, a decrease in another asset, cash, of $200, and an increase in an equity, notes payable, of $200. The transaction would then be recorded by a left-hand entry in the supplies account and right-hand entries for the appropriate amounts in the accounts receivable, cash, and notes payable accounts. The left-hand entry amounts to $500, and the right-hand entries total the same sum. Consequently the equation is still maintained.

An indefinite number of these "mixed" transactions may occur in business practice. In some cases it is very difficult, especially for the beginner, to disentangle the various elements and recognize the appropriate entries. Careful analysis is all

---

[14] It would be possible, of course, arbitrarily to divide such a transaction in two parts; i.e., to say that the receipt of $100 in cash (referring to the above illustration) measured the increase in ownership, and that the balance of the transaction involved merely an exchange of assets.

that is required in such a case, however, as no principles of procedure are required which have not been discussed fully in the earlier sections of this chapter. Accordingly no more space will be devoted here to illustrations of these combination situations.

SUMMARY—DOUBLE AND SINGLE ENTRY

To sum up: The accounting transaction in a broad sense is any happening, process, or circumstance which affects the status of property or equity items in the business enterprise. All possible cases can be classified in terms of effect upon the fundamental classes under four heads:

1. The exchange of one property for another asset of equal amount.
2. The exchange of one equity for another equity of equal amount.
3. An increase or decrease of a property accompanied by a corresponding increase or decrease of an equity.
4. A combination of two or more of the other three cases.

These fundamental situations may, of course, appear in an endless variety of amount, circumstance, and combination, but all cases can be placed without distortion under the above groups. A study of illustrations under each of the various divisions shows that every possible accounting transaction is *two-sided;* i.e., there is always an equal left-hand entry (or entries) for every right-hand entry (or entries) and vice versa. Hence the original equation existing between the sum of the left-hand (asset) balances and the sum of the right-hand (equity) balances is continuously maintained.[15]

The characterization, "double-entry system," undoubtedly finds its origin in this fact of equal and opposite entries for

---

[15] In bookkeeping practice this continuous equality of opposite ledger column totals furnishes an important test of accuracy through the use of the trial balance.

TYPES OF TRANSACTIONS

every transaction. As we have just seen, *double entries*—i.e., an entry in each of the parallel columns—must be recorded to give effect in the accounts to any happening, operation, or financial process. Yet the designation is not altogether happy, as its significance is widely misunderstood, even by those who are supposed to have some knowledge of accounting. The double-entry scheme seems to be popularly conceived as a system of *duplicate* entry, a plan by which every essential fact is recorded twice. This device, it is carelessly supposed, derives its chief virtue from the fact that having entered all data in two places the bookkeeper can, by comparing his duplicate lists, insure clerical accuracy. The preceding discussion should make it evident that such a conception is quite erroneous. The double-entry method is not a scheme by which all data are recorded *twice;* rather it is a system by which each essential amount is recorded *once*. Special features of conventional accounting (e.g., the use of the parallel-column account) are no doubt somewhat arbitrary; but in the main double-entry accounting is a rational and inevitable plan which is founded in the very nature of the business enterprise and business operation. In broad terms, the double-entry system is *any scheme of accounting which exhibits all of the property and equity facts of the business enterprise and registers, at least periodically, the changes therein;* in a narrower sense double entry is a device which accomplishes this purpose through the use of parallel-column accounts (in the manner outlined in this chapter). Every transaction requires at least two entries because there are at least two distinct value facts involved therein. A change in a property item can only be effected through a change in the opposite direction in some other asset or through a corresponding change in an equity. Similarly a change in an equity can only occur as there is an equal change in the opposite direction in some other equity or an equal change in the same direction in some property. There is nothing mysterious about this, and no duplication. It is an entirely matter-of-fact situation. A *complete* record of any business transaction requires at least two equal entries. Double entry in this sense must persist regardless of the nature of clerical methods adopted in practice.

In this connection the ghost of "single entry" should be laid. Single entry, so called, is generally discredited, yet many textbooks on accounting (most of the recent ones included) devote one or more chapters to a discussion of single-entry procedures and the relative merits and disadvantages of this system as compared with double-entry bookkeeping. A clear recognition of the essential nature of the account structure renders all consideration of single-entry methods entirely unnecessary. Evidently no possible transaction can actually be recorded by a *single* entry. Any other system than double entry, accordingly, represents merely *incomplete* accounting. There is no such thing as "single-entry" bookkeeping in any proper sense of the term.

It is of course a familiar fact that the accounts of many business enterprises are inadequate and imperfect at various points. In some cases actual accounts are set up covering only cash, customers, and creditors—a highly abbreviated and incomplete system. In other instances the only element not specifically recognized is the residual equity, in whole or in part. There is no standard incomplete system; rather there is an endless variety of ways in which the accounting structure may be organized imperfectly.

It is no doubt possible to characterize some particular incomplete method as "single entry"; but it should be clearly recognized that this designation does not indicate any system which literally involves the procedure suggested by the name. In any case, to give the impression—as is sometimes done—that single entry is a distinct alternative plan is wholly unreasonable. Some writers have even gone so far as to suggest that there were further possibilities, such as "triple" and "quadruple" entry. As a matter of fact there is only one kind of complete accounting possible, the system which has been outlined in this chapter and which may be characterized, with some reason, as the double-entry method. As has already been emphasized this scheme is founded in the immanent nature of the business situation; and this is doubtless the reason that the method has persisted—and will persist—despite the very common failure to understand its "mysteries."

CHAPTER VI

EXPENSE AND REVENUE ACCOUNTS

The next step is the explanation of the supplementary, intermediate, and provisional classes of accounts. In this chapter the *expense* and *revenue* divisions, the most important and the most difficult to interpret of the subsidiary classifications, will be examined. It will be shown that these classes are definite phases or aspects of the fundamental members of the balance sheet. It will be discovered that, in a sense, nothing new whatever is involved in these additional divisions. Were it not for certain complexities in the business process, and some matters of expediency, these classes might indeed be dispensed with altogether; and in that event the analysis of accounts and transactions would be essentially complete with the last chapter. As has been pointed out, all possible types of occurrences and processes, in all business enterprises, *can* be dissected into property and equity elements if all necessary data are immediately available. This being the case, expenses and revenues can be rationally explained as *phases of the properties and equities.*

As a preliminary to this explanation, the conditions of the business process and the practical requirements of an accounting system which occasion the use of these and other supplementary classifications will be restated and emphasized.

THE NEED FOR SUPPLEMENTARY ACCOUNTS

It has been indicated several times in the foregoing pages that certain transactions present themselves in virtually all businesses of such a character that it is not possible, or at least not feasible, to resolve them, immediately, into their lowest terms, positive and negative property and equity facts. The fundamental elements are present, but cannot be conveniently "precipitated" in the case of each individual transaction.

In the first place the transformation of assets within the business in the furthering of manufacturing operations cannot always be followed continuously in the accounts, both because of the clerical work involved and because of the inherent difficulties in the way of the ascertainment of the facts. The gradual utilization of fuel, for example, could only with great difficulty be concurrently exhibited by the accountant. Similarly, changes in fixed properties resulting from the conditions of operation, and changes which are a reflection of price movements, improved technique, and other external economic tendencies and developments over which the management may have little or no control, can hardly be reflected continuously in the records.

The translation of value processes within the enterprise, or economic movements of consequence without the business, into definite accounting entries as a rule can only be attempted *at intervals,* and at the best is always based to a large degree upon more or less reasonable estimates and judgments. Some of these processes of asset transmutation, occurring in time, can be viewed as constituting an infinite series of minute transactions. Obviously it is only periodically that specific accounting recognition can be given to such movements. And if the expirations of particular assets are not concomitantly or exactly recorded it is evident that the correct property balances will not be continuously exhibited in the accounts.

In attempting to deal with these asset changes, the accountant finds it necessary to extend his system of accounts far beyond a list of pure property headings. The complexities of the situation require the use of subsidiary or supplementary accounts. Special *phases* of the properties must be set up;

certain tentative, provisional classifications of asset data must be given accounting recognition.[1] Further, in this connection the accountant is obliged to make use of purchases accounts which have, temporarily, a somewhat dubious significance. Does a particular account at a particular moment of time represent an asset, an expiration of asset values, or what?[2] It is not always easy to answer such a question.

Again, in the periodic "closing" of accounts, i.e., in the process of reducing an entire system to its lowest terms, the balance sheet, it is often necessary to open up temporary accounts for purposes of summarization, and to indicate the amount and disposition of income. Still further, the practice of restricting the amounts presented in the principal equity accounts in the case of the corporation to formal par figures makes it necessary that special offset and surplus accounts be introduced which constitute adjuncts of the main equity accounts, the amount in such subsidiary account in any case representing the difference (positive or negative) between the formal figure and the complete "book" value of the equity.[3]

More important for our immediate purpose, however, is the fact that the determination of the *cost of product* is a problem which presents peculiar difficulties. Not only is it hard to follow the transformation of particular asset values within the business but it is especially difficult to discover the amount of asset values which finally disappears from the business, embodied in finished goods, when a sale is made. As was pointed out in the preceding chapter, the sale transaction consists at bottom of genuine property and equity elements and could be recorded directly in property and equity accounts, *provided the essential facts could be immediately ascertained at the time of the sale.* As a matter of fact, the cost of the

---
[1] See the discussion of valuation accounts in Chapter VII.
[2] In Chapter VIII this problem of account classification is further considered.
[3] The net revenue and surplus accounts will be briefly considered in Chapter VII.

individual sale, arising out of the expiration of assets incident to the product involved in the sale, cannot as a rule be determined with even approximate accuracy. In attempting to deal with this situation the accountant finds it necessary to set up intermediate, provisional classifications and accounts, from which, periodically, the underlying facts may be determined. The essential accounts required in this connection are the *expense* and *revenue* accounts. Unanalyzed phases of the assets and equities are poured into these accounts and the resulting amalgam is later resolved into its intrinsic elements.

It should be noted that there are other reasons for the use of these subordinate types of accounts than actual necessity. Such temporary divisions are of great inherent importance from the standpoint of the management. Even if it were possible to reduce each transaction to balance-sheet terms immediately it would still be desirable to set up certain temporary classifications for managerial purposes. The history of the business, the processes by which changes have been brought about, must be shown in the accounts with some degree of elaboration if the system is to be of the utmost utility in guiding the management. And it must not be forgotten that this is one of the most important, perhaps *the* most important, use to which modern accounts may be put. Thus expense or cost in its various aspects is a matter of such consequence to the directors of an enterprise—regardless of the fact that from the standpoint of the theory of accounts it is merely an ephemeral phase of something more fundamental—as to justify, in some circumstances, the use of a complex system of "cost accounting." Similarly gross revenue is an important criterion of business activity, and accordingly may well be given independent accounting recognition even though it is but an intermediate classification arising in the process of determining true financial condition. Hence, even if it were always possible to bring together individual sales and the costs thereof (and the cost accountant might argue that this is possible under approved cost methods with the possible exception of certain very general items), it would still be desirable in many cases to accumulate revenues and costs *en masse* in distinct groups of accounts, and to classify and reclassify the data contained therein in such a manner as to show various relationships in which the management might be interested.

Still further, even if it were actually possible to reduce the sale and every other accounting occurrence and process immediately to its lowest accounting terms, it might be clerically inconvenient to attempt to do this. Certainly it would involve a multiplicity of entries. It is simpler from the bookkeeping standpoint to build up subsidiary classes, which are analyzed only in total, at intervals, than it would be to carry each happening through immediately to its ultimate conclusion. This point will become clearer as we proceed.

In the following sections the precise nature of the expense and revenue classes and accounts as used in modern accounting will be made clear. The way in which these accounts fit into the system already outlined will be explained; and it will be shown that these new groups conform to the simple principles of account construction and entry already demonstrated.

THE REVENUE DIVISION

It was shown in the last chapter that the sale from one point of view consists in the exchange of finished goods (plus shipping and other marketing costs) for cash or receivables of equal value. It was pointed out, however, that prior to the actual completion of the sale it is not considered good accounting practice to recognize property values on the books in excess of the effective costs of *purchased* commodities and services involved.[4] In other words, the net increase in property values,

---
[4] A donated commodity or service would, of course, also be recognized; but as donations are not typical commercial transactions, the statement made is sufficiently exact.
The nature of the expense and revenue accounts and the procedures that would

and the consequent *net income* or increase in equities, which may be thought of as a payment for the peculiar economic functions of the enterprise itself,[5] is usually not recognized prior to the final sale of product. Accordingly, the properties received at time of sale exceed by the income margin the properties involved in the sale (whether all combined under the single head of finished goods or scattered throughout various original or intermediate accounts). In other words, the sale transaction involves (presumably) a net earning or income, an increase in equities or ownership.

The nature of the essential, residual element in gross revenue from an accounting standpoint may be brought out by a rather extreme illustration. If the necessary commodities and services which a business enterprise acquires were imperishable (in the economic as well as the physical sense) and hence could be used indefinitely in productive operations without replacement, there would be no such thing as expense and the sale of product would give rise on the one hand to a direct increase in assets and on the other to a direct increase in ownership. Although it is difficult indeed to discover an actual enterprise which even approximates this condition, a consideration of a supposititious case of this type will serve to throw light on the true significance of net revenue from the standpoint of the balance sheet.

A has $10,000 on deposit in a savings bank; and he has no other assets and has no liabilities. Viewing this situation as a business enterprise it might be said that *A*'s business con-

---

be involved in case finished goods were valued on the basis of selling price according to percentage of completion (which is sometimes done in the case of long-term processes) will be dealt with a little later. Economically, the accruing of business income (capital and enterprise cost) as the commodity passes from the raw stage to completion is as sound as the accruing of any element of material or labor expense. In a later chapter there will be further discussion of this point. For the present we will assume that there is good reason for the attitude of accountants in this connection.

[5] This difference in values may, of course, be exceptional, and hence exceed any price-determining cost of the services performed by the enterprise in furnishing the capital and ability necessary to draw together and properly co-ordinate the purchased commodities and services.

sists in furnishing the use of capital, and his balance sheet would appear somewhat as follows:

Properties		Equities	
Bank Account........	$10,000	A, Ownership	$10,000

The bank involved, it will be assumed, pays interest on deposits at the rate of 4 per cent per annum. At the end of a year, then, interest to the amount of $400 has accumulated. A's balance sheet, corrected to date (and assuming no other transactions), would evidently stand as follows:

Bank Account............ $10,400   A, Ownership $10,400

Here the increase in assets, $400, is accompanied by an equal increase in equities, since there are no expirations or costs. Revenue in this case is *net*. The original investment remains intact and hence this increment of $400 constitutes at once a net increase in properties and an equal net increase in equities. Two accounts, "bank account" and "A, ownership," would suffice to exhibit the entire situation, and the year's business might be recorded by a single pair of entries: a left-hand entry of $400 in the bank account and an equal right-hand entry in the A, ownership account.

For emphasis another hypothetical illustration will be given. B, a farmer, owns a very rocky hillside tract much favored by picnickers. Having no other use for the property B permits its occupancy by outing parties at a rate of 25 cents per person per visit. There are no maintenance costs and taxes are negligible. On a particular Saturday twenty persons make use of the grounds; and B's small son collects $5 in fees. Evidently this transaction likewise results in a net increase in assets and proprietorship; and, if B were keeping accounts, it might be recorded therein by a left entry of $5 in the cash account and an equal right entry in an appropriate net income or capital account.

The income is again net, as there are no expirations of value connected therewith.

The typical business situation, of course, is not at all represented by such cases. Even an individual, firm, or corporation engaged primarily in loaning capital would commonly incur certain costs, such as rent, labor, stationery, etc., incident to operation. And in a trading or manufacturing enterprise as much as from 60 to 90 per cent (or even more) of the funds received from the sale of product may be necessary to replace the outlays required in the production of that product. This means, in other words, that large deductions must be made from *gross* revenue, through the expense accounts, before the net return to ownership is determined.

Even where assets are consumed in the production of product, and the revenue is consequently gross, it should be emphasized that the entire situation *can* be recorded directly in property and equity accounts. It was shown in Chapter V that the sale transaction, while complex, presents no real difficulty provided the underlying facts are known. To stress this point we will consider a very simple situation, not at all typical of trading or other enterprises of any consequence, and yet which involves the same fundamental accounting classifications as all of them. Suppose for example that A, a schoolboy, has a capital of $5 cash. It is the day of one of the big football games; and A invests his entire capital (except 50 cents reserved to make change) in peanuts and pop which he expects to sell at the game. For the sake of simplicity we will assume the unlikely, that A is very successful, selling his entire stock for $9 in cash. No other costs are incurred aside from the original expenditure for merchandise. A furnishes all services himself. There are no liabilities outstanding at the end of the day, no receivables, no stock on hand.

In this very simple case A could, if opening up a double-entry set of accounts to record the day's happenings, reduce the entire situation immediately to pure asset and equity terms and strike a new balance sheet. The first transaction, the purchase of goods, would be an exchange of assets, and would be recognized by a left-hand entry in the merchandise account of $4.50 and an equal right-hand entry in the cash account. The business for the day could be viewed, in summary, as a single transaction consisting in an increase of assets, cash, to the amount of $9, a decrease in assets, merchandise, $4.50, and an increase in ownership, A's capital, of $4.50. This would be recorded by a left-hand entry of $9 in the cash account, a right-hand entry of $4.50 in the merchandise account, and a right-hand entry of $4.50 in A's capital account.

A's balance sheet, before the day's business, would stand as follows:

Cash .... $5 A, Capital $5

At the conclusion of the above transactions it would show:

Cash .... $9.50 A, Capital $9.50

In such a situation in practice A would doubtless keep no accounts whatever. Indeed it would be absurd to attempt any regular accounting for such a case. A count of cash and goods is all that is necessary to determine condition. Nevertheless, in getting at the real essence of more complex accounting situations and procedures a consideration of such cases is of value. All important operations are involved in this simple enterprise; assets are purchased, are converted (with respect to time and place), and are sold. And evidently all of these operations can be reflected directly in pure balance-sheet accounts.

Just how does the typical trading enterprise differ, with respect to our present purposes, from the case just discussed? The answer is that in the ordinary retail or wholesale store it is not feasible to ascertain the precise costs of each sale or of each day's sales. It may in some instances be expedient to follow closely the *material* costs of product sold, but evidently it would be very difficult, if not entirely impossible, in the average store, to state correctly the amount of clerk hire, light, depreciation, insurance, etc., which is consumed incident to a single sale or to the sales of a very short interval. Hence, the net income element, the increase in equities or ownership, cannot be precisely isolated in each transaction. It is only at more or less infrequent intervals that it is feasible to attempt this; and even then the result always depends to some degree upon estimates, judgments.

As has already been indicated, where cost accounting is attempted a considerable part of the costs applicable to a particular sale may be collected in a "finished stock" account. But certain costs connected directly with selling cannot be so assigned, and some general and administrative items are usually omitted. Further, as has been emphasized several times, the gross revenue figure is of intrinsic importance to the management as a criterion of operation, and should therefore be preserved for a time. In the manufacturing enterprise too, then, a direct accounting for sales in terms of pure property and equity accounts is not expedient. The accountant has need of further devices.

This situation is temporarily met by the accountant through the use of the *gross revenue* account. Gross revenue is normally the amount of sales. A wholesaler, for example, who sells a shipment of goods amounting to $1,000 on account records the transaction by a left-hand entry of $1,000 in the accounts receivable account and a right-hand entry for $1,000 in the *revenue* or "sales" account. The increase in assets, measured by the left-hand entry, is registered immediately. The accompanying decreases in cost values and (supposedly) increase in ownership, however, are not recognized explicitly. Instead we have a right-hand entry in a provisional, temporary account, gross revenue. In a sense the accounting equation is maintained, for equal entries are made in opposite columns; but although the left-hand entry (showing the increase in assets) presents a definite balance sheet fact, the right-hand entry is simply an unanalyzed, conglomerate figure.

What is the nature of this right-hand entry to revenue? It consists intrinsically in the two elements mentioned above: (1) subtractions from assets, and (2) additions to equities. Both of these elements, according to the scheme presented in Chapter IV, belong in the right-hand column. Hence there is no real disturbance in the fundamental structure. As far as columns are concerned the entries are entirely correct. The provisional aspect of the case lies in the fact that the revenue entry of $1,000 consists of an amalgamation of two very dissimilar things, expirations of properties and increase in equities. Later the two must be divided, for otherwise a correct new balance sheet could not be prepared.

This may be made very clear by reference again to the situation of A, the pop vender. According to the conventional accounting plan, A's sales for the day would be first recorded by a left-hand entry of $9 in the cash account and an equal right-hand entry in the revenue account. How does this differ from the procedure which used only property and equity accounts? Evidently the left-hand entry is the same according to both plans, but the entry in the revenue account in the second case takes the place, temporarily, of the right-hand entry in the merchandise account of $4.50 (a subtraction from assets) and the right-hand entry in A's account of $5 (an increase in an equity).

It is not irrational to consider the revenue classification, for convenience, as measuring *gross increase in equities,* and to explain the right-hand entry in terms of this designation. It is for the purpose of disclosing the pure equity element in the revenue account that most of the later efforts of the

EXPENSE AND REVENUE ACCOUNTS 153

accountant are undertaken. Perhaps the most important single purpose of accounting is the determination of net revenue. The net increase in ownership is the residual element in the revenue account, the element which the accountant is working toward. Nevertheless it must not be forgotten that the designation "gross increase in equities" can be no more than a caption of convenience. Revenue includes, in combination, the expirations of all the multifarious structures, commodities, and services embodied in the product sold together with a more or less important pure equity element.

THE EXPENSE DIVISION

This brings us to a consideration of *expense*. Suppose, for illustration, that during six months a wholesaler makes total sales amounting to $50,000, and that at the end of this time he "closes his books," i.e., takes inventories, determining the value on hand of each and every kind of property and thus, indirectly, the amount of the expirations involved in making the sales of the period. When these expirations are ascertained the accountant is in a position to resolve sales into their intrinsic elements and precipitate the pure net revenue. Let us assume that they total $40,000. Right-hand entries amounting to $40,000 would then be made in the various accounts recording the numerous commodities and services required to conduct the business—merchandise, transportation service, insurance, advertising, labor, rent, etc.—and an equal left-hand entry in the revenue account. The revenue account would now stand as follows:

	Revenue	
$40,000		$50,000

The balance of this account now represents the net equity increase and can be transferred to another account having an appropriate title.

Just what is the significance of this subtraction from revenue and how can we explain this entry in terms of our fundamental scheme? As was stated above, the original right-hand entry to revenue includes the indeterminate, unassigned expirations of properties (assuming the sales are not made at a net loss). As soon as these expirations are actually determined (by inventory and estimate) the accountant is in a position to distribute this provisional entry among the numerous specific fixed and current property accounts involved. In other words, he is then able to return, or allocate, to the various accounts recording specific structures, commodities, and services acquired, the temporary record of these subtractions, *en masse,* under the revenue heading. And since, as was noted in an earlier connection, it is a fundamental rule of bookkeeping, an innate feature of the two-column scheme of accounts, to indicate a subtraction in any case by placing an appropriate entry in the opposite column, the amount of $40,000 is subtracted from the revenue entry of $50,000 by an entry in the left-hand column of the revenue account. Concurrently, as was stated, right-handed entries would be made to the various accounts representing costs incurred or properties acquired, thus completing the redefinition and distribution of this part of the provisional revenue entry.

Strictly speaking, this left-hand entry of $40,000 represents a *subtraction from a subtraction from assets* (the first subtraction being involved in the provisional revenue entry), and since a subtraction from an asset is recorded in the right-hand column a subtraction from such a subtraction is properly placed in the left-hand column. Thus the expense charge represents the assignment to the various asset accounts involved of that part of the conglomerate revenue figure which covers the cost of goods sold.

But this left-hand entry to revenue is more than a mere subtraction from revenue. It also constitutes the *expense* or *cost* of production for the period involved; and, as was pointed out above, this figure is of the utmost intrinsic importance from the standpoint of the management. Expense represents in itself an important accounting division; and consequently the accountant is justified in giving it independent recognition. Thus a separate expense account or accounts may well be used, the expense and revenue classes being later combined under a summary account.

It should be emphasized, however, that entries in the left-hand column of distinct expense accounts have precisely the same underlying significance as if made directly in the left-hand column of the revenue account. Revenue is the dominant of these two classifications from the standpoint of the theory of accounts. An expense item, whatever its precise location, represents essentially a deduction from revenue. The expense accounts, strictly speaking, constitute merely the left-hand side of the revenue accounts and should be so conceived. The relationship may be shown graphically as follows, using the figures given above:

	Revenue	
		$50,000
	Expense	
$40,000		

On the other hand, it should be recognized that while the nature of these provisional classes can well be explained in terms of a single account, it is precisely here that a system of accounts may be extended and elaborated almost indefinitely. Revenue may be split up into several separate classes of sales, each of which is represented by a distinct account, and expense may be still more completely subdivided, first in terms of the many classes of original structures, commodities, and services acquired, and later on a functional basis. The detail classification of expense and revenue accounts will be briefly discussed in Chapter VIII.

Expense and revenue accounts, even when set up separately, are nevertheless essentially one-column accounts, the two-column form being preserved simply for convenience. Aside from transfer entries and adjustments a revenue account should have entries only in the right-hand column. A genuine expense account, similarly, has entries normally only in the left-hand column. If expense and revenue be combined in a single account, however, both columns are of course used. The right-hand column of such an account registers gross revenue; the left-hand column exhibits the subtractions from that revenue, the expenses which must be deducted before the net balance can be disclosed.

In the manufacturing establishment, where the process of production involves heavy costs and a considerable period of time, the determination of expense or cost of sales involves special difficulties. Here, as has already been pointed out, three merchandise classes are commonly recognized: materials, work in process, and finished stock. The cost accountant assumes that the costs of material, labor, etc., consumed inhere first in goods in process (throughout the various stages), later in finished stock, and disappear finally from the business as "cost of sales" as the product of the enterprise is disposed of. Manifestly if the entire cost of each sale could be thus determined as the sale was made there would be no absolute necessity for the use of distinct expense and revenue accounts. Instead each transaction could be reduced at once to its lowest terms and recorded in pure asset and equity accounts as has been explained. But in practice, to reiterate, the "indirect" costs (the "burden" or "overhead") can only be allocated to operations and products on more or less arbitrary bases; and in few cost systems is the attempt made to distribute literally all of such costs. Further, packing and transportation costs, for example, are commonly incurred subsequent to the technical completion of the product and incident to the actual sale transaction; and such costs are evidently not a part of the cost value of finished goods except, perhaps, during the very instant of sale.

Consequently, even with an elaborate system of cost accounting in use, it is not expedient in the typical manufacturing enterprise to avoid using the revenue account and a few concluding expense accounts. Genuine expense and revenue accounts are needed. The gross amount of sales for a period is entered in the revenue or sales account; the specific costs incurred during the period in producing the product involved in sales, in so far as these costs have been thus far collected under the head of finished goods, are transferred to a "cost of sales" (expense) account; selling and shipping costs, together with any general or administrative items which it was not considered feasible to attempt to allocate to specific operations and products and finally gather under finished goods, are likewise carried to this account; and net income is periodically determined by combining the sales and cost of sales accounts. The assets received in exchange for product are, of course, recognized as received, as in the case of a trading or other enterprise. A specific illustration of the entries involved in such a case will be given in a later section.

In this connection it should be again emphasized that even if all costs could rationally be collected under the finished goods account it would still be desirable to stress *cost of sales* as a distinct managerial figure. Further, to avoid the necessity for numerous cancellation entries the amalgamation of cost of sales and sales should only be made at intervals.

It has been stated that one of the bases of accounting in general is the assumption that finished product ready for sale is never worth more (on the books of the producer) than the sum total of all purchased costs which have gone to create it. If the theory were adopted that the finished article should be valued on the basis of all purchased items required plus the significance of the producing company's own function (assuming for convenience that the net earnings are not accidental surpluses but a payment by the consumer for real economic services), the nature of expense and the procedures relating thereto would be altered somewhat. In this case left-hand entries would be required in the finished goods account covering all original purchased items converted to that form plus the estimated accrued significance of the producer's own function (presumably on a percentage-of-completion basis). The corresponding right-hand entry for this last amount would be to a net earnings account. When sale was made it would still be convenient to enter the full amount first in a gross revenue account, the concurrent left-hand entry appearing under accounts receivable or cash, as the case happened to be. After selling and shipping costs were determined these items, as well as the proper amount of the finished goods balance, could be transferred to cost of sales. Finally, by combining cost of sales and revenue the additional net earning, probably a very small amount, would be discovered.[6]

A final point in connection with the character of expense should be noted in this section. It was stated that the original right-hand entry in the revenue account covers the then indeterminate subtractions from assets involved in the goods sold. In case the business is unsuccessful this may not be

---
[6] See Chapter XIX.

the case. In other words, the expirations, when determined, may *exceed* the total revenue figure, no equity right-hand balance remaining. Under these circumstances the concluding account would have a left-hand balance, which would become a *net decrease in equities,* a reduction in original capital (as of the beginning of the period), an operating deficit. Thus if expense exceeds revenue, the difference passes into still another classification, loss, which will be considered in the next chapter. Further, it could not be said in such a case that *all* subtractions from assets embodied in product were recognized provisionally in the revenue entries. Evidently the limiting figure for revenue is the amount of asset values (cash, accounts receivable, etc.) received in exchange for product. The excess of expirations over such receipts (if any) is not recorded in any form until later.

EXPENSE, EXPENDITURE, AND COST INCURRED

According to the explanations given above expense measures the *cost of producing the quantum of revenue arising in a particular period.* Expense is thus in nowise identical with: (1) the total of *costs incurred* during the period, (2) the amount of the *expenditures* for current commodities and services made during the period, or (3) the amount of values *utilized* or converted during the period. Even if two or more of these facts should happen to be approximately identical in amount in a particular case they would nevertheless be quite distinct in principle. In view of the considerable confusion in theory and practice on this point the matter deserves brief consideration.

It has been pointed out that asset values in a business enterprise pass through three distinct stages: (1) purchase or acquisition; (2) utilization or conversion to new form; (3) transition to expense or final disappearance from the business embodied in product. The failure to observe carefully the distinctions between these three operations is a common source of error in accounting theory and practice. Clearly true expense or cost of sales in any case is the amount of value passing through the third stage, not that appearing in the first or second operations. Cost incurred, the amount of commodities and services purchased or otherwise acquired during a given period, differs sharply from expense in several particulars. First, it does not include that part of the expiration of both fixed and current assets previously acquired which is properly chargeable to current revenue. Second, if any fixed properties are acquired during the period it is obvious that their cost has little or nothing to do with immediate sales. Third, the cost of all current commodities and services which are not completely utilized in current production and, further, in connection with the fabrication of goods which are currently sold, should not be included in expense. When the situation is carefully analyzed in this way it becomes evident that there is no identity whatever, exact or approximate, between periodic cost incurred and periodic cost of sales in the typical case.

It is possible, of course, to conceive of a situation where these elements, although quite diverse in principle, happen to coincide in amount. Suppose a newspaper dealer, for example, operated in a rented building, owned no equipment whatever, began the period with no stock of goods and disposed of all purchases during the period, and incurred costs for rent, light, and all other items only in connection with current business. In such an extreme situation, evidently, the total of costs incurred during the period would also be the proper cost of sales figure; since all commodities and services acquired —no more and no less—have been utilized and have completely expired.

It should be admitted that in the trading field, where fixed asset costs are often small or nil, the periodic cost of current commodities and services acquired may *approximate* a legitimate cost of sales figure—especially where the rate of turnover is high and the accounting period fairly long. Nevertheless it is careless and dangerous accounting, even in the typical retail establishment, to consider the amount of current costs as also the revenue charge. As a matter of fact all three stages mentioned are present in the trading enterprise in nearly every case. Merchandise (the raw material in this case) is purchased; the goods are delivered, uncrated, marked, shelved, and otherwise prepared for sale; placed upon the housewife's doorstep in convenient quantities and at convenient times they become the finished product. And ideally the accountant should recognize this process and the different classifications involved. It may even be important as a practical matter, especially if monthly statements are involved. If a retailer, for example, were stocking up in November for the holiday trade, incurring heavy carriage and handling costs, it would certainly be a serious error if he should include all labor and transportation costs incurred during November—to say nothing of merchandise costs—as charges against November sales. In other cases, where payroll in a particular period largely covers salesmen's services and freight charges constitute primarily payments on outgoing shipments, it would involve no serious mistake to consider the amount of these costs incurred as also current expense items.

It should be noticed that if inventories are the same in amount at both the beginning and end of a particular period the *amount* of purchases coincides with the amount of expense, although the particular items that make up one amount will not be the same throughout as those which constitute the other. In such a case it may be expedient, from the standpoint of clerical efficiency, to determine cost of sales directly from the purchases accounts; and no fault can be found with such a procedure as long as correct conclusions result. On the other hand, it should be emphasized that unvarying inventories, either in quantity or value, are not characteristic of actual business conditions.

It is in the manufacturing field, of course, that the importance of recognizing the three distinct stages with respect to asset values becomes clear. The extreme case is found in enterprises engaged in the fabrication of buildings, ships, and other elaborate structures. Evidently there is little danger that the management of the shipbuilding company, for example, will identify expense and cost incurred. Here it is plain that the cost of labor, materials, etc., acquired within the period, is unlikely to coincide with the cost of construction work carried on in the same period; and certainly neither of these will either constitute or express the cost of sales for the same interval. In such an enterprise purchase, utilization, and final expiration must each be given independent accounting recognition.

Not all asset items, in each and every enterprise, pass through all three steps. Some costs become expense at the instant of utilization. The cost of paper and twine used by a retailer furnishes an example. As purchased such items clearly represent an asset; as utilized they leave the business attached to product and hence give rise directly to an expense charge. Further, as has already been noted, costs may be discovered which do constitute expense immediately. Shipping costs and salesmen's salaries are important examples. Here acquisition, use, and final expiration are virtually simultaneous processes; and hence such items may reasonably be charged to expense at the time of their initial appearance.

The foregoing should make it clear that the numerous "cost" accounts of the manufacturing establishment and the current "expense" accounts of the trader represent for the most part costs incurred or values converted rather than genuine expenses. The pure expense account is the exception rather than the rule. This does not mean, however, that business men and accountants are seriously mistaken in conceiving of current accounts with labor, supplies, insurance, etc., as expense accounts. As will be shown in a later chapter, it may be reasonable to define an account in terms of its predominating element at crucial times rather than with reference to the precise character of the items entered in the account at the moment of original entry. As long as the proper interpretations are made periodically such a view with respect to some of the current accounts need not be considered hopelessly unreasonable.

Finally, in this connection, it should be emphasized that periodic cost incurred and periodic cash expenditure are by no means identical, either with respect to totals or individual classes. All sorts of commodities and services may be acquired on account. This means that cash payments in the particular period include payments of liabilities arising in a preceding period as well as the costs of labor, materials, etc., currently acquired. Further, cash may of course be paid to retire long-term equities, to distribute income, and for other purposes having no direct connection with current costs incurred.

AN ILLUSTRATION

To make this discussion of expense and revenue quite clear, and to show emphatically the relation of expense and revenue entries and accounts to the entire system, it may be well at this point to introduce a rather complete illustration. Referring to the X Co., and the outline of accounts presented for this enterprise in Chapter IV, let us assume that this company operates for one year, and, to take care of the situation, let us open four additional accounts,—work in process, finished stock, cost of sales, and sales. The first two titles indicate property accounts; the third, expense; and the fourth, revenue. These expense and revenue accounts, although relating to both fundamental categories as explained above, can for convenience be placed under the equity classification, since it is essentially their purpose to disclose the residual net earning figure.

We will assume that during the year the X Co. incurs labor cost amounting to $200,000, acquires materials, $100,000, pays insurance premiums, $2,000, buys fuel, $5,000, and purchases miscellaneous commodities and services amounting to $20,000. Sales of product are made totaling $425,000. Of these cash sales amount to $50,000, the balance being on account. Buildings and equipment depreciate during the period $4,000 and $10,000, respectively. Patents are amortized to the extent of $6,000. The values of work in process and finished stock at the end of the year are $20,000 and $15,000, respectively. Materials on hand at the end of the period amount to $50,000. Unexpired insurance is $500. Fuel on hand amounts to $500. Miscellaneous supplies and services not used or prepaid total $1,000. For convenience it will be assumed that there are no unrecognized costs incurred. It will also be assumed that all costs are of such a character that they can be rationally included in the work in process account. Collections, borrowings, payments of liabilities, etc., will be ignored.

In summary form the effects of the above transactions upon the accounts of the X Co. will now be stated. Assuming the labor services were acquired on account, the transaction would be recorded by a left [7] entry in the labor account and a right entry in a liability account, accounts payable,[8] an increase in assets and an equal increase in equities. Later, when payment was made, a left entry in accounts payable and a right

---

[7] Hereafter simply the words "left" and "right" will be used to designate the opposite account columns and the corresponding entries.

[8] For convenience all current liabilities involved in the illustration are entered in the accounts payable account. A more appropriate title in this case would be "wages payable," or "payroll."

entry in the cash account would be required, an equal decrease in properties and equities. The purchase of material, if on account, would likewise be recognized in the accounts by a left entry in the materials account and a right entry in accounts payable account. Similarly the acquisition of insurance services, fuel, and miscellaneous supplies and services would be registered by left entries in the appropriate asset accounts and right entries in current equity accounts, or, if payment were made immediately, in the cash account. In this case it will be assumed that cash was immediately paid for all these items.

The total of sales, $425,000, would, according to the explanation given in the preceding section, be entered in the right column of the sales or revenue account. This right entry, to repeat, represents provisional subtractions from costs incurred, assets purchased (whether or not collected under the head of finished goods), as well as a supposed, hoped-for element of net return or net increase in ownership. And since both of these elements, according to the scheme outlined in preceding chapters, belong in the right column, the entry in the sales account is properly located. The concurrent left entries would be distributed between the cash and accounts receivable accounts in accordance with the figures given above.

The conversion of properties as originally acquired to work in process and later to finished stock constitutes, as already explained, transpositions or exchanges of asset values within the enterprise. Right entries would be necessary in the labor, materials, buildings, equipment, patents, insurance, fuel, and miscellaneous supplies and services accounts, for the amounts of $200,000, $150,000,[9] $4,000, $10,000, $6,000, $1,500, $4,500, and $19,000, respectively; and a left entry for the sum, $395,000, would be made in the work in process

---

[9] The materials account as originally exhibited in Chapter IV showed a balance of $100,000. Adding the purchases, $100,000, to this balance and subtracting the amount now on hand, $50,000, gives the amount converted, $150,000.

account. The right entries in this case represent subtractions from asset values as they appeared in the original purchase accounts; the left entry represents the addition of this sum of values to the work in process, another kind of property.

The next step, the conversion of work in process to finished stock, ready to ship, is registered in the accounts by a right entry of $375,000 ($395,000, the total cost incurred, less $20,000, the balance in work in process at the end of the period) in the work in process account, and a left entry for the same amount in the finished stock account. Again we have an exchange or transposition of asset values.

The final step, the disappearance from the business of these values in product, would be reflected in the accounts by a right entry of $360,000 ($375,000 less $15,000) in the finished stock account (a subtraction from an asset) and a left entry in the cost of sales account (an equal subtraction from revenue). This left entry cannot, without a bit of roundabout reasoning, be attached directly to the fundamental categories. It is most reasonable to conceive of it as a deduction from, or cost of, revenue; and since revenue is a right-hand classification (for reasons fully explained above) any subtraction from revenue involves a left entry.[10]

The above illustration shows again how the three principal steps in production, from an accounting standpoint, are reflected in the accounts by means of the parallel-column scheme which has been outlined. First, values are acquired, other assets being given in exchange or new equities being recognized. Second, values are converted, an internal transposition of assets. Third, values finally disappear from the business embodied in product. This last step, as has just been explained, can be most conveniently handled by means of supplementary classifications and accounts, expense and revenue. And it is

---

[10] In the next chapter the completed scheme of accounts for the X Co. will be shown, the entries here mentioned being included in the proper columns.

now fully evident that all these situations can be rationally explained and entered in the accounts according to the simple rules and principles laid down in preceding chapters. In Chapter IX certain special cases involving expense and revenue entries, particularly those arising at the time of closing, will be considered.

EXPENSE AND REVENUE, AND PROPRIETORSHIP

The usual explanations of these provisional classifications, expense and revenue, are highly irrational. In many discussions of the theory of accounts no serious attempt is made to state the underlying reasons for the use of the supplementary accounts, or to explain the application of the double-entry system thereto. Arbitrary and sometimes meaningless terms and rules are offered in lieu of real explanation. To consider expense and revenue accounts as "nominal," opposed to "real," for example—which is still probably the most commonly accepted view—is to bar the way to any thorough understanding of the intrinsic character of these classifications. Any account which represents an aspect of the financial situation of an enterprise is essentially as "real" as any other such account. It is true that expense and revenue accounts are temporary, intermediate structures, which may, by combination, be later reduced to lower terms; but there is nothing unreal or "nominal" about them or the specific facts which they include. Expense and revenue facts constitute essential accounting data, phases of the properties and equities which are intrinsically important as managerial statistics and which must be determined if periodic net income and current financial status are to be disclosed.

Hatfield defines expense and revenue accounts as direct adjuncts of proprietorship, revenue representing additions to and expense subtractions from the proprietary interest; and this view is followed by several recent writers.[11] This doctrine, while a step in the right direction, is not strictly accurate. In the first place the assumption that gross revenue is a direct addition to the proprietor's account is evidently only one of convenience. Even if the proprietor were the sole owner, the *gross* amount of sales would measure profit, and hence an addition to his capital, only in the event that there were *no costs*. As was pointed out earlier in this chapter, such a case is seldom even approximated in practice. Accordingly, to enter gross revenue in the right column of the proprietor's account and the amount of expense in the left side, would involve a somewhat unfortunate padding of the two columns, although the net result might be correct (in case total ownership resided in the proprietor). Revenue, as was emphasized above, covers, in large part, merely substractions from assets. It is only the right *balance,* after the costs are deducted, which indicates increase in ownership.

The more serious objection to this theory, however, is based on the fact that in the case of the corporation (and to a lesser degree in the case of the sole-proprietorship and partnership) the residual equity is only one interest, one element of ownership. The corporation certainly is a definite entity; and it is the business of the corporate accountant to keep *its* books, not those of the common stockholder. It seems clear that in such a case the accounts must be constructed from the point of view of the corporation as an operating unit, an economic entirety. It is the function of the corporate accountant to keep a record of the amalgamated funds of the company as they take shape in manifold structures, commodities, services, and rights, and to disclose periodically the correct status of these funds in total, their distribution under specific asset headings and the net change therein. This net change (dis-

---

[11] In practice the terms "loss and gain" or "profit and loss" are more common than "expense and revenue." The use of these expressions is in accord with the doctrine that these items are direct accessories of proprietorship.

covered by the combination of expense and revenue) measures the enhancement in ownership which has come as a result of the period's transactions, an increase which must be parceled out *equitably* among all the various security-holders who have contributed funds to the enterprise. In other words, net revenue represents the increase in *all* equities, not merely the change in the residual interest. In the case of contractual investors this increase may be currently retired; in the case of the residual or proprietary equity it may be in part retained in the business, properly accounted for. Thus bond interest, preferred dividends, and other contractual distributions of income are none the less a part of the earnings of the enterprise as an operating unit.

This view is required if the expense and revenue classifications, the "operating" accounts, are to be considered as representing in any sense the results of management. Evidently the immediate managers of a corporation are not responsible for its plan of capitalization. Hence, to include in expense interest return on a part of the investment would destroy the significance of cost as a managerial figure. If expense and revenue are considered to be direct adjuncts of the residual interest this means that expirations of purchased assets, contractual elements of the net return on the funds which were required to make these purchases, and even such an item as income taxes, are all viewed as homogeneous facts. All represent deductions from the standpoint of the common stockholder; hence if expense is defined from his standpoint all constitute expense.

Net operating revenue should be defined from the standpoint of the business in its entirety, regardless of its particular scheme of capitalization. The basis for comparison of expenses between businesses and between years for the same business would otherwise be destroyed. Suppose, for example, that the *A* Co. during 1920 had outstanding an issue of

$1,000,000 in convertible bonds carrying a 6 per cent rate. Suppose further that at the beginning of 1921 the issue was reduced to $500,000 by conversion to common stock. Would the *expenses* for 1921 thereby be reduced by $30,000? Evidently any such conclusion would be ridiculous.[12] And yet if interest on contractual securities constitutes a corporate expense this conclusion would be correct.

The view here emphasized is in general recognized as having validity in discussions of corporate finance. It has not been fully applied, however, to the theory of accounts; and professional accountants have been slow to adopt it as a basis for the arrangement of the income sheet. In a later chapter this matter will be considered somewhat further, and a schedule showing a rational adjustment and dispersion of net operating revenue for income-sheet purposes will be exhibited.

---

[12] A certain motor car company at one time did advertise that it could sell at lower prices because it had no bonded indebtedness. A little thought will suffice to show that any such statement is thoroughly unsound. Specifically, capitalization has no effect whatever on costs or prices. For industry as a whole the fact that the specialization of securities enables corporations to secure part of their capital from low-return security issues *lowers* capital costs and hence prices. In other words, sane security specialization is a productive device from the social standpoint.

CHAPTER VII

OTHER TYPES OF SUPPLEMENTARY ACCOUNTS

The expense and revenue classifications, discussed in the last chapter, are undoubtedly the most important of the various types of provisional or permanent supplementary accounts required in the case of the typical business enterprise. There are, however, certain other important cases which any complete study of the theory of accounts cannot ignore. Following expense and revenue in the scheme of registering the net increases in ownership and its dispersion come the *net revenue* [1] and *surplus* groups. In addition we find, introduced into the accounting structure at various points, many subsidiary *offset* or *valuation* accounts. In the present chapter all of these further types of accounts will be considered.

THE NET REVENUE CLASSIFICATION

In Chapter VI the general significance of the net revenue figure was explained. It was pointed out that net revenue represents the excess of gross revenue over expense, or, in other words, the pure equity element that is involved in the revenue total, the net increase in ownership. It reflects, from the standpoint of ownership, the element of net increase in properties resulting from the transactions of a particular period (after allowing, of course, for changes due to direct increase or decrease of equities occasioned by new investment,

---

[1] A clear-cut net revenue classification is not in general used by accountants. The need for such a division nevertheless exists; and its independence is often more or less imperfectly recognized. In the Interstate Commerce Commission's classifications we find Expense and Revenue, Income, and Profit and Loss groups. Gilman suggests the use of a "profit and loss allocation account." (See his *Principles of Accounting*, p. 213.)

distributions, retirements, etc.). The *net revenue account,* the account in which this balance of expense and revenue is set up, is, accordingly, a genuine equity account, the right column of which is used to register positive items, the left column, decreases.

The need for such an account, or, in the case of large and complex enterprises, a system of net revenue accounts controlled by a master account, is undoubted; although, as was noted above, its use is as yet inadequately developed. Not only must the dispersion of the net return among the various interests involved be shown, but special adjustments of net operating revenue may be necessary which may well be made directly in the net revenue group instead of being carried through expense and revenue. In the case of the typical sole-proprietorship or partnership, of course, a minimum of "net revenue" transactions will arise; and here, consequently, the importance of this classification is likely to be negligible. In the case of the large corporation with a highly complex ownership, on the other hand, there may be many transactions affecting net earnings, and a need, therefore, for a distinct account or division of accounts in which to record them A corporation may have outstanding several distinct issues of bonds and other contractual securities as well as, perhaps, two or three classes of capital stock. In this event a separate account will be required to show accruals and appropriations of net revenue in connection with each distinct type of security.

The hypothetical balance sheet of the X Co., presented in Chapter II, showed equities as follows: common stock, $200,000; preferred stock, $200,000; mortgage bonds, $100,000; debenture bonds, $100,000; notes payable, $100,000. The Company's sales and cost of sales for a year, as given in Chapter VI, amounted to $425,000 and $360,000, respectively. Let us now assume that the X Co. opens, for summary purposes, an expense and revenue account, and that the cost of

OTHER TYPES OF SUPPLEMENTARY ACCOUNTS 173

sales and sales figures are carried to this account for combination. This transfer of items to the summary would be accomplished by left and right entries for $425,000 in sales and expense and revenue, respectively, and right and left entries for $360,000 in cost of sales and expense and revenue, respectively. The next step would be the opening of the net revenue account, and the transfer thereto of the operating net revenue balance of $65,000 appearing in the expense and revenue summary. This would be accomplished by a left entry of $65,000 in the expense and revenue account (the withdrawal of the pure equity balance contained therein) and an equal right entry in the net revenue account (an addition to equities under this title).

It will be assumed further that the three contractual issues, mortgage bonds, debentures, and notes, draw 5, 6, and 7 per cent rates of return, respectively; that the preferred stock calls for a distribution of 8 per cent; and that the directors declare a 10 per cent dividend on the common stock. For convenience it will be assumed that the dispersion of net revenue among the various security classes is recognized simultaneously, at the end of the year. To recognize these accruals and declarations left entries in the net revenue account totaling $54,000 would be required, and right entries aggregating the same amount in accounts showing mortgage bond interest payable, debenture interest payable, note interest payable, preferred dividends declared, and common dividends declared. These transactions are further illustrations of the interequity case discussed in Chapter V. A conglomerate figure (net return to the business as an operating economic unit) is reduced and definite liabilities in favor of bondholders, noteholders, and stockholders are recognized. When these liabilities are paid left entries would be made in the various liability accounts affected and right entries for the sum in the cash account.

In practice, of course, the quarterly rather than the yearly dividend is common. Interest in connection with bonds and similar securities is usually on a semiannual basis. The essential nature of these accruals and payments from the standpoint of the technical accounting structure is sufficiently exhibited, however, by the above simple illustration.

Even if there were no net increase in ownership in a given period—i.e., no net revenue balance—it might still be necessary to meet the current claims of the various classes of contractual and preferred equities. In such a case the interest involved would be appropriated from the original or accumulated share of the residual equity. That is, if cash or other property is disbursed when there are no current earnings it is evident that the total of original ownership (with respect to the beginning of the current period) is thereby equally reduced; and the loss involved must fall upon the buffer equity. No argument is required, however, to substantiate the statement that, in general, returns to all equities must be drawn from net earnings. Specific distributions of *investment*—"liquidating dividends"—are not, of course, included in this class of disbursements.

Direct additions to net revenue by way of interest or dividends are of course possible. Thus if an enterprise owns stocks, notes, bonds, or other securities, the true income on such assets as accrued is immediately *net* rather than *gross* revenue.[2] That is, there are virtually no expenses in connection with such earnings; they constitute, essentially, clear gain.

Perhaps the best illustration is the interest accruing on a savings account, as in this case there is practically no question as to the integrity of the principal. The interest on a bank balance clearly constitutes at once a net increase in assets and a net increase in ownership. Thus if the X Co. were

---

[2] Assuming, of course, that proper adjustments are made for accumulation of discount, amortization of premium, and other variations in principal.

allowed interest on its bank account amounting to $500, the transaction would be recorded by a left entry of $500 in the cash (bank) account and an equal right entry in the net revenue account (or in a special interest revenue account from which the amount could later be transferred to the summary account).

It is not intended to urge strongly that such items of net earnings should be excluded from gross revenue. To amalgamate gross revenue from sales and miscellaneous net earnings and deduct from the sum the total of expenses may not be a seriously irrational procedure in some cases. Nevertheless, if the expense and revenue classifications are to be of the greatest utility for managerial purposes it would seem to be more reasonable to first combine all revenues which involve costs, then deduct all such costs, and finally add to the residuum any items of income arising without expense.

It should be noted that miscellaneous or ancillary revenues are by no means always net. A company may lease certain properties, for example, and thus earn rent revenue. But such revenue is not a costless item; maintenance, insurance, depreciation, etc., are involved in its creation.

In the next section will be considered certain special transactions and accounts which may be viewed as adjuncts of the net revenue classification.

NET GAINS, LOSSES, AND TAXES

Donations and appreciations may in some cases be viewed as bringing about direct increases in net revenue. An interested municipality, for example, might donate a site to a manufacturing company. Such an increase in assets, unaccompanied by outgo or additions to liabilities, evidently involves an equal expansion in the residual equity. This increase might be thought of as a kind of net gain, a gain arising, however, entirely outside of regular operation.[3] Similarly appreciations, whether realized through sale or not, may be considered as giving rise to net gains. And if the change in value is current, i.e., has arisen during the latest accounting period, it would seem to be logical to enter its ownership reflection, in the first instance, in a subsidiary net revenue account. Thus if the securities owned by a certain company had advanced in value during the current period to the amount of $15,000, the situation might be registered in the accounts by a left entry of $15,000 in the securities account and a corresponding right entry in the net revenue account. On the other hand, if an increase in value which has been accruing through several accounting periods is finally recognized it would be more rational to use—as far as the equity side is concerned—the surplus classification.

Another type of happening which may be placed under the net revenue division in certain circumstances is the actual *loss*. The term "loss" is often used indiscriminately in accounting to include ordinary operating expense as well as true loss. This is unfortunate. The preservation of the integrity of the expense and revenue groupings should be one of the main objects of the accountant; for only as these classes are restricted to genuine expense and revenue items can they be used to the greatest advantage as a basis for managerial judgments. A loss measures the disappearance of some asset value for which no valuable consideration is received in return. In other words, if any of the assets of a business are lost, destroyed, or otherwise consumed without in any way entering into the productive operations of the owner, a loss has occurred. In principle the distinction between *loss* and *expense* is very clear. The value of the ton of coal burned in the manufacturer's furnace constitutes, presumedly, a legitimate cost of

---

[3] It would doubtless be better to use some special surplus account to reflect this increase in proprietorship.

product; the value of the ton of coal stolen, on the other hand, is a loss. Any value which is absorbed as a necessary incident of production, any cost which must be incurred if product is to result, becomes a cost of revenue, an expense. Any item which disappears as a result of inefficiency, accident, fraud, natural catastrophe, etc., without in any way facilitating the purposes of the enterprise, is a pure loss.

It should be admitted that, although the distinction between loss and expense in theory is sharp, it is not always easy to draw the line between the two classes in practice. The more or less technical process of production is in every enterprise bound up almost inextricably with the stream of general economic processes and with that of purely fortuitous circumstances. Is a particular item an expense or a loss? Often it is hard to answer. Many costs incurred by the average enterprise may be unnecessary from an ideal standpoint. Labor may be inefficient with resulting waste of materials and high labor cost; the management may be unsound; lack of proper co-ordination, delay, minor accidents, etc., may greatly increase costs; maintenance charges may be unduly high. Are such items losses or expense? Is obsolescence an expense or a loss? What is the nature of fire loss? From the standpoint of the entire industrial community such losses have to be borne and are conditions limiting supply. To some degree they doubtless constitute costs from the price-determining standpoint. On the other hand it is doubtful if they always have specific effect upon the selling prices of the individual enterprise. The mere fact that a company is obliged to abandon costly but antiquated equipment, for example, does not enable it thereby to raise its selling prices, especially since it may be competing with new enterprises in the same field which have not been obliged to undergo such losses.

Needless to say the accountant in practice cannot be guided by an ideal state of affairs in making his classifications. Every business falls far short of this condition. As long as expirations relate to production in a fairly reasonable way, and are not quite abnormal, they may be placed in the expenses. But a line must be drawn somewhere. Certainly a large embezzlement by a trusted officer is not a typical cost of doing business.

It is possibly even more difficult in some cases to distinguish between a loss and an asset balance. Experimental costs and reconstruction outlays furnish difficult cases. Has a particular outlay resulted in something of value from which the benefit will not be exhausted for some time or has the money virtually been thrown away? A company spends $100,000 on an advertising campaign, for example. The accountant is called upon to decide whether this value is a loss, a cost of producing current revenue, or an asset balance. Perhaps the most troublesome problems along this line arise during the period of organization and construction. In a later chapter some of these questions will be dealt with.

It is entirely beyond the scope of this study to discuss in detail the practical problem of distinguishing between asset balances, expenses, and losses. It is intended simply to emphasize roundly the essential nature of each classification and the way in which it relates to the technical structure of the accounting system. What is the character of a true loss in terms of two-column accounts and the fundamental equation? If an asset expires without any compensation, it is evident that a corresponding diminution of ownership must occur. What is the specific nature of this decrease in ownership? Is it an offset to original investment, accumulated net earnings, or current net revenue? If the asset lost were an original asset, that is, an asset secured from original invested funds, it might seem most logical to deduct the amount through the accounts representing the initial equities. In practice, however, it is usually assumed that losses absorb ownership in the order of its currency; that is, that expirations should be charged first against the most recently

OTHER TYPES OF SUPPLEMENTARY ACCOUNTS 179

accumulated amounts. This assumption is particularly convenient in the case of the corporation, for it is deemed desirable not to disturb the formal statement of the stockholders' equity unless specific shares are retired. In any case it is of course the residual equity which is *first* reduced by losses.

If a loss be assumed to be properly deductible from net revenue, the occurrence would evidently be recorded by an appropriate left entry in the net revenue account (a subtraction from an equity) and a corresponding right entry in the asset account affected (an equal subtraction from an asset).

In the event that expenses exceed gross revenues for a given period it is evident that the expense and revenue summary will have a left balance. When this is transferred to the net revenue account the account becomes a net *deficit* or net loss account, measuring the amount by which ownership has been reduced as a result of the operations and circumstances of the past period. If such an item is maintained for some time on the books we have a special case of the valuation account. This type of account is considered in a later section of this chapter.

One further transaction should be discussed in connection with the net revenue classification, the tax payment. What is the nature of governmental levies on the private enterprise and what, accordingly, is the character of the accounts in which such levies are recorded? It is difficult to answer these questions satisfactorily. Taxes are an anomalous element in business and hence in accounting. If we conceive of the government as furnishing protection to the business enterprise, stabilizing contracts, setting the level of competition, preventing unfair practices, etc., it might be argued that taxes constitute, first, the price of a composite of valuable services, and, finally, a cost of sales or expense. But one need not be an anarchist to exclude this conception of the case as a basis for the explanation of the tax account. Taxes do not represent a payment for definite commodities, services, or conditions required by the enterprise making payment to further its operations. The payment is coerced, entirely outside of managerial control. The purchasing department has nothing to say as to taxes.

Even if the broadest possible view be taken it could not reasonably be said that the enterprise pays taxes directly in proportion to benefits conferred by the state. The fundamental conditions contributed by government are of course of immeasurable value to business; but these conditions are an underlying part of the situation, to be taken for granted. The government's contribution to the success of the particular business is a factor entirely outside market laws. Taxes are in no sense a "price" for specific services. Taxes in general are not apportioned in accordance with benefit received. Hence we cannot view tax payments as measuring the value of services received and, later, a cost of production or expense.[4]

The most reasonable interpretation of the situation is that taxes in general constitute a coerced levy on net earnings (or capital if no net earnings are available). As was indicated in an earlier chapter, the state virtually has a latent prior equity in the properties of every business enterprise; private ownership is not absolute. As far as its explicit accounting recognition is concerned, this equity may be viewed as a continuously recurring claim. Taxes accrue; payment is made; the government's equity in dollars and cents is thereby momentarily extinguished. If at the time the accounts are "closed" the tax liability for the period is determinate, a left entry for the amount should be made in the net revenue account (or in a subsidiary tax account) and a right entry in the taxes payable account, a preferred liability account. If the tax is indetermi-

---

[4] Special fees, licenses, improvement assessments, etc., may with some justification be viewed as true costs. Certainly in so far as a tax payment represents the value of definite improvements added to property it constitutes an addition to assets, and, as the asset expires with use, an expense. There is likewise some force in that view that property taxes during a preliminary or construction period represent proper charges to property. See Chapter XIV.

OTHER TYPES OF SUPPLEMENTARY ACCOUNTS

nate at that time, the amount may nevertheless be estimated and the same entries made. When payment is made a left entry would be made in the liability account and a right entry for the same amount in the cash account.

Income and excess-profits taxes furnish, of course, a clear case. Here the state is levying specifically upon net earnings (derived, in general, from the stockholders' standpoint) and consequently such levies from an accounting view represent distributions of net revenue.

Taxes must either represent expense (the expiration of assets used in producing revenue), loss, a distribution to an equity, or an entirely distinct item which cannot be put under any general head. According to the above discussion the tax payment can best be considered a loss (which it is from the standpoint of the private owners) or a distribution in favor of the underlying equity of the state; it cannot reasonably be viewed as an expense. As stated above the tax transaction is anomalous; there is no other similar situation. But no serious mistake is made if the above analysis is adhered to.

In Chapter XI (and later chapters) there will be further consideration of net revenue, its essential accounting significance, its relation to the residual equity, its economic elements. In these connections further light will be thrown upon some of the matters raised in this section.

THE SURPLUS CLASSIFICATION

The essential function of the *surplus* division is to register the undistributed balance of the net revenue accounts. In addition, however, it should be recognized that certain transactions may occur which can rationally be reflected directly in surplus (as far as the equity side is concerned) without intermediate effect upon either gross or net revenue.

At the outset it should be noted that the distinction between the net revenue and surplus groups is not as important as the line between gross and net revenue. Because of the importance of these figures from a managerial standpoint, to reiterate, the maintenance of the integrity of the expense and revenue divisions should be a primary consideration for the accountant. Distributions of net revenue and appropriations of surplus must not be entangled with genuine expenses. But many items may be charged either to net revenue or to surplus, well-nigh indifferently. It is not considered bad practice, for example, to appropriate dividends from the surplus or undivided profits account. Indeed some companies follow the practice of transferring the adjusted net proprietary income figure to surplus account and making *all* proprietary appropriations at that point. The undivided profits or surplus account may thus be used as a reservoir for dividend declarations. It is evident that, if the accounting is reasonable, net revenue will commonly fluctuate from period to period.[5] But it may be desirable, in the interest of the stockholders, to stabilize dividends. This can be accomplished—as far as the *appropriation* of the dividend is concerned—by transferring all balances of net revenue to surplus and basing the declarations on the latter account.

In practice the surplus account is used almost exclusively by the corporation. It represents the accumulated profits, the addition to the residual equity. In general the surplus constitutes a partial measure of the common stockholders' equity, the preferred stockholders rating essentially with the other contractual interests as far as this account is concerned. In particular cases, of course, the preferred stockholder may have an interest in surplus. The need for such an account evidently originates in connection with the view that the capital stock account itself must be restricted to par. In the partnership,

---

[5] In this connection it should be emphasized that all accounting policies which tend to iron out the real fluctuations in net earnings are unreasonable. It is peculiarly the course of this figure which registers the history of the business, its successes and failures. The juggling of depreciation charges or any other practice which tends to "equalize" the showing of net return cannot be condemned too strongly.

OTHER TYPES OF SUPPLEMENTARY ACCOUNTS 183

frequently, little distinction is made between the partner's original investment and his accumulated profits. The extensive use of the surplus account even in the case of the corporation is perhaps intrinsically unreasonable; although there is clearly some advantage in preserving the figures showing initial investments intact. As a matter of fact several current practices result in obliterating the distinction between the original equity of the stockholder and the amount of the change therein.[6] Further, the actual figure for undivided profits tends to be obscured—at least as far as the layman is concerned—by the practice of segregating and "earmarking" surplus under unintelligible titles so as to reflect certain prognostications and impressions of the board of directors.

The explanation of the entries involving surplus furnishes no difficulties. For an illustration let us refer again to the X Co. The balance of the net revenue account, after the distributions mentioned in the first section of this chapter were recorded, would be $11,000. This represents the increase in the common stockholders' interest [7] which, for the time being at least, is retained in the business. To close the net revenue account it would be necessary to make a left entry of $11,000 therein, and an equal right entry in the surplus account. This transaction is evidently simply a "book" happening; an equity balance has been transferred from one account to another. Many of the transactions affecting surplus, it may be noted, are of this type, equity transpositions.

Suppose further that the directors of the X Co. now decide to appropriate or "earmark" the amount of $10,000 as a reserve for possible obsolescence. To give effect to this decision in the accounts it would be necessary to make a left entry of $10,000 in the surplus account (a subtraction from one equity heading) and an equal right entry in a "reserve for possible obsolescence"

---

[6] See the next section for a discussion of one of these practices.
[7] Assuming the preferred stock to be non-participating.

account (an addition to another equity title). This transaction evidently does not disturb any of the assets; there is no actual occurrence; the total amount of undivided profits is unchanged. But the directors have indicated their intention to retain profits to the amount of $10,000 in the business as an offset to possible losses.

The policy of appropriating surplus under special headings has been carried far in modern corporate accounting. All sorts of "reserves" are met with in corporate balance sheets. "Reserve for additions and betterments," "reserve for extensions," "reserve for improvements," "reserve for inventory shrinkage," "reserve for sinking fund," are common titles. This process of subdividing surplus gives a large number of the interequity transactions mentioned in Chapter V. Evidently there is virtually no limit to the use of subsidiary accounts in this connection. Surplus in general represents the excess of the common stockholders' equity over the nominal (par) value of the common stock. At the whim of the board of directors it may be subdivided almost indefinitely.

This practice of appropriating surplus under various headings is not entirely rational. Except as it insures the retention of undivided profits in the business it evidently affords no real security. Losses are not prevented by surplus appropriations. The accumulation of plain "undivided profits" is as satisfactory as the use of a multitude of reserves. The significant thing is the decision not to pay all the profits as dividends; the appropriation of reserves is a matter of minor importance. Where a very definite contingency is involved, such as arises in connection with endorsed notes, the true situation is perhaps reflected more accurately if a portion of surplus is specially labeled. In general, however, there is little point in anticipating losses in a particular direction by attaching dubious titles to sections of surplus. The entire equity may of course be wiped out by losses; but it would hardly be good accounting to anticipate

OTHER TYPES OF SUPPLEMENTARY ACCOUNTS

bankruptcy in the balance sheet. Certainly with respect to reserves for improvements and extensions, it is the foregoing of dividends, not the earmarking of surplus, which is important.

The practice is also somewhat unfortunate because the titles used are likely to be misunderstood. The term "reserve" suggests surplus, but it is not used exclusively with that connotation. Accrued liabilities are sometimes designated as "reserves." Reserves for wages and taxes should not be confused with true surplus. More serious is the fact that asset valuation accounts are commonly labeled "reserves." As will be shown in a later section of this chapter such balances are in no sense surplus.

A common misapprehension in connection with surpluses and reserves is the confusion of such items with cash and other liquid funds. This matter deserves brief consideration and can be conveniently discussed in connection with the sinking fund reserve, an important case of subsidiary surplus. Such a reserve may arise where a bond contract carries a sinking fund provision, or where the directors decide of their own volition to provide for the payment of the bond by the sinking fund method. The building up of the sinking fund reserve indicates the earmarking or appropriating of surplus to accompany the accumulation of the actual fund of liquid assets. It insures the accumulation of the fund "out of profits." It should be emphasized, however, that from the viewpoint of the accounting structure the two transactions are entirely distinct. The setting aside of a fund is reflected in the accounts by a left entry in the fund account and a right entry in the general cash account—an exchange of assets. The appropriation of the reserve is registered by a left entry in the general surplus account and a right entry in the reserve account—a transposition of equities. One transaction involves the subdivision of cash, the other the subdivision of surplus; the two processes are quite distinct.

This may be emphasized by noting that either transaction may be carried out independently. The only thing that is absolutely necessary to the accumulation of a fund is the availability of cash or other liquid property. The requisite condition for the building of a reserve is the retention of profits in the business. If the fund is accumulated without the reserve, the bondholder has thereby no assurance that the capital of the enterprise in its entirety is being maintained; as even a dying enterprise may be in a position to accumulate liquid funds. If the reserve alone is being built up, on the other hand, the bondholder has no assurance that any liquid assets whatever are being accumulated, but he does know that not only is the capital of the business in its entirety being maintained but that it is being increased (ignoring possible retirements of the liabilities); or, more accurately, he knows that the stockholders' equity, his margin of safety, is being widened. Evidently the building of the reserve, in general, is a greater protection to the bondholder than the mere accumulation of liquid assets; the "cushion" upon which his equity rests is being steadily increased thereby. The increase in assets corresponding to this increase in the stockholders' equity, however, is not likely to be solely or even largely in the form of cash. If the business is expanding, the retention of profits, as far as the assets are concerned, will probably mean enlarged plant, additional equipment, increased stock of merchandise, a larger total of outstanding customers' accounts, and more cash.

It was emphasized in Chapter IV that, in general, no particular equity balance bears any inherent and inevitable relation to any particular property. The only necessary relationship lies in the equality of balance-sheet totals. The total of assets is affected only when the total of equities is affected, and vice versa. This point may now be emphasized in connection with the surplus accounts. The "surplus" equity of the stockholder is no more related to one asset than to any other. It simply measures an *element in the asset total*. Consequently we need not expect to find the precise amount of surplus in the cash balance or in any other asset account.[8] Thus it often happens that a company is "making money" rapidly, i.e., is accumulating a large undivided profit or surplus balance, but is not in a position to pay dividends. The stockholders' equity is being increased, but liquid assets do not happen to have increased correspondingly. Businesses which have made large profits are sometimes obliged to borrow money to meet the claims of contractual equities and of the state.

Direct losses and net appreciations and donations may be reflected (on the equity side) in the general surplus account or in special accounts subsidiary thereto, as was noted in a preceding section. Such changes in asset values may not relate precisely to the period in which the change is finally recognized; and in this case it seems clear that it is best to carry the transaction directly to surplus. Further, if the loss or gain as the case may be has nothing to do with the ordinary operations of the business, is entirely outside the control of the management, it may well be urged that its effect should not appear in the expense and revenue or net revenue accounts. A large loss of property due to earthquake, the failure of a banking house where funds were deposited, a defalcation, etc., may thus be recorded by a left entry in the surplus account and a corresponding right entry in the asset account affected. Similarly, a direct gain due to appreciation of land, the payment of a supposedly worthless account, etc., may be registered by a left entry under the appropriate asset heading and a right entry to surplus.[9]

---

[8] Where an enterprise were neither enlarging nor decreasing the scope of its operations, there would of course be some practical force in the view that undivided profits were tied up in cash, accounts receivable, and other current assets.

[9] It may be well to note in this connection that for tax purposes virtually all losses are "allowable deductions" in the year in which they occur and nearly all gains (except unrealized appreciation) are similarly returnable income. It should be emphasized, however, that while an important advantage of accounts in these times lies in their use as a basis for the tax return, it would be entirely unreasonable to attempt

SPECIAL SURPLUS SITUATIONS

The issue of a stock dividend is an interesting surplus transaction, widely misunderstood. From an accounting point of view such a transaction involves essentially the amalgamation in whole or in part of the surplus and capital stock accounts. To record such an occurrence it would be necessary to make a left entry for the amount in the surplus account and an equal right entry in the capital stock account. (An intervening account—stock dividend payable—may be used.) Evidently this is another illustration of the interequity transaction. An item of ownership is transferred from one account to another. The assets are untouched; the total of ownership remains the same. Surplus has merely been carried from one accounting compartment to another; a new label has been placed upon a section of undivided profits. Each stockholder stands in essentially the same position as he did before the transaction; his fractional interest in the business is unchanged. The transaction consists simply in the division of the equity represented by the capital stock and surplus accounts into a greater number of aliquot parts. Naturally the value per share is lowered by such an occurrence.

It may not be out of place to point out that the stock dividend is not an entirely rational device. The desire on the part of the management to "cover up" surplus, to increase the showing of investment, or to still the clamor of stockholders for dividends, may be responsible in a particular case. On the other hand, the issue of capital stock to cover undivided profits effectively prevents the use of such profits as a basis for dividends; and hence the stock dividend may be reasonable

---

to organize the fundamental classifications of accounting strictly in terms of the classifications of Regulations 62. "Allowable deduction" and "expense" are not synonymous terms. "Gross income" for tax purposes and "operating revenue" are not identical. Accounting has many functions outside of taxation; and while the regulations and rulings of the Bureau of Internal Revenue are bound to exercise a marked influence on the development of accounting procedures, the fundamental principles of accounting will probably not be seriously disturbed thereby.

when there is a real need for expansion. The significance of dividends in stock and other securities will be further considered in Chapter XVI.

In many corporate balance sheets accounts are found which have doubtful significance. A company engaged in a legal controversy, for example, may decide to "set up a reserve" to cover the probable loss involved if judgment is rendered against it. What is the character of such an account? If appropriated from surplus it may be urged that it simply represents a segment of the general undivided profits. On the other hand, if an adverse decision seems likely it might be urged that the loss is really *accruing,* and the reserve balance is a "valuation" account, somewhat analogous to a depreciation reserve.

Another illustration of an account of somewhat uncertain character arises where a company attempts to carry its own fire risk. A particular corporation may decide, for example, that when the books are closed each month earnings to the amount of $1,000 shall be labeled as a fire insurance reserve. What is the character of this item? Is it an appropriation of true *net* earnings or surplus, or is it an "accrued" offset to property? If the latter, then the appropriation was really made (or should have been made) from gross revenue. That is, if the average fire loss is actually $1,000 per month—all reasonable precautions having been taken—there is some justification for the assumption that each month's business should be charged with a cost of that amount, regardless of the actual value of property destroyed by fire in the particular period. Yet at any one moment of time the balance in such an account —all estimated losses not having actually occurred—might with some justification be designated as surplus.

Various accounts arise in connection with the original issue of securities which are sometimes included in the surplus classification. When the original investment of the stockholder exceeds the par or formal value of his interest, it is customary to use a special account to register this excess equity. In bank accounting this additional amount is entered in the "surplus" account.[10] Evidently this account in such a case shows a part of the original equity or interest of the stockholder. Because of the wide use of "surplus" to indicate the enhancement in this equity resulting from successful operation, it is desirable in general to use some other heading to designate the difference between true investment and formal capitalization. "Premium on capital stock," the title required by the Interstate Commerce Commission's classifications, more explicitly suggests the true character of this item. The use of no-par stock, a highly rational development in corporate finance, obviates entirely the necessity or excuse for two accounts in connection with the original investment of the stockholder.

Another case of surplus, so-called, arising during the organization period, is the "donated" surplus. Where original subscribers relinquish a part of their holdings to be resold by the corporation to raise working capital, an apparent surplus balance is created. Such a surplus is usually purely fictitious because of the gross overvaluation of the original assets received. In any case it is again an item that relates to the original equity rather than indicating the enhancement thereof through the accumulation of earnings. It is simply a special case of premium on stock.

Again, a corporation by acquiring its outstanding stocks, bonds, or other securities at less than "book" value, evidently thereby increases the interest of the remaining stockholders. The surplus account is usually used to reflect such an increase.

Still other cases of surplus arise through forfeited instal-

---

[10] On the bank balance sheet we commonly find three main equity accounts to show the stockholders' interest, capital stock, surplus, and undivided profits. The surplus account is used in general to show stock premiums and such earnings as are to be retained definitely in the business (either because of statutory requirement or the volitional policy of the directors). "Undivided profits" is used to designate such part of the earnings as still may form a basis for dividend declarations.

ments, dividends uncalled for, etc. The point to be emphasized here is that all adjustments of the stockholder's interest, regardless of the peculiar circumstances surrounding a given case, can be rationally recorded in the surplus or related classifications according to the rules of procedure repeatedly stressed in the foregoing pages. Some of the peculiarities of accounting for capital stock and its subsidiary headings will be discussed in Chapter XVI.

VALUATION OR CONTRA ACCOUNTS

In an analysis of the structure of a system of financial accounts and the principal types of situations to be dealt with therein, a careful statement should be made of the nature of "valuation" accounts, so-called. Not only is the fundamental balance-sheet statement extended into a complex system of individual accounts falling into several important general classifications, but many specific accounts of virtually all classes may be used in connection with special subsidiary "offset" or valuation accounts. A valuation account is a device for registering special *subtractions* or offsets from some main heading, either asset or equity, or one of the important phases of the fundamental classes. Where for some reason it is desired to give special accounting recognition to certain subtractions from an important balance, we have a need for the valuation account. Such accounts are an extreme extension of the bookkeeper's practice of postponing actual subtraction. As they permeate the whole system of modern accounting, and are very commonly misinterpreted, their rational explanation is a matter of importance.

A significant illustration of a valuation account is the "allowance for depreciation" of fixed property. It is almost universal practice to enter the estimated expiration of plant and equipment assets for the period in the right column of a special offset account instead of the right side of the asset accounts. In other words, the special reduction in fixed assets occurring as a result of operation and the passage of time is shown in a subsidiary annex account, the original cost of units still in use being retained intact in the main property account.[11] Thus the true status of the asset (as estimated) does not appear in either account. It can only be determined by comparing the parent asset account with its subsidiary allowance for depreciation.

For a specific illustration let us refer to the figures given in Chapter VI for the depreciation of the X Co.'s buildings and equipment during the first year of operation. The assumed amounts were $4,000 and $10,000, respectively. Using valuation accounts, this depreciation would be recorded by left entries totaling $14,000 in expense accounts (or first in goods in process and later in expense if we adhere to the assumption laid down in the earlier discussion of this case), a right entry of $4,000 in the allowance for depreciation of buildings account, and a right entry for $10,000 in the allowance for depreciation of equipment account. The relationship of these asset accounts and their subsidiaries may now be shown graphically thus:

BUILDINGS

$200,000	ALLOWANCE FOR DEPRECIATION OF BUILDINGS
	$ 4,000

---

[11] It will be assumed in this discussion that original cost is the proper basis, as a starting point, for the valuation of fixed assets.

OTHER TYPES OF SUPPLEMENTARY ACCOUNTS

Equipment		
$100,000	Allowance for Depreciation of Equipment	
		$10,000

What is the nature of these special right-hand balances? It cannot be stated too emphatically that these right entries represent merely *estimated subtractions from assets*. Their significance is essentially the same as if they were recorded directly in the main property accounts. The "allowance" account is merely a section of the right side of the main asset account. To determine the real status of property (as near as may be) the two accounts must be read in conjunction, regardless of their physical separation in the ledger. The appellation "reserve," commonly used, is rather unfortunate. This title suggests "surplus," which is also a right-hand balance; and here we have the source of the common misinterpretation of such accounts. As a matter of fact there is essentially no more relation between such balances and true surplus than between *any* subtraction from property and a positive equity item. Subtractions from assets and additions to equities are fundamentally distinct, despite the fact that both classes of data appear in the right column. To confuse such diverse elements involves the ignoring of one of the underlying distinctions of the double-entry system.

The bookkeeping practice of listing asset valuation items on the right or equity side of the balance sheet has contributed to the current confusion on this matter. Strictly speaking such items do not belong in the balance sheet at all; they should be canceled against the gross asset balances and the net property values should be exhibited in the left column. However, if, as is advised by some accountants, the valuation balances are shown as deductions from gross asset figures on the left side of the statement (by means of an auxiliary column), no harm would result in the presentation of estimated expirations in the balance sheet.

Why use special accounts for depreciation allowances? One reason for this practice lies in the uncertain character of the depreciation figure. Even under the most favorable circumstances depreciation is a tentative, provisional figure. It represents the result of a judgment. It is an estimate, not a certainty. Fixed assets are used in their entirety throughout considerable periods to give off series of similar services. They are not consumed in units (from the standpoint of the ordinary accounting period) as are the current properties. Consequently there is something to be said in favor of the valuation account practice in this connection. The uncertain, provisional character of the depreciation figure is well indicated (if the situation is understood) by the use of a subsidiary account. The amount in the main asset account less the estimated expiration gives the supposed current value of the asset.

Further, the use of the valuation account permits the retention, undisturbed as long as the units involved are in use, of the original base figure. This is especially convenient in connection with the "straight-line method," the commonly accepted plan of apportioning depreciation between periods. The main asset account shows continuously the sum on which the annual rate is to be taken.

If the depreciation allowances are reasonably estimated, it is evident that the amount in the valuation account will steadily increase until, at the end of the life of the asset involved, the two balances are approximately equal (allowing for scrap value). When the asset is actually abandoned a final determination of total depreciation is clearly possible. At that time the provisional allowances may be given finality by being returned to the parent account, there showing, with the proper adjustments, the ultimate disposition of the property. The entries are of interest. Suppose for illustration, that a company has a machine account showing a total of original values acquired amounting to $10,000, and a valuation account connected therewith showing a total estimated depreciation of $9,000. If, now, the asset is abandoned or junked, a net salvage of $1,000 being realized, the transaction would be recorded by a left entry of $1,000 in the cash account (if the salvage value were realized in cash), a left entry of $9,000 in the allowance account and a right entry for $10,000 in the machine account.

What is the precise explanation of these entries? Evidently, since the machine is being definitely removed, there must now be a right entry for $10,000 in the machine account—to record this definite lapse of property value. But this subtraction, to the amount of $9,000, was *provisionally* recorded in a special offset account. The left entry of $9,000, accordingly, indicates the return of the provisional entry to the main account. It is a *subtraction from a subtraction* from assets; and hence it is registered in the left column. The subtraction in provisional form is transferred to the main account, and is thereby given finality.

In practice an allowance account would seldom be used in connection with each individual asset unit. But it is desirable to have an allowance account in connection with each main type of asset. Otherwise the situation is likely to become obscured; for it would be impossible to determine directly from the accounts the estimated net value of each important class of asset. And subsidiary records may well be kept, showing the cost, estimated life, probable salvage, depreciation rate, etc., in connection with each asset unit so that the amount in the reserve or allowance properly applicable to a particular unit may be deducted from the valuation account at the date of abandonment. If this scheme is carefully worked out the amount in the main account is continuously the cost of units still in use, and the amount in the valuation account is the estimated depreciation on these same units.

It should be emphasized in this connection that *abandonment* and *replacement* in connection with fixed assets constitute two distinct and independent accounting transactions. The practice of charging to the allowance account the cost of a new unit acquired, which is recommended by some accountants, is thoroughly unreasonable. Unless the new item happens to be identical in value with the unit it is replacing (an altogether unlikely occurrence) such a practice will shortly result in a serious misstatement of asset values. Further, in any case abandonment is one thing, acquisition another. An asset is discarded; it may never be exactly replaced. If, however, it is essentially replaced by a new unit it should nevertheless be emphasized that this is a transaction entirely independent of the abandonment, occurring, perhaps, weeks or months later, and having nothing to do with the accounting record of earlier properties. The only safe rule is always to treat the disposal of a unit of property as a happening entirely separate and apart from the acquisition of a new unit, regardless of their relation from the standpoint of physical operation.

When an asset is scrapped on which depreciation has not been adequately accrued to date it is evident that the deficiency constitutes a loss, a reduction in net revenue or surplus (to the extent that it has nothing to do with the current period of operation). Similarly, if the final determination of values shows that an excessive allowance has been made for depreciation the amount of the excess constitutes an heretofore concealed item of surplus and should be transferred to that account. It is in this connection that the only relation between a valuation reserve and true surplus obtains.

Another important illustration of the valuation account arises in connection with estimated uncollectibles. It is often considered desirable to attempt to correct the sales figure for the period by subtracting therefrom an estimated amount for customers' accounts which will not be paid. If the estimated figure is based on a careful study of past experience this procedure has much to commend it. Evidently, however, the specific accounts of the customers cannot be written down on the basis of a "blanket" estimate. Instead, a valuation account, which might be styled "allowance for estimated uncollectibles" is needed to show, in a tentative, lump-sum form, the offset to receivables. In this case the preservation of each customer's account until its status is definitely known, and the maintenance of the consistency between the customers' ledger and its control, accounts receivable, necessitates the use of the special offset account.

The explanation of the allowance for depreciation applies essentially to the allowance for uncollectibles. Nevertheless there are certain differences between the two cases requiring mention. In the first place the allowance for uncollectibles can be built up most accurately by basing the estimated loss on the total of credit sales for the period rather than on the mere outstanding balance at the end of the period. Second, while allowance for depreciation tends to show a steady accumulation, allowance for uncollectibles will commonly show a relatively small balance. As the credit or collection department comes to a decision as to the status of each dubious account the allowance is reduced by the amount involved in each case and the account is written off. Final determination in this case follows closely the provisional entry.

The *allowance for maintenance* is another interesting case.

This account arises where it is desired to apportion repair charges. The value expiration made good by repairs may be assumed to be as steadily accruing as is the residual depreciation which cannot be prevented by upkeep. The actual expenditures for repairs, however, may be highly irregular. If the cost incurred is assumed to accrue evenly it will be necessary in each period to make a left entry in the appropriate cost account and a right entry in the allowance for maintenance. When the value expired is replaced by actual repairs the transaction would be recorded by a left entry in the allowance account—the cancellation of the provisional offset to indicate that the value temporarily expired has been replaced—and a right entry in the cash account (assuming cash to be paid). Evidently such an accounting procedure is only of real importance where the accounting period used is very short and maintenance outlays are highly uneven in time. The peculiarity of this case lies in the fact that the repair cost, by definition, replaces but a part of the expired outlay in connection with some asset unit, and hence may be deducted directly from the allowance. Evidently anything in the nature of an "improvement" should not be handled through such an account.

A valuation account might be used in connection with almost any asset account. Shortages in cash due to thefts and other causes, for example, might be shown, provisionally, in the right column of a "cash shortage" account. The use of such an account would, of course, serve no purpose except to focus attention upon the fact of shortage and to exclude this fact from typical subtractions from cash, viz., expenditures. It should be emphasized that wherever a valuation account is used the entries can be made therein in accordance with the principles stressed in connection with regular balance-sheet accounts. No new lines of analysis are required. The asset valuation item will naturally appear on the right side since positive asset balances are listed on the left; and to determine

OTHER TYPES OF SUPPLEMENTARY ACCOUNTS 199

the correct status of any asset in connection with which such an offset account is used the two accounts must be read together.

As stated above, valuation items may likewise arise in connection with equities. Since an equity balance is on the right side any offset thereto, whether in a special account or not, must be registered in the left column. The deficit account as sometimes used is an example of an offset account in connection with the stockholders' equity. Special loss accounts are in essentially the same class. Discounts on stocks and bonds are valuation items. Since the treatment of discounts is discussed in some detail in later chapters it will not be necessary to consider illustrations in this connection.

Valuation accounts also arise in connection with the more current classifications. Purchase and sales returns and discounts are examples. Discounts on current loans is another case. These items are very commonly misunderstood and Chapter XVII is largely devoted to a careful consideration of their character. Even the expense accounts may be thought of as offset accounts subsidiary to revenue, as already explained. Because of the intrinsic importance of the expense classification, however, it is probably best to think of it as constituting a distinct case.

In practice left-hand valuation balances, showing deductions from various equity headings, are frequently listed among the assets in the balance sheet. This confusion is illustrated in the balance sheet prescribed for the railways by the Interstate Commerce Commission. On the asset side genuine assets, such as "rents and insurance premiums paid in advance," are grouped with such obvious offsets to equities as "discount on capital stock." This is a highly unfortunate practice. If offsets to equities in the case of which, for some reason, it is desired to postpone final cancellation, are placed in the balance sheet, each offset should be shown in connection with the equity heading to which it relates on the *right side of the statement*. Otherwise equities are misstated and the assets are padded.

GRAPHIC SUMMARY

It will be convenient, in concluding this chapter, to exhibit the various accounts of the X Co. mentioned in preceding pages, and the essential transactions relating thereto, in graphic form. All important types of accounts are illustrated in this exhibit; and the relationship of each case (and the entries involved) to the underlying equation is shown. Our explanation of the technical structure of the double-entry system in terms of the fundamental classes of data and underlying situations of the business enterprise is now essentially complete. It should be evident at this point that *every possible transaction* arising in the conduct of business can be reported and classified according to the principles that have been emphasized, rationally, without the use of blind rules-of-thumb or unreasonable figures of speech.

The expense and revenue accounts used in the illustration are shown under the equity side. As explained in Chapter VI, these accounts relate to both of the fundamental classes; but since their main purpose is to disclose the net revenue figure it is not unreasonable to list them in this way. Individual accounts payable and receivable are not shown although such accounts would of course be required in practice. This illustration, it should be emphasized, is highly hypothetical, no attempt being made to introduce the necessary details of an actual business history. The illustrative transactions of Chapter V, in so far as they relate to the X Co., are omitted, but the summary data given in Chapter VI and the present chapter are entered in the appropriate accounts and columns. In addition it has been assumed that the payroll [12] liability has been reduced by cash

---

[12] The accounts payable account, as used in Chapter VI, is at this point separated into wages payable and accounts payable headings.

payments of $150,000, that accounts payable have been liquidated to the amount of $40,000, that all interest accruals have been met, and that customers' accounts to the amount of $200,000 have been collected. Depreciation is shown in the allowance accounts mentioned in the preceding section.

The X Co's Accounts

Properties		Equities	
Additions	Subtractions	Subtractions	Additions
Land		**Capital Stock—Common**	
$100,000			$200,000
		Common Stock Dividends Declared	
			$ 20,000
Buildings		**Capital Stock—Preferred**	
$200,000	Allowance for Depreciation of Buildings		$200,000
	$ 4,000	**Preferred Stock Dividends Declared**	
			$ 16,000
Equipment		**Mortgage Bonds**	
$100,000	Allowance for Depreciation of Equipment		$100,000
	$10,000	**Mortgage Bond Interest Payable**	
		$ 5,000	$ 5,000
Patents		**Debenture Bonds**	
$100,000	$ 6,000		$100,000
		Debenture Interest Payable	
		$ 6,000	$ 6,000

Properties		Equities	
Additions	Subtractions	Subtractions	Additions
ORGANIZATION COSTS		NOTES PAYABLE	
$ 25,000			$100,000
		NOTE INTEREST PAYABLE	
		$ 7,000	$ 7,000
MATERIALS		ACCOUNTS PAYABLE	
$100,000 100,000	$150,000	$ 40,000	$100,000
CASH		WAGES PAYABLE	
$ 75,000 50,000 200,000	$ 27,000 150,000 40,000 18,000	$150,000	$200,000
LABOR		SALES	
$200,000	$200,000	$425,000	$425,000
		Cost of Sales	
		$360,000	603$,000
FUEL		EXPENSE AND REVENUE	
$ 5,000	$ 4,500	$360,000 65,000	$425,000
INSURANCE		NET REVENUE	
$ 2,000	$ 1,500	$ 54,000 11,000	$ 65,000

OTHER TYPES OF SUPPLEMENTARY ACCOUNTS

Properties		Equities	
Additions	Subtractions	Subtractions	Additions
MISCELLANEOUS SUPPLIES AND SERVICES		**SURPLUS**	
$ 20,000	$ 19,000	$10,000	$ 11,000
ACCOUNTS RECEIVABLE		**RESERVE FOR POSSIBLE OBSOLESCENCE**	
$375,000	$200,000		$ 10,000
WORK IN PROCESS			
$395,000	$375,000		
FINISHED STOCK			
$375,000	$360,000		

After the year's operations have been recorded as shown above a new balance sheet of the *X* Co. may be prepared by collecting the balances of all the accounts. It would stand as follows: [13]

Properties			Equities	
Land		$100,000	Capital Stock—Common . .	$200,000
Buildings—gross .	$200,000		Common Dividends Declared...	20,000
Less Allowance for Deprec. .	4,000	196,000	Capital Stock—Preferred . .	200,000
			Preferred Dividends Declared..	16,000
Equipment—gross .	$100,000		Mortgage Bonds	100,000
Less Allowance for Deprec. .	10,000	90,000	Debenture Bonds	100,000
			Notes Payable	100,000

[13] No attempt has been made in this exhibit to arrange account titles in approved balance-sheet form. The order shown in the above system of accounts is followed.

Patents	$ 94,000	Accounts Payable	$ 60,000
Organization Costs	25,000	Wages Payable	50,000
Materials	50,000	Surplus	1,000
Cash	90,000	Reserve for Possible Obsoles-	
Fuel	500	cence	10,000
Insurance	500		
Miscellaneous Supplies and Services	1,000		
Accounts Receivable	175,000		
Work in Process	20,000		
Finished Stock	15,000		
Total	$857,000	Total	$857,000

Thus it appears that a preliminary balance sheet may be extended into a system of parallel-column accounts (asset, equity, expense, revenue, net revenue, surplus, and valuation), according to the principles developed in the foregoing discussions, a system which may later be resolved again into its fundamental balance-sheet elements.

Indeed, if the double-entry system were carried to its extreme conclusion, as has sometimes been done in practice, an account entitled "balance sheet" or "X Co., financial condition," might now be opened. By means of actual entries all other accounts might then be merged into the master account. Later, at the beginning of the next accounting period, it would again be necessary to extend the summary account into a system of subsidiary units. The process of double entry may thus be envisaged as essentially a succession of balance-sheet extensions and contractions.

CHAPTER VIII

ACCOUNT CLASSIFICATION

In the preceding chapters accounts have been classified in terms of the fundamental groups of the balance sheet, or special phases, positive or negative, of these classes. In other words, each of the important accounting divisions has been thought of as attaching to a *distinct* group of accounts. Thus we have asset, equity, expense, revenue, net revenue and surplus accounts. Each account in turn has been conceived as representing a definite type of accounting data.

Now while this analysis is of primary importance in that it furnishes a rational basis for the explanation of the essential nature of a system of double-entry accounts, it should be recognized that no specific set of accounts in practice can be expected to conform thereto precisely. Actual accounts do not as a rule represent continuously and purely a single accounting element. In terms of the specific accounts in any case there is much overlapping among the various fundamental divisions. Many obscure and dubious situations must be dealt with. Further, special groups of accounts are required at the time of the periodic closing, to show certain classes of expense and revenue not distinctly recognized earlier and to permit of summarizing and reclassification by the double-entry method. Again, in attempting to answer detail questions of management the accountant may find it desirable to organize an accounting system on some functional basis, especially in connection with the asset, expense, and revenue groups. Still further, various other important, though less fundamental, principles of classification arise in connection with the preparation of the financial statements. These aspects of account classification will be very briefly considered in this chapter.

THE OVERLAPPING OF ACCOUNT CLASSES

As has been already noted, many kinds of commodities and services required by business enterprises are highly current in nature. The status of such items as fuel, supplies, labor services, advertising services, etc., is only momentarily maintained. Accordingly, the accounts in which such items are recorded may not stand continuously in any one of the fundamental divisions. In so far as the product for the creation of which these costs are required remains in the business, in either inchoate or finished form, these values may perhaps be said to exist as assets. But the titles used would be no longer appropriate; at intervals the change in form should be recognized by the transfer of values to work in process headings.

In the trading field, where the technical period of production is short and costs incurred may be viewed largely as costs of current sales or expense, the current assets merge into the expense classification. Indeed many commodities and services in such a case are so transitory in character as to constitute essentially expense at the moment of acquisition. That is, although strictly speaking, any valuable consideration is an asset *as acquired,* it may become an expense shortly after—or even before—it is convenient to register the item in the accounts. Thus the services of the special salesman whom X, a retailer, secures to help handle a Saturday's business are in a sense an asset as furnished. X assumes that he is getting full value for his expenditure. The $10 paid, let us say, might then be entered in an *asset* account, the transaction being viewed as an exchange of asset values. But it is evident that this cost is also a cost of Saturday's sales, an expense. Accordingly, if the account in which the value of this service is registered be viewed from the standpoint of the destination of the item, it may be designated an expense account. In such an extreme case it is evident that, as a practical matter, the entire transaction should be viewed as a direct cost of sales. To recognize separately *cost incurred* and *utilization of services in producing revenue* in such a case would evidently be unreasonable from the bookkeeper's standpoint.

Thus in accounting practice the accounts designated as current asset accounts in an early chapter are often thought of as expense accounts. This is no very serious error in the trading enterprise if it is clearly recognized that all the items involved in such an account are really asset values as acquired, not losses, and give rise to expense items only as they facilitate the making of sales. Whether or not such a view is justified in a particular case depends upon the *normal* condition of the account in question. If the fuel account of a trader, for example, shows fuel acquired with a value of $500 and an examination of the bin shows fuel on hand of but $50, it is evident that, at this instant of time, the fuel account is primarily an expense account. Of the total entries in the left column of the account the amount of $450 is an expense (or at any rate no longer represents fuel except from the expense standpoint); the balance of $50 constitutes an asset. Both items are properly in the left column; but one heading is not sufficient. At this moment expense and asset figures with reference to fuel are amalgamated, and in order to state the financial condition of the business correctly it would be necessary to separate the two amounts.

Plainly, then, a distinction must sometimes be drawn between the precise nature of the individual *items* in a business transaction and the character of the *accounts* which are used to record the transaction. For convenience an account may well be defined or classified in terms of its predominating element, or, in other words, from the standpoint of the destination at the end of the accounting period of the principal sum involved in the account. Thus the acquisition of assets may be registered in an "expense" account, so-called because at the moments of closing a large proportion of the amount shown therein constitutes expense.

In a lesser degree the accounts which represent the more permanent assets of an enterprise present the same difficulties of classification. An equipment account for example may show at a particular date a left balance of $100,000. But if an appraisal or careful judgment discloses the fact that the current value of this property is but $99,000, it is evident that the account does not represent an asset alone. An element of expense is involved (assuming this depreciation relates to current sales). And since depreciation is assumed to accrue continuously it is not convenient to follow it concurrently in the accounts. Consequently, virtually all property accounts, in practice, fail to represent steadily a single class of data. Just as the fuel account at a particular instant may represent coal consumed as well as coal on hand, so the equipment or other durable asset account may show, in one conglomerate figure, depreciation as well as property value.

Some accounts become "mixed" in practice in the sense that more than one element is specifically recorded in a single account. The "merchandise" account as sometimes kept by the retailer is an example. Such an account is an asset, expense and revenue account combined. The left column is used to show purchases of merchandise (the principal "raw material" of the enterprise); the right column is used to show sale of "finished product" (retailed merchandise). That is, one column represents, initially, an asset, the other, revenue. As the goods are sold the amount in the left column passes into the expense division.[1] It is interesting to note in this case that the revenue entry can also be thought of as in part a direct sub-

---
[1] This account is further considered in the next chapter.

traction from goods acquired, since it is placed in the right column of the merchandise account. Nevertheless the two sides are quite distinct in their accounting significance, as cost prices are shown in one column, selling prices in the other. Such accounts are not to be recommended, but as long as items are entered in the appropriate columns, and their character is clearly understood, they can be handled without serious confusion.

The practice of listing several elements in a single account might be carried very far. Indeed, as already noted, the balance sheet itself may be conceived as an account showing all the assets and equities in the business. The degree to which classes and subclasses should be broken up under separate headings depends primarily upon the size and complexity of the enterprise. The application of the principles of double entry to the closing of mixed accounts will be illustrated in the next chapter.

The discussion has now been carried far enough to suggest the problems that arise if a strictly logical classification of accounts is attempted in practice. The fact that such a classification cannot be precisely and continuously adhered to does not destroy the significance of the underlying divisions we have been discussing. In no field except a purely imaginary one can a classifier follow exact lines of cleavage. There are always connecting links, grounds of dubiety, points at which one class shades into another. But these difficulties do not destroy the value of classification. Classifications are primarily for purposes of convenience; a particular grouping is adequate if it satisfactorily serves the purpose in hand. For some purposes distinctions may well be observed, for others, similarities. Controversies concerning the legitimacy of this or that line of demarcation frequently arise because the fact that various reasonable purposes are involved is not appreciated. The essential aim of the preceding discussion is the rational explanation of the double-entry system; and it seems clear that for the purpose of such an exposition accounts must be conceived in terms of the underlying classes of data with which the accountant is concerned

FUNCTIONAL CLASSIFICATION

The most convenient initial classification of property accounts is in terms of *kinds* of structures, commodities, and services acquired. Thus we have such titles as "land," "buildings," "machinery," "tools," "materials," "insurance," etc., or, where the system is somewhat elaborate, more specific headings such as "factory site," "warehouse," "lathes," "No. 6 castings," "insurance on office building," etc. The "investment in road and equipment" division prescribed by the Interstate Commerce Commission for railways under its jurisdiction illustrates a fairly detailed classification along this line. Thus we find under the general account, road, such "primary" headings as "grading," "underground power tubes," "tunnels and subways," "ties," "rails," "ballast," etc.

Another method of classifying properties frequently stressed is in terms of use or *function*. For managerial purposes a classification which shows the amount of property applicable to each department or phase of the business and to the production of each type of commodity or service, is often desirable. Such an arrangement would aid in the securing of the data required in making comparisons for the purpose of determining the relative efficiency of specific plants, departments, processes, etc. In this connection a functional classification of expense and revenue accounts is more important; but such a scheme is facilitated by a corresponding grouping of the asset accounts.

In a manufacturing enterprise, for example, an attempt might be made to collect in a particular group of accounts all property values devoted to technical manufacture as opposed to administration and selling activities. Thus the value of *factory* buildings, equipment, and materials might be set up separately. Or, carrying this plan of classification still further, the value of the buildings, equipment, etc., devoted to the manufacture of a particular type of product might be segregated. Evidently this last would be very difficult to accomplish, rationally, in many cases. Where a particular building or other property is used in connection with several products, the assignment of its value to the various functional property accounts would be likely to require the use of more or less reasonable arbitraries. Yet such an assignment would be a necessary preliminary to any apportionment of depreciation cost on a similar plan.

The point should be emphasized that however fully the properties be classified according to either kind or use, no new principles are required in recording all transactions which may be involved. The double-entry system can be applied as well to an extensive as to a simple system.

As was stated above, detail classification is of especial importance in the expense and revenue divisions. Here is one of the points at which a system of accounts may be greatly extended. In the case of an enterprise of any complexity it is not sufficient that total expense and total revenue be correctly shown in the accounts (although it is doubtful if these totals are exhibited with precise accuracy in a majority of cases). The net earnings of the business can be determined by combining these figures, and a rough test of efficiency may be had by comparing the expense and revenue totals in a particular period with the corresponding figures for preceding periods. But the management of a business of any size should have at its disposal more information than this. The expenses applicable to each kind of asset, each department, process, or phase of the business, or to each kind of product manufactured, may well be shown separately. In connection with types of assets it may be desirable, for example, to open such accounts as "fuel expense," "depreciation of factory," "maintenance of equipment," "materials expense," "labor expense," etc. Possible accounts corresponding to phases of operation in the broad sense are "buying expense," "manufacturing expense," "selling expense," and "office and administrative expense." Such designations as "prime" or "direct" cost and "overhead" or "indirect" expense are common. The supposed cost of making and selling a particular kind of product may be collected under various combinations of the above and similar titles.

It is evident that in attempting to apportion expense charges between departments and phases of an enterprise difficulties of a serious nature arise. A power plant, for example, may be used to furnish heat and light to the office building as well as to the factory. In such a case the distribution of fuel, labor, and other costs incident to the operation of the power plant between the two phases of the business on any but an arbitrary basis is a troublesome matter. Further, added problems arise in the determination of the expenses incident to particular classes of sales. Many kinds of current services and commodities as well as fixed properties are normally utilized in the production of more than one line. A particular type of labor—or even a specific laborer, for example, may be employed at different times upon work connected with several products. Evidently considerable clerical work would be involved in following such labor costs. The allocation of general items, such as supervision, maintenance, depreciation, etc., is of course still more difficult.

It is entirely beyond the scope of this study to consider the problems of cost accounting. It is merely intended to emphasize the possibility of superimposing a functional classification of expense accounts upon the underlying divisions emphasized in preceding chapters.

The revenue accounts are normally fewer in number than the expense accounts. The production of almost any commodity or service requires a relatively long list of commodities and services. In some cases, however, several distinct lines are handled, and the use of several revenue accounts may be desirable. In fact the collection of expense in terms of separate classes of sales presupposes the subdivision of revenue. The classification of revenue is largely a clerical matter. While it may be very difficult to apportion expenses to particular classes of sales, it is evident that the gross sales figure may be subdivided almost indefinitely if desired. The sale, like the purchase, is an explicit transaction, and hence these transactions may readily be grouped by departments, principal lines, or detail classes. The only limitation on such classification is its clerical cost.

STATEMENT CLASSIFICATION

Certain further lines of division, of especial importance in the preparation of financial statements, should be mentioned in a statement of accounting theory. On the asset side the distinction between tangible and intangible items is of some consequence, although there is not complete agreement among accountants or engineers as to just what are the essential characteristics of each group. The most logical view is to consider as intangibles all immaterial properties, such as patents, leaseholds, goodwill, trade-marks, copyrights, royalty rights, etc., and all other rights or claims, such as securities and open customers' accounts. Accounts receivable are certainly as fully immaterial in nature as patent rights. And securities, such as stocks, bonds, and notes, can hardly be said to constitute or express physical properties. They are rather merely *evidences* of legal rights. The document itself is a tangible thing, of course, but the property is only *represented by* the paper and does not inhere therein.[2] Cash itself is indeed largely intangible. A major part of the cash resources of a company usually consists in various bank deposits. These really represent not tangible property but highly liquid accounts receivable. Even cash in hand may consist primarily in undeposited checks and other instruments having no intrinsic value. It should be noted, however, that accountants commonly rate cash as a tangible; and many would also place securities, notes, and open accounts in the same class, restricting intangibles to the more general items such as those listed above.

It is usually conceded that the non-physical properties should be exactly labeled and segregated in the balance sheet. This opinion is due in part to the peculiar susceptibility of such assets to overstatement. The more dubious intangibles arise primarily during the preliminary period of organization, construction, and development. Certain special questions involving the intangible assets during this period are dealt with in Chapter XIV. Goodwill and related intangibles receive especial consideration in Chapter XIII.

As was pointed out in an earlier connection, value is an essential aspect of every asset. Strictly speaking the accountant's asset is the value inhering in some structure, commodity, service, right, or condition. A value having an immaterial residence may accordingly be fully as bona fide as that involved in a physical object. Nevertheless there are important reasons for drawing the distinction in the accounts as far as possible.

Another important balance-sheet classification divides all properties into "fixed" and "current" assets. This distinction has been recognized in preceding chapters as having an important bearing on accounting, but it will not be out of place

---

[2] In the case of a coupon bond, payable to bearer, the value might perhaps be said to attach to the document itself, since, if lost or stolen, the asset is presumably destroyed as far as the original holder is concerned.

to emphasize it here. What constitutes a fixed asset, a current asset? Four points of difference (not all applicable to every case) may be noted. First may be mentioned normal *length of life* within the business. A fixed asset is one that normally will remain an economic factor within the particular business for at least two or more accounting periods (assuming the period to be one year), such as a piece of durable equipment, a fireproof building, a leasehold, a long-term security bought for investment. A current asset, conversely, is one that will normally reside in the business less than one or, at the most, two full periods, such as fuel, stationery and postage, materials, work in process, finished stock, accounts receivable, insurance.

A second consideration is *liquidity*. From this standpoint a current asset is one which may or will shortly be converted into cash. A fixed asset, accordingly, is one which may or will with difficulty, or only in a roundabout fashion, be liquidated. The same examples may again be used except that it should be noted that long-term investments, such as bonds, which the management fully intends to hold, may, if necessary, be converted to cash very readily. An account receivable, on the other hand, is inevitably soon realized in cash (payment in other form being rare) in the normal course of events. An item of equipment is commonly converted to cash only through a long period, and indirectly, as the product to which it contributes is exchanged for legal tender.

Third, a current asset is one which passes rapidly into the expense division, while a fixed asset is transferred to expense account over perhaps many accounting periods. This point evidently applies only to those assets which are actually consumed (at least from the economic standpoint) in the process of production. Securities, receivables, and cash never normally become expense. When such items expire they are exchanged for other properties or are used (in the case of cash) to retire equities. The value of a machine (except salvage), on the other hand, is gradually carried to expense. Current supplies and services in some businesses are likely to constitute expense almost as soon as acquired.

Finally, a typical fixed asset, such as a machine unit, is used in its *entirety* to furnish a series of similar services. The business man in buying the machine acquires, essentially, a bundle of services. A current asset such as coal, however, is actually consumed in instalments. The fixed asset is not used up bit by bit, each of essentially the same significance. Instead the whole item is used more or less continuously until its efficiency is so impaired that it is no longer economical to repair it and continue it in operation. Of course if a long enough view be taken one can imagine a succession of specific machines being acquired, operated, and discarded. Nevertheless the accounting period is not ten or twenty years in length; and at any rate there is a real difference in the technical way in which such assets as plant and equipment on the one hand and raw material on the other enter into production. This last consideration also only applies to assets actually used in the technical processes.

Subclasses under both fixed and current assets are needed in the preparation of a detailed balance sheet. Four principal groups of fixed assets may be distinguished, natural resources, plant and equipment items, investments, and general intangibles (patents, leaseholds, etc.). Under current assets such subdivisions as "liquid," "working," and "deferred" assets may well be used. Cash, current receivables, marketable securities, and, perhaps, finished stock, may be classed as liquid items. Materials and work in process are the principal examples of working assets. Prepaid insurance, rent, etc., items which will be liquidated with services rather than by cash payment, are often labeled "deferred charges."

Similarly the equities, especially those of a contractual type, may be classified into fixed and current groups. Here length of life or term is the controlling consideration in every case. No important principles of classification not already sufficiently discussed arise here. The collection of all surplus accounts into one group is a matter which might well be more carefully observed. "Accrued" liabilities is a designation commonly used to indicate contractual accruals of interest, rent, etc., which have not matured. Liabilities which are to be retired with commodities or services instead of cash are sometimes labeled as "deferred revenue" items.

The supplementary groupings of the balance sheet mentioned above represent simply collections of account balances which are useful in any case in bringing out important aspects of the financial position of the enterprise. This kind of classification, as well as that discussed in the preceding section, is evidently not in conflict with the principles of the accounting structure stressed in preceding chapters. Once all transactions throughout a period have been recorded in the proper account columns and under appropriate titles, it should be clear that extensive classification and reclassification is possible without disturbing in any way the underlying equation, and without the introduction of new principles or rules of procedure.

CHAPTER IX

PERIODIC ANALYSIS AND SPECIAL CASES

The nature of the various important types of data with which the accountant is concerned, the structure of the corresponding groups of accounts, and the application of the principles of the double-entry plan to the main kinds of explicit and implicit transactions arising in the business enterprise, have been considered in the foregoing pages. There are, however, a few additional situations requiring attention if our examination of the theory of modern accounts is to be quite complete. The more important of these arise in connection with the process of analysis at the end of the accounting period.

The explanation of the procedures adopted by the bookkeeper in closing a system of parallel-column accounts presents certain difficulties. The balancing and summarizing entries made at the close of the accounting period—at which time an attempt is made to reduce the entire system again to its lowest terms, to reconvert the financial data of the situation again to balance-sheet form—are very commonly misunderstood. Rational explanations of these procedures seem to be lacking; rules-of-thumb are usually offered instead.

No attempt will be made here to go into any full description of the technique of closing accounts. A discussion of bookkeeping procedure—the methods and forms used in journalizing, posting, balancing or closing—is entirely outside the plan of this book. It will be endeavored, however, from a discussion of a few cases, to indicate that each step in the bookkeeper's procedure *can* be rationally interpreted, that every balancing and closing entry is entirely consistent with

PERIODIC ANALYSIS AND SPECIAL CASES 219

the scheme for recording business transactions which has been stressed in this study. In addition a few miscellaneous transactions, involving special difficulties of interpretation, will be briefly examined. The explanation of these cases will furnish an additional test of the principles which have been outlined.

CLOSING CURRENT ASSET ACCOUNTS

Let us first consider the case of the current asset accounts, such as fuel. The fuel account of the B Co., for example, at the end of the year shows entries in the left column totaling $5,000, and—assuming no record of coal consumed has been kept—no entries in the right column. An inventory now discloses the fact that fuel on hand amounts to $1,000. How is this situation to be dealt with? During the period only explicit business transactions affecting the status of fuel have been recognized; no record of the use of coal—the transformation of this value within the business—has been maintained. Consequently the fuel account as it stands simply shows acquisitions, current purchases plus the preceding balance if any. At this instant the nature of the fuel account is not clear. It shows a balance of $5,000 but only a part of that amount still represents fuel as an asset. The bookkeeper is now faced with the task of splitting this sum up into its underlying components, of showing the correct value of fuel on hand and the proper disposition of the amount that has disappeared—as fuel.

The procedure adopted by the bookkeeper in this situation will (or should) depend upon the interpretation which he attaches to the fuel account. If he defines this account in terms of the balance on hand, i.e., considers it to be an asset account, he will make a right entry therein for $4,000 (the amount expired) and a left entry for the same amount in some expense account (assuming that this expiration had to do with current sales).[1] After *balancing*, the fuel account would appear somewhat as follows:

Fuel

$5,000			$4,000
		(Inv.)	1,000
$5,000			$5,000
Inv. $1,000			

This balancing procedure requires a few comments. The bookkeeper first enters the amount of the inventory (the difference between the two sides) in the right column. Evidently this cannot be intended as a deduction from assets as the full amount of the expiration has already been recorded. What is, then, its explanation? This procedure illustrates the particular method of subtraction followed by the bookkeeper. It is his task now to show the correct present status of the fuel account. If all transactions, both explicit and implicit, have been recorded, this status is represented by the difference between the two sides, the difference between the total additions to the asset and the total of subtractions therefrom. The bookkeeper foots up the two sides. Then, instead of subtracting the smaller from the larger total in the usual way, he adds enough to the smaller side to equate the two. A single line is then drawn under this balance and the work is checked (or may be) by actually combining the balance and the smaller total. Double lines are written beneath the grand totals on each side to indicate that the calculation is complete. The balance is now written under the double line on the left side,

---

[1] If a part of this expiration may be viewed as still in the business in the form of work in process or finished stock, such amount would of course be charged to the appropriate asset accounts. The amount transferred to expense may be first set up in a special account such as fuel expense, be later transferred to a more general heading such as manufacturing expense, and finally be closed into a summary account, expense and revenue. The nature of each enterprise and the needs of the management will determine the particular procedure followed. Evidently all such transfer entries may be made without the introduction of any new principles.

where it actually belongs. This cancels the balancing entry on the right side (of which the nominal character may be shown by parentheses, as above) and at the same time shows the present status of the asset in a single figure. The final effect upon the account of the two inventory entries is thus nil; yet by means of these entries the actual balance of the account is shown in one figure.[2]

If the fuel account is viewed as an expense account, on the other hand, the closing procedure would be somewhat different. In this case the first step would be the transfer of the asset balance, $1,000, to some property account. In case there were several small property items, and it was not considered necessary for balance-sheet purposes to give separate recognition to each, a "sundry assets" account might be opened to show, temporarily, these miscellaneous asset balances. A right entry in the fuel account for $1,000 (a subtraction of the asset element) and a corresponding left entry in the sundry assets account would then be necessary. Later [3] the expense balance would require transfer to (finally) a summary expense and revenue account. This would be accomplished by a right entry of $4,000 in the fuel account (a subtraction from expense under one title) and an equal left entry in the expense and revenue account (an addition to expense under another title). The fuel account would then have no balance, and would stand as follows:

FUEL

$5,000	$1,000
	4,000
$5,000	$5,000

---

[2] In this simple illustration the balance is evident without computation. In practice, however, an account would frequently show many individual entries on each side and hence the computing of the actual difference would be a matter of clerical importance.

[3] The order of these operations is not of importance.

This simple illustration will be sufficient to suggest the essence of the procedures involved in analyzing a current asset account, or an expense account containing a minor asset element.

CLOSING THE LABOR ACCOUNT

As has been emphasized several times in this book, labor services constitute a valuable consideration as received. The account in which such services are first recorded may, accordingly, be deemed an asset account. In practice, however, especially in the trading field, it often happens that no account is taken of this flow of value into the business until payment is made. In other words the labor account at the end of a period is likely to represent simply the total payments to employees during the period. It approaches the nature of an expense account, but requires adjustment before its balance-sheet significance can be determined.

For an illustration of this case let us assume that the *A* Co., a trading enterprise, has been in business for a single period and has expended on payroll account $5,000. It will be further assumed for convenience that all labor services acquired are utilized almost immediately in making sales and hence constitute expense directly following receipt. At the end of the period, accordingly, the labor account without adjustment shows entries in the left side totaling $5,000. Now let us suppose that the *A* Co. has acquired a total of labor services during the period of $5,500, the amount of $500 not having been booked as yet because payment has not been made. In other words the *A* Co. owes certain employees $500 on account of services actually rendered. How is the labor account to be adjusted?

The significant thing about such an accrual is its *two-sided* character; it affects the accounts in two distinct directions. From one point of view it means that the labor cost of the period as recognized to date is understated; labor services have been acquired and utilized to the amount of $500 and no record has been made of that fact. Further, it means that equities are understated correspondingly. The employees have furnished the services amounting to $500 for which payment has not been made and consequently have a current claim in the business for the amount. In other words, the business has purchased services valued at $500 *on account*; and this credit purchase has been temporarily neglected as far as the books are concerned.[4] Values are received and corresponding liabilities are thereby incurred; both sides of the equation are affected.

If the A Co.'s bookkeeper for convenience uses the single labor account to show payments, accrued payroll, and labor expense, the account, when closed, would appear as follows:

LABOR

	$5,000	$5,500
(Inv.)	500	
	$5,500	$5,500
		Inv. $ 500

Just what is the explanation of this procedure? The first step is the recognition of the additional cost incurred. This is accomplished by a left entry of $500 in the labor account. The corresponding right entry to indicate the liability involved

---

[4] Such inexact accounting is common. In manufacturing enterprises which attempt a fairly complete cost accounting, however, the acquisition of labor services is followed closely, regardless of the date of payment. Certainly the purchase of ordinary services on account is a universal business transaction; and it is really just as unreasonable to ignore such a transaction as it would be to ignore the acquisition of commodities on a credit basis. The only essential difference between the two transactions from a bookkeeping standpoint, aside from the difference in kind, is that labor services are acquired in a stream of small units, perhaps from thousands of employees, while purchases of commodities are received in terms of comparatively few distinct shipments from a smaller list of creditors.

is postponed for a moment; and the next step consists in the transfer of the total labor cost, $5,500, from the labor account to the expense and revenue account (or other appropriate title). The two sides are then footed and the double lines ruled. Finally a right entry of $500 is made to show the current equity previously unrecognized. This completes the record of the accrual transaction. The labor account now represents a liability, a liability which is closely analogous to the merchandise creditors' balances. The account has thus represented successively wages paid, labor cost, and wages payable.

In this case the accrual entries of $500 are more than mere balancing figures. They represent an actual transaction, the purchase on account of labor services worth $500. The left entry increases the labor cost to the proper figure; the right entry shows the actual liability. The nature of the transaction is shown more clearly if an actual liability account is opened. Suppose, for example, that a special payroll account is used to show the liability balance. In this event a left entry of $500 would be made as before in the labor account and a right entry for the same amount in the payroll account. To finally close the labor account the further entries noted above would then be made.

The essence of these procedures is seen more clearly when their effect upon the next accounting period is seen. In the succeeding period the expenditures for labor are again charged to the labor account. Presumably the accrued payroll will be the first met. From the standpoint of the following operating interval, accordingly, the right entry of $500 constitutes essentially an offset to what would otherwise be an overstated cost; it cancels that part of the current expenditures for labor which are on account of labor acquired in the preceding period and included in its costs. It represented a liability momentarily; it later constitutes an adjustment of cost. In case the accrued item were not met throughout the following period, it would again constitute an accrued balance and the correct labor cost would still be shown. If the accrued payroll account were used it would evidently be necessary, to accomplish this adjustment in the labor account, to return the amount of the liability again to the labor account.

A more elaborate treatment of the case would of course be possible. One alternative would be the use of three (or perhaps four) distinct accounts, wages paid, labor cost incurred (and a labor cost of sales account as well if there were a distinction here), and accrued payroll. More entries would be involved in this event; but they would simmer down to essentially the same procedures as just discussed. As was noted above, the most accurate policy would be to record the value of all services as acquired and show the corresponding liabilities. Wage payments would then represent the retirement of these equities.

In conclusion the practical significance of the recognition of accrued payroll (or other similar accrual) in connection with the financial statements may be emphasized. Evidently unless such items are considered at the end of the period costs will not be correctly presented and net income will accordingly be more or less seriously misstated. And even if expenditures happened to be identical in amount with labor costs (because of the coincidence of the accrued item at the beginning and at the end of the period) in a particular case, so that net income would be unaffected by an ignoring of accruals, it would still be important from the standpoint of the balance sheet to show such amounts. Otherwise current liabilities and current assets would be understated.

THE MIXED MERCHANDISE ACCOUNT

The accounts discussed in the two preceding sections are evidently "mixed" in the sense that at various times they show more than one element. One main fact predominated in each case, however, the cost of the class of commodity or service involved. Other accounts are more specifically mixed; i.e., are used to record, concurrently, more than one class of data. A much discussed example is the merchandise account, so-called, which is used to register purchase, sales, and—at intervals—merchandise inventory. Such an account has been discussed in some detail by Sprague but there are one or two points in connection therewith which may well receive brief attention.

The *B* Co., it will be assumed, uses a single account to show all the three classes just mentioned. During the Company's first accounting period purchases total $50,000; and this amount is entered (in a sequence of smaller items of course) in the left column. Sales amount to $60,000 and are entered in the right column. At the end of the period an inventory shows merchandise on hand with a value [5] of $5,000. The account in these circumstances would be closed by an entry of $15,000 in the left column of the merchandise account, and a corresponding right entry in the expense and revenue summary (or in some appropriate intermediate account) and by a right inventory entry of $5,000 above the double lines in the merchandise account and a balancing entry to correspond on the left side below the double lines. After closing, the account would stand as follows:

MERCHANDISE

	$50,000		$60,000
	15,000	(Inv.)	5,000
	$65,000		$65,000
Inv.	$ 5,000		

[5] We will not consider the problem of the determination of such a value. An adequate study of merchandise pricing would make a volume in itself.

Precisely what is the proper explanation of this procedure? In the first place it must be clearly understood that when purchases and sales are shown in the opposing columns of a single account two distinct classes of data, from an accounting standpoint, are being recognized; viz., cost and revenue. On one side is being recorded purchases of the principal raw material; on the other we find sales of product, gross revenue. It may be true in a trading establishment that goods on the shelf and goods on the housewife's back doorstep are essentially the same from a physical standpoint; but the accountant must here adopt the economist's view that the middleman performs a distinct productive function, that there is a "process of production" in retailing as in manufacturing. "Raw material" and "finished goods" are just as distinct for the accountant in one case as in the other. Accordingly, separate accounts may well be used for costs and revenues in the trading field as elsewhere.

If purchases and sales figures are placed in one account, however, this means that as goods are consumed in the selling process (i.e., as merchandise is sold) the values thereof become an expense,[6] cost of producing revenue, which must be deducted from gross sales (along with other expenses) if the net revenue figure is to be determined. Evidently from this standpoint the merchandise cost of goods sold is properly a charge against the gross revenue. In the above account, therefore, *at the end of the period,* such part of merchandise purchases as represents an expense is already set against revenue, and need not be transferred to other accounts for that purpose. Ignoring the cost of goods still on hand the account has now become a partial expense and revenue summary. Its concluding or balancing figure from this stand-

---

[6] The merchant is inclined to define his "expense" as all costs of producing sales *other than* merchandise cost. This view is consistent with the mixed merchandise account usage, as merchandise expense tends to be obscured by such a practice. Evidently a conception of expense as the *total* cost of producing a particular volume of sales is, in general, more satisfactory for the accountant.

point is evidently gross revenue less the *merchandise* cost of producing this revenue, an intermediate revenue item. Before final net revenue can be determined, of course, all other expenses must be deducted.[7]

Merchandise expense for the period evidently consists in the opening balance (if any) plus purchases less the value of goods still on hand. For the above case this would be $50,000 minus $5,000, or $45,000. Deducting this figure from gross sales gives $15,000, as the intermediate revenue figure which must be transferred to a final expense and revenue account. This computation may evidently be easily made without reference to technical accounting devices. The bookkeeper, however, is faced with the problem of registering the proper effect with respect to expense and revenue in an account which also includes an asset balance. The difference between purchases and sales as they stand is but $10,000. This *would be* the correct intermediate revenue figure if all goods acquired had been disposed of. But there is still a balance on hand amounting to $5,000. The bookkeeper accordingly makes a right entry in the merchandise account *to offset what would otherwise be an overstatement of expense.* This entry of $5,000 subtracts the amount of the asset contained in the total on the left side from that total. Since a subtraction from assets must be entered in the right column, this inventory entry is entirely rational. Now the merchandise account shows a right-hand balance of $15,000, the correct figure. This balance is transferred to some special or summary revenue account by the entries noted above. It should be emphasized that the entry of $15,000 in the left column is not an addition

---

[7] To the extent that freight, costs of handling, revenue stamps, etc., are included in purchase figures, the merchandise expense is not a mere matter of invoice price. As a matter of logic it might be urged that the value of all commodities and services used by the trader except those connected immediately with sales might be charged—as consumed—to merchandise (the trader's goods in process). In practice, however, it would not be expedient or desirable to attempt anything of this kind. The selling activity here predominates; and hence it is reasonable to charge most "overhead" expenses directly to sales.

PERIODIC ANALYSIS AND SPECIAL CASES   229

to amounts already appearing in that side, but a *subtraction of the intermediate revenue* from the figure appearing on the right side.

After footing and ruling the account the bookkeeper enters the inventory balance on the left side, thus restoring the merchandise account to its status as an asset account. In other words, the asset balance, which was temporarily deducted, is now returned to its proper position.

The use of separate accounts for purchases, sales, and periodic inventories, is now more common than the device just discussed. Nevertheless such a mixed account can be dealt with rationally according to the principles of double entry. As long as the various items are correctly interpreted, and the proper relationships between columns are maintained, accurate conclusions may be drawn.

CLOSING THE RENT ACCOUNT

As a final illustration of the application of double entry to the process of closing, a complex rent account will be considered. The *B* Co., it will be assumed, operates in a leased building, paying therefor at the rate of $300 per month. One floor is sublet to the *C* Co. at $100 per month. The entire situation with respect to these leases is recorded by the bookkeeper of the *B* Co. in a single account. At the beginning of a certain period this account shows a balance on the left side of $300 and a right balance of $100. These amounts, it may be assumed, represent rent paid in advance to the *A* Co. (the owner of the building) and rent prepaid by the *C* Co. to the *B* Co. on the sublease, respectively. The first amount is an asset; it represents the claim for service (not money) which the *B* Co. has against the lessor. The second amount is a liability; it represents the claim for service which the *C* Co. has against the *B* Co. As the *B* Co. receives the

the use of the building for which it pays rent the asset claim expires. As the *B* Co. furnishes the use of a part of this property to the secondary lessee the liability is extinguished. During the period the *B* Co. pays $3,000 on its lease contract and receives $1,000 from the *C* Co. At the end of the period, when the accounts are closed, it is found that the *B* Co. owes the *A* Co. for one month's rent, $300, and the *C* Co. likewise owes the *B* Co. for a month's rent, $100. This gives again both asset and liability accruals in connection with this account; although in this case the receivable (the claim against the *C* Co.) calls for payment in cash and the payable (amount owing the *A* Co.) is a liability which must be settled with cash.[8]

After closing, the rent account of the *B* Co., under such circumstances, would appear essentially as follows:

RENT

Asset	$ 300	Liab.	$ 100
	3,000		1,000
	300		100
			2,400
	$3,600		$3,600
Asset	$ 100	Liab.	$ 300

What is the explanation of such an amalgam? In the first place the original asset item of $300, which represented a month's payment in advance to the *A* Co., will evidently become a rent cost incurred—i.e., the value of a service received—as the month expires. From the viewpoint of the ensuing period (the period following payment), accordingly, this item may still remain in the left column of the rent account if we now consider it to be the main function of this column

---

[8] Evidently two kinds of assets and two types of liabilities are possible in connection with such an arrangement.

to show rent cost. Similarly the original liability item (the prepayment to the *B* Co.) becomes a genuine revenue as the *B* Co. furnishes the service for which this payment was made. Hence this balance may with reason be left in the right column of the rent account if it is now the principal purpose of this column to show rent revenue. Payments to the *A* Co., presumably covering building service acquired during the period, are entered in the left column; and the amount of cash receipts, presumably representing largely the sale of building service, are placed in the right column. (Concurrent entries in the cash account would of course be required.)

But now the bookkeeper finds that a month's service has been received (although not paid for) of which no record has been made, and that a month's service has been sold (although not paid for) which has received no accounting recognition. Evidently, to bring the account down to date and show all values acquired and all revenues earned, an entry of $300 must be made in the left column to cover values received but not booked and an entry of $100 must be made on the right side to cover service sold but not recognized as yet. The total of the left side now stands at $3,600, the value of a year's building service received; and the right side shows $1,200, the value of building service sold during the same period. Assuming that building service received during the period has finally expired incident to the production of the year's sales,[9] the two sides may now be combined to show the net rent cost to the *B* Co., $2,400. This balance is then transferred by making a right entry for the amount in the rent account (a subtraction from the net expense as shown by that account) and a left entry under the expense and revenue summary (or other appropriate title). Finally, it is necessary to show the liability incurred because of service received

---

[9] An assumption not likely to be strictly correct in the case of a manufacturing enterprise.

but not paid for; and a right entry for the amount is accordingly placed below the footings. This side of the account now shows simply a definite liability, a special account payable. On the left side is likewise entered the amount of rent receivable from the C Co. This side of the account now registers an asset.

It is again of interest to observe the effect of these sub-footing entries upon the conclusions of the succeeding period. Presumably the first receipt of rent will constitute a retirement of the receivable against the C Co. rather than a revenue. The asset balance will accordingly serve to cancel what would otherwise constitute an overstatement of revenue; or, to put it differently, among the credits to the rent account in the next period will be one which is merely a subtraction from an asset, not a revenue. The liability—rent due the A Co.—will likewise presumably be retired by the first payment in the ensuing period. In other words, among the debits to the rent account entered in the next period will be one which constitutes a subtraction from a liability, not a cost of additional service. Thus the liability item will offset properly what would otherwise constitute an overstatement of cost.

It is not intended to suggest that such a complex account is a desirable device. Such conglomerate and chameleonic accounts are to be avoided. A clear presentation of these data would require the use of several distinct accounts. A more adequate procedure in this case would be to enter the value of service received each month (or other convenient period) in an account entitled, perhaps, "building service received," and, similarly, to register at regular intervals the sale of building service in another account. Concurrently accounts showing indebtedness to the A Co., and the indebtedness of the C Co., should be built up. As payments are made or received the current liability and the current asset, respectively, would be extinguished. The following exhibit shows the way these accounts would appear, if this method were followed, at the end of the period.[10]

Building Service Received		A Co.—Rent Payable	
$3,600		$3,300	$3,600

C Co.—Rent Receivable		Building Service Sold	
$1,200	$1,100		$1,200

Closing by this scheme would then consist simply in balancing and transferring the expense and revenue items to a summary.

However, these mixed accounts may be handled in accordance with the principles stressed in the foregoing chapters if, as was emphasized before, each item is correctly interpreted and the proper *column* distribution is observed. The "interest and discount" account as often used in the small business presents a case much like the one we have been considering.

SOME MISCELLANEOUS CASES

It is not intended to attempt to show the application of the principles emphasized in this study to each and every kind of situation arising in business practice. The reliability of these principles has already been rather thoroughly tested in terms of all fundamental classes of accounts and transactions. In concluding this chapter, however, a brief statement of a few miscellaneous transactions will be added.

---

[10] Strictly speaking, two other accounts would be needed for balances such as were assumed for the beginning of the period, entitled, for example, "*A* Co.—rent advanced to" and "*C* Co.—rent advanced by."

BOND PREMIUM AND DEFERRED REVENUE. The issue of a bond or other contractual security at a premium brings about an interesting situation and one which is commonly given a careless interpretation by the accountant. In this connection one or two fundamental conceptions should be emphasized. The bona fide sum of values received by the issuing company in such a case, either in cash or other properties, constitutes the effective initial principal. The difference between this sum and the grand total of all payments made to the investor throughout the life of the security constitutes the total interest or income. Thus when a bond is issued at a premium the actual amount received by the corporation is the only principal and liability which the accountant should recognize at the outset. In such a case the sum paid at maturity and the original investment differ. It is the business of the accountant to handle the situation in such a way that the integrity of each net revenue figure and of each balance sheet, prepared during the life of the security, will not be impaired.

Suppose the X Co. issues a block of 20-year bonds carrying a semiannual payment of $4,000 and calling for the payment of $100,000 at maturity. The Company receives, it will be assumed, $123,114.77, which gives a 6 per cent basis. Assuming for convenience that the bonds are dated as of the beginning of an accounting period, and that the books are closed and statements prepared once every six months, then the first payment to the bondholders should be recorded by a left entry of $3,693.44 (interest on $123,114.77 for six months at 6 per cent) in the net revenue account (or appropriate subsidiary), a left entry of $306.56 in the bond liability account,[11] and a right entry for the sum in the cash account. That is,

---

[11] This entry may be recorded in a special bond premium account if par and premium are shown separately. The only reason for separating the two is that the premium represents a liability which will be gradually extinguished while the par will be retired at maturity with a single payment. See Chapter XVII for a discussion of what constitutes the effective liability from an accounting standpoint in case true principal and par or face value differ at the outset.

since the principal invested is greater than the lump sum which will be paid at maturity it is evident that the difference is returned in the series of semiannual payments; and it is entirely reasonable to assume that it is returned throughout the period on a basis consistent with the original valuation. Consequently the left entry of $306.56 is a subtraction from an equity, and has nothing to do with the net revenue account.

The usual, or at least a common interpretation, however, is to consider the amount of the premium as a "deferred revenue" which may gradually be transferred to income. On the other hand the entire payment is viewed as a deduction from income. While this procedure does not disturb the final net revenue figure, it does uselessly pad both sides of the income account. And it needs to be emphasized that the presentation of the integrity of subsidiary groups of data, such as income and deductions therefrom, is a matter of importance. The correct treatment of bond premium is the one illustrated above.

The true "deferred revenue" balance arises where customers deposit cash in advance of the delivery of the commodity or service involved. Such transactions are common in some retail lines, in the amusement business, in transportation, in the insurance field, and elsewhere. The Y Co., in the retail coal business, for example, receives from Z, a customer, $200 for coal to be delivered three months later. Evidently the transaction would be recorded by a left entry of $500 in the cash account (increase in assets) and a right entry for the same amount in Z's account (increase in liabilities). When the coal is delivered a left entry for $500 would be made in the liability account and an equal right entry in the revenue account. This simply means that the liability is extinguished by furnishing product instead of cash; hence it happens that the amount of the liability must virtually be transferred to the revenue account. This type of situation is entirely distinct, however, from the bond premium case.

ANNUITY ANALYSIS. Other cases arise where an explicit payment or receipt must be divided into a pure balance-sheet transaction on the one hand and an income transaction (indirectly affecting the balance sheet of course) on the other. The payment of an annuity is an important illustration. For an example let us assume that the X Co. acquires a patent valued at $73,600.87, agreeing to pay the inventor therefor, in lieu of a lump sum, ten annual payments of $10,000 each. This gives a 6 per cent basis. Assuming that these payments are made in each case at the end of an accounting period, entries should be made on the books of the X Co. showing the proper apportionment between return of principal and payment of net income.

If the patent was secured just at the beginning of a period the initial transaction would be recorded by a left entry of $73,600.87 in the patents account and an equal entry in the inventor's account.[12] This last might be headed "annuity payable." At the end of the year, when the first payment is made, an entry of $4,416.05 (6 per cent of $73,600.87) should be made in the left side of the net revenue account (to indicate the part of the payment which is virtually made out of current earnings), a left entry for $5,583.95 in the annuity payable account (a partial retirement of the original liability), and a right entry for the sum in the cash account. As time goes on it is evident that a larger and larger part of the fixed payment will be a return of capital, due to the decline in the principal.

STOCK SUBSCRIBED. A transaction rather difficult to interpret arises when a corporation receives subscriptions for its capital stock. It is customary to treat the subscriptions as bona

---

[12] The current effective liability is no more and no less than the actual amount invested. The inventor turns over to the corporation patents valued at $73,600.87; he thereby secures an equity with a present significance (from the standpoint of the corporate books at any rate) of just that sum. True, the corporation promises to pay in exchange a total of $100,000. But it would be ridiculous to contend that this is the correct present liability. One might as well argue that the current liability when a bond is issued is the par or face of the bond plus the grand total of all semiannual payments made throughout the life of the contract.

fide receivables, assets having about the same significance as promissory notes. Accordingly the amount is entered in the left column of the "subscriptions" accounts. But what right entry should be made at the same time? Usually the same amount is concurrently entered in the right column of the "capital stock subscribed" account, which is then viewed as expressing the corporation's "liability" or obligation to issue the stock. Evidently this is a very peculiar liability or equity account. It does not measure an amount to be paid in goods, services, or money, as is usually the case. Perhaps the most reasonable interpretation of this account is to consider it as a representation of the rights of the subscribers, through the corporation, in their own subscriptions.

When the subscriptions are once exchanged for cash, and the provisional "liability" balance is replaced by outstanding capital stock the situation has evidently reached a definite asset and equity stage. The difficulty that arises in this case is simply due to the attempt on the part of the accountant to reflect certain intermediate procedures in the regular double-entry form which hardly have a clear-cut balance-sheet significance. No doubt the stock subscription may with reason be recorded in the financial accounts; but there are many situations bearing upon the financial condition of the business enterprise, as was noted in Chapter II, which have no definite asset or equity meaning.

ADVERTISING RESERVE. One further kind of situation will be considered, the prorating of certain expenses by the "reserve method" in cases where a short accounting period is adopted. This plan is not wholly unreasonable in connection with such costs as maintenance and advertising. Suppose a manufacturing company, for example, which spends large sums for magazine advertising, wishes to close its books and prepare financial statements once a month. It is evident that the cost of advertising in periodicals (advertising which makes itself felt largely through the retail demand) is not an expense that can be related to specific sales on any but a purely arbitrary basis. It is fairly rational in such a case to assume that a year's advertising accrues evenly month by month; in other words, that the sales of each month require one-twelfth of the total advertising outlay for the year.[13] If this assumption is adhered to, and actual advertising payments are somewhat irregular, it will be convenient to open an adjustment or reserve account for advertising.

Each month, under this plan, one-twelfth of the estimated cost of the year's advertising program should be charged to expense and the same amount should be entered in the right column of the "advertising reserve" account. Later, when advertising costs are actually incurred, that is, when the advertising service is furnished, a left entry for the appropriate amount in the advertising reserve account and a corresponding entry in the right side of the proper liability account (or in the cash account if payment is made immediately) would be required.

What is the explanation of the preliminary entries in the advertising reserve account? This account does not show subtractions from assets since no assets have, at the outset, been given up. It does not represent a liability since no obligation is yet incurred. Strictly speaking it represents a part of the residual equity, a true surplus. From the long-run view any balance in this account does not represent income, however, because it is considered to be absorbed against excess advertising costs incurred in other periods. Thus if the actual costs incurred during the first month are less than one-twelfth of the estimated year's total by $1,000, net revenue for that month is in a sense understated by this procedure. If advertising costs incurred the second month exceed the regular allowance by

---

[13] It might be argued, of course, that advertising costs in 1921 may relate very largely to 1922 sales. In some cases this is doubtless true, but it is probably inexpedient for the accountant, as a rule, to start his analysis from this point of view.

$500, this excess is thrown back against the amount of revenue segregated in the preceding month under the advertising reserve heading. The balance in the right side of this account measures an amount of revenue which is being withheld from the concluding income account to cancel a probable excess cost of a later period.

It should be emphasized again that any considerable extension of such accounting would be unreasonable. Each period should stand on its own footing as far as possible. Earnings should not be equalized by juggling expenses. Nevertheless, in connection with certain classes of costs such apportioning entries have a justification from the practical standpoint.

Many other interesting cases might be studied. For the time being, however, the foregoing discussions in this and preceding chapters will be considered as an adequate application of the principles of the double-entry system as they have been set forth in this book.

CHAPTER X

DEBIT AND CREDIT

In practice the left column of all accounts is called the "debit" side; the right column is called the "credit" side. Similarly entries in the debit column are "debits"; entries in the credit column are "credits." To enter an item in the debit column is to debit or charge the account; to enter an item in the credit column is to credit the account. Is there any underlying significance to be attached to this nomenclature? What is the significance of the terms "debit" and "credit" as used in modern accounting? Is there any inherent reason for listing asset balances in the debit column and equity balances in the credit column?

Sprague and Hatfield have shown conclusively that these expressions in current usage have come to indicate essentially left and right columns—nothing more. In other words, debit and credit are conventional signs used to designate a spatial relationship between columns. "Left" and "right" would do as well, even better. This view has been adhered to in the explanation of the accounting structure given in this book. All main classes of data, all principal types of accounts, all important kinds of transactions, have been rationally explained without any resort to these technical expressions. The whole system has been stated in terms of numerical changes registered in parallel-column accounts.

A great many writers on accounting, however, have attempted to attach intrinsic significance to the terms "debit" and "credit" in their explanations of the double-entry system. Ingenious rules of debit and credit have been worked out in an endeavor to account for and explain the bookkeeper's various procedures. Needless to say, perhaps, the writer views all such efforts as hopeless and the resulting rules as misleading and inadequate. The rational development of accounting theory has been retarded rather than advanced by this method of approach. Yet debit and credit rules are widely taught and used; and in concluding this part of the present book it may be well to take a glance at some of the more important of these devices.

THE DEBTOR-CREDITOR EXPLANATION

In many attempted explanations of the double-entry system of accounts an effort is made to attach the significance of the words "debtor" and "creditor" to the terms "debit" and "credit" respectively, as used in modern accounts. Etymologically there is not doubt such a relationship. In their early use in financial statements (still commonly followed in the construction of bills) it is probable that the debit and credit abbreviations (Dr. and Cr.) were intended to signify debtor and creditor, respectively. In all personal accounts, i.e., accounts representing the relations between a business enterprise and outside individuals or other business entities, these meanings can with some respect be applied. The following, for example, may be assumed to represent the account of Y, a customer, with the X Co.:

Dr.	Y	Cr.
$500		$100

The amount of $500 entered in the debit column indicates the total claims accumulated against Y during the period. This measures *debts* incurred by Y in favor of the X Co.; Y is indebted to, is a *debtor* of the X Co. for the amounts charged to his account. The amounts entered in the credit column, on the other hand, express the sums paid by Y, which, accordingly, must be *credited* to his account; to the extent of these amounts he is a *creditor*.

This last, however, is not quite correct. Y is a debtor of the X Co. to the amount of the balance appearing in the debit column of his account, but as long as the credits are less than the total debits he does not, strictly speaking, become a creditor. It is more accurate to say that the credits in such a case merely represent the cancellation of a part of the total indebtedness.

Similarly in the case of the account of Z, a merchandise creditor of the X Co., it will be assumed, the amounts in the credit column represent claims which Z has acquired against the X Co., on account of goods furnished "on credit." Any balance in this column represents a current equity, a liability, the amount of Z's creditor position. But charges against the amount of these claims do not make Z a debtor until such charges exceed the original credits. It is more accurate to view such debits as subtractions from the current liability which has been incurred by buying goods and postponing payment.

Much the same analysis can be made in connection with all accounts representing, with respect to a particular business, other persons and businesses. In a sense all corporate equities, all the phases of corporate ownership, represent *creditors*. All individuals and businesses owing anything of value to the enterprise are *debtors*. As just noted, however, this applies essentially to debit *balances* and credit balances, in such cases. The subtractions from asset claims are credits as well as the positive additions to creditors' accounts. Yet these two are not the same thing.

Is there any reason whatsoever why debtors' balances should be set at the left and creditors' balances at the right? Apparently not. The reverse order would seem to suit as well intrinsically. English balance-sheet practice, as noted in an earlier connection, does indeed follow the alternative plan.

The debtor-creditor analysis is of little or no assistance in unraveling the intricacies of double entry because it has such a narrow application. Suppose it be conceded, by a great stretch of the imagination, to apply to all balance-sheet equity accounts and to all asset accounts which represent claims or rights against other business entities. It cannot possibly be said to have any rational application to all the other asset accounts, to the expense and revenue accounts, net revenue headings, and surplus accounts, no matter how ingeniously we employ terms and continually shift our viewpoint. As will be pointed out in a moment, rules of debit and credit are sometimes advanced which appear to say that there is some such application; but it is of course clear that this kind of thing is purely figurative. Cash, plant, merchandise, etc., do not represent debtors of the enterprise. They are assets fully and completely in the possession of the business and in no sense indicate legal claims against individuals or concerns for money or other values.

THE RESPONSIBILITY RULES

By means of a system of personification of accounts, and an especial glorification of the business-enterprise conception, an attempt is sometimes made to apply a modification of the debtor-creditor analysis to the tangible asset accounts. This scheme is made somewhat plausible by the fact that frequently in the large enterprise some officer or employee has charge of each important type of property. The cashier is responsible for cash, the stores clerk for merchandise, the engineer, possibly, for the power plant, etc. Thus it may be urged that whenever an asset account is debited this means that the account, personified, or the employee most closely connected with this asset, has become a debtor of—or indebted to—the business for the amount of the entry. A debit to cash means that responsibility has been conferred upon the cash account, the cash drawer, or the cashier. A value has been entrusted to an imaginary or a real person, as the case may be; hence the debtor relationship and the debit entry.

Similarly, a credit entry in the cash account may be said to indicate the giving up of responsibility. When the cash account is credited this means that the personified cash account, or the cashier, if there is such a person, has acquitted himself of responsibility; he has returned the value with which he was entrusted.

But while it may be one function of the property accounts to register the responsibility of officers and other employees, this function should not be confused with the significance of debit and credit. These terms are applied to the left and right columns of *all* accounts; and the above explanation fails completely if an attempt is made to apply it to the equity accounts, or to the supplementary expense and revenue divisions. A debit entry in a liability or other equity account indicates a reduction in the amount of the particular interest involved; and this, obviously, has nothing to do with the conferring of responsibility upon any person real or imaginary. A credit entry in such an account indicates an increase in the equity involved; but here again no responsibility is given up by any actual or fictitious person. The writers who adopt the "responsibility" scheme as a basis for the explanation of debit and credit usages consequently never get beyond the asset accounts. With respect to the application of debit and credit to other types of accounts they usually offer no rules whatever.

The familiar rule, "debit whatever account receives value and credit whatever account gives up value," represents a modification of this explanation which is still emphasized by many writers. This rule is extremely superficial. At best it involves unreasonable figures of speech; and it can only be used to explain the recording of transactions which consist in asset exchanges. It is difficult to see how either the student or practitioner can make any intelligent use of such a device.

DEBIT AND CREDIT, AND PROPRIETORSHIP

Attempts have been made to explain the modern use of debit and credit in terms of effect upon proprietorship. This type of device should receive brief consideration.

It has been shown in preceding chapters that it is not always possible in the case of the corporate form of organization to make very significant use of the proprietorship concept. But even if it be admitted that the conventional proprietary equity is of fundamental importance in accounting no consistent scheme of debit and credit rules can be worked out from this standpoint. In terms of effect upon the proprietor's position there is no possibility of attaching uniform significance to the expressions, debit and credit. In the case of asset and liability accounts debits (indicating additions to assets and subtractions from liabilities) might be said to represent facts favorable to the proprietor, and credits (indicating subtractions from assets and additions to liabilities) in a sense represent data unfavorable to proprietorship. In the case of the proprietary accounts and supplementary divisions such as the expense and revenue accounts on the other hand, debits indicate unfavorable changes and credits favorable changes. As a matter of fact most of these happenings have no real or direct effect whatever upon proprietorship. The exchange of assets, the incurring of a liability, the retirement of a liability, and the exchange of liabilities are all cases which give rise to no disturbance in the proprietary interest. Just as it is the entries in the cash account which show the changes in the cash balance, so it is the entries in the proprietary accounts—and not in other accounts—that specifically reflect the course of this equity.

An ingenious attempt has been made by C. M. Van Cleave[1] to write the language of debit and credit in terms of all these devices—debtor and creditor relationships, personification and responsibility, and effect upon and relation to proprietorship. This book is interesting primarily as an illustration of the extremes to which one may be carried in attempting to work out a theory of double entry along these lines. After criticizing the view that the "business" in a distinct entity whose financial conditions may be represented by a statement of assets and equities as an illogical position which requires one to face two ways at the same time, the author presents his scheme. It may be stated briefly. First he personifies all the accounts. Then each of these fictitious entities is considered as being in account with the proprietor. All asset accounts stand for persons owing the proprietor; all liability accounts represent persons owed by the proprietor. Various transactions are then explained on this basis. Thus, in the case of a sale, "the proprietor borrows $800 from Merchandise and lends it to Cash; therefore Cash owes the proprietor and the proprietor owes Merchandise." When an expense is incurred "we borrow from Cash and lend it to Expense. Expense owes us and we owe Cash; we debit Expense and credit Cash. The debt which Expense owes us is bad; it represents loss. The debt which we owe Cash is good; it is a liability." In the case of an interest earning, "we borrow from Interest and lend to Cash; Cash owes us and we owe Interest. We debit Cash and credit Interest. The debt which Cash owes us is good; it is an asset. The debt which we owe Interest is bad; it represents gain."

Such explanations are evidently highly fantastic. In addition they are anything but exact, even if the propriety of the various figures used be admitted. A sale, for example, is

---

[1] In *Principles of Double-Entry Bookkeeping*, published by the author in 1913.

certainly not merely a change in the status of merchandise. Further, it may be noted that in order to carry out such a scheme it is necessary to reverse the order of statement in connection with the proprietary account itself. Thus "Cash" is conceived as "in account with the proprietor," while the "Proprietor" is represented as "in account with outside parties." This is certainly a case of "facing both ways."

CONCLUSION

Anyone who endeavors to grasp fully the scheme by which all possible transactions are recorded in a system of parallel-column accounts may safely ignore current rules-of-thumb. Even the bookkeeper might well abandon most of his "rules" and substitute a real understanding of the structure with which he is dealing in terms of the fundamental classes of data to be recorded therein. As has been shown in the preceding pages, there are at least two underlying categories, *properties* and *equities,* and several subsidiary and provisional phases of these classes which must be dealt with by the accountant. The entire record is made in a scheme of two-column accounts. Evidently, then, the meaning of a particular entry depends upon its effect upon the class involved. A left or debit entry thus may indicate several distinct kinds of happenings; it is out of the question to attach a uniform significance to this term. All accounts have left or debit columns. But not all accounts show the same kinds of data. A debit indicates an *addition to an asset* in the case of an asset account. It indicates a *subtraction from an equity* in the case of an equity account. These two happenings are fundamentally distinct; they cannot possibly be made to mean the same thing. How, then, can a debit be always conceived as having a uniform significance such, for example, as the "conferring of responsibility"?

As a matter of fact "debit" has more than two meanings

which the accountant must recognize. Signifying as it does all entries in left columns it covers:

1. Additions to assets.
2. Subtractions from revenue (or additions to expense).
3. Deductions from net revenue and surplus (either as special losses, an operating deficit, or income appropriations).
4. Subtractions from initial equity amounts.

Further, as there are several important groups of assets the first case evidently might be subdivided somewhat. Still further, in so far as the distinction between proprietorship and the liabilities in a narrow sense is viewed as of considerable importance, number (4) evidently includes two significant cases. The point should be emphasized that debit entries indicate two fundamentally distinct classes of facts, and several minor or supplementary divisions. It is accordingly best to think of debit simply as the sign of the left column, a column which covers several types of information since it attaches to several distinct classes of accounts.

Similarly credit entries—meaning all entries in the right columns of all accounts—indicate at least two entirely different kinds of facts, viz.: (1) subtractions from assets, and (2) additions to equities. Accordingly no uniform significance such, for example, as "the giving up of value," can be attached to the term "credit." The meaning of credit depends upon and varies with the character of the transaction. A credit entry in an asset account signifies one thing; in an equity account such an entry means quite another thing. Further, "credit" not only has the two underlying meanings given above but several supplementary meanings as well. Additions to gross revenue, additions to the residual and other equities as a result of new investment, increases in net income or surplus—all these situations require credit entries.

To reiterate, the accounts are built up to record the underlying equation representing the financial status of the business enterprise and to register any changes which may occur therein. The double-entry system consists essentially in a scheme of two parallel columns broken up into sections appropriately headed. The left column is characterized as the "debit" column, the right, as the "credit" column. A debit entry thus signifies any entry in the left column and a credit entry, any entry in the right column. Since there are at least two fundamentally distinct types of accounts the meanings of these terms vary with the type of account involved. "Debit" and "credit" thus become merely conventional signs indicating left and right columns.

PART II

SPECIAL PROBLEMS

CHAPTER XI

NET REVENUE

In previous chapters the nature and treatment of net revenue have been briefly explained. Likewise the importance of this figure in the accounting scheme has been stressed. It will now be necessary, however, to examine the net revenue concept more carefully.

Net revenue is the first significant conclusion drawn by the accountant at the end of the accounting period; and in this figure most of his periodic estimates, judgments, calculations come to a focus. From the accounting standpoint it is the paramount criterion of financial enhancement; it is the gauge or yardstick which measures the success of the business enterprise as an operating economic unit. Further, the theory of accounts developed in Part I is of especial consequence with respect to its bearing upon the definition and treatment of net revenue. This element of the accounting structure is certainly carelessly defined and inadequately emphasized in practice; and this is largely due to unsound theories. Again, the peculiarly difficult problems of accounting, such as the treatment of interest, the significance of goodwill, etc.—some of which problems will be dealt with in succeeding chapters—depend for their solution in part upon the views and interpretations underlying the conception of net revenue. These considerations warrant a further inquiry into this segment of the accounting system.

OPERATING NET REVENUE

Technically, operating net revenue is a *credit* balance, the excess of gross revenue or sales over expense or cost of sales;

and this balance expresses the increase in equities resulting from successful operation. Both members of the fundamental equation are of course expanded as a result of income-producing transactions. In relation to the balance sheet as a whole, accordingly, net revenue may be defined as a measure, from the standpoint of and in terms of the ownership, of the net change in the asset total, due allowance having been made for all investments and retirements. This is the broadest possible conception of net revenue; and, so defined, the net change in balance sheet totals would equal the amount of operating net revenue from a managerial standpoint only in the absence of actual losses and special gains. For the moment we will conceive of operation as being possible without such incidental concomitants.

The factor upon which net revenue intimately depends is *expense*;[1] the definition of the operating balance is closely related to the conceptions controlling the deductions. Hence we must begin with a further examination of expense, the accountant's cost.

As has been emphasized in preceding chapters, the asset division is conceived in this study to embrace all structures, commodities, and services having an economic character which are deemed necessary to successful operation.[2] From the standpoint of the private enterprise, then, the cost of the finished good consists of the amount of asset values which have been utilized in its production. This cost, as it is deducted from revenue, constitutes expense. But it has also been emphasized that the services of ownership itself are not recognized in the accounts as costs because the accounting structure is organized in terms of the needs and purposes of the private interests involved. Hence the "cost" of the business enterprise con-

---

[1] There is relatively little dispute as to the meaning of "gross revenue." See, nevertheless, Chapter XIX.

[2] "Operation" is used here in a broad sense. The production of any commodity or service requires operation. Even the holding company "operates."

sists only in the expiration of valuable goods and services *purchased* by the business and does not include any estimate of the value of services furnished by the various individuals and interests which have invested capital in the enterprise. In other words, expense is cost to the business, not cost to the buyer or consumer.

In this connection the accountant's expense and the economist's cost of production should be sharply contrasted. As has been stressed in preceding pages, the viewpoints of the economist and accountant must be, of necessity, very different. The economist is concerned with economic phenomena from the standpoint of an industrial community, of an entire market situation. He seeks to discover, for example, the laws which govern the determination of market prices, prices which are compounded of a complex of circumstances and conditions as reflected in the attitude of a myriad of buyers and sellers. He endeavors to resolve the economic personnel of the community into its primary functional elements—laborer, manager, capitalist, landlord, etc., disregarding, in large measure, the specific personalities of the business world. The economist, in short, attempts to analyze the fundamental processes of the *entire* economic structure.

The accountant, on the other hand, deals with the business situation on an entirely different level. As was emphasized in Chapter I and elsewhere, the unit of organization in accounting—as far as the field of competitive industry is concerned, at any rate—is the private business enterprise. No accounting procedure has meaning except as a particular business entity is assumed; every transaction, to have significance for the accountant, must be related to the specific enterprise. From the standpoint of the balance sheet, to put it somewhat concretely, it is the function of accounting to register the investment of an owner or group of owners in a particular business situation, and to follow this investment as it takes shape in manifold structures, commodities, services, rights, and conditions. Or, from the point of view of the income sheet, it is the task of the accountant to set up periodic statements of the gross value of the product of the specific business and to allocate thereto the cost of producing each particular quantum of revenue, so that the net change in the situation through a particular period may be stated, and its apportionment indicated.

In other words, to apply this particularly to the matter in hand, while the economist is engaged in a disinterested study of the forces that control prices in the general market, the accountant is endeavoring to show what the particular net income of his particular enterprise is. As a result the economist considers everything as cost which makes up the necessary supply price of goods in the long run, including the necessary rewards of all the factors of production. The accountant, on the other hand, draws a line between the factors of production furnished by the members of the concern and those furnished by outsiders. The rewards of the latter are costs of the enterprise, and the rewards of the former are the income the accountant is undertaking to report.

This contrast has been pointed out many times in this book and elsewhere; yet it requires this additional emphasis. Many of the current controversies concerning accounting procedures seem to arise out of a confusion of economic and accounting concepts and points of view. Accountants often make use of statements of economic principles to justify certain accounting theories, although in many cases the economist is talking about an altogether different situation, or is, at least, considering the situation from quite another angle.

Whether or not this income or net revenue which the accountant is trying to disclose is greater or less in the particular case than the long-run necessary supply price of the services involved, it is not his task, as an accountant, to decide. Undoubtedly net revenue includes in many cases a pure economic surplus or rent as well as a reward for the services of ownership. Nevertheless there is no great impropriety in viewing the net revenue balance as a return to the investors, an addition to equities, arising in large measure out of the value of the conditions and services contributed by the owners, those responsible for the capital of the enterprise.

Indeed, from the standpoint of the buyer—as was noted in Chapter V—the sale transaction constitutes simply an exchange of asset values. The buyer pays $10, for example, for a product which he considers to be worth, to him, that amount. But from the point of view of the selling enterprise the finished product is worth cost in purchased commodities and services utilized in its production, and the difference between this cost and selling price is net revenue, a payment for services and conditions furnished which have never been booked as costs. In other words the accounting scheme, organized from the point of view of managers and investors, is fashioned to disclose business income as a residuum, a difference between expense and sales price, and not as a payment for services rendered, however indubitable their economic significance.

The following diagram may serve for emphasis:

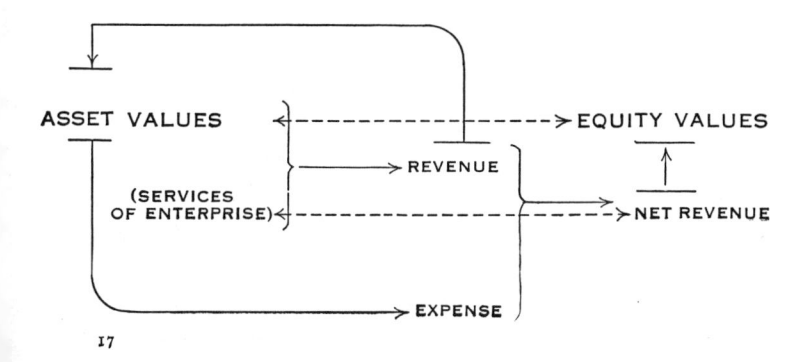

```
          ┌─────────────────────────┐
          ↓                         │
ASSET VALUES  ←───────────┬────────→ EQUITY VALUES
 ─────────                │          ─────────────
                          │               ↑
                ┌────────→ REVENUE         │
   (SERVICES    │                          │
   OF ENTERPRISE)←──────────────┬─ ─ ─ ─ →NET REVENUE
                                │
                                │
          └──────────→ EXPENSE ─┘
```

17

The peculiar services of the enterprise itself, as indicated by the parentheses in the above diagram, are not formally recognized in the accounts. The excess of the value of the product over the amount of asset values consumed constitutes a return for these services, however; and this margin first appears in the asset accounts as a part of the cash or other property received from customers, and in the equity accounts it is initially reflected by the net revenue balance.

If industry were organized in socialistic units, the antithesis between consumer's cost and enterprise expense would not be so clear. If there were no private owners as such in industry, the services of capital might conceivably be acquired by purchase in much the same manner that the private business enterprise now acquires the necessary commodities and labor services. To the socialistic business unit, then, these capital costs would be viewed as necessary operating expenses, and cost and selling price would doubtless be approximately equal.[3]

It may be desirable to carry yet a step further this comparison of economic and accounting conceptions with respect to income. The "net product" of industry from the economist's point of view is the product (or value thereof) available for distribution in a given market, community, industrial or political territory among *all* human agents in production, due allowance having been made for all capital goods expired and natural resources consumed. This net product is commonly conceived as being divided into four main distributive shares: wages, interest, profits, and rent. Evidently the accountant's net revenue is not closely related to any of these elements or to the total. The accountant, to repeat, is engaged in computing the income for a specific business concern. His scheme is organized not from the point of view of all human agents concerned but from that of the individuals and interests having

---

[3] Unless selling prices were arbitrarily advanced to cover the costs of non-productive state operations, or to permit the state to accumulate capital.

consequential property rights. Thus wages do not constitute a characteristic element of net revenue,[4] although all of the other functional shares may be present. Further, if all business enterprises and individuals kept accounts and computed periodic net revenue, a summary of all these income balances would contain much duplication from the standpoint of the community as a whole. A particular company or individual, for example, may receive income in the form of dividends paid by another enterprise. Thus, a particular item of income, from the standpoint of industrial society, may appear in two or more systems of accounts as an item of net revenue.

The conception of net revenue that has been developed here is essentially the managerial, and is especially applicable to the large corporation. The view that net revenue expresses the increase in *all* equities, not that of a particular interest, coincides in the main with the standpoint of the hired manager, a standpoint that is steadily becoming more important in these days of the specialization of the executive function and general emphasis upon efficient management. To the manager the particular manner in which the company is capitalized is a matter entirely outside the determination of operating net income. He looks upon his enterprise as a definite entity or situation into which are poured the funds of various classes of investors. With all the resources at his disposal, however secured and amalgamated beyond all hope of distinguishing the source thereof, he acquires the various structures, commodities, and services to carry on the operations of the business. Net operating revenue is then the excess of values received over purchased assets utilized in connection with product sold, and represents the increase in capital to be apportioned or distributed among all the individuals or interests who have committed cash funds or other property to the undertaking.

---

[4] This may not be true where the owners also furnish important labor services of one kind or another. This matter will be discussed further a little later.

CURRENT LIABILITIES AND NET REVENUE

But can we reasonably insist that net revenue must be literally defined in terms of *all* equities, the entire right-hand side of the balance sheet? Are employees, trade creditors, and others having current claims to be viewed as contributing capital to the business, or are the commodities and services furnished by such interests *purchased* by the enterprise? According to the view that has been adopted here, expense consists in the amount of purchased commodities and services expired, and net revenue constitutes the return to the equities which have furnished the necessary funds. Just where is the line to be drawn between purchased services and equity services? This question will be considered with some care.

The typical business enterprise requires a fairly steady flow of *personal* services in carrying on its operations. The term "labor" is often used as a general designation to cover all such services, and wages and salaries constitute the compensation therefor. In practice, payment for such services, however, is commonly deferred for some time. That is, the service furnished is frequently utilized and its value becomes embodied in raw material or goods in various stages of completion, or even in goods sold, before the actual disbursement to the furnisher. Thus, as was indicated in an earlier chapter, the employee comes to have a bona fide equity in assets; and it might therefore conceivably be urged that his wage is, in whole or in part, a return to this equity rather than an expiration of valuable purchased services, an expense.

The apparent difficulty is not a very serious one, however. Admitting that the laborer, through waiting for his compensation, does carry in some cases a not inconsiderable part of the capital burden of production, and that his compensation hence includes an element of true interest or capital income, it may still be strongly urged that, from the accounting standpoint, transactions with employees—the purchase of personal services—do not give rise to net revenue charges. Labor services, in their entirety, flow specifically into the asset classification and later into expense, cost of sales. No part of the payment therefor need be considered a return to an equity. The employee unquestionably obtains an equity, an equity requiring definite recognition in the balance sheet; but this claim is not an explicitly income-bearing interest.

A distinction must be drawn between an equity which is secured through the *sale* of some specific commodity or service for which payment is not immediately secured, and the right which is conferred upon the individual or interest furnishing capital to the enterprise to be used for a more or less lengthy period, periodic payment for the use thereof meanwhile to be made. The employee sells his service to the enterprise; he does not contribute capital thereto with the understanding that he is to share in the net return. True, as was stated above, he undoubtedly does share the capital burden through waiting for the price of his service, and that price, presumably, is affected by this fact of waiting; but throughout the transaction the value involved is considered to remain unchanged, no fluctuation occurring to indicate either income or loss.

No doubt some slight logical scruples must be ignored in coming to a decision in this case. But it seems eminently sound to conclude that the accountant's net revenue figure does not relate in any significant way to the laborer's equity. As was stated in Chapter I, the cleavage between the owners and employees may some day become less sharp than at present; others than those investing capital in significant amounts may come to share in net earnings; but these possibilities need not seriously disturb our interpretation of the current situation.

If payment for personal services were made in advance —as is the almost universal practice in the case of insurance services—or immediately upon receipt of the service, the employee would have no explicit accounting equity. As it is, the amount of wages and salaries payable at any one date is commonly a relatively small amount. The employee might be said to have a constantly recurring equity, seldom large in amount. Services are furnished; a liability is thereby incurred; the liability is shortly liquidated. And so on.

The same line of reasoning holds in the case of the merchandise creditors. The total of accounts payable because of goods acquired on credit is likely to be a considerable amount in each successive balance sheet; and, as was pointed out in a previous chapter, this means that, although particular bills are shortly paid, the enterprise is virtually securing—continuously —a considerable slice of its capital from the concerns from which it buys goods. That such outstanding balances constitute genuine equities is undeniable. They represent sources of asset values; they constitute liabilities which must be paid. Unquestionably all such equities should receive careful recognition in the accounts and statements. Yet again it may be insisted that the merchandise creditors do not as a rule obtain income from the enterprise to which they ship goods on account; they do not share explicitly in its net revenue. While they carry a part of the capital burden of production without question, and the price of the goods involved doubtless includes an element of true economic interest, their claims do not call for definite income accruals for the use of the funds tied up in the goods furnished, and they have no share in residual profits.

Exceptions to the above statement can be cited. Occasionally merchandise accounts payable draw a stated rate of interest from date of shipment or from a definite date thereafter. There are also cases where the merchandise creditors hold contracts which make them essentially a controlling interest and sharers in net revenue. Still more important in this connection, perhaps, is the fact of cash discounts. Alternative terms of settlement, of course, are very commonly offered in merchandising transactions. If payment is made within ten days a 2 per cent discount from the gross price is sometimes allowed, for example. Undoubtedly there is some justification for viewing such an arrangement as involving not merely a purchase of assets but also an income adjustment. It might be argued that when an account is settled after the discount has lapsed the amount of the discount neglected is a deduction from net revenue in favor of the account-holder, and not a cost of goods and subsequently an expense. However, in view of the fact that the discount rate is commonly far above ordinary contractual income rates and is not viewed in practice as an income rate by either party to the transaction, the current practice of treating these additional payments to the creditor as costs of goods rather than income distributions cannot be severely criticized.

Rent [5] charges and credits require further analysis in this connection. Rent debits represent the cost of using property, the title to which resides in an outside individual or enterprise. Such charges represent the acquisition of a definite service necessary to production and hence constitute initially an asset value and later an expense. This situation is analogous to the purchase and expiration of any asset. Again it must be admitted that the income element is present in a fundamental sense in such transactions, especially if the rent is not prepaid and the lessor is obliged to wait a considerable interval for his compensation; but *net* income does not specifically accrue in favor of the equity so created, and it would be quite fantastic for the accountant to attempt to divide the total rent charge between value of service received or cost and an estimated net return for the use of capital funds. We have here simply another example of an equity which has no share in accounting net revenue.

---

[5] Rent in the sense of "hire," not the economist's "rent."

Similarly, rent credits are not net revenue items. If an enterprise leases a part of its building to outside interests, for example, the revenues accruing in this connection are not net. Rent commonly covers maintenance, depreciation, insurance, and taxes, as well as a net income element. Rent revenue is consequently a gross rather than a net credit.

All other current liabilities that arise as a result of the purchase of commodities and services "on time" may likewise be considered as bearing no significant relation to net revenue. They represent equities, but not income-bearing interests.

Evidently, then, net revenue may be defined essentially from the standpoint of the relatively long-term, capital-furnishing, income-bearing equities. Net revenue measures the increase in these equities, the amount available for apportionment or distribution among the various classes of investors.

The treatment of tax accruals and payments should be again mentioned in this connection. As has already been explained, taxes constitute an anomalous element in the accounting structure. The state secures an enforceable equity without furnishing capital funds and without selling to the enterprise any commodities or services. Consequently the tax levy means essentially confiscation, a loss. Federal income and profits taxes are evidently in nowise a return to an investing equity. Yet by definition such taxes constitute a share in net revenue; and after being assessed the amount of the tax in any case constitutes a preferred current liability until paid. Evidently we are obliged to treat some taxes, at any rate, as net income charges, despite the fact that the government's share in the income has an entirely different basis from that of the investor's equity.

NET REVENUE AND PROPRIETARY PROFIT

The conception of net revenue that has been developed in this book is quite distinct from that of proprietary or residual "net profit." According to our view, expense or cost of sales classification should be restricted to the expirations of purchased structures, commodities, and services, and should not include any interest or other appropriations in favor of contractual or residual equities. Thus a sharp distinction is drawn between distributions of net revenue to equities and costs of gross revenue or expense. But it is precisely at this point that accounting practice is most irrational. In the typical income sheet the line between charges against gross revenue and appropriations of net is very imperfectly indicated. Actual expenses, losses, taxes, interest charges, etc., are commonly thrown together in a single hodgepodge profit and loss statement, which emphasizes, as it stands, but one concluding figure, the profit of the proprietary interest.

This unsatisfactory condition of income-sheet practice can be traced directly to overemphasis of the doctrines of proprietorship. If the entire accounting structure is organized around the proprietary as a pivotal concept, if all accounts and accounting procedures and classifications are constructed and defined solely from the standpoint of proprietorship, a nonclassified income statement is the natural result. From the point of view of the final residual equity there *is* no essential difference between net revenue and gross revenue charges, with the exception of proprietary appropriations. To the common shareholder federal taxes, bond interest, losses, etc., are in exactly the same class as labor and material costs—deductions which must be recognized before his available profit is disclosed. Yet from the operating, managerial standpoint these charges are entirely incongruous and should be carefully divided into at least two main groups.

This matter is of especial importance in the case of the corporation, and hence it will be desirable to center the further consideration of the question around this type of enterprise. As was pointed out in Chapter III, the corporate form of organization, by means of security specialization, makes possible the gathering of capital from various types of investors. An almost endless variety of stocks, bonds, and notes are found in corporate finance. Each company, indeed, discloses a more or less distinctive scheme of capitalization. In this welter of equities, as was stated earlier, proprietorship is commonly considered to be represented by the stockholder's interest. All other equities—bonds, mortgages, notes, etc.—are viewed as liabilities, the claims of creditors. From the standpoint of the stockholder, accordingly, it appears that all distributions to prior equities are deductions which, as far as the determination of his profit is concerned, are in essentially the same class as operating expenses.

But can the corporate accountant accept the view that material cost, for example, is congruous with interest paid to bondholders? Should he organize his income classifications solely from the standpoint of the residual interest or should he base his scheme upon the corporate enterprise as an operating unit? Should the income sheet be constructed exclusively with reference to the buffer equity or in terms of all long-term, income-bearing securities, the corporate investors as a body?

In attempting a decisive answer let us first consider the entries required in the accounts when the different classes of securities are emitted. The X Co., for example, issues additional capital stock for cash to the amount of $25,000. How are the accounts thereby affected? Evidently the effect of the transaction, in summary, would be indicated in the accounts by a charge to the cash account and a credit to the capital stock account. The funds of the corporation are increased; its equities are correspondingly expanded. Similarly if the Company emits additional bonds to the amount of $25,000 for cash the transaction would be reflected by a charge of $25,000 to the cash account and an equal credit to the bonds account. Again resources are enhanced and equities are increased a like amount.

Certainly there is a fundamental similarity between the two transactions. In each case the corporation as an entity enters into a relation with the individual investor. In one case the investor with speculative leanings is appealed to, and capital is secured through a stock issue; in the other case the conservative investor is induced to furnish capital on the basis of a bond issue. In neither instance does the corporation *buy* the services of anyone as it purchases services from the employee and goods from the merchandise creditor. Instead each transaction involves the raising of income-bearing capital. The corporation undertakes to preserve the investment of each class, and to return income for the use of funds to each. In one case the rate is fixed and the risk relatively slight; in the other (if common stock) the return is elastic and the risk of loss more serious. But these are differences in degree and not fundamental distinctions, as was emphasized in earlier statements.

Accordingly, there is no fundamental antithesis between payments to the stockholder (dividends) and return to the bondholder (interest). Both represent distributions of income. By no reasonable line of analysis can the interest paid to the bondholder be classed with operating expense while the return to the stockholder is treated as a distribution of net revenue. To reiterate, expense measures the expiration of purchased items, and the corporation does not buy anything from the bondholder any more than it does from the stockholder. Certainly the stockholder does not purchase the services of the bondholder. The corporate entity intervenes as fully in one case as in the other.[6]

To the extent that bond interest and similar charges are

---

[6] In a sense it may doubtless be said that the corporation buys the use of capital from all investors. From this standpoint, as was noted in a previous chapter, the corporate balance sheet consists of three classes: (1) properties, (2) corporate owner, and (3) sources of funds or equities. For convenience the accountant expresses the fact of the business entity in the heading of the balance sheet, thus, "The X Co., Statement of Financial Conditions, Dec. 31, 1921," and juxtaposes assets and equities. This represents, clearly, a very reasonable interpretation of the situation. The services of the investor are not purchased; but the joint funds of all classes are used to buy the necessary assets.

treated as corporate expenses it is evident that expense and operating net revenue are dependent upon the particular scheme of financing which has been adopted. But it ought to be obvious that the method of capitalization cannot reasonably alter the cost of product. The distribution of investment among different classes of securities is a fact entirely outside of production and expense. The operating management is not interested in capitalization and is often not responsible therefor in any way. A change in capitalization does not affect costs of labor, material, etc. If the accounts are to be used as a criterion of and a guide to the management, it is surely evident that all distributions to the equities, contractual or otherwise, must be excluded from gross revenue charges.

In comparing the results of different periods and in scrutinizing the operating figures of various plants and enterprises, mere method of capitalization must be ignored if entirely irrational conclusions are to be avoided. This may be emphasized by an illustration. Suppose that two enterprises, A and B, are organized at the same time to operate in identical lines. Each company, it will be assumed, starts with a capital of $5,000,000 and each has exactly the same opportunities for success as the other. But in the case of A all funds are secured through stock issues while B issues $2,000,000 in bonds carrying a 6 per cent rate of return. If in this situation the doctrine that interest charges are an operating expense be accepted we are forced to the ridiculous conclusion that the expense of B each year exceeds that of enterprise A by $120,000. An illustration of the way in which a reduction in contractual capital during a particular period would likewise alter expense—if interest were rated as an expense—was given in Chapter VI.

This point of view has long been recognized in corporate finance but has been very imperfectly applied to accounting practice, and has scarcely penetrated at all the pall surrounding the theory of accounts. The classifications of the Interstate

Commerce Commission, which perhaps show the furthest development in this direction, do treat interest charges as deductions from "income" rather than "revenue." But rents and some other true expenses are unfortunately brought into the same division. In other words the Commission seems to be emphasizing primarily the distinction between "operating" and "non-operating" charges in a technical sense, rather than the line dividing true expense and distributions of income to equities.

The following outline of income-sheet headings may serve to emphasize the above discussion. This exhibit begins with the operating net revenue balance, the schedules of expense and revenue accounts being omitted. It is not intended to suggest that this arrangement is entirely satisfactory for every case. The peculiarities of each situation obviously demand variations in procedure. Except for the fact of income taxation, preferred stock dividends might better be deducted immediately after interest charges. Further, according to legal priority, taxes should be placed before any interest charges; but since interest accruals are an "allowable deduction" the arrangement as given is more convenient. There are other doubtful points and imperfections in this suggestion; but it is believed that it indicates the way to a marked improvement over the typical schemes now followed in practice.

NET REVENUE DIVISION, INCOME SHEET OF X CO., DEC. 31, 19—
OPERATING NET REVENUE............................ $......
   Interest Earned................................. ... $......
   Fire Loss....................................... ....
NET REVENUE TO ALL EQUITIES, Before Deducting Taxes........ $......
   Interest on Mortgage Bonds...................... $ ....
   Interest on Debentures.......................... ....
   Interest on Notes............................... ....
                                                                        $......
   Federal Income and Profits Taxes........................... .....
                                                                         $......
   Preferred Dividends....................................... .....

Net Balance for Common Stock.............................	$.....	
Common Dividends...	.....	
Undivided Profits..	$....	
Surplus Balance, Jan. 1, 19—...................................	.....	
	$.....	
Reserve for Contingencies...................................	....	
Total Unappropriated Surplus, Dec. 31, 19—.................	$.....	

    The above conclusions with reference to the treatment of interest charges do not, of course, apply with equal force to the sole-proprietorship and partnership. In such cases, as has already been admitted, the doctrines of proprietorship have considerable force. Net return to the "proprietor" is often the only significant income figure in the unincorporated business. Interest charges are likely to be small in amount and relate largely to current liabilities. To include interest with operating expenses in such cases, evidently, is not seriously unreasonable as a practical matter. On the other hand, if there are any important long-term, income-bearing equities other than the proprietary in a particular case, the net revenue division as developed above should be recognized.

    To deny that explicit interest in the particular business is an expense is not inconsistent with the view that interest in the fundamental sense of a price for the use of capital is an economic cost of production in the industrial community. As was emphasized in a preceding section of this chapter, prices as a rule must be sufficiently high to cover the necessary competitive return to capital as well as all the expenses of the enterprise. Interest is unquestionably a price-determining factor and constitutes an element in the "normal price" which the producer must, in the long run, obtain. But in the particular enterprise, to repeat, the accountant is endeavoring to disclose all income elements as a residuum, a difference between revenue and expense. Interest on capital is here not an expense but simply one element in the margin which represents the return to all equities. Accounting attempts to present this margin not as a cost but as a difference, a balance, in which is found not only interest but profits and vestiges of other functional income elements.

In this connection the controversy with respect to the inclusion or exclusion of "interest on investment" in manufacturing cost should be referred to. For some years certain teachers and professional accountants have been advocating vigorously the affirmative of the proposition and the negative has been upheld quite as strongly by others. It is not intended to discuss here the details of this problem, long since worn threadbare by disputation. It may be well, however, to indicate its relation to the matter in hand. In the first place the view that interest on all investment, whether actually accruing by contract or not, should be included in the accounts as a cost, undoubtedly derives considerable encouragement from the theory that all explicit interest charges constitute expense, and is certainly not supported by the analysis of net revenue here developed. On the other hand it should be admitted that an estimated interest charge might be included in the factory accounts without disturbing the ultimate integrity of operating net revenue, provided some final revenue account were credited for the same amount. The propriety of any such procedure can be criticized on other grounds, however, as will be shown in the following sections.

Unquestionably interest, both explicit and estimated, must be taken into consideration in the solution of certain managerial problems. The manager is called upon to make an efficient use of all assets purchased by the enterprise, and this means that the administration of capital itself is in his hands. In securing productive efficiency, comparisons between employees, machines, departments, plants, processes, products, and periods, are necessary. And a comparison of alternative methods involving different amounts of capital cannot well be made without recognizing the interest element. But it does not appear at all clear that such calculations require, or are facilitated by, specific charges to cost accounts covering estimated interest. The fact that capital should yield a return wherever used can be recognized by the manager without the introduction of fictitious charges to expense.

The proponents of the doctrine that estimated interest is an expense, it may be noted finally, have made little headway in securing the adoption of this view in practice. The American Institute of Accountants has always refused to endorse the theory; the accounting profession in general has not adhered to it; and the Bureau of Internal Revenue, in its regulations with respect to the valuation of inventories for tax purposes, specifically excludes interest on investment as an element of cost. The practical difficulties involved in estimating interest (e.g., the determination of the amount of capital to be included in any case and the selection of a rate) have no doubt weighed most heavily in the establishing of this attitude, but the theoretic objections to the doctrine are clear-cut and convincing.

PROPRIETARY SALARIES

As has already been suggested, the function undertaken by the owners or investors in a typical business includes several important elements. In all cases it involves the furnishing of capital, with the attendant risks; in all cases it involves a certain amount of responsibility and final control with respect to financial policies and the direction of production; in many instances it also covers the furnishing of managerial and ordinary labor services. These various phases of the owner's function are measurably distinct from the standpoint of economic theory, but in actual practice they are often more or less inextricably tied together. Even the distinction between capital services and personal services is a little hard to draw in some cases. The principal owner of a large business, for example, may take no part whatever in the immediate management; he may furnish no ordinary labor services; and yet his function may be much more complex than that of simply furnishing funds. He may decide certain residual but important questions of policy; his personal reputation may be a large factor in attracting business; his personal "credit" may be important in securing the funds necessary to initiate and carry on the venture. All these are conditions bearing intimately upon business success; and the income paid the owner in such a case may be said to cover remuneration for these services as well as a return on the capital invested *per se*.

The underlying economic significance of net revenue, then, varies between enterprises according to the nature of the owner's function. At one extreme is the minority stockholder who furnishes funds but no personal services beyond filling out a proxy for the annual meeting. At the other extreme stands the proprietor of a small retail establishment who works from ten to twelve hours per day at his business, thus not only carrying the burden of general management but furnishing a large part of the necessary labor services as well. Net income in the first case is largely interest and profits on capital invested; in the second case it includes an important element of wages.

In this situation the question arises, should not a fair allowance for the personal services of the owners be charged to operating expense? If the accounts are to be of the utmost service to all concerned should not the income figure be restricted to a return for capital services, the reward for personal services being excluded? As this question is of especial importance in the case of the unincorporated business attention will first be directed to the significance and treatment of owners' salary allowances in the sole-proprietorship and partnership.

How shall the accountant conceive of the operation of the unincorporated business? Evidently, since the partners or proprietor commonly represent the lion's share of the income-bearing equities in such cases, he must read the situation largely through the eyes of the principal proprietors, from the standpoint of the owners. The owners invest their funds in a variety of structures, commodities, and services. The combination of these with their own efforts results in a salable product. The cost of producing this product, *to the owners,* is the expiration of *purchased* items. This is their *expense.* The deduction of this amount from gross revenue leaves the net operating income. If there are no consequential preferred equities this is likewise essentially the net return to the proprietors.

According to this view no allowances for owners' services should be charged to operating expense. The owner does not purchase his own personal efforts any more than he does his capital services. He contributes to the success of his business capital, managerial skill, labor, etc. Consequently his return is an amalgam of various economic elements. But no part of his return is a cost to him, a payment for something which he has purchased to carry on operations. The value of the owner's personal services may be rated, of course, as a part of the economist's "cost of production." But so are the interest and profits elements, at least in the marginal instance. As has been emphasized above, price-determining cost and specific business expense are quite distinct.

In sole-proprietorships and partnerships, in other words, where the point of view of the accountant must be essentially identical with that of the principal owners, the charging to expense of an estimated allowance for the personal service of the owners amounts to the transfer of an item of net earnings to the expense classification. If a concurrent credit is made to some nominal revenue account, as has been sometimes advised, the final effect upon the net income figure is nil, and the whole procedure is thereby shown to be entirely fictitious. If the owner's personal or capital account is credited with the amount of the salary charge, on the other hand, this means that an item of income has been transferred bodily from gross revenue to capital without having been shown anywhere as income—a most questionable procedure.

But, it may be argued, is this not inconsistent with the thesis that the accountant must construct his classifications in terms of the managerial, business-entity point of view? The writer does not believe so. An emphasis upon the conception of the business enterprise as the accounting unit need not lead to a blind, unreasonable glorification of this idea. As was indicated in Chapter III, the organization of accounts and procedures in the unincorporated business from the point of view of the partners or the sole-proprietor in their business capacities is essentially consistent with the managerial standpoint. The assumption of a business enterprise in such cases is largely one of convenience; there is no legal entity. To insist that the Jones' grocery business buys the services of Jones, the proprietor, is quite fantastic. Nothing of the kind occurs; and it is the business of the accountant to record the facts of the actual business process, not a lot of purely imaginary transactions.

Instead of clarifying the situation for the owner the charging of an estimated salary allowance to expense is quite likely to mislead him. He wishes to know in the first place what has been the result of his business activities, the net return for his efforts and capital. He is bound to be quite aware of the extent of his personal services. If he works in his store from morning till night he requires no fictitious accounting charge to inform him of the fact. If the net earnings of his business do not yield a reasonable rate on his investment and decent wages for his work the fact will be quite apparent without the use of a special ledger account. Indeed, as was indicated above, if expenses are padded with a "fair allowance" (whatever that may be) for the owner's personal services, he is quite likely to misinterpret the situation completely and imagine that the business is less successful than it really is.

This does not mean that the business man should attempt no analysis of net revenue. Quite the contrary. But the figure from which all such analysis should start should be the true, actual net income. This net result may then be divided up in various ways, if this seems expedient. An owner with a net income of $10,000, for example, might reason about it as follows: "Let's see, if I had put my capital in the savings bank and had taken that job with the Blank people I would have made $7,000; evidently, then, I am ahead $3,000 as a result of staying where I am besides being independent. On the other hand if I had put my money into U. S. Steel preferred and taken the job I would have made $8,000 and wouldn't have had to worry so much and work so hard." And so on. Evidently there may be any number of hypothetical situations the owner may wish to compare with the actual in coming to a decision as to the direction of his further efforts. But it is the business of the accountant to report the actual, not the purely hypothetical. Hence he should not calculate expenses on the basis of the assumption that the owner is working for himself at some estimated salary.

An accounting apportionment of net revenue into its important economic elements would not be unreasonable, of course, if there were anything to be gained by it. This might be done by charging actual net revenue successively, and crediting the principal equity accounts (if there were no withdrawals) with amounts for salaries, interest, and pure profits. This would focus attention upon the question as to whether or not the business were paying more or less than a mere wage, for example. Thus the proprietor often says that he is "not making anything," when he simply means that the business is not yielding what he considers to be a reasonable return. And an apportionment of net revenue by the accountant would stress such a fact.

In some cases, true, the owner decides actually to draw a certain sum regularly from the business as a "salary." But this procedure does no more force the conclusion that the salary is a true expense than does the mere estimating of such an allowance. Obviously if the salary is sufficiently handsome all actual income and more may be so drawn. If there were no net earnings in a particular case the "salary" would evidently be drawn from capital. A drawn proprietary salary is not an expense. An expense can only arise as a result of the expiration of purchased structures, commodities, and services; and when the proprietor draws money from the till there is no such expiration.

The proper way to account for a drawn salary—if it is desired to focus attention upon the amount—is to charge first a proprietor-salary account and credit cash. Later, the proprietor-salary account should be credited and the amount charged either to a current or a capital equity account. In no case should such a salary account be closed against operating revenue. A similar procedure would be possible if it were desired to introduce a purely hypothetical salary allowance into the accounts; but in such a case the concurrent credit entry in the first instance would be lodged in the owner's drawing or capital account.

It should be admitted that certain doubtful cases arise in partnership accounting. If one partner, for example, is much more "active" than the other, or contributes peculiarly valuable services, some adjustment is obviously necessary to preserve equity between the two. A favorite scheme for dealing with such situations is to allow a "salary" to the active partner or, if both draw regularly, to proportion drawings to the estimated values of services rendered. Are such salaries, or such an excess salary, properly chargeable to operating expense? It is hard to come to a decision in this case. This is one illustration of the fact that every principle of accounting, however substantial, is at some point confronted with a situation to which the application is not quite clear. The writer believes that, on the whole, it is more rational to treat all partners' salaries as adjustments of net revenue between partners rather than as operating expense. In this way the conclusion that the partnership is buying the services of a partner is avoided. On the other hand the partnership to some extent actually exhibits a business enterprise condition more or less independent of the person of the individual partner. Especially is this true in the case of the large partnership with several members. Some further light will be thrown on this matter in Chapter XV.

In the case of the corporation our conclusion on this question must be somewhat altered. A corporation is a legal entity, and the investor who is also an employee of the company may be viewed, in this capacity, as a distinct outsider. Further, in the case of the large corporation at any rate most of the necessary personal services are furnished by persons who are not investors, except perhaps in a small way. Even the managerial staff of the big company is often composed largely of people who are no more than minor stockholders, if that. In other words, in the open corporation the investor furnishes capital but little in the way of personal services. Such services as he does furnish are actually *purchased* by the corporation as from one who furnishes no funds whatever. Consequently payments to corporate investors for personal services may legitimately be charged to expense. The net revenue of such an enterprise naturally includes little in the way of compensation for personal services.

Again we find doubtful cases, however, in the close corporation. It must be remembered that the "open" company— the large enterprise in which control is vested in hundreds or thousands of scattered stockholders and in which the general officers and other managers are engaged by the directors by a process of arm's-length bargaining—is hardly the most common case. A great many corporations are simply incorporated partnerships. Many are family affairs, in which three or four relatives own all or at least a controlling interest in the capital stock. Not infrequently we meet the essentially one-man company, with a single individual holding from 50 to nearly 100 per cent of the outstanding shares. And it may be added that even among the larger companies actual control sometimes resides in a small coterie of stockholders, from among whom are likely to be selected the general officers and perhaps certain other important employees.

Evidently, in such cases, salaries, so-called, may be really distributions of net revenue in disguise. Wherever a corporate officer or other employee is in a position, through his control of the company, to dictate the amount of his "salary," the transaction requires careful scrutiny if its true essence is to be disclosed. This question will be further considered in Chapter XV.

The relation of federal taxation to this matter should be noted here. Undoubtedly the income and profits taxes have encouraged business men to include as liberal salaries as possible in "allowable deductions." It should be emphasized, however, that since there are at present no such taxes levied upon the partnership or sole-proprietorship as business entities there is in the fact of taxation no practical reason whatever for the inclusion of estimated proprietary salaries in expense in the unincorporated enterprise. It is only in the case of the corporation that there is now any possibility of reducing taxes by increasing investors' salaries.

PROPRIETARY INTEREST AND RENT

Precisely the same line of argument as the above may be advanced against the inclusion in expense of estimated interest on investment and rent of assets owned. Indeed the case is here even clearer. To include an element of capital return in expense is still more irrational than to include an estimated remuneration for personal services. It is surely hard to see any justification for some of the proposals which have been made with respect to interest and rent. The business man is often advised to charge to expense an allowance for "interest on capital owned" and "rent of building owned." This is the height of questionable accounting. In the first place such a procedure involves an entanglement of actual and imaginary transactions, and is open to all the objections which have been advanced above with respect to the recognition of proprietary salaries. Second, it is likely to lead to sheer duplication. Manifestly the value of a building or other asset constitutes a part of the "capital owned." Further, maintenance, depreciation, insurance, etc., the *actual* costs incurred in connection with the use of any building, and which are bound to appear in the accounts, will be duplicated by the imaginary rent charge.[7] The result is a thoroughly unreasonable padding of expense charges by means of non-existent items. And even if these charges are offset, as they must be, by equally fictitious revenue allowances, the procedure has no real justification. An accounting practice which disturbs the integrity of one of the important interior divisions, such as gross revenue or expense, even though it does not distort the final net figure or the balance sheet, is thoroughly vicious.

But, it may be argued, admitting that the introduction of a fictitious rent charge—which duplicates under another heading certain actual expenses—is unsound, is it not important to include a fair rate of interest for the use of capital involved in order that the management may know what true costs are so that proper prices may be set and managerial efficiency promoted? This brings us back to the old question of the pro-

---

[7] This duplication may of course be avoided in a measure by deducting the value of real estate from the investment on which interest is figured, and by charging maintenance, depreciation, etc.—the *actual* costs arising in connection with buildings—to the fictitious revenue account which is used to offset the imaginary expense charges.

priety of treating interest on investment as a cost. The question has already been answered on a logical basis in the foregoing discussion of salaries. With respect to price-fixing the writer holds to the familiar view that in most lines price determination in the long run is a matter of market processes, processes which give little heed to the expense of the particular enterprise. The specific enterprise holds no guaranty of any rate of interest on its investment. The proof of the pudding is in the eating. If all goes well sales will exceed expenses by a goodly margin. If circumstances are unfavorable, on the other hand, the operating sheet may show even a debit balance. The inclusion of an arbitrary capital return in cost will advantage the merchant not at all. He will get all he can in any case, and will naturally be pleased if his accounts show a good return.

Even if price-fixing were a matter of specific business expense plus the business man's idea as to what his return should be—a wild assumption—it would still be hard to see how any part of this return could reasonably be included in expense or cost. Prices could certainly be fixed very nicely by the addition of the proper margin without the introduction of fictitious debits and credits in the accounts. And the use of estimated interest as a cost would inflate inventories and result in other technical difficulties which could just as well be avoided.

However, it is not intended to discuss this matter at all exhaustively. Enough has been said to indicate the principal objections. The introduction of estimated interest charges into the cost of manufacturing or trading is not a common practice and is not likely to become popular. In contract work, where cost no doubt plays a part in the fixing of specific bids, interest and other elements of income must, of course, be reckoned. There may even be cases where the accountant can with advantage make use of explicit entries in the ledger covering hypothetical interest adjustments. But in general the case against the practice seems clear.

In conclusion it may be reiterated that the character of net revenue varies with the functions performed by the owners or investors. In virtually all cases it may be said to include some compensation for personal services as well as a return to capital. In general, however, it is not the business of the accountant to attempt to impute to each fundamental functional factor its share in net income; and in no case should any part of the return to the owners or investors, however realized, be charged to expense. Padding of expense with hypothetical allowances for proprietary salaries, interest, etc., is thoroughly illogical accounting and on the whole unfortunate from the practical standpoint. The accountant should confine himself to the task of reporting the actual net revenue resulting from the transactions and processes of the particular period, a task sufficiently difficult without the introduction of unnecessary and unreasonable complications.

CHAPTER XII

INCOME PRIOR TO OPERATION[1]

It is now desired to apply the line of reasoning followed in the preceding chapter to a special problem. What is the significance to the accountant of the "interest" actually accruing, or which might be assumed to be accruing, during the period of organization and construction? To what extent and in what manner should income on investment prior to the operating period be recognized?

It is of course a familiar fact that to promote the large-scale enterprise, obtain the necessary capital, build the plant, acquire raw materials and supplies, organize personnel, etc., is an undertaking requiring considerable time. In the case of a large public utility or railway enterprise several years may elapse between the time the project is initiated and the date upon which operation really begins. The question then arises, should not interest for the use of capital during this preliminary interval, whether actual disbursements are made or not, be taken into the property account in some fashion? In the case of the public utilities the affirmative side of this proposition has received strong support; and some authorities appear to be inclined to defend this position for industry in general. The more conservative view that only interest actually accruing or disbursed by contract should be included in the cost of properties is also common.

This is one of the most difficult questions in the field of accounting analysis. It is indeed hard to come to a definite

---

[1] Adapted in part from "Interest During Construction," *Journal of Political Economy*, vol. XXVIII, pp. 680-695.

conclusion as to how the accountant should view this matter. It would seem that at the least he should be fully alive to the consequences and implications of his decision. The problem need not be settled in an arbitrary manner; it should be possible to relate it to underlying points of view and reach a solution which is thoroughly consistent with the standpoint that is adopted. In this chapter, to repeat, the writer wishes to examine this question carefully in the light of the principles stated and positions taken in the preceding pages.

IN THE UNINCORPORATED COMPETITIVE ENTERPRISE

In endeavoring to answer this question attention will first be directed to a simple illustration of the typical, unincorporated, competitive business. Suppose, for example, that X decides to start in business as a manufacturer. He has a capital of $100,000 which he places on deposit in a commercial, non-interest-bearing account. As funds are needed for organization, building, and other operations, he draws upon this account. At the end of a year, it may be assumed, the plant is completed, machinery has been installed, materials are in stock, operatives have been engaged, managerial organization has been perfected, and X is ready to begin manufacturing. During the year, however, not a wheel has turned; there have been no sales; no income in the ordinary sense has been realized. Expressed literally the situation is summed up in the statement that X has invested during the year $100,000 in a business undertaking, and is finally in a position to begin production.

The sharp distinction here assumed between the construction and operating periods, it should be remarked, does not always, perhaps not often, hold good in practice. In the building of a railway line, for example, certain units of the road are likely to be turned over to operation before the entire property

INCOME PRIOR TO OPERATION 285

is completed. Further, some revenue may be earned by trains which are primarily engaged in construction work. Similarly, construction period and operating period may overlap somewhat in the case of a manufacturing or mercantile company. In the very large corporation, construction—in the sense of addition, extension, etc.—is likely to be more or less steadily in progress for an indefinite period. And even in the case of the single plant there may be no hard and fast line dividing the preliminary work from operation; thus operations are often started in the new factory before construction is fully completed.

But, it may be argued—to return to the illustration—the finished plant with all the attendant conditions is now actually worth more than the $100,000 invested. X has had these funds tied up for the year;[2] and if he were to dispose of the completed property he would normally expect more, and would probably receive more, than $100,000 therefor. He has borne the burden of management, risk, and waiting for a year, and would not now relinquish the enterprise for the bare amount of his investment. In other words, it might be urged, an interest on the investment has accrued, and the value of the plant and all that goes with it is enhanced by the amount of such accrual.

However, even if the truth of this statement be admitted, does it follow that this supposed accrual should now be recognized on X's books of account? Let us assume for the moment that an affirmative answer is correct, and note the effect of the entries which would be required. The value of the completed property, it will be supposed, is enhanced as a result of the use of these funds for a year by $6,000, interest on $100,000 for one year at 6 per cent. To recognize this accrual it would be necessary to charge the factory account (or some special asset

---

[2] For convenience the probability that these funds, in practice, would be gradually invested is ignored in the illustration.

account) with the amount of $6,000 and credit X's capital account (or a special supplementary equity account) with the same amount.

What is the effect of this procedure upon X's balance sheet? Evidently his assets are increased by $6,000 and the amount of his ownership or capital is expanded by a like amount. Properties have apparently been augmented without any accompanying reductions, and the owner's equity is therefore enhanced correspondingly. But this is exactly the same effect as follows successful operation. Asset values have increased; no liabilities are incurred thereby; the owner has invested no further funds; therefore income has accrued.

But what was said in the preceding chapter and elsewhere concerning the unit with which the accountant deals should now be recalled. We have here not the general economic situation but X's particular investment and business. Doubtless interest in general is required for the use of capital. Interest as a cost of capital is a price-determining element. But can this lead the accountant to conclude that in the case in hand there has been a genuine, explicit increase in the assets of the X manufacturing enterprise because considerable capital has been in use during the construction period? If it be insisted that there has, is this not taking the position that each and every specific investment in the business world *inevitably* increases with the lapse of time? This proposition could not, of course, be maintained. While investments frequently may so increase as a result of successful operation or definite contract, there is no guaranty that any specific investment will even remain intact. Actual losses of investment are unpleasantly common. Success or failure depends upon the concrete circumstances of each case. Money invested in business is not money invested in the savings bank. Certainly if X were to continue in business year after year and be unsuccessful with respect to operation he would not be justified in complacently assuming that interest was steadily accruing on his investment because of the burdens of risk and waiting which he was carrying. And this is as true of the construction as of the operating period. It is sometimes assumed that a business cannot start operations with a deficit; in other words, that all charges prior to operation must be to asset accounts. This position is not sound. There is nothing about the preliminary period which renders a particular group of assets, a particular mass of funds, inviolate. Illegitimate expenditures, inefficiency, or accident in construction may cause large losses prior to operation.

But even assuming that there were no losses during construction and that successful operation were assured—a postulate not supported by actualities—should the assets be definitely written up by the amount of an estimated interest accrual? There is good reason for an answer in the negative. The recognition of such an accrual would have the effect of increasing the apparent amount of the investment and consequently of lowering the *rate* of the return realized in the later years of successful operation. Is this reasonable from the owner's standpoint? Is not the preliminary period literally a lean year, for which X expects compensation in the form of a relatively high rate of return in later periods? A genuine economic cost from the standpoint of the buying community may, of course, be involved; but this fact alone would not justify the accountant in capitalizing the preliminary services of the owner as a furnisher of capital on the owner's own books. X does not furnish the use of capital to himself. Rather he invests a certain sum in purchased commodities and services. His service as a capitalist consists in doing just this and is not in itself a part of his investment. He naturally wishes his books to register his investment as it takes shape in purchased items, not this amount plus an estimated allowance for the function he is thereby performing.

Thus far in the illustration it has been assumed that no withdrawals were made by X, the owner, during the construction period. Let us now alter the case by supposing that X drew $6,000 (assuming for the moment that this is a fair return on his capital for the year) at the end of the year. What effect would this have upon his balance sheet? According to the view here adopted this is purely a withdrawal of capital from the standpoint of X's accounts and not a payment for the use of his capital during the construction period. The transaction would be recorded, then, by a charge of $6,000 to X's capital account and a similar credit to the cash account.

If, however, it be admitted that interest for the use of capital during construction should be recognized as an addition to the value of property, we should be obliged to conclude that a drawing by the owner not exceeding a reasonable rate of return did not diminish the amount of the initial investment. This view would mean, in the hypothetical case in hand, that X's investment in the business remained at $100,000 notwithstanding this withdrawal of $6,000; and the transaction would accordingly be booked by a credit to the cash account and a concurrent charge to some *property* account.

But the above argument against the recognition of a property value of more than $100,000 in the case where no drawings from original funds were made by the owner during the preliminary period would hold with equal force in favor of the proposition that the return of $6,000 to X would reduce the amount of the actual investment in the business to $94,000. In any case it is the net investment which should finally appear in the asset accounts, the amount which is actually invested in labor, materials, etc.

ACTUAL COST VERSUS SELLING VALUE

If estimated interest during construction is to be accrued as a concrete accounting fact, what rate should be used? In the above illustration, for example, X might have left his money in the savings bank drawing possibly 3 per cent; he might have invested in substantial securities yielding 7 per cent; or he might, perhaps, have taken a "flyer" in speculative stocks and made (or lost) 50 per cent or more. Almost an endless number of alternatives face the man with funds. What is the effective rate involved in view of his decision to embark in a manufacturing business on his own account? Evidently the only rate which can have any reality or meaning is the one implicit in the "market" price of completed establishments of this type. This could only be determined by the securing of bona fide bids for the finished plant. In the absence of abnormal conditions figures could doubtless be obtained in this way indicating the "true" value of the property and, if this were above cost, the amount and rate of enhancement. In case such a value were below cost this would be concrete evidence that no interest had accrued from any standpoint.

This brings us to another aspect of the question. As was admitted above, the completed plant and all attaching appurtenances and conditions (assuming these can be transferred) would normally sell for more than $100,000—the bare cash investment of X—to another manufacturer who wished to begin operations directly without going through the process of organization and construction. But such selling value would probably be $115,000 or more, rather than $106,000. In other words, the selling value would tend to exceed cost by the market value of *all* the services, functions, and burdens furnished and assumed by the original organizer and builder, X. Pure interest, profits, wages, and other elements would be involved. If this were a normal price-determining instance the selling value might be said to cover just the amount of the investment plus the market rate of interest and the effective values of other capital and managerial services performed. If this were a supramarginal case—i.e., if because of special efficiency or other circumstances the cost of construction had been peculiarly low—the selling price would include an especially high rate of enhancement. Similarly, the inefficient constructor would realize a low rate of return.

Indeed, it should be emphasized that there is no assurance in the specific situation that the selling value of a new property or enterprise will be even equivalent to the amount of the actual investment. In addition to the possibility of inefficiency or accident, with accompanying high costs, there are innumerable other possible circumstances which may make it out of the question to dispose of the new plant on a profitable basis. In short, the selling price of a new property may be above or below actual cost, depending upon the particular conditions surrounding each case.

At all events any *effective* value enhancement is a matter of possible selling price; and, as has just been indicated, the difference between actual investment and selling value is not merely the amount of a normal interest accrual. If, then, any charge should be made to property on account of the services furnished by the owner during the construction period, it would seem that the amount thereof should be based upon probable selling value. But this would be inconsistent with an essential feature of the scheme of modern accounting. In the main the accounting structure is organized in such a way as to disclose the return to the owners or investors as a balance or residuum, a difference between cost and selling price. This means that in general the buying market and not the selling market is the effective basis for accounting charges. As between enterprises, accordingly, the very same article, physically, will appear in accounts at different values. This gives in some cases an apparent violation of the law of single price but is, nevertheless, an entirely rational situation from the accountant's standpoint. B, for example, buys materials, labor services, etc., and manufactures a linotype machine. Value on *his* books is not probable selling price but cost. But C, a publisher, who buys the machine from B, values it initially at selling price to B, which is, nevertheless, cost to C.

In other words, finished goods in the balance sheet of the producer are commonly valued at cost (a possible adjustment of original cost figures to cost of replacement or effective cost not being thereby precluded), and on the books of the buyer these same goods are charged to the appropriate accounts at this cost plus income to the seller (which includes interest and all other elements of net revenue), if there is any such income involved, plus transportation, handling, and installation charges. The economic character of the article may, of course, be assumed to have undergone a change as a result of the transfer with respect to ownership and location, but the physical character of the article may be altered by such transfer very little if at all.

The still more striking case of variation in accounting values between enterprises is discovered when we compare the accounts of different producers in *the same line*. Suppose, for example, that D is a competitor of B's, being likewise engaged in fabricating linotype machines. It is exceedingly unlikely that costs will be identical in the two cases. Variations in labor and material costs, differences in general efficiency—these and other circumstances are bound to give rise to a diversity of total costs per unit. Yet, in the absence of very striking evidence as to its unreasonableness, the accountant is very strongly disinclined to abandon the specific cost in favor of some other basis of value.

In certain special cases, it should be noted, inventories based upon selling prices are approved by the accountant. Where goods are being produced to order and a binding contract covers the transaction, and where the process of production covers more than a single period or season, accounting values exceeding cost are sometimes recognized.[3] In general, however, no rule of accounting is more strongly supported than that which denies the validity of selling price as a proper basis for the valuation of materials, work in process, finished stock, or other assets.

Now should not the question of the proper treatment of income during construction be settled in accordance with this point of view? The difference between the manufacture of an intricate machine on the one hand and the organization of a business and the construction of a plant on the other is one only of degree in size and complexity. If property charges should not be based upon selling prices in one case, is it not reasonable to hold that the same principle applies to the other? This will, of course, give rise to discrepancies with respect to capital values between enterprises in like physical circumstances, discrepancies entirely rational from the accounting standpoint, however, as has been indicated above. X builds and equips his own factory at an actual cost to him of $100,000. Then the amount of $100,000 is the correct property charge. Y buys a duplicate plant and accessories from a construction company for $120,000. Actual cost to the ultimate owner is again the proper basis for the entries. From the standpoint of the general market situation both establishments doubtless have the same economic significance, but from the accounting standpoint X has assets of $100,000, Y of $120,000. X has invested in raw materials, labor, etc. Y has purchased these same elements, indirectly, and the services of the construction company as well.

If operation is equally successful in both cases, the *rate* of return subsequently realized by X will, of course, be somewhat higher than the rate earned by Y. But this is precisely what the accounts should show. The true situation would be obscured rather than illuminated if a sufficient amount were

---
[3] This matter will be dealt with somewhat further in Chapter XIX.

added to capital in the case of X to equalize the rate of income for both enterprises. It cannot be stated too emphatically that any accounting policy which tends to eliminate differences with respect to rates of net income between years for the same enterprise or between enterprises for the same period should be condemned. The accounts should show the peculiar situation of each enterprise. If X actually earns 30 per cent on his investment and Y realizes but 25 per cent, this condition should be revealed by the accounts. The capitalization process, although it may be quite reasonable from the standpoint of an investor buying a security, should not in general be used in arriving at asset values for balance sheets.[4] This matter will be further considered in the discussion of goodwill in the next chapter.

It should be admitted that even actual cost is only a tentative figure. Accounting deals largely with judgments and estimates, not with certainties. Values are always more or less conjectural and unstable. But an exhibit of cost is in itself a significant statistical record; it gives a fairly reasonable starting point, at least. There is always a possibility in the particular case that a large part of the asset values will soon disappear; but this would not justify the recognition of possible bankruptcy in the current balance sheet. The accountant could make little headway without the fundamental assumption that costs give values as a matter of preliminary record. The accountant assumes that the values of labor and materials expended for a certain purpose pass into the resulting commodity, structure or situation, not as a final conclusion but for purposes of initial statement and until decisive evidence to the contrary is adduced. It would doubtless be impossible to demonstrate the absolute truth of this assumption; indeed we know that as a principle of price determination it is not strictly true; never-

---

[4] Where an asset consists in the right to a definitely known series of incomes, as in the case of certain leaseholds, its value for purposes of purchase and record and also for purposes of periodic extinguishment on the books may, of course, be obtained by capitalization.

theless most would agree that it is a reasonable basis for accounting procedure.[5]

To capitalize the services and conditions furnished by the owners themselves would be to introduce a still more tentative and provisional fact into the accounts; yet this alone would perhaps not be sufficient ground for their exclusion. It must be recognized that in a sense the values of these services do accrue, at least during the operating period, just as surely as do those of purchased items. The economic history of a business enterprise is a more or less continuous stream, and when the accountant attempts to break up this flow of transactions and processes into years, half-years, quarters, months, or other periods, and—putting a balance sheet stone wall at each end—allocate to each period the data truly appertaining thereto, he must, of course, proceed in a more or less arbitrary fashion and sever many real connections. Thus, if a unit of raw material as it makes its way from the storeroom through the various stages of manufacture and finally to the warehouse as a finished article ready for shipment draws unto itself the values of all purchased services and commodities which are consumed as necessary factors in the process, then, it might be argued, so do the economic significances of the various services and conditions furnished by the owners themselves also attach to the finished article. Or, in other words, the value of the finished product ready to ship is virtually selling price, regardless of the fact that an actual sale has not been effectuated.

This may all be admitted, however, and we can still return to the fundamental proposition that the point of view of the accountant must be essentially that of the particular enterprise and its owners and not that of an entire market situation. As has been emphasized repeatedly in the foregoing pages, the accounting scheme is organized on the basis of a sharp distinction between commodities, services, etc., which are acquired from

---

[5] See Chapter XX, pp. 489-490.

outsiders, and which are booked as costs, and services and conditions contributed by the owners themselves, which are taken for granted without explicit recognition until they become reported as a balance, income. Adhering to this position we can conclude that the functions of ownership, however and whenever furnished, never give rise to asset values or expense charges.

This same line of analysis can be applied to settle a minor problem. How should equipment or other assets built by an operating company for its own use be valued for purposes of book charges? What is the correct figure, actual cost to the company, or the amount required to buy or otherwise acquire the asset elsewhere, its market price? According to the above argument actual cost is the proper charge. In practice, however, the mistake is often made of including only the direct costs in labor and materials. All indirect—but actual—costs properly applicable to the construction work should also be added. A portion of the ordinary cost of operating the power plant should be included, for example, if power from this plant is used in construction operations. A small element to cover a part of the depreciation of structures in which construction work is housed should likewise be added. In fact, any part whatever of the ordinary costs which can reasonably be assigned to the special work, should be transferred from the current operating accounts to the account representing the cost of the new unit. Such allocation is, of course, a difficult technical problem in many cases.

IN THE INCORPORATED ENTERPRISE

In the case of the corporation it is somewhat more difficult to establish the proposition supported above. Here is met the legal business entity, and instead of "drawings" by the proprietor we have "payments" made by the corporation to its members. But it should be emphasized that the introduction of the corporate entity does not alter, as a rule, the essential nature of a transaction as far as its effect upon the balance sheet is concerned. Transactions between a corporation and its members are quite distinct from dealings between corporation and outsiders. "Dividends" paid by a corporation to its shareholders are not a payment for services purchased but represent rather a distribution of income or capital to investors. And any such payments which may be made prior to operation would seem to be best interpreted as constituting a reduction in capital—since no income exists at that stage—rather than a payment for services which can be charged to property account.

As a basis for further discussion let us consider an illustration similar to that used above. Suppose the X Co. is organized, issues capital stock to the amount of $100,000 for cash, has the use of these funds for a year, and builds and equips a plant therewith. Would the arguments and conclusions presented in the foregoing sections still apply and hold? It would seem as if this query could be safely answered in the affirmative. The bare introduction of the corporate form, other conditions remaining the same, would scarcely justify a fundamental revision of property values. The X Co. can hardly be said to buy the capital services of its stockholders. There is no sharp antithesis in this connection between the investors and the corporation. The stockholders furnish the funds; the corporation acts as their agent in carrying on construction operations. It seems clear that the resulting property charge would be again $100,000, neither more nor less. This would be as true if there were a long list of members as in the event that X, for example, were the sole shareholder.

A difference between the two cases may reasonably arise, however, in the treatment of payments for personal services. In the case of the sole-owner organization X may furnish personal services in organizing, supervising, etc. And, according to the view above presented, the result from the accounting standpoint is simply a lower cost. In the case of the corporation, on the other hand, any payments allowed to *particular* investors as compensation for personal services furnished in organization work and in managing construction operations might reasonably be treated as costs of property rather than as distribution of capital. As was indicated in the preceding chapter, the corporation usually does *buy* for the most part the necessary personal services required. There is certainly some tendency under the corporate form of organization for the investors to content themselves with the furnishing of capital and ultimate management, other necessary services being obtained from those who are not primarily shareholders.

Further, if particular investors are employed by their company at a reasonable rate of compensation such transactions can legitimately be viewed as purchases. That is, the fact that an individual corporate employee likewise is a shareholder does not stand in the way of the conclusion that his remuneration is a proper cost of construction or operation as the case may be. The corporate entity, the body of the investors, the business enterprise, is here quite in contrast with the particular shareholder-employee. If, however, because of his control of the governing board, a particular investor were in a position to have himself granted entirely unreasonable compensation, it could not be concluded that the full amount should be charged to property; ideally the excess of the payment over a fair value for the services furnished should be treated as a dissipation of capital funds.

Suppose that the X Co. pays its shareholders a "dividend" aggregating $10,000 during the preliminary period.[6] Can this amount be charged to some asset account on the theory that it is a payment for a necessary service, the use of capital, for one year? In this case the position already taken can certainly be reasserted. The net result is exactly the same as if the in-

---

[6] Such a disbursement, of course, would in general be illegal.

vestors had deposited but $90,000 at the outset. The mere deposit of an additional $10,000, which is later—upon the authority of the investors' own duly elected representatives—returned pro rata, is a transaction which cannot possibly be held to involve the acquisition of property. To say otherwise would be a step in the direction of the theory that the return of funds to the investors, whatever the amount, never results in a diminution of assets. As a matter of fact the return of initial funds is a transaction exactly the reverse of their receipt, and entries should be made accordingly. When the shareholders invest money the final accounting result is a charge to cash and a credit to capital stock. Similarly, when original funds are returned pro rata the transaction should be recorded by a credit to cash and a debit to capital stock (or some valuation account indicating a diminution of capital equities).

Thus far a homogeneous group of owners or investors has been assumed. A serious complication arises where the capital used in construction is secured from several more or less distinct sources. This is especially likely to be true in the case of the large corporation. In such circumstances various alternative points of view offer themselves; it is somewhat difficult to decide who are the owners *per se;* the line between *purchased* commodities and services and services *furnished* by the investors is harder to draw.

Suppose the X Co., to alter the illustration again, secures $100,000 in cash from two classes of investors, preferred and common stockholders. Each issue, it will be assumed, is for the amount of $50,000. The funds secured from both classes of stockholders are deposited in a single account, and are disbursed by the corporate treasurer to promoters, brokers, contractors, jobbers, etc. It will again be assumed, for convenience, that organization and construction cover the period of one year and that the full $100,000 is secured at the beginning of the year.

Let us now assume that the preferred stock is issued with the definite understanding that a dividend of 6 per cent per annum shall be regularly paid to all holders thereof. In this case, evidently, a sum of $3,000 must be paid to the preferred stockholders during the year in addition to the other necessary outlays. What is the significance of this transaction? A cash payment of $3,000 has been made to one class of investors, themselves stockholders and rating legally as members of the corporation; but those representing the other half of the capital have received no return whatever. Evidently the disbursement must have been made from the joint funds, as there is no other source. How should the transaction be treated in the accounts?

According to the view that all required disbursements (or definite contractual accruals) during the preliminary period in favor of investors are the cost of an essential service—the use of capital—the amount of the payment in this case ($3,000) should be charged to some appropriate asset or property account and credited to cash. Such a conclusion is supported by the doctrine which envisages the common stockholders as the essential nucleus around which and from the standpoint of which all accounting principles and procedures should be organized and interpreted. According to the theory that a "fair return" on *all* capital used during the construction interval should be charged to the cost of property, a debit of $6,000 should be entered in an asset account, cash should be credited with the amount of $3,000, and a further credit of $3,000 should be entered in some income or surplus account attaching to the common shareholder's interest. The propriety of this procedure depends upon the validity of the conception of the business enterprise as an entity entirely apart and distinct from the body of investors, a conception sufficiently dealt with in earlier paragraphs of this section.

If the view adopted thus far in this chapter be adhered to, on the other hand, the payment of $3,000 results simply in a *reduction in capital or investment,* and cannot be considered as a payment for property. Evidently if the Company had secured all its capital from a homogeneous body of stockholders and had made no dividend payments (as in the first illustration in this section), an additional sum of $3,000 would have been available for investment in plant and materials. A more extensive and *more valuable* property would have been the result. If, then, an estimated interest during construction is not an asset in the first case, the amount withdrawn by the preferred stockholders prior to operation in the second instance is a retirement of capital.

But if this is the case, whose equity is thereby impaired, the common or preferred stockholder's? This is an exceedingly difficult question and perhaps cannot be definitely settled. If the preferred members have prior rights to assets this payment, from the point of view of possible dissolution at any rate, would appear to result in a loss from the standpoint of the common shareholder. Yet the transaction is entirely voluntary and it is quite possible that the residual investor would view the whole arrangement as a very sensible one. He may be quite willing to make this apparent concession for the sake of inducing his preferred partner to accept a fixed rate of return, hoping thereby to secure later a much higher rate on his own investment. It is indeed a troublesome point to decide.

What standpoint shall the corporate accountant accept as a basis for his report of the cost of property, that of all investors as a body, the enterprise as a whole, the operating management, or that of the residual equity, of the common shareholders? From the point of view of the investors as a body the actual cost of property in this case, according to the opinion we are trying to establish, is $100,000 less $3,000, or $97,000. From the point of view of the common stockholders there is some reason for saying that the true investment for accounting purposes is the full $100,000, since by permitting the preferred stockholders to draw the sum of $3,000 in advance the residual investors are obtaining a privilege, a speculative opportunity, which they doubtless consider worth the amount paid. The problem simmers down to the question, can the accountant rate the preferred stockholders as mere outsiders—like laborers—rather than as capital contributors and owners and take the position that the business unit whose accounts he is preparing actually *buys* certain valuable services from these stockholders during the construction period, or should he take the position of the investors as a body and accordingly hold that the cost of the completed property is the net amount actually invested by stockholders of all classes?

It would seem necessary to conclude, if the logic of the case is not to be ignored, that dividends paid to preferred stockholders during the prerevenue period must be treated as reductions in capital, not as payments for asset values, provided it is held that dividends to such stockholders disbursed during the period of operation should be viewed as distributions of income, not as operating expense charges.

If these preferred dividend payments constitute a retirement of capital what entries should be made to recognize them? Accepting the conventional view that the capital stock account should not be charged unless actual shares are retired, it would be necessary to debit a special subsidiary account. "Advances to preferred stockholders" would be a possible caption, an account which might later be closed against accumulated surplus, or which, conceivably, might be retained indefinitely to indicate a voluntary organization "deficit." This would constitute a peculiar kind of valuation account, an account which represented an offset to a nominal capital equity from one standpoint, and yet which indicated or suggested a speculative advantage residing in one class of investors.

The still more difficult case arises where part of the capital is secured by means of bond issues or other contractual securities, and is disbursed or accrues in connection therewith prior to the operating period. Suppose, for example, that the X Co. secures its $100,000 through a stock issue of $50,000 and a bond issue for the same amount, and that during the construction year interest amounting to $3,000 is paid to the bondholders. How shall this transaction be interpreted for accounting purposes?

Here again, if the point of view of all long-term investors as a body be adopted, this payment constitutes a decrease in initial capital funds, a reduction which—from the standpoint of possible dissolution at any rate—bears first upon the stockholder. To take this position is to assert that the business does not *buy* the services of the bondholder. The issue of both bonds and stocks means simply that the corporation is securing funds from two classes of investors. As has been demonstrated in preceding chapters the bondholder's equity is essentially just as much an element of the corporate capitalization as is the stockholder's interest. If funds are disbursed to any of these investors prior to operation they must come out of capital; there is no other source unless we assume the enterprise to be earning income during the organization and construction period. The question again is, what point of view shall the accountant take? From the standpoint of the stockholders, the residual equity, it does not appear entirely unreasonable for him to hold that these interest payments do not reduce the investment, or, in other words, measure a part of the cost of the completed property. The broader view forces the conclusion that such payments reduce the final net investment.

Again, to be consistent, it is necessary to conclude that if interest paid to the bondholder during the operating period is a distribution of net revenue, "interest" paid to such an investor before income begins to accrue constitutes a retirement of capital.

IN THE PUBLIC UTILITY OR RAILWAY

In concluding this discussion of the significance and treatment of preoperating "interest," particular attention should be directed to the quasi-competitive, publicly regulated enterprise. To refer to the railway field, for example, it is clear that the determination of the cost of property is in this case a problem of especial difficulty and moment. In the first place it is particularly in this field that the construction period is normally of considerable length, a fact which directly contributes to the difficulty of ascertaining a rational cost-of-property figure. Further, the measurement of true initial investment or sacrifice is here a matter of especial consequence because of the importance that investment has come to assume in the determination of rates.

In the field of competitive industry the cost of original property bears little or no relation, in the specific case, to the prices which will be received for product; and hence a careful accounting for investment—as far as effect upon gross revenue is concerned—does not appear to be of great importance. In the railway field, on the other hand, the prominence given to the dictum that the investor is entitled to a "fair return on a fair value" of his property, coupled with a stressing of the theory that initial investment is intimately related to fair value for rate-making purposes, has naturally resulted in an emphasis upon construction accounting. That is, in the case of the enterprise whose rates are regulated by the state property values have an added significance in that they may be used to some extent as a basis for price determination.

The classifications prescribed by the Interstate Commerce Commission include a property account entitled "interest during construction." This account is charged with all interest accruing during the construction period on bonds and other contractual securities, and "this account shall also include reasonable charges for interest, during the construction period before the property becomes available for service, on the carrier's own funds expended for construction purposes." [7] Evidently, then, the railway enterprise is permitted to add actual accrued interest, together with an allowance for estimated interest, to the cost of property. Is this reasonable, and if so how can we justify the contrary position taken in the preceding sections?

There is at least something to be said in support of the Commission's attitude. It must be remembered that the railroads have become quasi-public institutions. Their operations and rates are quite largely regulated by the government; and, as a result, the investor in railroad securities is restricted pretty largely to a non-speculative rate of return. In equity, accordingly, it would seem that the investor should be allowed to earn this lower rate from the time his funds are first deposited. That is, if the speculative opportunities are removed, the burdens and risks should likewise be eliminated or minimized. If, then, it is advisable to construct the accounts in the case of a railroad in such a way as to show the value upon which the investor should be allowed to earn, interest during the preliminary period of waiting should be added to the cost of property.

It should be noted that the Commission provides for the inclusion in "interest during construction" of both interest paid and specifically accrued and estimated "interest" on capital not explicitly interest-bearing. In other words, not only is investment not to be considered as impaired by interest payments to bondholders prior to operation, but the cost of road and equipment is to be charged with a fair interest allowance

---

[7] *Classification of Investment in Road and Equipment of Steam Roads,* account number 76.

on the funds contributed by stockholders. This is logical. If interest on any part of the capital invested accrues as a property charge, interest on the entire investment, regardless of its source, so accrues. The part of such accrual which is not accompanied—or shortly followed—by actual disbursements, must, of course, be credited to some income, surplus, or capital account as was indicated in a preceding section. There appears to be no definite provision in the Commission's classifications covering the location of this credit. Probably it is intended that it should be absorbed in some account in the profit and loss group.

Perhaps, then, certain practices can be justified in the field of regulated enterprise which are quite unreasonable in the accounting for the ordinary private business in the competitive field. As was noted in an earlier connection, in the case of a completely socialized enterprise it could with some reason be held that the state actually purchased the services of capital, as well as the other necessary commodities and services. In other words, wherever the investors are virtually outsiders instead of the all-important element in the ultimate control of operation the accountant may perhaps shift his viewpoint with respect to the determination of costs. If the railroad accountant were to organize his system entirely from the standpoint of the private investors it would evidently be unreasonable to charge to assets an allowance for the investor's own services; for this would be assuming that the owner were buying these services from himself. But in view of the peculiar situation in the public utility field—a condition of state regulation if not of absolute state ownership—the adoption here of a somewhat different attitude by the accountant need not be surprising.

On the other hand, there is much to be said in favor of the use in the regulated enterprise of essentially the same scheme of accounting principles and procedures as are suitable to typical competitive business. The net income of the public utility is still reported as the net income of the private investors. Dividends and interest are viewed as distributions of income rather than expenses. The management must go out on the open market to buy goods and services of all kinds; and the criteria of successful management are about the same here as in the unregulated field. Should the one striking fact of rate determination be permitted to affect the accounting structure and the viewpoints on which it is based? Is there good reason for holding that it is the function of the accounts to exhibit original sacrifice because of the importance of this fact in price-fixing? Should not the business of the accountant rather be restricted to a presentation of the actual net investment of the private owners as it takes shape in manifold structures, commodites, and services, and *as it is varied*—increased or decreased—as a result of specific value changes in the concrete asset items flowing through the enterprise? In other words, should the accounts even purport to show values for rate purposes?

In view of the conflicting ideas held by regulatory bodies with respect to valuation for rate-making and the muddle the whole matter is in it would seem as if the accountant might well avoid any attempt to exhibit such values or to modify his balances in view of particular decisions concerning rates. From the standpoint of the immediate management, certainly, the asset accounts should be charged initially with the cost of purchased items; and no revisions should be permitted that do not reflect specific economic change. Values for rate purposes are figures determined by courts and commissions in the light of various considerations with respect to public policy, and might, with reason, be entirely ignored by the accountant. This matter as it arises in connection with the capitalization of early losses and similar procedures, will be considered further in the next chapter.

CHAPTER XII

GOODWILL AND GOING VALUE

Some of the considerations stressed in the preceding chapter have an important bearing upon the interpretation of certain intangible assets and the accounting treatment which should be accorded the same; and hence these topics may well be studied at this point. No attempt will be made to present an exhaustive discussion of the various intangibles. Rather it is intended to emphasize only those phases of this subject which are particularly related to theoretic points of view adopted and utilized extensively in the foregoing explanations of the accounting structure. Goodwill and going value will receive especial attention in this connection. To begin with, and in view of the prevailing confusion of opinion on this matter, a statement of the essential characteristics of the intangibles as a class will be given.

A DEFINITION OF INTANGIBLES

Among the classifications of which the accountant makes considerable use is that which divides the properties into tangibles and intangibles. It follows a quite basic line of cleavage and is often given little or no explicit recognition in the balance sheet. As was indicated in Chapter VIII, the fixed and current divisions, together with certain subsidiary classes, are the groups most strongly emphasized in the preparation of the financial statement. Nevertheless the distinction between tangibles and intangibles weighs heavily in the literature of accountancy and has a measurable significance in practice.

There seems to be quite a diversity of opinion as to what

constitutes an intangible property for accounting purposes. The word "intangible," according to the usual acceptation, is synonymous with "impalpable." It means, then, "incapable of being touched or perceived by touch," immaterial. If this signification, without qualification, is carried over into accounting, an intangible asset becomes any valuable consideration, factor, or element of significant duration attaching to a business enterprise but having no specific material residence therein; and an intangible asset account is any account which is used to exhibit the amount of such an element. According to this strict view of the case only physical, material properties, such as natural resources, structures, equipment, tools, materials, merchandise, etc., could be rated as tangible assets; and only accounts representing such items could be viewed as tangible property accounts. Accounts receivable, notes, securities, insurance prepayments, leaseholds, and all other valuable rights, privileges, and conditions would, consequently, constitute intangible assets.

The use of the phrase "significant duration" in the above definition should be explained. It might be urged, in accordance with the insistence in Chapter IV that current services are assets as purchased, that all such elements constitute intangible assets, since they are obviously immaterial. However, while services may undoubtedly contribute to asset values from the standpoint of cost and hence for purposes of debit and credit analysis can be treated as "additions to assets," it should be emphasized that current services for the most part can hardly be said to exist disembodied, independent of any material object. That is, as was emphasized in preceding connections, the accountant ordinarily assumes that the value of labor services, for example, passes over into and attaches to the goods upon which the employee is working. On the other hand, it must be admitted that the values of such services as insurance, advertising, supervision, management, etc., which enter into production in a general way and can hardly be conceived as attaching specifically and immediately to goods in process or other tangible elements, may be viewed as constituting, for an appreciable period of time, intangible assets.

As was indicated in Chapter VIII, there is some force in the view that where any valuable right, claim, or privilege is represented by a definite instrument, such as a note, mortgage, bond, certificate, or other document, the asset is actually tangible, since it is evidenced or expressed by a material thing. And undoubtedly this opinion finds considerable justification in the case of bank notes, and readily negotiable securities such as coupon bonds. The business man naturally comes to view such papers as having an intrinsic value; and, indeed, they do have an intrinsic value from the private standpoint in so far as they are payable to bearer and if lost, stolen, or destroyed, cannot be replaced (the rights involved being thereby canceled as far as the original holder is concerned). On the other hand, in the case of accounts receivable, bank deposits, stock certificates, registered bonds, etc., the mere loss of documentary evidence will not as a rule annul the effective validity of the right involved. The documents in these cases are merely *evidences* of assets and do not constitute properties in themselves.

In part, as was noted before, the intangible asset accounts exhibit the duplicate representation of wealth which arises out of the fact that accounting is based upon the point of view of the specific enterprise rather than that of the community. Rights and privileges and claims, from the standpoint of the accountant, constitute assets to the beneficiary enterprises. But fundamentally, of course, the entire structure must be based upon tangible properties. Society's wealth, at any one instant, consists in land, buildings, equipment, and commodities —tangible assets. The capital of the particular business, on the other hand, may be made up in large measure of valuable rights, securities, claims, conditions.

The nature of the problem of valuation as it arises during the preliminary period in which a company is organizing and acquiring its principal initial properties suggests a possible way of interpreting the intangibles as a whole. During organization and construction—in the case of the large and complex undertaking—considerable sums are spent which can scarcely be said to result in definite tangible assets, or in an addition to the values of such properties. Accordingly, from this standpoint the intangibles as a whole may be defined as the excess of the total cost of bringing into being the enterprise *in its entirety* over and above that part of such cost as can reasonably be allocated to specified tangible properties. This is a kind of negative conception, but it has distinct value for the accountant. (In the succeeding chapter this problem of determining initial property values will be further considered.)

A modification of this definition gives a useful starting point in the analysis of intangibles in general. The intangibles are the residuum, the balance of the legitimate values attaching to an enterprise as a totality, over the sum of the legitimate values of the various tangible properties taken individually. That is, the intangibles measure that part of a company's asset total which might be said to reside in the physical situation viewed as a whole, but which cannot be considered—except upon some highly arbitrary basis—to inhere in, or have a residence in, specific units of plant, equipment, etc. Or, to put it still differently, the amount by which the total of the values of the various physical properties within the enterprise, inventoried unit by unit, falls short of the legitimate asset total for the entire business, expresses the intangible asset value.

To some extent, evidently, the contrast between tangible and intangible is analogous to that between specific and general, direct and indirect, assignable and unassignable. From the standpoint of the entire enterprise it might perhaps be said in the typical case that all the assets are tangible. That is, if the entire left side of the balance sheet were viewed as a single account, "all assets," there would be no good reason for excluding any one element more than any other; and there would be no good reason for considering this single account as an intangible property account. As soon as the attempt is made to isolate certain specific tangible properties, however, the intangible classification appears.

The following graphic representation may serve to emphasize this point:

TOTAL ASSETS OF THE X CO.

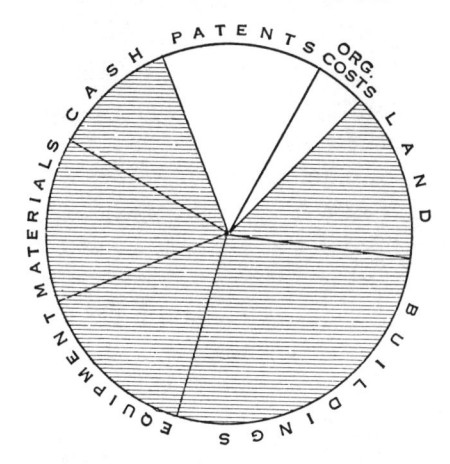

The total of the assets of the hypothetical X Co., as given in Chapter II, is represented by the area of the entire circle. That part of the total assignable to particular tangible asset accounts is represented by the shaded area. The unshaded area indicates the amount not so assignable, the intangibles. Cash is here treated as a tangible although, as has been indicated, this asset is commonly—in large measure—a special kind of receivable.

The commonly accepted views do not adhere closely and consistently to the foregoing suggestions. Starting with a conception of intangibles as immaterial assets, the accountant usually abandons this position more or less completely when he attacks concretely the problem of asset classification. In practice, accounts and notes receivable, stocks, bonds, and other securities are seldom listed as intangible assets. Rather arbitrarily the designation is reserved for goodwill, patents, trademarks, copyrights, franchises, and going value. The values of leaseholds, prepaid royalties, etc., are also sometimes treated as intangibles. Evidently this means that materiality is not being insisted upon as a test of tangibility; for certainly an account receivable is a highly immaterial asset. It is a view which includes in the tangible properties all definite, certain, easily valued rights and claims, and restricts the caption "intangible" to more or less vague, dubious, uncertain rights, conditions, and privileges.

A definition of intangibles suggested by some engineers and accountants, particularly in the public utility field, makes this class of assets consist in the excess of the appraised value of an enterprise in its entirety over the cost of all assets. That is, an intangible property value is one which originates without direct cost. Franchise and going values of various kinds are usually intended. It is surely evident that in general cost is not a satisfactory evidence of intangibility. Goodwill, patents, and other intangibles may be purchased on a cash or equivalent basis.

If, as an expedient, the accountant wishes to treat as intangibles only those somewhat dubious and special properties mentioned above, there can be little solid objection. It may well be emphasized, however, that this means that the classification is then not being used to designate the non-physical or immaterial assets as a group.

AN ANALYSIS OF GOODWILL

"Goodwill," in the broadest possible sense of the term, indicates the estimated value of future excess income. This interpretation of goodwill gives a convenient starting point; and the first step in dealing with it involves a consideration of the phrase "excess income."

It is a familiar fact that the *rate* of return realized on capital invested in business varies sharply between enterprises. Even in the particular line the rate of net revenue is likely to range from a negative figure to perhaps 100 per cent or more. One company will operate at a loss; another will earn a modest income; still another will realize a very favorable rate of return. Between periods, between companies, between industries, the rate of net income is subject to wide variation. This is one of the striking facts of business. The conditions leading to success are exceedingly complex. The amount of capital invested in any case is only one of the elements determining the amount of periodic net revenue. Managerial ability, methods and processes, territorial location, trade-name—these and numerous other factors may contribute to financial success. Further, purely external and fortuitous circumstances over which the particular management has no control whatever may be the dominant conditions, for a time at least, in the determination of profit and loss. With respect to these collateral factors and conditions some enterprises are more favorably situated than their representative competitors. Such businesses may be said to have *goodwill*.

To put it precisely, goodwill from this standpoint may be defined as the capitalized value of the excess income which a particular enterprise is able to earn over the income of a representative competitor—a "normal" business—having the same capital investment, the rate used in capitalizing being the rate realized by the representative concern. The representative concern—a more or less imaginary entity—may be defined for this purpose as a business which earns a typical or reasonable rate on its investment, a rate which is recognized as adequate, a rate high enough to insure the maintenance of the capital of the industry and reasonable additions thereto as demand for product increases.

Suppose, for example, that the X Co.—a representative business—has a capital of $100,000 and earns $10,000 per annum; and that the Y Co.—a favorably situated competitor—likewise has a capital (according to the same principles of valuation) of $100,000 but earns $20,000 annually. The permanence of the income rate and all conditions of risk, it will be assumed, are essentially identical in both cases. Now, under these circumstances, it is evident that the property of the Y Co.—with all attendant factors and conditions—is worth, from the standpoint of earning capacity, $100,000 more than that of the X Co. In other words, a prospective investor would naturally be willing to pay twice as much per share for the stock of the Y Co. as for that of the X Co. (assuming the number of shares to be the same in both cases). The capitalized amount of the excess of the income of the Y Co. over that of the X Co. constitutes goodwill according to the above definition.

The interpretation of goodwill as capitalized differential earning capacity restricts this value to the favorably situated, the supramarginal enterprise. That is, no goodwill can reside in the representative business according to this view. This position, at first sight, may appear quite unreasonable. The professional accountant would be likely to urge that even the moderately successful business may possess a modicum of goodwill. It must be remembered, however, that the representative concern as defined above is a highly hypothetical entity; and if such a case were actually discovered it is doubtful if anyone would be willing to pay an additional sum for goodwill in the purchase of the business in whole or in part. Further, it is of course necessary to assume that the representative business and all enterprises that are being compared with it have never been sold, reorganized, or otherwise revalued in such a way as to include a goodwill element.

Goodwill, according to this conception, is closely related to the producer's "rent" or "surplus" of economics. The producer who has monopolistic advantages, is especially efficient, or is unusually well situated for some other reason, is often said to realize a special surplus or rent. Viewing the "representative business" as essentially the counterpart of the marginal, price-determining producer, leads to the conclusion that goodwill expresses from the standpoint of the particular enterprise the capitalized value of economic rents enjoyed.

A permanent exceptional rate of income is not essential to the creation of goodwill as above defined. If unusual earnings are assured for several years, or even for a single year, the enterprise as a whole has an added value from the standpoint of capitalized income.

Before taking up definitely the accounting treatment of goodwill it will be desirable to examine more carefully the factors and conditions which contribute to the creation of this element and to indicate the more narrow significations which are adopted in practice.

Goodwill may be said to be brought about by three main classes of factors, conditions, and circumstances: (1) services and conditions contributed directly by the principal owners themselves; (2) definite rights or other elements secured by the enterprise which are quite external as far as the owners personally are concerned; (3) indefinite, general, collateral privileges and circumstances which nevertheless have a decided bearing upon successful operation. Examples in the first group are special skill and knowledge with respect to technical processes of production, high managerial ability, exceptional selling capacity, personal credit, social and business connections, general reputation, attractive personality, etc. In the second class may be listed patents, trade-marks, copyrights, trade-names, and similar specific rights and conditions. To suggest the character of the third group established clientele, location, and established staff may be mentioned. Favorable trade developments and other highly external and general factors may also give the particular enterprise a temporary advantage.

It should be emphasized that none of these rights, conditions, or favorable circumstances can reasonably be said to contribute to goodwill or any other value except as they give the particular business an advantage over the basic representative concern. Obviously many of these things mentioned above —as well as specific assets—must be present in some degree if operation is to be carried on in any fashion. For the most part these factors are to be taken for granted; they constitute a part of the accessories and setting required for every business undertaking. It is only when some of these elements have such a character as to give the particular enterprise with which they are associated a special position financially that they can possibly give rise to an intangible property.

In accounting literature and in professional work the view seems to be common that the use of the term "goodwill" should be restricted to the value attaching to an enterprise because of its superior endowment with respect to the first and third classes of conditions mentioned above. Specific rights and privileges supported by governmental grants are ordinarily given independent consideration and recognition under appropriate captions. This attitude, on the whole, is a reasonable one, as patent rights and similar privileges are sufficiently distinct from the more implicit and personal elements and may require a different accounting treatment. Much stress, however, has been laid upon the conception of goodwill as the value of all income-producing factors which are independent of and in addition to the ordinary purchased assets; and this interpretation probably gives the most satisfactory starting point for an analysis of the principal intangibles.

THE TREATMENT OF NON-PURCHASED GOODWILL

According to the general definition developed in the foregoing section goodwill may come into existence as an economic fact without being acquired by purchase as is the typical asset. It does not follow, however, that goodwill in such circumstances should be given explicit accounting recognition. It has long been an accepted rule of orthodox accounting—a rule which has nevertheless been frequently violated—that goodwill or related intangibles should in no case be recognized definitely in the accounts unless acquired by bona fide purchase on a cash or equivalent basis, and should then be entered as an asset for only the amount actually paid.

This rule may appear at first sight as somewhat irrational and as in conflict with conceptions stressed in preceding statements, especially in view of the suggestion in Chapter V and elsewhere that valuable considerations and objects coming into the possession of the particular enterprise without cost should none the less be recognized as properties. It is believed, however, that this principle of practice is thoroughly sound, and is not in conflict with the theories emphasized in this study. On the contrary the points of view which have been stressed throughout the foregoing pages, and especially in the last two chapters, furnish a logical basis from which the attitude of the accountant can be defended, at least as far as the narrower conception of goodwill is concerned.

Goodwill, as has been indicated, expresses the value of an excess earning power. It represents the capitalization of the peculiar rights and advantages enjoyed by the supramarginal enterprise. Evidently, then, if goodwill were completely recognized as an asset in the accounts of all businesses in a given industry all unusual *rates* of return would be thereby annihilated. The most successful company would earn no more than the ordinary competitive rate, the percentage realized by the representative concern. As far as net income rates were concerned all particularly successful businesses would be reduced essentially to the normal or representative level.

This, it seems clear, would seriously obscure the true situation. The accounts should show the investor the actual rate of net revenue realized on the objective economic resources possessed by the enterprise. If this rate is 50 per cent in a particular period the asset values should not be juggled in such a way as to obliterate this fact. If the true rate is 5 per cent, the accounts should again conform to the real situation. Any accounting procedure which resulted in eliminating the periodic fluctuations in income in the specific business, or in equalizing the rates realized by different competing enterprises, would be quite unreasonable.

The adoption of an accounting policy which necessitated the adjustment of asset values in such a way that no enterprise in a particular field earned a rate of above 10 per cent, for example, would destroy an important basis for comparison. It would result in an apparent uniformity of earning power when actually no such uniformity existed. Thus it would involve an obscuring of the very facts that the plan would be supposed to be emphasizing. The *rate* of net income to total properties is a fact of first importance. The owner, prospective investor, or other individual concerned naturally wishes to know just what is the earning power of the particular business in which he is interested, and how this earning capacity compares with that of competing companies. Obviously any universal recognition of the goodwill element, any general introduction of the capitalization process into accounting, would tend to obscure rather than clarify these facts.

This position may be strengthened if goodwill is considered to represent merely the significance of the services and special conditions furnished by the owners themselves. To capitalize an excess earning power due to such services and conditions would be a practice similar to the recognition of income prior to operation. The objections to the latter procedure which were urged in the last chapter can be applied with equal force here. To recognize goodwill in this sense as a definite asset would mean again the accruing of the services and conditions furnished by the owners themselves as a property value on the books of their own enterprise. But, as has been urged repeatedly in the foregoing pages, the owners do not buy their own functions and services as they do other valuable considerations; hence to include the estimated value of such factors as properties would involve an absurd shifting of viewpoint.

It is the function of the asset accounts to exhibit continuously the actual investment of the owners as it is manifested in various commodities and services purchased, but it is not their function to include an estimated allowance for either capital or personal elements—however important they may be —which are furnished by the owners themselves. The value of the owner's functions is first definitely reported by the accountant as income; in the nature of the case it cannot likewise appear as an asset cost if the viewpoint of the owners is accepted as the controlling principle. The rate of return on the actual value of capital as invested in purchased assets is the significant percentage for the owner. If this rate is reduced to a nominal level by the recognition of an intangible asset based upon the value of that part of the owner's technical skill, general ability, and reputation which ranks above the similar endowments of a representative competitor, the true situation is concealed rather than clarified.

In economics it is usually insisted that skill, health, education, and other personal attributes cannot be regarded as a part of the wealth or capital of the individual or community, regardless of the fundamental importance of such factors in financial success. Similarly, the various special abilities and qualifications of the owners of a business enterprise cannot reasonably be viewed as in whole or in part giving rise to definite asset values on their books of account.

To the extent that goodwill depends upon personal services and attributes it is evidently hardly transferable. Where unusual success is intimately associated with the abilities and connections of a particular individual or group of individuals, as is very often the case in sole-proprietorships and in partnerships, a transfer of goodwill from one business to another is out of the question unless the persons responsible for the success are brought over into the new undertaking in the same capacities. Thus certain kinds of goodwill, at any rate, can rarely if ever be validated by actual purchase.

It is not intended to deny the importance of the capitalization process as an economic fact, but it does not seem rational or practicable to recognize in the asset accounts of an enterprise the capitalized value of a part of its probable future income. In the nature of the case the revenues of the specific properties of the business world are largely indeterminate; and it would be difficult indeed to settle upon capitalization rates if future revenues were known. Cost (or adjusted cost) is the natural basis for the accountant's entries; to leave this basis would be to throw open the entire accounting system to a maze of conjecture and uncertainty. But even if the capitalization or discounting calculation were to be used in obtaining the book values of purchased assets—and to a limited extent it may be—no warrant for the capitalization of a part of the *net* income of the enterprise would be thereby obtained.

It is doubtful if this conclusion may be extended, however, to cover patents, copyrights, leases, and other rights which are definite and objective as far as the persons of the owners are concerned. Special privileges granted by the state to specific enterprises often give rise to exceptional earning power and hence may come to have an important value. There are cases where the value of a company's patents far outweighs the significance of all tangible properties. And the real test as to a patent's value is perhaps seldom its cost. It is considered advisable in orthodox practice to enter a patent in the accounts of the patentee at only the amount of the cost of experiments, models, etc., and legal fees and expenses. This figure is likely to bear no relation whatever to reasonable value once the particular device has proved its merit.

There is at least something to be said in such cases in favor of the proposition that selling value, bona fide market value, is the most valid basis for accounting entries. Would it not be quite absurd for a company possessing patents with a demonstrated value (based on reliable offers, for example) of $25,000,000 to show a value in its patents account of but $50,000, the cost of experimentation, etc.? It appears reasonable to conclude that genuine intangible assets of this class may arise without cost or with a value in excess of cost, just as tangible assets may so appear. Surely no one would argue that a railroad company which receives a gift of land with a value of $100,000 should neglect to book this asset simply because it originated without cost, or that a prospector who discovers a mineral deposit worth a million should value his find in his accounts at the cost of food, equipment, filing expenses, etc.! Similarly it may be urged that patents, copyrights, and similar definite and objective privileges and rights may come to have a legitimate accounting value greatly in excess of cost.

THE TREATMENT OF PURCHASED GOODWILL

If, on the other hand, a particular enterprise actually buys on a cash or equivalent basis the properties of another company and pays something in excess of the sum of the values of land, buildings, equipment, merchandise, receivables, and securities in order to secure location, clientele, trade-name, etc., this means that an investment is actually being made in goodwill and it accordingly becomes a legitimate intangible asset on the books of the purchaser.

This is not inconsistent with the conclusions reached above. As was explained in Chapter XII, an enterprise which invests $100,000, for example, in the construction of a plant has a property which should be entered in the accounts at that figure. But if at the end of the construction period the completed property were sold to another company for $115,000, the new concern should enter the property on its books at the full amount of $115,000, for it has actually invested in the services of the construction company. Similarly an enterprise, which is especially endowed with respect to location, reputation, etc., and because of these exceptional advantages earns a very high rate of return, is not justified in capitalizing a part of such income despite the fact that it might be possible to sell the business on a favorable basis because of these factors. But an enterprise which actually buys out the old business and voluntarily pays a price in excess of the sum of the values of the ordinary assets has thereby made a definite investment in goodwill—has *purchased* goodwill—and hence can properly recognize this asset in its accounts. This rule leads to a variation in asset values between otherwise similar companies; but such a variation is quite reasonable from an accounting standpoint, as was indicated in the preceding chapter.

Despite the rules of the accountant, goodwill which is quite fictitious is often recognized in practice. It has been used freely in corporate organization and reorganization to give a nominal validation to security issues which had a par value exceeding the reasonable value of properties received. Often when a partnership or corporation is taken over by another concern payment is made for goodwill in securities having a value much below the amount stated in the agreement; the result is the recognition of goodwill as an asset for an amount which is in part or even largely a mere discount. Further, the entire transaction is frequently nominal as far as the change in ownership is concerned. If a partnership, for example, is converted into a corporation in which the original partners are sole investors, the recognition of goodwill is of doubtful propriety; in such a case no real purchase and sale has occurred and no reliable criterion of goodwill value would appear. If, on the other hand, considerable new capital is contributed by individuals not connected with the partnership, even though the partners become the principal stockholders, it may be urged that a recognition of a reasonable amount of goodwill as a purchased asset may be justified. The clear case is found where the buying business is entirely distinct from the selling with respect to ownership. It is here that an outright and bona fide purchase and sale of goodwill may occur. In Chapter XV some further considerations will be given to the problem of revaluation induced by a partial change in ownership.

Evidently, then, goodwill can never arise as a legitimate asset unless the factors responsible for this element are definitely transferable without loss in significance. Further, unless a positive change in ownership takes place, it is doubtful if a transaction in goodwill should be recognized. Accordingly it appears that the personal attributes and services of owners can seldom be capitalized with propriety. Special cases may of course arise where the original owner becomes attached to the new enterprise, although the ownership as a whole is essentially new. The owner of a small business which is sold to a large corporation, for example, may contract to remain as resident manager for a period of years and receive, as a consideration for this agreement, an additional amount of stock in the purchasing company. The reasonable value of this stock may then be charged to goodwill on the books of the vendee. If the consideration were cash, there would of course be no question as to the amount of this goodwill. Even in this case the interest of the former owner is quite likely to wane to such an extent that the special value of his connection with the business largely evaporates in a short time.

It should be evident that the exact determination of the effective amount of goodwill in a particular case may be a matter of considerable difficulty. According to the definition of goodwill given at the outset it would be necessary to ascertain the normal competitive rate of income in the industry in question, the amount of the excess income for the business under consideration, and the number of years during which this excess may be expected to accrue. Obviously no precise discounting calculation is possible. As a result of the bargaining between vendor and vendee a figure is obtained which is compounded from the opinions of both parties and involves judgment and conjecture rather than exact mathematical computation. An assumption that the current favorable situation will be maintained from two to five years is common. Clientele, trade-name, etc., are more or less ephemeral aspects of the business enterprise, and can only be maintained at all by continuous effort and expense.

This raises the question of the subsequent treatment of goodwill in the accounts, assuming such an asset to have been properly handled in the first place. If the special advantages purchased are permanent the goodwill item evidently need not be amortized. It would be dangerous, however, to assume that goodwill were ever of such a character. As was just suggested, the more reasonable view considers purchased goodwill as a terminable asset which is later replaced by a new—but not recognizable—element created by the efforts of the new owners. This view is definitely supported by experience.

Very often we see the new doctor or merchant using the phrase "successor to ———" on signs and letterheads for two or three years, after which the old name is dropped. Certainly when the special factors for which additional payment is made disappear or lose their potency, the goodwill should be written off. A more or less arbitrary assumption with respect to length of life is often needed. If goodwill value is based upon definite rights, such as patents, or upon terminable contracts, it should evidently be amortized in an orderly manner during the period of such rights and contracts, unless circumstances indicate a more rapid lapse in value.

It is sometimes argued that goodwill should not be written off when revenues are declining as this further impairs net revenue, but should be amortized by charges to revenue during boom years as rapidly as possible. This position can hardly be commended. The accounts should show as nearly as may be the actual situation. Goodwill should not be left on the books when it is known that the asset no longer exists, and it need not be extinguished unless expiration of value actually occurs.

If goodwill is not a legitimate asset except when purchased it may be urged that goodwill can never appreciate. Any added earning power over and above the return secured through the purchase of original goodwill should be attributed to the efforts and connections of the new owners, and should be reflected by a higher rate of return rather than by additional charges to asset accounts.

In the valuation of the goodwill of a corporation for purposes of purchase some clue is obtained from the going market prices of the company's securities. Stock prices naturally are based to some extent upon the capitalization of income principle. The individual investor attaches considerable weight to the past showing of income and the probable future trend of earnings. The excess of market value over book value is thus one measure of goodwill. Nevertheless it should be emphasized that the influences affecting security prices are so numerous and often external to the particular business that it would be entirely unsafe to gauge the value of goodwill on this basis alone.

GOING VALUE

For purposes of considering the significance and treatment of going value the history of the business enterprise may be divided into three periods. The first is the organization and construction period, extending from the time the undertaking is first projected by the promoter to the date when the business is ready for regular operation. Next in order comes the developmental period, the interval during which the business is being built up, extending from the date of the initial sales to the time a normal rate of return is first realized. The third period is that during which the company is successfully operating at least on a level with the representative concern in the particular line of industry involved. The first period is more or less common to all enterprises—although it may be of insignificant duration in some fields; the second, the pioneering and experimental period, does not confront all enterprises, especially in old-established lines; the third stage is only reached by those businesses which at some time in their history attain a fair degree of success.

This classification is of course somewhat artificial. The history of a business is a more or less continuous stream, and there are no sharp dividing lines between these various periods. Nevertheless it conforms measurably to realities, and is an essential preliminary to an analysis of *going value*.[1]

According to one interpretation, going value relates to the

---

[1] "Developmental" value, "pioneering" value, and "going" value are expressions which are used more or less synonymously.

first period mentioned above. Costs of promotion, incorporation fees, underwriter's charges, etc., are essential outlays required during organization and construction, as will be shown in the next chapter. Such charges may be considered to be quite as legitimate costs of property as are the labor and material costs contributing directly to the tangible asset values. They constitute an intangible asset only in the sense that, although attaching to the property as a whole, they cannot be conveniently distributed among the individual tangible units. To designate as "going value" the total of these general costs of getting the business going, ready to operate, is a procedure not without justification.

More commonly, however, the term is used to express the capitalized value of early losses and unrealized income. It often happens in the development of a new business that there is a considerable interval between the time that operation actually begins and the time that a normal or representative rate of income is first earned. A lean period of several years may follow the completion of the plant before the enterprise reaches a paying basis. This is particularly true in industries which are in a distinctly experimental stage. Many of the electric power companies, for example, failed to earn a reasonable rate of income in the early years of the industry; and in some cases serious capital losses were suffered. This was due in part to the lack of a brisk demand for electric light and power, to the excessive outlays necessitated by rapidly changing technical methods, and to the high costs due to inexperienced management.

On the basis of the theory that the investor is entitled to a fair return on his investment, it has been urged that there is, in such cases, a developmental or going value representing the capitalized early losses and income deficiencies. From this standpoint, to put it precisely, going value in a particular case is the amount of the capitalized values of the sums by which actual revenues during the developmental period have fallen short of the amounts required to produce representative returns on the investment, the capitalizing rate being the fair, normal, or representative percentage.

Let us test the validity of this value, first, in the case of the typical competitive enterprise. Does an additional intangible value attach to the typical competitive enterprise which has weathered a period of pioneering without disaster and is finally on the road to success, a value which just equals capitalized losses and income deficiencies? Does such a value exist from the standpoint of any reasonable test? And in any case should such value receive explicit accounting recognition as an asset? A negative answer would seem to be required.

In the first place it is extremely doubtful if the investor in a competitive enterprise is able to recompense himself for early income deficiencies by means of later higher prices; and if he cannot, the supposed going value surely disappears. If *all* the early investors in an industry started operations at the same moment—an assumption wide of the facts—and suffered losses or failed to realize adequate returns concurrently for a definite period, it might seem reasonable to conclude that competition between them would be of such a character as to make prices high enough to cover the early deficiencies. But even in this extreme case such a conclusion would be questionable. In the first place it ignores the effect of demand and a possible competition among producers to avoid further losses. Further, once the industry in question became established the early investors would not be in a position to charge higher prices because of previous hardships. The competition of newcomers would have to be faced. Capital would flow into the then established field and force prices to a point at which a more or less normal return were realized by the representative producer.

There is certainly no definite assurance in the market situation that the investor in the specific enterprise will be able to recoup early losses in later prosperous years. To so insist would be virtually to deny the plain fact of business losses. One enterprise may be ultimately successful while another may never yield a fair return. It is a familiar fact that in certain hazardous lines more capital is dissipated in unsuccessful ventures than is earned by successful undertakings. In such a case the industry as a whole is operating at a continuous net loss.

Even in the case of a completely monopolized business it is very doubtful if it may fairly be said that an intangible asset exists which offsets early losses. In the nature of the case the monopolist will charge the most favorable price (barring the control of public opinion, law, etc.) which the conditions of demand make possible. This need not be the highest price, but would be that price which produced the greatest possible net income for the monopolist. Evidently there would be no early losses or income deficiencies in such a case if the producer could possibly prevent it. And the fact of such losses does not put the owner in a position to charge any more satisfactory a price than he is bound to charge anyway.

Early losses, whether due to experiments, inefficiency, inadequate demand, or to some other cause, cannot be recovered by the specific enterprise bearing the same. The possibility of these losses is among the risks of ownership which require at least the *prospect* of income to attract capital. Net revenue in general, it is true, is the economic burden which the community bears in order to secure the services of ownership and allied functions. The possibility of initial losses or ultimate failure is one of the reasons for the existence of this net revenue element in general. But net income is by no means guaranteed in the specific instance; and indeed if it were one of the reasons for the existence of this residuum over expenses would be removed.

But even if it were true that the representative competitive enterprise were able to realize an income in later years sufficient to include a fair return on a going value as above defined, it would not follow that this value should be entered as an intangible asset in the accounts. So to recognize it would involve again the accounting capitalization of an element of income, a procedure which is open to the various objections already urged against the recognition of non-purchased goodwill and interest during construction. It is doubtless true that the investor hopes and expects to realize finally a return sufficient to make up for the lean periods; but even if the future large earnings are positively assured it would obscure the actual situation to book such income prior to its realization. Any such accounting procedure, as previously explained, is unsound in that it tends to obscure the true record of income. Further, the funds of the individual business are certainly not accruing willy-nilly each year at the normal competitive rate of interest.

When we turn to the publicly regulated enterprise the case is not quite so clear. Going value, franchise value, and related intangibles have had their principal practical application in this field. In connection with rate regulation the valuation of railway properties and those of other regulated enterprises is a matter which has been very much in the limelight. It has been repeatedly urged that the public utility investor is entitled to a "reasonable return on a fair value" of his property. In this connection the courts and commissions have more or less unanimously taken the general position that the rate should be a conservative, non-speculative one, and that some provision should be made to preserve the integrity of the investment. This attitude has been very imperfectly adhered to by the regulating bodies, but has nevertheless persisted and gained in favor. A fairly complete adoption of the "guaranteed industry" principle in the railway field seems to be impending.

If the public utility is not "guaranteed," it would seem that rates should be so adjusted that the investor in such properties would be neither discriminated against nor advantaged as compared with his fellow investor in competitive lines which involve the same burdens with respect to risk and other aspects of ownership. If the investor in these competitive lines were able to recover pioneering losses, then the investor in public utilities should be allowed to do so. In any event the investor in the regulated field should not be made to undergo early losses and lean years and then in addition be forced to submit to a nonspeculative rate of income in later more prosperous periods. If the rates prescribed by the rate-making authorities result in a net return which is lower than that which would normally be earned, and no adjustment is made to cover risk, the legitimate rights of the investor are evidently being infringed upon.

As was stated above the tendency has been to restrict the rate of net income allowed the public utilities below the normal income rates in other fields, and to recompense the investor in a roundabout fashion by permitting him to earn this restricted rate upon an additional value, the capitalized amount of early deficiencies and losses. If this principle is carried out to its logical conclusion it means that the valuation of a public utility for rate purposes simmers down to a record of initial investment coupled with a compound interest calculation. (Ideally the change in the value of money should also be taken into account.)

It is not intended to discuss the propriety of going value as a basis for rates, or the desirability of the complete adoption by regulatory bodies of the guaranteed industry principle. This is quite beyond the scope of this study. A question may be raised, however, as to the feasibility of actually entering in the accounts the values which are determined by courts and commissions as a basis for rate calculations. Such values, it would seem, might well be given no explicit accounting recognition. They are a matter of governmental determination, are quite apart from commercial principles of valuation, have little or no significance for the operating management. No fundamental objection, perhaps, can be urged against their appearance in the accounts under appropriate captions; but it may be insisted that their inclusion as assets is somewhat inconsistent with certain fundamental conceptions of the accountant, and in any case can serve no essential purpose.

CHAPTER XIV

PRELIMINARY VALUATION PROBLEMS

In Chapter XII the treatment of interest and other phases of income during the preoperating period was fully discussed. There are other difficult questions arising during the preliminary period, however, problems which have to do especially with the initial valuation of the assets. The setting up of the asset accounts and the preparation of the first balance sheet are matters which involve peculiarly troublesome analyses. This is particularly true in the case of the large enterprise. Here an elaborate financial program is needed; the properties required may be numerous and complex; the organization and construction period may be of considerable length. The problems of valuation arising under these circumstances relate distinctly to considerations stressed in the two preceding chapters and hence may well be examined at this point. There is a special need for a careful treatment of this subject in view of the extent to which these questions of initial valuation have been ignored by writers and professional accountants.

GENERAL INITIAL COSTS

It was indicated in Chapter XIII that from the standpoint of the construction period all costs can be divided between direct and indirect charges, those which are assignable to specific physical objects and those which are assignable only to the enterprise in its entirety. It will now be necessary to consider this classification somewhat further.

As the important example of the indirect or general costs, organization outlays may be given. Payments to promoters, incorporation fees, legal expenses, costs of prospectus, certificates, etc., commissions to underwriters and salesmen, outlays for preliminary advertising—these are all items falling into this class. Evidently such costs must be incurred in the launching of any elaborate undertaking; but it is also quite evident that they are not direct costs of buildings, equipment, merchandise, or other physical assets. This does not mean, however, that such costs do not result in legitimate asset values. They are not a jot less significant in their contribution to the asset total and the investment total than the costs of brick and lumber. They measure a legitimate part of the properties in the broadest sense. And they require explicit recognition in the accounts.

In view of current misconceptions this matter needs emphasis. In the first place it should be reiterated that whether or not a particular outlay results in an addition to the value of a specific *tangible* asset is a point of little significance as far as its fundamental accounting character is concerned. Securities and customers' balances are highly valid assets and yet are obviously not closely associated with particular physical properties. Further, even the direct cost value of the tangible asset such as a building can be resolved into other elements than those pertaining to physical things. Labor as well as material cost is required in the fabrication of any structure or piece of equipment. Material cost in turn can be dissected again into labor and material cost. And so on. Value from the cost side is primarily the summation of the costs of a series of services, the value of the physical elements involved, in their primal raw state, being commonly a small or even negligible factor. The asset category, as has been emphasized repeatedly in the foregoing pages, is based primarily upon economic rather than physical concepts.

The necessity for undergoing these general organization costs seems to be clear. Financiering is as essential as engineering. The building of a railway, for example, could never be accomplished by the construction engineer alone. The capital of the investor must be drawn to the task; and it may be necessary to interest a multitude of individual investors. Hence promotion and other preliminary costs may be considered quite as legitimate as the costs of surveying, grading, etc.

Incidentally it may be noted that there are some costs which have to do with technical construction that are so general in character that their allocation to specific units of tangible property can scarcely be accomplished except on a purely arbitrary basis. The salaries of supervising architects, surveyors, and managers, and the necessary clerical costs, for example, cannot easily be distributed in a rational manner in the case of a large undertaking with numerous and complex initial properties. A problem of cost accounting is here involved which is closely analogous to many questions of cost allocation arising during the operating period. The loading of general asset costs into specific asset accounts, like the distribution of overhead to specific jobs and processes, involves judgment and estimate at various points. Cost values on the books of the fabricator seldom if ever, throughout the field of accounting, have any entirely independent validity. The cost of a particular fixed asset or an elaborate plant is, like the cost of an operation, simply a sum of values drawn from a more or less conglomerate mass of figures on the basis of the best possible judgment available.

It might be urged that such services as promotion, underwriting, etc., do not have definite prices as do the services of architect and builder, and hence that expenditure for such services are peculiarly susceptible to inflation. This may be readily admitted, however, without accepting the conclusion that no explicit recognition as assets should be given to such costs. It is merely a question of degree. Technical construction costs as well as outlays for organization and financial requirements are often quite unreasonable.

In determining the valid property charges during the organization and construction period each outlay might well be tested on this basis: Does the cost in question represent the price of a commodity, service, or condition *necessary* to the initiation of the enterprise, and was the price paid a *legitimate* one under all the circumstances? It must be recognized, of course, that the values of initial properties cannot be determined ideally. Especially in the case of the large undertaking it is evident that the property accounts will exhibit only substantially correct figures at the best. The peculiarities and accidents of the particular situation coupled with the errors in judgment on the part of those immediately concerned preclude the possibility of discovering ideal asset values. Nevertheless, as was indicated above, it is no more difficult to ascertain the legitimate cost of property in a given case than it is to determine the cost of producing a particular product. The question as to what are and what are not legitimate property costs will be further considered in a later section of this chapter.

We have now to deal with the express accounting treatment of these general organization costs. One solution would be to charge them to the accounts with buildings, equipment, etc., in proportion to the direct costs of such properties. This is objectionable, however, in that it involves an apportionment on a purely arbitrary basis and obscures the direct costs of the tangible assets. Organization costs are really not even indirect costs of *specific* tangible properties. They are a cost of the business institution as an entity which is something more and beyond the sum of its layout of physical assets. Consequently it is hardly reasonable to distribute such costs among the accounts with material properties. Further, so to apportion these general charges would require an adjustment of depreciation rates, and might result in an amortization of such costs in an illegitimate manner.

The better procedure is to charge costs of promotion and organization to specific accounts restricted to such general charges. This gives a kind of intangible asset, applicable to the business as a whole but not assignable to tangible properties. This practice—especially when carried into the balance sheet—has the desirable result of causing attention to be focused upon the amount of the organization cost. If this amount is unduly large a question is at once raised as to the legitimacy of the outlays, and the stockholders and all others concerned are in a position to judge for themselves as to the care with which their funds have been handled. There is, of course, a general prejudice in favor of definite tangible assets, and hence the temptation to charge all these costs to plant and equipment accounts is strong. But to do so makes it possible to cover up unreasonable allowances to promoters, construction company profits, extraordinary underwriting costs, etc., and to present a thoroughly unreasonable and misleading balance sheet. An honest presentation of these general outlays is much to be commended, and should inspire confidence in the management rather than distrust. As has been emphasized above, organization costs need not be viewed as uncertain, dubious, and ephemeral values, and hence need not be secreted under improper account titles.

Even if the physical property in a particular case consists essentially in a single important asset, such as an office building, for example, the organization costs may well be segregated in the ledger and in the balance sheet. They are no doubt a part of an "all assets" account; but their distinctive character makes it highly desirable to give them a special recognition.

The classifications of the Interstate Commerce Commission prescribed for the use of steam railways recognize the need for special organization and construction accounts. In the classification "investment in road and equipment" under the head "general expenditures" are found such account titles as "organization expenses," "general officers and clerks," "law," and "stationery and printing." This is highly commendable practice.

Assuming that organization costs constitute legitimate asset values at the outset and require separate accounting recognition, how should these costs finally be disposed of? This is a difficult question. In general the professional accountant supports the opinion that these charges should be amortized against operating revenues as soon as there is an excess of revenues available for this purpose, or within from two to five years if this is feasible. This view is unreasonable. It is based upon a conception of organization costs as an uncertain, dubious item, a necessary evil, which should be eliminated as soon as possible. Such costs must be recognized in the first place, so they argue, to avoid imperiling the credit of the enterprise through the appearance of an initial deficit; but this preliminary inflation of property values should be extinguished just as rapidly as operating conditions warrant. Plainly, in view of the discussion above, such an interpretation of *reasonable* organization costs is not sound. Further, it can hardly be urged that it is rational accounting to cover up losses to begin with, even though the perhaps praiseworthy intention to correct the overstatement as soon as possible through concealed profits is a part of the plan of procedure. As will be emphasized a little later, initial losses should be shown as such, and should only be written off against accumulated surplus, never against operating revenues.

An extreme position in the other direction is the opinion that organization costs are a bona fide value throughout the legal life of the enterprise, and should only be extinguished if the business is liquidated and its existence terminated. This view would mean that wherever a corporation, for example, was chartered for a definite term of years, its organization costs should be amortized in an orderly fashion during the specified period. This principle would evidently be hopelessly unsound if carried to extremes, as there are hundreds of corporations in some states which still exist as legal entities because the necessary steps have never been taken to destroy them, but which are fully defunct from an economic standpoint.

A reasonably conservative plan would be to extinguish these general costs in a systematic way during the life of the principal physical properties for which the initial funds were expended. Organization costs, in a sense, are incurred because they are required in getting the enterprise started and raising the necessary capital. Therefore it might be urged that, while not assignable to specific tangible asset accounts, they are related to the total of such assets in such a way that they expire as this original total disappears.

A modification of this rule is perhaps the most sound from a theoretic point of view. The mere fact of organization, unaccompanied by any properties other than organization expenses, can hardly be held to indicate the existence of property values. But as long as the *total* of asset values is at least maintained, regardless of the fact that initial items of equipment and other assets have disappeared, it might be reasonably urged that in general the significance of these original organization outlays is unimpaired. To the extent that this total is reduced, organization costs should be amortized accordingly. Thus a mining company which is steadily consuming its deposits should extinguish its promotion and organization costs in proportion to such expiration; for as a rule the complete exhaustion of the ore bodies will mean virtually the economic extinction of the enterprise.

One further plan which has a limited application should be mentioned. The cost of raising capital by means of a terminable security should be written off in an orderly manner during the life of the security; for the presumption in such a case would be that it would be necessary to incur similar costs in refunding. No doubt the cost of replacing the capital would not coincide exactly with the cost of issuing the original security; but it could surely be held, under such circumstances, that the significance of the first expenditures had completely disappeared.

PRELIMINARY DEPRECIATION

The significance and treatment of preliminary depreciation is a special problem in valuation which arises during the organization and construction period. Whenever the construction period is of any considerable duration, deterioration of tangible assets inevitably occurs. The question arises as to whether or not such deterioration is to be considered as giving rise to expiration of property value, and as to how such expiration—if any—is to be recognized in the accounts.

To be consistent with the view emphasized above that all legitimate outlays for commodities and services normally considered necessary for the initiation of an enterprise constitute costs of property and may be charged to asset accounts it must be insisted that no lapse in value with respect to the property as a whole can occur as a result of normal deterioration during a normal construction period. Reasoning by analogy may serve measurably to support this conclusion.

In the first place much material is economically consumed in the erection of buildings and other structures which is not embodied in the ultimate tangible result. The "forms" necessary in concrete work are an example. This material is later taken down and perhaps permanently discarded, but its cost (less salvage value) is naturally considered to be a part of the cost value of the completed structure. Again, in handling lumber and other construction materials the workmen are obliged to "waste" more or less significant amounts; raw

PRELIMINARY VALUATION PROBLEMS

materials are seldom if ever of ideal size and shape as far as the particular job is concerned, and hence there are bound to be virtually worthless remnants. But the fact that but 95 per cent of the lumber purchased for a particular job, for example, actually becomes a part of the finished building does not lead to the conclusion that the lumber cost value of the property is but 95 per cent of total cost incurred on this account. Further, the costs of the small tools and implements that are consumed in construction work are always treated as a part of the cost of the final asset resulting; although it is obvious that such items do not become attached to the object for which they were utilized in a tangible sense.

These cases are all clear. And it would seem to be no less evident that no loss in value occurs because there is deterioration during the construction period with respect to the final tangible properties turned over to the operating officials. The partial decay of physical items which inhere in the completed structure is one of the inevitable requirements of construction akin to the physical consumption of items necessary to the result but not embodied in a physical sense therein. During a reasonable construction period it is possible for a property as a whole to *deteriorate* but not to *depreciate*. At the beginning of the operating period a property should always be reckoned at 100 per cent of its legitimate cost, even if its physical and service life fall quite short of the technical ideal. If, for example, a property is of such a character that its condition when ready for operation is inevitably but 90 per cent of perfect from an engineering standpoint, the conclusion none the less follows that it has a value of 100 per cent.

This does not mean that there need be no accounting for depreciation during construction. While the properties of the enterprise as a whole cannot normally so depreciate it must be recognized that particular units can and do lose their value as a result of preliminary wear and tear.

This is most clear in the case of an elaborate undertaking such as a railway enterprise, for example, which requires perhaps several years for organization and construction, and will finally be made up of a great many distinct asset units. The railway company, ready to begin operations, will have tracks, bridges, buildings, locomotives, etc., etc. Further, each important class of property—or even each significant item—may require a distinct account. The accountant, under these circumstances, faces the problem of maintaining the integrity of each account as well as the asset total. If particular asset units have suffered especial deterioration in construction work and have a noticeably curtailed service life remaining, it would be a mistake to insist that no depreciation had occurred as far as the *specific items affected* were concerned. Suppose, for example, that cars used in hauling construction materials have but 60 per cent of their service life remaining when turned over to the operating department. How should this situation be analyzed and recorded? Clearly these cars have *depreciated* 40 per cent (on the straight-line plan, and ignoring salvage value), and if the cars account is to exhibit a reasonable current value (either directly or by means of a modifying contra account), it would seem to be necessary to record a credit to this property class for the proper amount.

In what account should the concurrent charge be entered? As has been emphasized, this item of depreciation does not constitute a lapse in value from the standpoint of the property as a whole. The cars have virtually given up their value in constructing the finished roadbed, tracks, etc., in the same manner as have the spades and other small tools utilized. Hence this depreciation (with respect to cars) is not a loss and is obviously not an expense and should be charged to some appropriate asset account. If a reasonable basis for allocation appears, the charge should be distributed among the accounts representing the more permanent property items in the erection or construction of which the depreciated cars were used. If such a distribution is possible only on an arbitrary basis, the situation calls for a special asset account which might be entitled "depreciation during construction." Such an account would be charged with the total expiration of cars and other properties partially depreciated during construction which could not reasonably be apportioned among the accounts representing the still more permanent assets.

How should such a special property charge be finally disposed of? A fairly satisfactory plan would be to amortize this value by charges to operating expense based upon a rate which was calculated in terms of all the rates applicable to the various properties resulting from the construction operations in which the initially depreciated assets played a part. In so far as the resulting property were roadbed or other highly permanent asset, a relatively low rate of extinguishment would evidently be applicable to depreciation during construction account.

Conceivably an accounting for depreciation during construction might be attempted in connection with more permanent assets. Suppose, for example, that the completed property of the *Z* Co. consists in three plants, *A, B,* and *C,* and that construction operations—carried on concurrently in each case—have required a period of two years. Evidently wear and tear in construction, the action of the elements, etc., will bring about some deterioration, and as a result the finished structures will not be technically perfect. Basing service life on an ideal engineering condition in such circumstances would make it necessary to recognize preliminary depreciation as having an application. Credits might be made to the three plant accounts (or to appropriate contra accounts) to cover depreciation so calculated, and the sum might be charged to a special asset account. This procedure, however, would seem to serve no useful purpose. The special asset value so created would of necessity be extinguished as the remaining plant values were written down, and the periodic distribution of depreciation during operation would hence be unchanged by the recognition of this preliminary depreciation. The more rational plan for such a case would seem to be to permit the plant values to remain unchanged until operations begin (assuming a reasonable construction period), after which time depreciation should be recognized on the basis of an operating service life based upon actual rather than ideal conditions.

PRELIMINARY LOSSES

Thus far stress has been laid upon the importance of including in the cost value of new properties all legitimate items. There remains to be considered another side of preliminary valuation. What costs should be *excluded* from property values as unreasonable? Under what circumstances are preliminary losses possible? How should excessive payments for construction materials and services be treated? Should the accountant take cognizance of inflation due to dishonesty and inefficiency?

The attitude of the professional accountant on the question of valuation is interestingly inconsistent. As a rule he concludes that all outlays during the preliminary period, regardless of their reasonableness, give bona fide property charges. This is surely a rather non-conservative position. Once revenue begins to accrue, however, the accountant reverses his attitude and holds that property charges should be written off rapidly; that all items in any way dubious should be extinguished as soon as revenues are capable of bearing the burden; that the utmost conservatism should be insisted upon in all revaluations.

As a matter of fact preoperating losses are a distinct possibility. There is nothing about the preliminary period which renders the funds of the investor inviolate. Assets can be dissipated just as easily during construction as at any other time. The enterprise may be forced to languish for long intervals because of an insufficiency of capital; and this will mean an unreasonable deterioration and excessive cost at various points. If the construction force is inefficiently handled the length of the building period may be unreasonably extended and labor and other costs consequently inflated. Materials may be carelessly used and material cost may thus be unduly high. Unusual accidents, strikes, delays in deliveries, bad weather conditions— all such circumstances may contribute to an extraordinary expenditure for initial properties. Further, dishonest and careless handling of funds and incompetent buying may result in the acceptance of prices for materials and services which are quite unreasonable.

The fact that an actual transaction has taken place and that a "cost" has been incurred does not force the conclusion that the amount of the outlay is a proper charge to an asset account. Unless a reasonable value is received for the particular expenditure a loss of capital is the result. It is quite possible for a company to begin operations with a deficit, that is, with a true asset total less than the sum of the funds actually invested. And if the viewpoint be accepted that it is the business of the accountant to report as nearly as may be the actual situation, then the initial balance sheet should show reasonable figures for the values of completed properties.

On the other hand the accountant can hardly set himself up as an absolute judge of values. The accounts cannot be expected to exhibit ideal figures. In general it is necessary to assume that in the case of a voluntary, bona fide purchase of material, services, etc., a value equivalent is received for the expenditure. It is only when it becomes clearly evident that this assumption is false that a revision is in order. Thus, in the construction period, unless circumstances make it clear that the initial price paid is quite improper or that values are being lost by accident, fraud, or inefficiency, it is quite reasonable for the accountant to view all outlays as legitimate costs of property. It should still be insisted, however, that when the circumstances are such as to indicate sharply the fact of loss it is quite unreasonable to fail to recognize the true situation in the accounts.

It is especially during the preliminary period that asset values are often dubious and uncertain. It is during this period that many transactions occur which are value-determining only in a nominal sense. It is often almost out of the question to ascertain legitimate values. What is the proper erection cost for an elaborate new property? There may be no adequate basis for comparison which makes a rational answer possible. A bridge across the St. Lawrence, to cite an extreme example, is not a standard article with a standard price. Is the fair accounting value of such a property, when complete, its actual cost or what it should have cost under other more perfect conditions? As far as possible comparison with representative cases should be relied upon. All normal and necessary items of cost can be charged to property; all unreasonable and superfluous outlays should be deducted from capital. But it should be recognized that frequently no solid basis for assaying construction expenditures is available. In principle the distinction between an addition to assets and a subtraction from equities is clear, as has been emphasized; but cases arise during the preliminary period which are almost insolvable.

As was indicated in the immediately preceding chapters it is not always easy to delimit the construction period. In some cases organization and construction gradually merge into operation, no hard and fast line of cleavage appearing; in other instances, especially where the enterprise rapidly develops, financing and building go on more or less indefinitely as concomitants of continued operation. This difficulty of determining a normal or legitimate preliminary period is a main reason for the uncertainty with respect to reasonable asset values.

In the case of railways and other public utilities it is an especially troublesome task to set the limits of the construction interval. In attempting to pass upon this question in any case it would be necessary of course to canvass the whole situation. All unavoidable obstacles to speedy construction would require recognition. But the preoperating period must not be unduly lengthened. To argue that the cost of an abandoned curve line is a legitimate part of the construction cost of the new and straightened roadway and track—as has been done—is quite unsound; it involves a thoroughly unreasonable extension of the conception of construction.[1] It is but a step from such an argument to the position that early losses from operation should be capitalized in the accounts as going values or under similar head—a thesis rejected in the last chapter.

The building of a modern enterprise is a complex process. It involves more than mere physical construction; organization and development are required. Preliminary period gradually gives way to regular operation. After, or along with, construction come preliminary advertising, establishment of sales connections, organization of operating force, etc. In this situation practical rules and expedients must be resorted to in distinguishing between asset charges, loss of capital, and costs of revenue. Before revenues appear there are but two alternatives open: A particular outlay results either in an addition to properties or a reduction in investment. Here it is perhaps expedient to exhibit losses only when the case is clear. Once revenues appear another alternative presents itself. From this point on it is doubtless sound accounting from a practical standpoint to charge all doubtful items to revenue or accumulated profits.

---

[1] Nevertheless, under certain conditions the Interstate Commerce Commission permits the railroads to treat the cost of abandoned property as a deferred charge extinguishable against later operating revenues.

PROPERTY VALUATION AND SECURITIES

A final topic should be briefly considered before this discussion of preliminary valuation problems is closed. In the case of the corporation, funds are secured primarily through the issue of securities. These securities commonly have a par value, and their total par value constitutes the formal capitalization. But it seldom happens that the value of properties constructed or otherwise acquired (even assuming that all legitimate costs are included) exactly equals the par value of the securities issued; usually nominal capitalization exceeds the actual investment. This need not be viewed as an improper situation. It simply means that in American corporate financing it is common practice to emit securities at a discount. Unfortunately, however, the fact of nominal capitalization has been frequently misunderstood and improperly entered in the accounts. It is customary to book securities at par and inflate property values accordingly in an effort to give formal capital a specious validity. That is, par values are frequently taken as the real basis for the valuation of assets in the balance sheet. The securities are placed on one side of the statement at par; the asset items are listed on the other side at figures totaling the same amount. In other words, discounts are covered up by charges to property.[2]

Such a practice, of course, is entirely improper. Sums appearing in the asset accounts under these circumstances may bear little relation to bona fide property values. The par of securities issued is a formal fact which reflects investment only in the most general way. In particular cases nominal capital is an amount of little significance. Indeed, for accounting purposes par value with respect to securities having no repayment date might well be eliminated entirely. The abandonment of a

---

[2] In Chapter XVI the accounting for stock discounts will be further discussed, and in Chapter XVII brief consideration will be given to the significance and treatment of contractual discounts.

formal stated value would naturally require a shifting of emphasis to the amount of funds actually invested and actual costs of construction and purchase. The equity values would then tend to become merely the equitable dispersion of the asset total. In this connection the development of no-par stock is a healthy tendency. There is no temptation to book such stock at a figure above actual investment. The proper treatment of such stock is analogous to that applied to sole-proprietors' and partners' equities: The capital account is made to reflect objectively determined asset values.

There are some objections to no-par stock, no doubt; but none of these have much significance from the accounting standpoint. A share of stock may be conceived as a fractional part of a book value as easily as in terms of an arbitrary par value. Dividends may be declared in "dollars per share" as readily as in percentage of a nominal capital; and the rate of dividends to true book value is certainly a much more significant and less misleading fact than the relation between dividends and formal capitalization.

If the par value of capital stock is placed in the balance sheet and this figure exceeds actual investment on a cash basis or its equivalent, the difference should be shown under a separate head as discount on stock—a special valuation item as previously explained. Such a contra balance does not represent a dissipation of capital; it is not an organization and construction deficit or loss. It is merely an offset to formal capital, the difference between a nominal equity and the amount actually invested.

Property values are often particularly uncertain where securities are issued directly in exchange therefor. Suppose, for example, that the owner of a patent turns his rights over to a new corporation in exchange for a thousand shares of stock. How should the purchasing company register this transaction on its books? The value of the patents (as an independent fact) may be quite uncertain and the stock may likewise have no established market price. In such a situation valuation might reasonably be attempted from either direction. An appraisal of the patents might be made and the resulting value used for the accounting entries; or reliable bids for the stock might be secured and the value so indicated employed in the accounts. If trustworthy market prices are available as a basis for gauging the value of a security which has been emitted in exchange for a property of uncertain significance, such prices give probably the most reasonable clue to asset values which can be found. While in general accounting values cannot be based upon market prices for outstanding securities, it is not improper, in the case of a new enterprise, and where asset values are obscure, to proceed from this standpoint.

An especially difficult and interesting problem of valuation arises with respect to commissions paid in connection with the issue ("sale") of new securities. It was indicated in the first section of this chapter that such outlays, being necessary costs of raising capital, can be charged to a property account. In this connection, however, a number of questions present themselves which can best be settled by reference to theoretic points of view stressed in preceding chapters.

Suppose, to take a concrete example, that the A Co. sells its stock through hired salesmen, the ultimate investor paying $90 per share and the salesman receiving a commission of $5 per share. If this, under the circumstances, is a reasonable method to follow in securing the necessary funds the transaction should be recorded (in summary) by a credit to the capital stock account of $100 per share (assuming par to be $100 and that it is desirable—in conformity with current usage—to preserve par value in the accounts), a debit to discount on stock—a valuation account—of $10, a debit to organization costs—an asset account—of $5, and a debit to cash or equivalent of $85

PRELIMINARY VALUATION PROBLEMS 351

This conclusion seems reasonable enough, but some doubt as to its propriety is raised when the circumstances of the illustration are slightly altered. Suppose the B Co. disposes of its stock by selling the entire issue outright to an underwriting or investment house for $85 per share. All other conditions are the same as in the preceding case. The transaction would be recognized in the accounts in this case by a charge to cash of $85, a debit to discount of $15, and a credit to capital stock of $100.

A comparison of the two cases now discloses the fact that in the first asset values of $90 have been recognized, while in the other the funds received total but $85. Is this discrepancy legitimate? The only difference between the two cases seems to be that in the first the enterprise is undertaking for itself the task of raising the capital from the final investor, while in the second the company is dealing directly with a securities middleman. This minor variation in procedure, it might be urged, does not justify a 5 per cent difference in the amount of capital investment recognized in the accounts.

The comparison may be made still more difficult by assuming in the first instance that the A Co. engages an underwriter to market the stock, all risk being assumed by the A Co.; and that the underwriter sells the stock for $90, deducts an agreed commission of $5, and forwards the remaining $85 to the A Co. The second case is as before, the underwriter actually buying the stock for $85 directly from the B Co. With this alteration the two situations would seem to be almost identical, in essence; and yet the accounting suggested above would give a variation in asset values between the two.

The question involved is, should the issuing company consider the amount of capital raised to be determined by the sum paid by some final investor, or by the price received from the first party to whom title to the security actually passes? In answer it must be urged that the initial amount of the corporation's funds is the amount paid by the first stockholders, regardless of the permanence of their tenure. Thereafter the stock may pass through many hands at varying prices, but these subsequent transactions in nowise affect the books of the issuing company. If a company sells its stock outright at a net price, there being no commissions or fees, then there is no direct cost of raising capital in that case; the company buys no services of salesmen or underwriters and hence cannot recognize any such values in its accounts. The fact that the security is later "retailed" at a higher price does not alter asset values on the books of the original issuer. The manufacturer who sells goods to the wholesaler does not receive the retail price. Nor can he say that he has purchased the service of the wholesaler in such a case. If, however, he engages the wholesaler to act as his agent at an agreed compensation, he is thereby acquiring the services of the wholesaler and the value thereof becomes a cost to the purchaser. Similarly, the company which issues securities can treat as legitimate initial values only the sum received from the immediate subscriber; and if a part of this sum is paid for necessary services in arranging the transaction the full amount is none the less a cost of property in the broad sense. If, on the other hand, the amount received from the subscriber is net, no service in connection therewith has been purchased and hence none can be recognized in the accounts.

This conclusion means that apparent discrepancies in asset values *between enterprises* will arise. But as was pointed out in Chapter XII and elsewhere, such discrepancies are quite rational when the purposes and nature of accounting are considered. It is the business of the accountant above all to adhere to the actual record for the particular enterprise. If one company buys the services of a construction company in acquiring its plant it will probably pay a higher price, and there will be a resultant higher charge to asset accounts, than in the case of the company which erects its own properties. And if one company undergoes a cost of raising capital while another does not, the legitimate cost of property is accordingly higher in one case than in the other.

CHAPTER XV

RELATIONS BETWEEN OWNER AND BUSINESS

It has been urged at various points throughout this study that the personification of the business enterprise is a reasonable, indeed indispensable figure for the accountant. It has also been insisted that the entire group of long-term investors or owners constitutes the most concrete manifestation of the business entity, and that, accordingly, the accountant should develop his classifications and organize his procedures from the point of view of the owners as a body, in terms of the needs and purposes of those furnishing the bulk of the capital of the business. On the other hand it has been indicated in several connections that while the enterprise may be viewed as something beyond and in addition to the persons of the investors, care must be exercised in setting up owners and business as distinct entities capable of carrying on commercial relations. Thus it has been pointed out with respect to proprietary salaries, interest during construction, goodwill, etc., that the assumption that the business buys the services of the investors seldom indeed has any proper validity from an accounting standpoint.

Uncertainty with respect to the fundamental starting point, a shifting of emphasis from owner to business entity and back again to owner, is responsible for much of the confusion in the field of accounting analysis. In the present chapter this question will be further considered in connection with some particularly troublesome types of transactions, and with reference to the four cases, sole-proprietorship, partnership, close corporation, and open corporation.

OWNERS' BORROWINGS

A situation very difficult to interpret in terms of fundamental accounting classes is presented by the transaction which consists in a "loan" by the business to an owner. Such transactions are especially common in partnerships but are also found in other cases. What is the essential nature of a "borrowing" by an owner? How shall such occurrences be analyzed and recorded in the accounts?

In the case of the sole-proprietorship the answer seems clear and unmistakable. Here there can be no such thing as a loan by the business to the proprietor. In this case there is no sharp differentiation for accounting purposes between "business" and principal owner. If the owner takes funds or other property from the business this constitutes simply a reduction in business assets and an equal diminution in capital or equities. By whatever manner the owner is pleased to label such an occurrence its essence is unchanged. From the standpoint of management, ownership, customers, prospective creditors, or other important interest it would be quite out of the question to conclude that the proprietor could borrow funds from the business without reducing business assets and capital. Proprietary borrowings under such circumstances are simply proprietary drawings. And such transactions should be recorded by appropriate credit entries in the cash or other asset account affected and equal charges to the owner's equity account. In no case should the assumption that the transaction constitutes an exchange of assets—cash for receivables—be permitted.

In the case of the partnership the situation is by no means so clear; and it is here that borrowings by owners are especially common. In current discussions of this topic it is usually urged that these transactions between partner and firm should be interpreted and recorded just as are occurrences between firm and outsiders. But there are serious reasons for questioning the propriety of such recommendations. Partners' borrowings to some extent may be considered in the light of drawings, and their record as an exhibit of adjustments between partners. The two points of view will be examined with some care.

Let us consider an illustration. Suppose that X and Y are equal partners in some commercial undertaking and that Y finds himself in need of funds for outside purposes. Suppose further that there are no profits available from which to draw and that Y accordingly borrows $10,000 from the firm, giving his promissory note for the amount. How should this transaction be interpreted and recorded? According to the orthodox view the amount of the note should be charged to the notes receivable account as in the case of a note made by a customer. That is, the transaction is interpreted as an exchange of assets, asset and equity totals—and therefore financial status—remaining unchanged.

But do these entries and this interpretation express the true condition of affairs? Does the note receivable signed by Y replace the cash withdrawn in any but a formal sense? Are the business assets truly maintained? The point of view of the creditor may be first considered. Here the fact of unlimited liability is an important matter. If the X and Y firm is of the usual type the creditors depend for security not only upon the assets of the business but ultimately upon the entire personal estates of X and Y as well. In other words, the law does not consider a part only of the assets of X and Y as subject to the just claims of the contractual investors; all their properties are involved. As was pointed out in Chapter III, a two-section balance sheet would be desirable from the point of view of the creditor, a statement exhibiting the business assets and equities as well as all outside properties and rights. Under these circumstances the depositing of Y's note, clearly, does not maintain the business assets and protect the creditor in at all the same way as would the receipt of a note signed by a responsible outsider. As to whether or not the loan to Y actually diminishes the creditor's security depends primarily upon the disposition Y makes of the borrowed funds. If he invests the $10,000 in other property without loss in realizable value the position of the creditor is essentially unimpaired. If, on the other hand, he spends or loses this sum his total wealth or estate is reduced accordingly and the security of the firm's creditors is disturbed.

It should be emphasized that the creditor's position is essentially the same after this loan has been made as it would be if no note were deposited and the sum of $10,000 were treated as a partial retirement of Y's capital investment in the partnership. On the other hand, in the case of liquidation the availability of a note signed by Y might be of minor advantage to the creditor.

Likewise from the point of view of the partners and their business interests it is doubtful if Y's note can be considered a bona fide asset. The partners naturally wish to have the accounts show the history and periodic standing of the enterprise as a distinct business unit. Their point of view is closely akin to the managerial. But borrowings or other drawings by the partners surely reduce the effective business assets, and are likely to impair the enterprise as an operating entity. This may be shown by a rather extreme illustration.

Suppose that the X and Y firm is engaged in cutting a definite tract of timber, and that as the original capital becomes available in current funds the partners "borrow" from the funds from time to time the amount of the depletion, depositing their promissory notes for the appropriate amounts. Assuming that this plan is continued until all capital assets are completely liquidated, that all net income is divided and withdrawn, and that there are no liabilities, the final balance sheet of the firm—just before dissolution—would show on one side the partners' notes and on the other the capital accounts. Evidently in this case the partnership as an enterprise has no true assets; the items on one side of the balance sheet are merely offsets to the amounts appearing on the other side. The business has virtually ceased to exist and its assets have been distributed. The notes are merely an expression of proprietary drawings; they are not assets. And if partners' borrowings are not assets in this extreme case where all capital is so drawn, it may be argued that any step in this direction involves a decrease in true capital.

The accounts to which these notes are charged may, with some propriety, be viewed as capital adjustment accounts rather than asset headings. The making of these notes is one way of preserving equity between X and Y. If drawings have been unequal a payment will have to be made by the deficient partner. Each might of course insist upon the payment of the gross amount of the notes and the subsequent equal division of the funds thus raised; but this procedure would be equivalent to a payment by one partner to the other for the net amount—the excess of his drawings.

Returning to the first illustration—a loan of $10,000 from the firm to Y—it is interesting to note the relation of the individual partner to the situation. Y has drawn $10,000 from the joint funds, 50 per cent of which were contributed by himself. Accordingly, from his point of view, he is borrowing $5,000 from X and withdrawing an equal sum of his own. X, analogously, views the transaction as the equivalent of a personal loan to Y for $5,000. Y's $10,000 note then constitutes an asset of $5,000 from X's point of view and a liability of $5,000 from his own standpoint. If it be insisted that the note is an asset of $10,000 from the standpoint of the firm as a whole the conclusion is forced that Y is a part owner in a right against himself—a somewhat fantastic conception.

On the whole it would seem to be safer to conclude that partners' borrowings are very closely allied to proprietary drawings from the accounting standpoint, and that the superficial legal distinction that exists between the two cases should be ignored when one is assaying the accounts from the standpoint of the actual financial status of the partnership. A note drawn by a partner in favor of the partnership should be viewed, not as an asset similar to a note signed by a customer, but as primarily a proprietary adjustment between the partners. A special account title, such as "loan to Y," for example, should be used to cover such borrowings. The designation "notes receivable" is quite misleading.

In the case of the "open" corporation the situation would be quite different. A note drawn by a stockholder in favor of the corporation would here be as legitimate a corporate asset as the note of any equally responsible outsider. Such a note puts the corporation in possession of a right entirely in addition to and distinct from any rights it previously had against the stockholder as a member of the company. The fact of limited liability means that the stockholder usually only jeopardizes the amount of his investment and that the creditor, consequently, has no rights against any other property the stockholder may have. But a note gives a definite additional receivable. From the standpoint of the company, then, a loan to the stockholder does not impair the assets any more than would a loan to any other party. The stockholder's note is in nowise a reduction of capital, but is a genuine addition to assets. The corporation, a distinct legal entity, has an enforceable right against a supposedly responsible party for the amount of the loan.

A loan to a stockholder in a close corporation, on the other hand, gives another doubtful case. If the borrower is a stockholder with a controlling interest, a question is at once raised as to the validity of the whole transaction. Legally the close corporation is of course a distinct entity and its formal assets are unimpaired by a loan to a stockholder. But as a practical matter such a loan may approach in character a plain retirement in capital. Suppose, to take a striking example, that Z owns 99 per cent of the stock of the Z Co. Evidently this gives him virtually complete control. Under such circumstances the acts of the corporation are essentially Z's acts; a loan by the corporation to Z becomes essentially a loan from Z to himself. As to whether the integrity of the corporation is endangered by such a loan depends entirely upon the extent and character of Z's other resources. If the process is carried very far, so that, for example, a major part of the company's capital consists of notes signed by Z, the situation becomes highly questionable. Certainly the cautious auditor in such a case would take good care to exhibit these notes for exactly what they were, and would not allow them to be treated as ordinary notes receivable.

ADJUSTMENTS FOR INTEREST

Interest payments and accruals on owners' borrowings likewise call for special treatment. In this connection it will be necessary only to examine the situation in the case of the partnership, the relation of the problem as it arises in the other cases to the conditions of the partnership having already been indicated. It is commonly held that interest accruing on loans to partners should be credited to the regular interest account, should be viewed, in other words, as an earning in the same class as interest on customers' notes. To the extent, however, that the view developed above to the effect that partners' borrowings are very similar to drawings is correct, it is evident that interest on such loans calls for a special interpretation.

Suppose, for example, that in the first illustration mentioned above interest on the loan to Y is due at the end of a year, the rate being 7 per cent. Suppose further that Y for some reason finds it inconvenient to make the payment, and that it is agreed between the partners that a charge be made to Y's capital account for the amount of interest due, $700. According to the conventional method of procedure the concurrent credit would be placed in the interest revenue account. But is this supposed revenue item actually an earning? A careful examination of the case discloses the fact that no revenue whatever is involved; the transaction is in essence simply a capital adjustment between the two partners. Assets are unaffected by the occurrence and total proprietorship is unchanged. This can perhaps be best shown by an examination of hypothetical balance sheets as affected by this transaction alone.

The balance sheet of X and Y just after the loan is made, it will be assumed, appears as follows:

Sundry Assets..........	$ 90,000	X, Capital...............	$ 50,000
Loan to Y...............	10,000	Y, Capital...............	$ 50,000
	$100,000		$100,000

Now if all other transactions for the period are ignored the item of interest revenue may be divided equally between the two partners by charging the interest account for $700 and crediting each of the capital accounts with $350. A new balance sheet, affected only by these interest entries, would stand as follows:

Sundry Assets...........	$ 90,000	X, Capital...............	$ 50,350
Loan to Y...............	10,000	Y, Capital...............	49,650
	$100,000		$100,000

A comparison of the two sheets shows very clearly that no income whatever has been realized by the firm as a result of the interest adjustment. Asset and equity totals are identical in the two statements, and, as was pointed out in Chapter XI, a transaction involving net revenue in the nature of the case enhances both assets and equities. Net revenue is the equity representation of the increase in asset values resulting from successful operation. Since this test fails here there has evidently been no income realized. The introduction of the interest account is a bit of formal procedure which has nothing to do with actual income. The net result of the entire transaction is a decrease of $350 in one partner's equity account and an equal increase in the other. Evidently we have here an illustration of an interequity transaction. Total proprietorship is not affected; asset values are unchanged; no income has been realized. X's equity has been increased; Y's has been correspondingly diminished; the firm as a whole has neither suffered loss nor realized gain.

The debit and credit entries to the interest account might well have been omitted. In this case the transaction would be recorded by a charge of $700 to Y, capital, and credits of $350 each to Y, capital and X, capital; or, more simply, the situation might be fully recognized by a debit of $350 to Y's account and an equal credit to X's account.

It might be urged that the introduction of the entries in the interest account serves a useful purpose in presenting in formal fashion the history of the transaction, and that the integrity of the final balance sheet is in no way disturbed thereby. The answer to this argument is that while such accounting does not impair the accuracy of the balance sheet it does distort the income statement. If credits to interest of this type are included with regular interest earnings they go to swell the final net income figure. The amounts involved will usually be small but the principle is of consequence. No accounting procedure should be approved which permits the shifting of an item of original proprietorship from one account

RELATIONS BETWEEN OWNER AND BUSINESS 363

to another to affect the showing of net revenue. Further, it may well be doubted if the true character of the transaction is more clearly exhibited by means of the entries in the interest account. If it is desired to display the history of the transaction very fully some account other than the general interest account might well be used. A temporary residence for such items might be labeled "partners' adjustments" or given some other appropriate title. Whatever the caption used it should be emphasized that the account does not represent income.

How would the situation be interpreted and recorded if Y actually paid $700 in cash when the interest fell due? Here we have an actual increase in assets, and it might accordingly seem reasonable to urge that an earning has been realized. Such a conclusion, however, is of doubtful propriety.

Let us examine the entries again. If the concurrent credit (when cash is charged) is entered in the interest account, the transaction would seem to have all the "earmarks" of a genuine income-producing occurrence. But it must be remembered that since Y has a half-interest in all income, the amount of $350 must ultimately find its way to his capital account as a credit. In summary, then, we have a debit to cash of $700, and a credit to each partner of $350. As far as Y is concerned this means that the amount of $350 is virtually transferred from one pocket to another—from outside interests to the partnership—and really represents not profit but new investment. The other $350 represents a payment made by Y to X for the use of $5,000 of X's money for one year. From X's point of view, analogously, an earning of $350 has appeared, 7 per cent on his loan to Y for one year. But has the *firm* earned anything? Has the partnership as an operating unit realized any income? Y has paid $350 to X and has invested an additional $350 in the business to preserve the equality in capital accounts. X has earned $350 in the collateral venture of loaning money to *y*. It is hard to see how it can reasonably be said that the firm has made a profit on this interowner transaction.

NEW INVESTMENT AND REVALUATION

A change in ownership, either partial or complete, may require a revaluation of the assets. The explanation of this fact lies in the natural divergence between book values and market values, both with respect to particular properties and to the enterprise and its assets as a whole. As has been emphasized repeatedly in foregoing connections, the accountant in general must start with cost. Ideally he should thereafter record all genuine changes from the standpoint of the going concern arising in connection with every asset item. But accounting in practice falls far short of this ideal; and even if it did not, there would still arise the problem of revaluation whenever the assets in their entirety were transferred to new owners. The new investor is almost certain to view the situation in a different light—either more or less favorable—than that which is expressed by the book values. Selling value on a big scale, both with respect to fixed and current assets, is bound to give figures quite different from those exhibited in the accounts. Forced liquidation values are of course likely to be much lower than book values for most kinds of property. Where the new owner expects to continue the use of the assets as before, on the other hand, the prices he is willing to pay may be more or less than book values depending upon circumstances. He may, for example, be willing to pay more than book value for the real estate and less for the merchandise.

Further, if the sale results in the transfer to new owners of the entire business, and all assets, conditions, and circumstances attaching thereto, the recognition of goodwill may be involved. As was pointed out in Chapter XIII, a genuine change in ownership may justify goodwill from an accounting standpoint. The new owners may actually pay for the exceptional services, conditions, or factors which attach to the business, and hence to them this outlay becomes a cost of property. The previous owner cannot recognize this excess value as an asset in his accounts, since this involves the capitalization of his own services and obscures the real situation as has been pointed out; but the new owner may reasonably treat all actual costs incurred in acquiring the business as accounting facts.

Where the change in ownership is complete and unqualified there can be little question as to the proper accounting procedure; the accounts should exhibit the situation from the standpoint of the new proprietors. In many instances, however, the change in the personnel of the owners is partial. In such cases two or more equally reasonable alternatives may present themselves. Especially is this true in the case of the unincorporated business. A new partner may be taken in, the business in other respects remaining unchanged. Strictly speaking this means a change in the identity of the firm: a new partnership. On the other hand the business may go on with no marked change in managerial or other policies. Such an occurrence savors in part of a transaction between proprietors personally; and it also may be viewed as a transaction between the business as an entity and a new owner.

An illustration will be needed to indicate clearly the nature of the accounting problem. Suppose that the balance sheet of the A and B firm, in summary, stands as follows:

Sundry Assets............	$100,000	A, Capital...............	$ 50,000
		B, Capital...............	50,000
	$100,000		$100,000

At this time B decides to sell out his interest to C for $55,000 cash. A, however, agrees to accept C as an equal partner only on condition that he pay $5,000 in cash into the firm. An agreement is consummated on these lines; C pays $55,000 to B and turns over $5,000 to the new firm.

How should the partnership accounts be adjusted to take care of this situation? Evidently three differing points of view are involved. *A* would doubtless be inclined to argue that no revaluation of the assets was necessary, that the book values should be allowed to stand. From this standpoint the transaction would be recorded (assuming a continuous set of accounts) by a charge of $5,000 to cash, a charge of $50,000 to *B*'s account, a credit of $52,500 to *C*'s account, and a credit of $2,500 to *A*. That is, *A* would naturally feel that the exchange between *B* and *C* in nowise affected the asset values, and that the only real change consisted in the increase of $5,000 in the cash balance and the consequent enhancement of his equity by $2,500. He would doubtless insist that the business had not sold its assets, and that there was accordingly no reason for a revision of asset values.

According to *B*'s viewpoint, however, the true value of a half-interest in the business prior to the receipt of the new cash is $55,000, the amount he realizes therefor. If this valuation be accepted, then the entire enterprise and all that goes with it is worth $110,000, and, after the $5,000 in cash is deposited, $115,000. This view could be written into the accounts by a charge of $5,000 to cash, a charge of $10,000 to goodwill (or to one or more specific asset accounts, such as real estate if it were decided that the increased value attached to some particular tangible property or properties), a debit of $50,000 to *B*, a credit of $57,500 to *C*, and a credit of $7,500 to *A*.

C, on the other hand, would consider a half-interest in the enterprise to be worth the total amount paid by him to secure such an interest, viz., $60,000. To adjust the accounts to conform to this interpretation it would be necessary to increase the goodwill valuation to $15,000. A balance sheet prepared in accordance therewith would appear somewhat as follows:

Original Assets	$100,000	*A,* Capital	$ 60,000
Cash	5,000	*C,* Capital	60,000
Goodwill	15,000		
	$120,000		$120,000

In practice the last valuation would doubtless be adopted. It seems to be natural for a management to be more than willing to revise values upward if a good excuse for so doing offers itself. The opinion of the retiring partner naturally would not have much weight; it is the attitude of the incoming owners that usually controls. In the above case, in view of the fact that *C* obtains a half-interest, it would not be unreasonable perhaps to view the transaction as the sale of business assets to new owners.

In the case of the corporation, likewise, the market values of securities are almost certain to be very different from either book or par values. Stocks and other securities in many companies are freely bought and sold. In such cases prices are affected by political developments, money rates, and manifold other general factors as well as by the specific developments in the particular company. To some extent the capitalization process is involved in the market valuation of securities. Thus a share of stock is extremely unlikely to sell for any considerable time at a price equivalent to the corresponding fraction of the stockholders' equity as exhibited in the accounts. The ordinary buying and selling of corporate stock, however, in no way disturbs book values. The assets are owned by the corporation, it must be remembered, and an indefinite number of transfers may occur among stockholders without giving any reason or occasion for revaluation. It is only where a reorganization brings about a change in the corporate identity, or where an entirely new company buys out the old, that asset revaluation is at all justified. In many cases, where the change is formal rather than literal, even such a transaction should doubtless be viewed as being merely an internal adjustment of ownership. It is only where there is a material change in the make-up of the investing body that a revision of property values is fully called for.

INVESTORS' SALARIES AND OTHER COMPENSATION

The significance and treatment of owners' salaries was considered at some length in Chapter XI, particularly with reference to the sole-proprietorship and partnership. It was pointed out that in the sole-proprietorship—indeed in the unincorporated business in general—the charging of owners' salary allowances to expense is a highly questionable procedure. It was further indicated that in the open corporation payments for the personal services of individuals who are also stockholders can, on the contrary, be legitimately included in operating charges. At this point a further discussion of this question as it arises in the close corporation will be undertaken. In view of the fact that the corporation is subject to federal income and profits taxes as a distinct entity the question of the treatment of payments for services and special functions undertaken by officers and other stockholders in the close corporation takes on a peculiar importance. Here it is especially hard to distinguish between the bona fide transaction between the business and the stockholder and the purely nominal occurrence.

The determination of an accounting standpoint is particularly difficult in the incorporated partnership, the "family" enterprise, "one-man" company, or other close corporation. The strict adoption of the legal point of view by the accountant is likely to lead to dangerous conclusions. The business-entity conception must be here accepted with a clear understanding of its limitations. The accountant cannot admit that transactions between principal stockholders and the corporation are on the same level with transactions between the company and genuine outsiders. The legal fiction must in some cases be brushed aside in order to get at the realities of the situation. The principal stockholders must be envisaged at times in lieu of the business entity.

Take the case, for example, where a single individual owns 99 per cent of the stock and in addition is in active control of all operations. To this individual the earnings of the corporation are essentially his earnings, and he may not be much concerned whether they are distributed in the form of dividends or salary. Such an individual would of course recognize the fact that the income of the enterprise was the result of his personal efforts in conjunction with the capital invested and other conditions; but he might not consider it necessary to make an accounting differentiation of earnings into compensation for personal services and return on capital invested. Indeed it could be argued, along the line of the discussion in Chapter XI, that since such a stockholder virtually determines and pays his own salary the amount of such allowance should not be charged to expense along with the cost of expired items purchased from outsiders.

The inauguration in recent years of federal taxes levied upon corporate incomes has of course made necessary a division between compensation to stockholders for personal services and dividends on capital. The tax is designed essentially as a burden on capital earnings and profits, and hence reasonable salaries for corporate officers are allowable in the calculation of taxable net income. Under these circumstances there has been a tendency for those in control of the close corporation to be unduly liberal with respect to stockholders' "salaries."

The officers of such companies are in a position where they may set their own compensation. The corporation as an entity may of course act with full formality and legality; the salaries may be duly voted and recorded; but it is evident that such transactions between company and stockholder are bound to be highly artificial.

It is not intended to undertake any serious discussion of the problem of determining reasonable stockholders' salaries. That is a problem of imputation and all sorts of difficulties are involved. For ordinary accounting purposes a precise separation of the earnings of the close corporation into service income and capital income is hardly more necessary than in the case of the unincorporated business. The point here to be emphasized is that a salary adjustment between the corporation and a controlling stockholder is largely a formal rather than a genuine transaction.

In some cases the principal stockholder is "paid" a special bonus, emolument, or royalty for furnishing some factor other than personal services in the usual sense. He may permit the company to use some secret process to which he has title, or a piece of real estate which he owns personally. The stockholder may make a contract with the corporation so favorable to himself that most of the earnings are disguised as costs of operation. Such a transaction, in reality, would seem to consist in the transfer of funds from one pocket to another under cover of the corporate entity. Here again the accountant is faced with a transaction which may have a formal propriety but is otherwise often quite unreasonable.

In the one-man company the owner may wish to charge large sums to expense to cover his personal services and yet may not wish to draw in cash the amount of such allowances. If such a transaction is explicitly introduced into the accounts it is necessary to credit surplus with the amount involved. This emphasizes the purely specious character of the adjustment;

an item of gross revenue is carried directly to undivided profits without appearing anywhere in the net income figure. This is certainly questionable accounting. Capital stock may be later issued for the amount of the allowance; and this means that a definite increase in corporate capital has been taken out of gross corporate revenue—a most peculiar transaction. It may be argued, of course, that this is new investment on the part of the stockholder, the net effect being the same as if the salary allowance were first withdrawn in cash and then immediately reinvested.

In conclusion it should be stated that it is not intended to minimize the importance of the corporate entity for the accountant—quite the contrary. The fact of the legal entity is of real significance, even in the close corporation. Its importance, on the other hand, should not be exaggerated; and transactions between stockholders and company—especially in the close corporation—should be recognized in the accounts in such a fashion that the true situation is not obscured.

CHAPTER XVI

PHASES OF CAPITAL STOCK [1]

There has been much discussion among accountants and others of the various phases of the stockholder's equity, and some disagreement with respect to the meanings of certain situations involving capital stock and their proper accounting treatment. The formality attaching to corporate procedures, and the use of nominal values for corporate securities, tend to obscure the essential accounting facts and raise difficult questions which do not appear in the case of the unincorporated business. The capital stock of a corporation may pass through several stages, have several manifestations; it is often expressed in the balance sheet by two or more accounts; numerous transactions of doubtful import may be associated with this equity. The accountant must deal with authorized, subscribed, and outstanding stock; unissued, purchased, and donated securities; stock discounts and premiums; subscriptions, calls, and assessments.

In this chapter no attempt will be made to discuss fully the subject of capital stock in all its aspects. Some phases of the stockholder's equity have received sufficient attention for our purposes in preceding chapters. It is intended to consider only three topics in this connection; first, the nature and disposition of stock discounts; second, the significance and accounting treatment of treasury stock in its various forms; third, the significance of "dividends" in stock and other securities. An examination of these matters will serve especially to illustrate and emphasize further the interequity class of transactions as

---

[1] Adapted in part from "Some Phases of Capital Stock," *Journal of Accountancy*, vol. XXVII, pp. 321-335.

found in corporate accounting. They may be conveniently considered at this point inasmuch as the second topic mentioned, in particular, is closely allied to questions discussed in the last chapter.

STOCK DISCOUNTS

Discounts on capital stock have been defined thus far, from the accounting standpoint, as valuation or contra equity items. Discount is the difference between the nominal capital and the amount actually invested and, in the accounts, constitutes a suspended deduction from an overstated equity balance, the par of the capital stock. The discount on stock account, from this point of view, is really but a section of the main capital stock account; and the two must be drawn together in any determination of the stockholder's equity.

This view is imperfectly reflected in accounting procedure, however, as is evidenced by the common practice of listing the discount balance among the assets or, worse still, including it under some individual asset caption. No doubt such usage is oftener a result of careless interpretation than it is an indication of a deliberate intention to overstate the properties. Discount on capital stock is a debit ledger balance, and the accountant often seems to fail to see any alternative to placing the item in the asset classification. Then, having once listed stock discount in the asset column—where it is combined with true assets to obtain the total of properties—he finds it easy to slip into the habit of assuming that this element is in some sense an asset, albeit one of a somewhat suspicious character.

Stock discount, evidently, must be interpreted as an asset, a loss, or—as above—an offset to nominal capital; there are no other possibilities. The second of these may be dismissed as quite unreasonable; discount in no sense expresses a loss of capital. There is a little more to be said for the theory that discount is related to the assets. A possible basis for this interpretation is found in the fact that the amount of original discount is supposed to represent assessments which can be called by the board of directors or, in the case of liquidation, by the court in charge.[2] It might be argued, accordingly, that unpaid discount is analogous to an unpaid subscription, is a bona fide receivable. Such a view, however, involves an unreasonable use of the term "receivable." Discount is simply a formal amount of capital which might conceivably be raised but which nevertheless has not yet been secured in any real sense. The amount of a subscription, on the other hand, is due on a definite date or dates, and payment is reasonably assured by means of a written contract. The difference between the agreed subscription price and par may never be called; it is only remotely available—a potential receivable but not an active current claim. Discount is thus a mere possible source of funds, not an effective asset. If an assessment is called, however, the amount thereof may legitimately be treated as a genuine receivable. An assessment called is a definite, explicit claim on stockholders, uncertainty of collection being the only factor which may modify its validity.

It was pointed out in Chapter II that not all conditions, factors, and circumstances which have a bearing upon the financial condition of an enterprise can be explicitly exhibited as assets or equities; and possible assessments on stockholders were mentioned as an illustration. Unpaid discount is not an asset, although in a sense indicating a potential source of funds.

It is the later treatment of discounts which it is particularly desired to emphasize here. The accountant, viewing stock discount as a dubious asset item, has in general adopted the rule that such a balance—a necessary evil to begin with—

---

[2] Stock which is formally full-paid is, as a matter of fact, often issued for overvalued property, and, hence, at a discount.

should be eliminated entirely as soon as revenues are adequate for this purpose. This rule, it is believed, is at least questionable, and its nature and consequences will now be carefully examined.

If discount on capital stock is written off in a manner at all legitimate it must be through charges to some account containing a positive element of the stockholder's equity; for such discount obviously bears no relation to the liabilities and to conceal it under an asset caption would, as indicated above, be quite improper. The classifications in which this positive balance may be found are revenue, net income, surplus, and capital stock. To dispose of discount by a charge to capital stock would be a mere reversal of the initial accounting procedure by which the discount was recognized; and if there was adequate reason for bringing such an item into the accounts in the first place it would be unreasonable to write it off by such means. The elimination of discount by charges to gross revenue would be out of the question since such a procedure would disturb the integrity of the net revenue figure. This would simmer down to a transfer of sales to capital stock, and would be the extreme of bad accounting. Evidently, then, if discounts are to be extinguished the concurrent charges must be to net income or accumulated surplus.

Such a disposition of discount would not disturb the net amount of the stockholder's equity but it would obscure two important facts, namely, investment and accumulated earnings.[3] Neither of these highly significant balances can be accurately determined from a financial statement if any stock discounts have been extinguished. As was indicated above,

---

[3] "The fundamental balances to which all accounting records contribute . . . are four in number, namely, the balance which measures the cost of the property, the balance which measures net operating revenues, the balance which measures the current surplus or deficit, and the balance sheet statement of accumulated profit or loss. . . . They are guides for the judgment of the investor and a measure for those who desire to know the degree of prosperity which has attended the operation of a property. . . . The degree of confidence which may be placed in the integrity of the four balances named is one of the accepted tests of sound accounting." (Adams, *American Railway Accounting*, p. 15.)

when stock has been issued below par and par is retained as a balance-sheet fact the original investment can only be determined by deducting the amount of the discount from the total par value of the outstanding capital stock, or, in other words, by reading the capital stock and discount on stock accounts together. If discount is eliminated by charges against earnings, accordingly, the balance sheet certainly will not exhibit, separately, the amount of the investment or the extent of incomes retained in the business. The total of the two elements is still correct, it is true, but the integrity of the two important divisions of the stockholder's equity is not individually maintained.

Suppose, for example, that a company were organized with a capital stock of $100,000, par, and that this stock were issued at a discount of 20 per cent. The actual investment, then, was $80,000. Suppose further that after a few years of successful operation the company had accumulated earnings to the amount of $50,000, and that at this point the discount balance were extinguished by a charge to surplus. The resulting balance sheet, evidently, would show an apparent initial investment of $100,000 and accumulated profits of but $30,000. As a matter of fact the true investment would be unchanged at $80,000, and the true undistributed earnings would still amount to $50,000.

It must surely be admitted that it is a primary purpose of the balance sheet to furnish essential data concerning the financial status of the enterprise to the present and prospective stockholder; and it appears from the foregoing that the elimination of stock discounts is a practice inconsistent with this purpose. Undivided profit is one of the most significant figures appearing in the corporate balance sheet; the amount and fluctuation of accumulated earnings is a fact of the utmost significance to the investor and all others concerned. It is evident that entirely erroneous conclusions might be drawn regarding the success of an enterprise between years if an accounting procedure such as was indicated in the above illustration were adopted. A few individuals might know the facts, but the average investor would be almost sure to be misled. The matter is the more serious in view of the fact that the balance sheet is by far the most "popular" form of financial statement. The balance sheets of leading companies are widely circulated and are eagerly examined by investors. The manager also depends upon the balance sheet for important general and specific impressions with respect to the financial condition of his enterprise. In view of the significance of the balance sheet as the fundamental accounting statement it surely requires no extended argument to demonstrate the impropriety of any accounting procedure which tends to disturb the essential elements of this statement.

The maintenance of the individual integrity of investment and surplus is a matter of importance. In the public utility these elements are highly significant factors with respect to the problem of rate regulation.[4] The adjudication of disputes between the business and its employees may involve reference to accumulated earnings. The present tax program of the federal government provides for a calculation of undivided profits in various connections. In view of these and other considerations any accounting practice which covers up or obscures either investment or surplus is of very doubtful propriety.

There are, of course, other procedures than the writing off of discounts which obliterate surplus more or less completely. Surplus is often subdivided into several accounts which— obscurely or improperly labeled—are scattered among the items on the equity side of the balance sheet in such a way as to confuse all but the trained accountant. Further, the issue of

[4] Nevertheless the rules of the Interstate Commerce Commission as stated in the classifications of 1914 permit stock discounts to be extinguished by charges against either current income or surplus.

dividend stock results in an amalgamation of investment and profits. This transaction will be discussed later in this chapter.

It might be objected that it is not essential that surplus and investment be segregated in the balance sheet since the manager or investor should be able to gauge the success of the enterprise from the data exhibited in the income statement, or, if they care for details, may discover the same by an examination of original entries and detail accounts. In answer it should be admitted that a careful examination of income and balance sheets in conjunction by a person with some knowledge of accounting would serve to explain the disappearance of a stock discount item (especially if a full statement of the surplus account were attached), but the difficulty is that the person interested is usually not sufficiently trained to trace such a technical procedure through the various statements. Further, as was indicated above, the balance sheet is often published as an independent statement, and is read by many interested parties without reference to other data.

Any examination of original entries and accounts is, of course, usually quite out of the question as far as the typical stockholder is concerned. Summary statements showing revenue, expense, net revenue, surplus, investments, and assets are prepared for the very purpose of obviating such examinations. Few if any of the interested parties have the time, opportunity, or skill to glean the desired information from a mass of underlying records. Omissions or distortions with respect to essential balances in the summaries, accordingly, cannot be excused on the ground that the correct data can be determined if necessary from the detail entries and accounts.

The fact that discounts may be called for under certain circumstances is an added minor reason for the preservation of such balances.

There would therefore seem to be good reason for the conclusion that the discount balance should be retained in the ledger indefinitely, or until called by assessments on the stockholders. If frankly labeled there need be no reason for viewing the item with suspicion. Discount on stock and undivided profits may well appear concurrently in the same statement, and indeed should so appear if it be admitted that the balance sheet should show investment and accumulated earnings as distinct facts. The discount figure should not be listed among the assets, however, but should be shown as a special deduction from the capital stock balance on the equity side of the sheet. This practice is now urged by many accountants and is highly commendable. By this device the par of the stock is shown for what that fact may be worth, and the actual net investment is also exhibited. Further, in this way the padding of the totals of the statement is avoided, and the stockholder or other person interested is not deceived as to the real situation.

What has been said about stock discounts may be applied in principle to premiums on capital stock. Such a premium is a part of the investment and should accordingly be treated in the accounts as a permanent adjunct of the capital stock account. Premium should be carefully distinguished from income or surplus balances. It is worth noting that accountants are almost in unanimous agreement with respect to the permanency of the premium account; and this state of opinion is an added argument in favor of a change in sentiment with respect to the disposition of discounts.

Thus far it has been assumed that stock discounts must be introduced into the accounts whenever the capital stock is issued below par, or, in other words, that the capital stock account proper must show par value. As a matter of fact it would be quite possible to record all the essential facts—the amount of funds received and the corresponding investment or equity thereby created—without any explicit recognition of discount. Par value, as was pointed out in Chapter XIV, is not a fundamental accounting fact. On the other hand it is entirely feasible to record capital stock at par provided the proper offset (or adjunct) account is set up.

To conclude and summarize, discount on capital stock should either not be introduced into the accounts in the first place, or, if brought in, should be retained undisturbed in the ledger as long as the stock issue remains unchanged or until assessments are called. The elimination of discount balances against surplus is objectionable because it obliterates in a measure the distinction between the two fundamental elements of the stockholder's interest, investment and accumulated earnings.

TREASURY STOCK

It is usually admitted that *unissued* capital stock is not an asset of the corporation involved and that, if shown in the accounts and statements in any form, it should be treated as an offset to the amount of authorized capital. Many accountants, indeed, prefer to begin the accounting record with stock subscribed rather than stock authorized, and such procedure results, of course, in the complete exclusion of unissued stock from the accounts. It is recognized that authorized but unissued stock may be a convenience in the event of future expansion, but that it cannot possibly be said to constitute a genuine asset. "Treasury" stock, on the other hand, has been held by some authorities to be a bona fide asset under certain circumstances. This opinion is especially common in the case of stock which was formerly outstanding and which has been purchased by the issuing company on a cash or equivalent basis. Such stock, it has often been urged, is a true asset, and hence should be sharply distinguished from the amount of unissued but authorized securities.

This position requires modification. As a matter of fact no security whatever—stocks, bonds, or notes—is a legitimate asset when in the hands of the issuing company, regardless of the circumstances of its acquisition. In this respect there are no fundamental differences between unissued stock, donated stock, or purchased stock; none of these can constitute assets. Such differences as exist between the various types of treasury stock are quite superficial as far as accounting is concerned. There is indeed even less reason for treating such a security as an asset than for considering discount on capital stock as a true receivable.

In attempting to substantiate this view the most extreme case will be relied upon for an illustration—that of stock bought outright on the market by the issuing company; for if it can be demonstrated that such stock is not an asset when in the possession of the issuer it surely follows that treasury stock is never a bona fide property, however secured. Suppose that the directors of a mining company decide to use $30,000 of available cash to purchase a part of the stock of the corporation from miscellaneous stockholders.[5] The capital stock of the company at this time, it will be assumed, totals $100,000 (par) and surplus amounts to $50,000. This gives a book value—on the basis of 1,000 shares—of $150 per share. For convenience it will be further assumed that the transaction is carried out exactly on the basis of book values—that 200 shares, in other words, are acquired at a cost of $150 each.

How should this transaction be recorded in the accounts? If this treasury stock is to be viewed as an asset it would be necessary to charge the amount paid, $30,000, to a treasury stock account, the concurrent credit, of course, being entered in cash. According to this interpretation the transaction consists in an exchange of assets, cash being paid for securities

[5] There are many possible conditions which may lead a company to traffic in its own securities. Preferred stocks are frequently callable under specified conditions; they are likewise sometimes acquired by purchase on the exchanges when circumstances are favorable. Interests having immediate control may desire for various reasons to eliminate other interests, and may use corporate funds for that purpose. And so on.

of equivalent value. The total of assets would be unchanged, and the total of the stockholders' equity would be in nowise affected. But does this give a correct representation of the facts from an accounting point of view? Should not the charges be made to capital stock and surplus in appropriate amounts rather than to treasury stock, thus reducing the stockholder's equity to $120,000? Or, if a treasury stock account is used temporarily should it not be viewed as a valuation account, an offset to capital stock and surplus balances, which, in the balance sheet, would be shown as a deduction from gross equity values rather than as an asset? In other words, has not the company used $30,000 to reduce its outstanding, effective capitalization rather than to acquire an asset of that amount?

In practice treasury stock is usually exhibited in the accounts at par, regardless of the price paid. In the above case the adoption of this rule would reduce the charge to treasury stock to $20,000, the balance of $10,000 being debited to surplus. This is not unreasonable in itself, as the true relationship between treasury stock and capital stock accounts is thus indicated in a measure. Such procedure, however, is quite inconsistent with the theory that treasury stock is an asset. In other words, conventional practice in itself presents an argument against the interpretation of treasury stock that often appears to accompany such practice. It would seem obvious that if any part of the cost of treasury stock can be charged to an asset account the entire cost must be so treated. And, analogously, if any part of the cost of such stock can properly be charged to equity accounts the entire cost must be so charged. Treasury stock is either an asset to the extent of the full amount paid—either more or less than par—or it has no asset significance whatever.

A coincidence between market price and book value would, of course, be very rare, particularly in the case of a series of transactions covering a considerable period. It may be well to interject here a brief statement of some other possibilities. If the stock were secured for less than book value but more than par the charge to surplus would be less than indicated by the percentage of stock being acquired. This would result in an increase in the book value per share of the outstanding stock; from the standpoint of book value the retiring shareholders are making a concession to those who remain. If book value happened to be just par and the stock were secured at a discount, the amount of discount would be an actual *credit* to surplus. If book value were less than par but above market price there would still be a credit to surplus for the difference between book discount or deficit and market discount. A surplus arising in such a way is of course not an accumulated earning; it indicates merely a transfer of a book equity from one group of stockholders to another. In the sense that the asset values are genuine this gives, none the less, a kind of advantage to the remaining investors. If the price paid were above par and above book value, on the other hand, the charge to surplus would exceed the amount indicated by the percentage of stock retired. Under these circumstances the remaining stockholders have made a concession to those retiring.

Suppose now that by formal action the capital of our mining company is reduced from $100,000 to $80,000, from 1,000 shares to 800, and that the stock certificates are canceled. Under these circumstances, clearly, the treasury stock would no longer have any value; for surely no one would have the hardihood to argue that unauthorized capital stock is an asset. At this point the reduction in the equity accounts could not be further postponed. If a treasury stock account had been used to record the initial transaction it would now be necessary to credit this account and debit the equity accounts for the appropriate amounts. The case is now clear; the net result of the whole transaction is a reduction in liquid assets of

$30,000 and a corresponding diminution in the stock equities. But, it may be asked, what change in the situation is produced by the actual cancellation of the acquired stock? Has this formal action destroyed anything of value? Was it this bit of red tape that brought about a decrease in assets and equities of $30,000? The answer seems to be unavoidable: The reduction of the capital and the cancellation of the certificates is simply the formal completion of a stock retirement which became effective from the accounting standpoint when the stock first came into the possession of the issuing company.

The argument may be made more emphatic by an extreme modification of this illustration. Suppose that the stock of the mining company is not canceled or acquired, but that more and more stock is bought up as funds become available through the wasting of the mineral deposits until the property is practically exhausted and stock to the amount of but 100 shares remains in the hands of individual stockholders. If it be insisted that the treasury stock is still an asset under these circumstances the conclusion follows that the property of the company is essentially unimpaired despite the fact that the mine is almost entirely depleted and has been replaced with nothing but the company's own stock—a conclusion manifestly absurd.

But, it may be urged, in the case of the active going concern treasury stock may be sold for cash as readily as any property item, and anything which is freely salable must surely be rated as an asset. This kind of argument is typical of the careless reasoning concerning treasury stock which is primarily responsible for the current misinterpretations. The acquisition of outstanding stock by the issuer does not represent a *purchase*—an exchange of assets—in the true sense; and similarly the reissue of such stock does not truly involve a *sale,* another exchange of assets. Instead, such transactions always affect both sides of the balance sheet. When stock is issued both assets and equities are increased; when stock is retired—temporarily or permanently—both classes are reduced. "Issue" and "retirement" express the real situation better than "sale" and "purchase." A corporation retires or pays its stocks, bonds, and notes; on occasion it issues such securities and raises new capital. One might almost as well say that the sole-proprietor *buys* his note at the bank when it matures, thereby acquiring an asset, as to urge that the incorporated business may treat its own securities as assets.

The law, of course, in some jurisdictions recognizes the right of a corporation to purchase and hold its own stock and other securities. And a smoke-screen of red tape often surrounds such transactions. An illustration of this is found where, in retiring securities by the sinking fund method, payments are drawn from the corporate funds to cover interest or dividends on the securities of the issuing company held by the trustee. But such transactions and occurrences are mere formalities from the accounting standpoint. The law sometimes carries the fiction of the corporate entity further than the accountant may safely follow. Certainly the accountant must treat a company's dealings with its own securities as on quite a different level from transactions involving the securities of other corporations. He cannot permit the corporation to count as an asset—in addition to all true properties—a liquidated equity in the business itself.

It should be admitted that the fact that a corporation has stock or other securities authorized which can be issued to secure additional funds when needed may be an advantage, since new authorizations may require special meetings, changes in the articles of incorporation, or other formalities. Further, it might even be admitted for the sake of argument that stock once issued and held in the treasury may, in certain circumstances, have some slight advantage with respect to marketability over authorized but unissued stock. But this would not in the least justify the conclusion that treasury stock is an asset. As has been pointed out before, an advantageous condition does not necessarily signify an asset. A bank's right to issue currency may be an advantage—one of the many conditions necessary to successful business operation—but cannot be counted as an accounting fact. Nor is a bale of notes fresh from the press in the hands of the issuing bank worth more than the cost of manufacture. The fact that a company can borrow needed current funds on its promissory note is an advantage but not an asset. A company under certain conditions may assess its stockholders, but, as was indicated in the preceding section, this possibility is not an asset. To sum up, it is quite illegitimate for a company to count as an actual property any condition which merely makes possible or convenient the raising of capital.

It is not intended to deny the importance of authorized securities as a legal fact. Particularly with respect to their bearing upon potential control are such authorizations of consequence. It may even be desirable from some standpoints to introduce such facts into the accounts. But if brought into the financial statement such items should be distinctly labeled as valuation accounts, or, better, treated as deductions from gross equity balances. The least dangerous practice is to exclude all these data from the balance sheet entirely. They may more properly be exhibited in reports, upon stock certificates, and elsewhere than in the strictly accounting statements.

The conclusion reached in the above discussion may be applied directly to the case of donated stock. There are, however, one or two interesting questions arising in this connection which should receive independent comment. In some cases capital stock once issued in a bona fide manner is returned to the issuing company without apparent compensation—is "donated" by the original subscriber. Such transactions commonly occur in states which do not permit the issuance of capital stock, initially, at less than par value. They are usually prearranged; and the underlying purpose is to make the stock nominally "fully paid" so that it may then be reissued at any price it will bring to raise working capital. An interested stockholder puts in a tract of land, a factory, a patent, or other property at a nominal valuation and later returns for resale a part of the stock issued to him in exchange. In such circumstances a reasonable interpretation of the financial condition of the enterprise is very difficult.

Suppose, for example, that an inventor turns over his patent rights to a corporation in exchange for $45,000, par, in the company's capital stock, and later donates $20,000 of this stock to the company to be sold for the purpose of obtaining the necessary liquid capital. Suppose further that the incorporators initially subscribe for stock to the amount of $5,000 at par, and that these subscriptions are paid in cash. The accounts of the company at the conclusion of these occurrences would stand (in summary balance-sheet form) somewhat as follows:

Patents	$45,000	Capital Stock	$50,000
Donated Stock	20,000	Donated Reserve	20,000
Cash	5,000		
	$70,000		$70,000

The donated stock is now reissued, it will be assumed, for 80 per cent of par, or $16,000. How should this transaction be recorded? The conventional procedure would be to credit donated stock to the amount of $20,000, debit cash $16,000 and debit donated reserve $4,000. According to this interpretation the inventor has paid a premium of $16,000—the balance in the reserve account—for his stock. He has not conceded this much to other parties, as he still holds 50 per cent of the total stock (more, if he is also one of the incorporators) and has a corresponding equity in the premium; but he has apparently contributed over two-thirds of the asset total and hence has made some apparent sacrifice.

This interpretation is at all legitimate only on the assumption that the owner of the patents has found it necessary to make this concession because of a scarcity of liquid funds and the absolute need for some cash resources. But are the patents actually worth $45,000 on a conservative basis? The key to the situation, evidently, is the value of this intangible; the validity of the reserve or special premium depends upon the value of the patents. And in the subsequent sale of the donated stock at a discount would seem to lie strong evidence that no true premium existed. If the inventor has really conceded anything of value to the company the stock should readily sell at a higher figure. A more conservative solution, accordingly, would involve the writing off of the balance in the reserve account, $16,000, against patents, or, in other words, a valuation of patents at $29,000.

A still more conservative and logical interpretation would be possible. In the absence of decisive evidence of the value of initial assets other than cash the bona fide cash value of securities at date of issue is usually conceded to be the most reliable criterion. In the above illustration two values for stock appear. The amount of $5,000 is subscribed at par while the amount of $20,000, par, is issued for $16,000, cash. Accepting the price of the larger block as the best indication of the value of the stock the entire issue is evidently worth 80 per cent of $50,000, or $40,000. Deducting the cash amount of $21,000 leaves $19,000 as the conservative figure for patents. A final balance sheet prepared on this basis would appear as follows:

Patents	$19,000	Capital Stock—Par...	$50,000	
Cash	21,000	Less: Discount.......	10,000	$40,000
	$40,000			$40,000

One further alternative may be mentioned. Assuming the value of the stock retained by the inventor (par, $25,000) to be 80 per cent, or $20,000, and that this discloses the value of the patents without reference to any other transaction, the final balance sheet should show an asset total of $41,000 and the discount on stock would accordingly be reduced to $9,000.

In conclusion it should be emphasized that donated stock is never an asset but should always be viewed as an offset to the total capital stock. The validity of the donated reserve as a true capital equity, on the other hand, depends entirely upon the bona fide value of the assets originally invested. If the donor has actually paid a premium for his stock this account measures an equity for the amount of the true premium. In the great majority of cases the amount of the apparent premium is undoubtedly best interpreted as an offset to an overstated property value. Not only is no true premium commonly involved but a reasonable valuation of the properties would often disclose an actual discount. In the absence of other conclusive evidence the cash value of the securities issued, at the time of issue, is the best criterion of the reasonable value of the property received in exchange therefor. Finally, since each aliquot share in a given issue has the same significance as every other similar share, the price of an important block (20 per cent or more, for example) is a satisfactory determinant of the value of the entire issue.

STOCK DIVIDENDS

The stock dividend and its accounting significance were briefly discussed in Chapter VII. Inaccurate interpretation of this "dividend" is so widespread, however, that a further consideration of this phase of capital stock seems advisable at this point. The issue of stock and other securities in lieu of cash dividends is a familiar corporate practice, but it is none the less persistently misunderstood, and in high places. The prevalent misconceptions, while extending far beyond the accounting aspect of these transactions, are in large measure grounded, it is believed, in a failure to appreciate what dividends in the form of a company's own securities mean in terms of the balance sheet; and hence the correction of opinion with respect to this matter may well be inaugurated by the accountant.

As was pointed out in Chapter VII, the declaration and issue of a stock dividend constitutes an interequity transaction —a transaction which in nowise disturbs the totals of the balance sheet, does not affect the assets in any way, and does not alter the equity class except with respect to individual headings. It involves merely a transfer of an element of the stockholder's equity from one account to another. Surplus is charged and capital stock is credited for the same amount. Accumulated profits are in whole or in part combined with original investment. The total of the stockholder's equity is not affected; it is simply cut up into a greater number of parts. The fractional interest of each shareholder remains the same (assuming that the new stock can be distributed *exactly* in proportion to the holdings of the various stockholders). Book value *per share* is proportionately reduced; and the market price per share is lowered (as far as the effect of this particular event is concerned). In no sense whatever does the corporation part with any funds or the stockholders receive any. Its effect upon the assets is nil; its effect upon equities is purely formal. If a single account were being used to represent the entire equity of the stockholder no accounting transaction whatever would be here involved and no entries would be needed. In other words, it is only as it is considered necessary to preserve the par of the capital stock in a separate account that the declaration and issue of a stock dividend can be considered an accounting transaction in any sense.

What, then, is the significance of such an occurrence? What purpose is involved? Let us attempt to answer this question first from the standpoint of the issuing company and its management. The principal legitimate reason for the issue of a stock dividend is the desire on the part of the board of directors to *insure* the permanent retention of profits in the business, or, to put it more technically, to make it impossible for the present board or any of its successors to base *cash* dividend appropriations upon the element of surplus in question. Once surplus has been capitalized—i.e., has been covered by an issue of additional capital stock—it cannot legally be made the basis for dividend declarations. To insure permanent expansion at the expense of cash dividends, then, the stock dividend device is sometimes utilized.

This should not be misunderstood. The stock dividend in itself does not bring about the growth of the enterprise. The fundamental thing is the decision on the part of the management to permit profits to accumulate. If the directors refrain from declaring cash dividends (or dividends payable in other assets) the enterprise will expand (if there are any profits) just as surely as if additional stock were issued to cover the profits. The stock dividend simply clinches the matter, makes it impossible to reverse or alter the decision to restrict or avoid altogether the disbursing of actual funds or other assets to the stockholder to retire the increase in his equity resulting from successful operation.

Less rational reasons or excuses for the stock dividend are common. The mere desire to obliterate or cover up the surplus account, to conceal the fact of profit accumulation, may be responsible. The needs of the business may make cash dividends out of the question, and the management may not care to permit the amount of undivided profits to remain a patent figure on the balance sheet. Unfortunately it is often true that the purpose actuating those having authority over the preparation of the financial statements is to obscure rather than to disclose. The directors may not wish to have the public, the employees, or even the scattered stockholders fully aware of the extent of profits.

To some extent, no doubt, the stock dividend has been used as a stockholder's pacifier. The clamor for dividends has been met in some cases with the stock dividend, a dividend in a purely nominal sense. If the stockholder were keenly appreciative of the true situation it is hard to see how he could derive any marked satisfaction from such a procedure, but the stockholder of course often entirely misunderstands the transaction. Still another excuse for the stock dividend has been the desire on the part of the directors to manipulate the market price of the stock; the rumor of a "melon-cutting" has long been used as a bull argument on the stock market. In the case of stock with a very high market value the stock dividend may be used to cut down this price to a more popular and convenient figure for trading purposes. Dividend stock may also play a part in fights for control if it applies to a particular issue among several outstanding stocks emitted by a single company, especially to one having a high voting power.

From an accounting standpoint the same argument can be made against the issue of the stock dividend which was urged in opposition to the erasing of stock discounts against profits. The elimination of a stock discount is essentially the same kind of transaction as the issue of a stock dividend. In both cases accumulated profits are attached to the accounts showing initial investment; in both cases the two important elements in the stockholder's equity—investment and surplus —are obscured. In this connection we find another excuse for the stock dividend. To increase the *apparent* investment and sacrifice of the investor so as to permit of a larger aggregate cash dividend without increasing the *rate* of dividend upon formal capitalization, the stock dividend has often been resorted to. This, like most of the other reasons given, exhibits the stock dividend in the light of a device or expedient of a somewhat questionable character.

It should be noted that, whatever the purpose involved, only the corporation having authorized but unissued stock (unissued, at least, as far as individual holders are concerned) may make use of the stock dividend. All others must either forego this financial operation or first take the steps necessary to increase the formal capitalization.

What is the significance of the stock dividend from the standpoint of the recipient stockholder? As already indicated, the individual shareholder's fractional interest in the enterprise is unchanged. The literal effect of the transaction is merely an increase in the number of shares which he holds. He receives an additional certificate to cover the new stock, or his old certificate is exchanged for a new one covering his entire holding. It is hard to see how he is in any way advantaged by the transaction. One would expect the total market value of his stock (both old and new) to be essentially unchanged as a result of the fact of the stock dividend alone. The effect of the stock dividend upon market prices could not, of course, be precisely ascertained in any case because the securities market is constantly subject to manifold influences. But only in so far as the insuring of the retention of profits in the business augured for a more marked success in the future could a legitimate bull argument be deduced from the fact of a stock dividend. It might happen in a particular case, of course, that the declaration was the first genuine assurance given the stockholders at large of the fact of accumulated profits, and in such circumstances some appreciation of the stock on the market might result; but in general it is the showing of net revenue and surplus in the financial statements rather than stock dividend policies which discloses the degree of success attending the operations of an enterprise. At any rate, the fact that the declaration of a stock dividend may be an indirect notification to the stockholder that the company is making money—a fact with which he should have been acquainted by other means—can hardly be held to be a point of importance in determining the essential character of such a dividend from the standpoint of the shareholder.

As has been stated above, the rumor or declaration of a large stock dividend may cause an upward flurry in the market price per share. But the actual *emission* of the new stock, it should be emphasized, is bound to result—in the absence of other potent influences—in a fall in price per share roughly proportionate to the percentage of increase in outstanding capitalization.

To the stockholder interested in immediate cash dividends, indeed, the declaration of a stock dividend should be a discouragement. Such an action serves notice upon the stockholder—if he understands the transaction—that to the extent of the new stock issued accumulated profits are permanently removed from the field of possible dividend appropriations. Profits so attached can *never* be distributed—except by final liquidation. It is only as these funds in turn earn profits that the directors can make any actual disbursements to shareholders in connection therewith.

The recipient stockholder might, of course, sell the additional shares. Such a procedure, however, would reduce his fractional interest in the enterprise. Further, if he sold the dividend stock he would realize no more surely than if—in the absence of a stock dividend—he disposed of sufficient shares to liquidate his equity in the possible stock dividend. In this connection it should be noted that in theory a stockholder is always in a position to "declare" his own dividend provided there is an active market for his stock. Ignoring other and possibly more potent factors it may be said that the effect of successful operation and profit accumulation will be reflected in an advance in the market price for the stock. If the directors do not disburse these profits to the shareholder he may none the less virtually withdraw his interest in the earnings by selling a sufficient amount of his holding. This will reduce his proportionate interest, but he may still retain an equity equivalent in value to his original investment. Indeed, if market values and book values were always identical the dividend policy of the directors would be a matter of complete indifference to the individual shareholder, aside from the single question of the maintenance of his fractional interest.[6]

Some light may be thrown upon the situation by contrasting the stock dividend, so called, with other dividends. The only true dividend involves an actual disbursement of cash or other corporate asset to the shareholders. Such a dividend extinguishes a part of the stockholder's equity on the corporate balance sheet—usually the increase due to successful operation—and reduces the property total accordingly. It is perhaps a mistake to conclude, however, that the wealth of the individual stockholder is increased by such a dividend. In a quiet market the payment of a cash dividend will commonly result in an immediate decline in the price per share (from the level reached just before the books are closed) approximately equivalent to the amount of the dividend per share. It should be emphasized that it is not the declaration and payment of a dividend that increases the wealth of the shareholder in the broad sense but the process of successful operation on the part of the corporation. The corporation to a degree is only the agent of the stockholder, using his funds and regularly reporting (supposedly) a record of stewardship. As the investor's funds are enhanced as a result of successful operation his equity in the company is increased correspondingly. From

---

[6] Strictly speaking this is true only on the basis of the assumption that the holding of the stockholder is indefinitely divisible.

time to time those in authority actually pay him sums based on the record of earnings. This act converts a part of the investor's wealth from an equity in a corporation to liquid assets. If the dividend is in actual cash this means an increase in the stockholder's purchasing power without the necessity on his own part of conversion, either by borrowing on his stock or actually disposing of it.

In a word, then, the dividend in cash or other corporate property involves a reduction in both sides of the corporate balance sheet and the actual receipt by the stockholder of cash or other assets covering a part of his equity in the enterprise. The stock dividend, on the other hand, has no essential effect upon the corporate balance sheet and leaves the stockholder in virtually the same position as before. In neither case does the transaction immediately affect the total wealth of the shareholder. In the case of the cash dividend the investor's position is altered only in that a part of his resources have been converted from the form of investment in a company to cash without changing his fractional interest in the enterprise. In the case of the stock dividend the investor has a new stock certificate but the amount and character of his wealth is quite unchanged.

What, to carry the problem a step farther, is the relation of the stock dividend to dividends in scrip, notes or other securities issued by the declaring corporation? Suppose, for example, that a company with an accumulated surplus of $100,000 issues a pro rata dividend for this amount in 10-year, 6 per cent notes. What is the effect of this transaction from the point of view of the issuing company? As far as the accounting is concerned the transaction would be recorded, in summary, by a charge to surplus and a credit to notes payable. This is evidently another interequity transaction which does not disturb the balance-sheet totals. No assets are eliminated; the equity total is unchanged. The essence of the operation is a reduction in one equity heading and an equal increase in another. The only immediate difference as compared with the stock dividend lies in the fact that the legal character of the equity has been changed. The amount of $100,000 has been transferred from the stockholder's interest to a liability account. The same people—initially—are involved, but they now have two kinds of equities in the company. Further, the company must ultimately pay the notes and thus actually distribute assets to the then noteholders. This might mean no permanent reduction in capital, however, as the company might borrow or issue new stock to secure the funds to retire the notes. Under this last condition such a note dividend, from the standpoint of the corporation, would be almost identical with a stock dividend, both immediately and ultimately.

In the case of a short-term scrip dividend the immediate effect of the transaction on the company's books would be as described above. The final effect, however, would be identical with that of a cash dividend. A genuine scrip dividend is essentially a postponed cash disbursement.

Turning now to the case of the individual stockholder—and continuing to use the illustration of the 10-year note issue, it appears that the recipient shareholder is in much the same position as that in which he would be left as a result of a stock dividend. He holds the corporation's promise to pay, but this cannot be considered as a disbursement by the company. Such a note is a resource about on a level with a stock certificate. Neither is legal tender. To realize on a stock certificate it would be necessary to sell, assign, or hypothecate the security; exactly the same situation holds in the case of the note. From the standpoint of the individual shareholder's immediate interest the difference between the stock and note dividends simmers down to one point: In the case of the note dividend the shareholder may realize by sale without reducing his fractional interest and control through stockholding, while in the case of the stock dividend the sale of the additional shares will disturb his relative position in this regard.

Where a corporation which is financially embarrassed issues a scrip dividend it often appears that the immediate effect from the standpoint of the shareholder is essentially the same as it would be if no dividend action were taken. The stockholder may of course endorse the scrip and obtain cash from some bank; but this amounts to a loan from the bank to the stockholder. Under these circumstances the investor is borrowing to pay his own dividend. True, the corporation is signing his note with him, but if the credit of the company is such that the directors do not consider it wise for the corporation to borrow the necessary funds for the dividend this fact is of small immediate advantage to the shareholder. If all goes well, however, and the corporation takes up the scrip when due it is clear that the ultimate result of the transaction is the same as brought about by the cash dividend.

In conclusion the practical question of federal taxation of dividends in the hands of the recipient should be commented upon. The Supreme Court has held that the stock dividend does not represent income to the recipient shareholder and hence is not subject to the federal surtax. This opinion conforms to the accounting interpretation of the case. The declaration and issue of a stock dividend, as has been just explained, cannot reasonably be considered as affecting the shareholder's wealth or income. On the other hand the foregoing discussion should make it clear that the act of paying the cash dividend does not in itself increase the wealth of the investor in a broad sense. The periodic income sheet rather than the dividend schedule expresses the movement of the stockholder's equity. Nevertheless the payment of the cash dividend is the act which places the resources in question in the shareholder's hands without restriction and in effective form; and hence there is some justification from a practical standpoint for the view that the dividend rather than the income report should be used as a gauge of the shareholder's personal income.

The chief criticism that can be advanced against the present attitude of the Treasury Department and the courts with respect to the taxation of dividends (aside from the general objection to double taxation) lies in the fact that the only dividend in securities of the declaring company which is held to be exempt is that which is essentially the same kind as the security held by the recipient. That is, dividends in notes or bonds—as well as dividends in cash—are held to be income to the shareholder. In view of the points emphasized above it would seem to be more legitimate to treat all dividends "paid" in the securities of the declaring company—notes, bonds, and stocks—as exempt from tax until the securities involved were sold by the recipient or liquidated or paid by the issuing corporation.

CHAPTER XVII

SOME VALUATION ACCOUNTS [1]

As was pointed out in Chapter VII, the separation of pluses and minuses with the parallel-column device has been carried very far in modern accounting practice. Not only is the individual account divided into opposing columns, but in many cases a parent account is separated into two or more sections, each of which rates as an independent account. Thus we have the *valuation* or contra account. Such an account is simply a subsidiary section of some main account, designed to show, in suspended form, certain special deductions from the principal balance. Securities issued, for example, are commonly credited in the accounts at face or par amounts, the difference between the nominal sum and the actual investment being charged to a discount account. Similarly, fixed assets are usually carried in the accounts at original cost figures, and accrued expirations are registered by credits to appropriate reserves or allowances. Indeed, the use of these offset or contra accounts permeates the whole system. In general there is a tendency to set up original, gross, par, and face values in the principal accounts, all discounts, allowances, and other offsets being entered in separate subsidiary accounts. Some of these contra accounts relate to fixed asset and equity items and are retained in the balance sheet. Others are associated with current items and are disposed of in the preparation of the income sheet. The principles of account construction involved, however, are the same in all cases.

This widespread use of valuation accounts is entirely legiti-

---

[1] Adapted in part from "Some Current Valuation Accounts," *Journal of Accountancy*, vol. XXIX, pp. 335-350.

mate in so far as it serves to emphasize certain kinds of data for statistical purposes. The practice has its unfortunate side, nevertheless, in view of the fact that such accounts are often misinterpreted by both accountants and laymen, and are commonly improperly placed in the summary financial statements. Allowances for accrued depreciation, for example, are still frequently exhibited on the equity side of the balance sheet grouped with true surplus balances; discounts on securities are often listed among the assets instead of being shown in conjunction with the main equity accounts to which they relate; allowances for uncollectibles are by no means always presented as deductions from the face of outstanding receivables. It is true that many professional accountants now urge the recognition of genuine offset accounts as deductions from the appropriate main headings in the balance sheet, but in a majority of cases such items are still permitted to inflate the asset and equity totals. Further, accountants in general fail to recognize and properly locate the current valuation items of the income sheet. Many contra accounts arise in connection with purchases and sales which are seldom correctly interpreted and which are almost always misplaced in the income statement. There is room for marked improvement in income-sheet practice in this and other particulars.

The allowance for depreciation account, the discount on capital stock account, and certain other important valuation accounts have been carefully analyzed in Chapter VII and elsewhere in this study. The current offset accounts, however, which relate especially to the operating classifications, have thus far been neglected. In the present chapter three main cases will be considered: (1) discounts and other allowances on sales; (2) discounts and allowances on purchases; (3) discounts on contractual securities. The first two of these are associated primarily with the expense and revenue divisions; the second case has an important bearing upon both financial statements.

SALES DISCOUNTS AND ALLOWANCES

A great deal has been written concerning the significance of cash discounts on sales and purchases and the treatment of such items in the accounts and statements. Probably no other minor accounting problem has aroused as much discussion as this. Various ingenious methods of accounting for purchases and sales and discounts thereon, designed to illuminate essential aspects of these transactions, have been proposed. It has been pointed out that there are several phases of discounts in which the management may be interested, such as discounts offered, discounts taken, discounts neglected, and—at the end of the accounting period—possible discounts outstanding and the probable extent of acceptance thereof; and there has been considerable controversy with respect to the relative merits of the several schemes for presenting this information which have been advocated. It is not intended here to go over this ground or to elaborate in detail still another system of accounting for discounts. This aspect of the subject has already been overworked. There is, however, a main theoretic question involved which seems to be still unsettled, viz., are discounts on sales deductions from nominal revenue figures or positive expense or loss items; and, analogously, are discounts and allowances on purchases deductions from nominal and otherwise overstated expenses or positive additions to income? In other words, are current discounts and allowances merely offsets or contra items subsidiary to the principal operating divisions, or are they in themselves intrinsically valid as positive elements of these divisions? It is this question in particular to which attention will be directed.

It should be admitted at the outset that however this question be answered the effect upon the final net income figure will be the same in any case, and that, consequently, the problem is not one of first importance. But it should be emphasized on the other hand that an accounting view or procedure cannot be approved merely because it does not disturb the integrity of the concluding figure of the income sheet. There are innumerable hopelessly inadequate ways of arranging the data of this statement which nevertheless give an accurate final balance. This may even be accomplished by as crude a device as two unclassified columns of debits and credits. Obviously a satisfactory operating report must stress a number of intermediate facts, scarcely less important than the final figure. Effective gross revenue, material cost of sales, and total expense, for example, are highly significant amounts; and with respect to such data the question as to whether a particular item should be treated as a positive revenue or as a subtraction from an apparent expense is not a matter of tweedledum and tweedledee. Even after the net operating balance is struck there are several important amounts to be disclosed, as was emphasized in Chapter XI.

Sales discounts result from the vendor's practice of selling goods on account with alternative terms of settlement offered. The vendor usually records the transaction on his books when the goods are shipped. But if a discount has been offered it is not known certainly in advance upon which basis the customer will make payment. He may settle promptly and take the discount or he may postpone payment until the discount privilege has lapsed and he is obligated to pay the gross price. In view of this situation how should the original sale be recorded on the vendor's books? In theory it would seem to be equally reasonable to use either alternative as a basis for the entries, since the amount which will finally be paid cannot be ascertained in advance. It would be conservative practice—especially if the proffered discount is commonly accepted—to charge the customer and credit sales with the smaller of the possible amounts; and, as has been pointed out by several writers, it would be thoroughly feasible to use the discounted price in making the original entries. As a matter of fact, however, it is almost universal practice to record the gross amount of the bill. And this procedure, while not strictly in accord with that conservatism so much advocated by accountants, is nevertheless fairly reasonable and probably the more convenient. The amount most prominently displayed in the invoice and other documents accompanying the transaction is usually the gross figure; and if legal proceedings should ensue the gross or face of the account would normally constitute the basis of the vendor's claim (although his collection of this amount would be not at all certain).

Later, if the customer pays only the net price, in accordance with the privilege extended to him, the difference is charged to a special account, discounts on sales. What is the significance of this charge? According to the view implied above, this allowance is not an expense or a loss but simply an offset to an overstated gross revenue figure. In other words, the amount of the credit to sales in excess of the net price is purely tentative, the gross figure being used for convenience, and when the customer accepts the discount the effective revenue involved in the transaction is disclosed and the nominal excess should be written off. Except in so far as it is desirable for managerial purposes to isolate temporarily the amount of discounts accepted by customers in a given period, it would be entirely proper accounting to charge such amounts directly against the gross sales. And in the periodic closing of the accounts the most rational procedure is to close the discount on sales account directly into sales. According to this interpretation discount on sales is really a subsidiary section of the sales account, in which are segregated for a time special offsets to nominal gross revenue figures.

The treatment of sales discounts as an expense or loss is the result of careless reasoning. As was explained in an earlier chapter, expense for a given period is the cost of producing the

SOME VALUATION ACCOUNTS 405

particular quantum of revenue arising within the period. In other words, expense (ideally) measures the value expiration of all the manifold commodities and services necessary to the creation of revenue. In what sense, one may ask, is a discount accepted by a customer a cost of revenue? What commodity or service is it whose utilization in production is measured by such an item? Similarly, the sales discount is not a loss. A loss arises because of the escape of some value from the enterprise without any accompanying compensation. What valuable consideration is lost simply because a customer is prompt in paying his account?

The view that sales discounts are simply offsets to overstated revenue conforms to the common sense of the case. The vendor simply has two sets of prices: one charge is made to all those who pay promptly; a somewhat higher price is required from those who are slow to pay. Both offers are entirely voluntary. Indeed, any merchant or manufacturer would be glad to make all sales on a cash basis; there is no loss involved for the vendor when a customer accepts a discount and thereby takes advantage of the cash price. If voluntary discount on sales is a cost or expense we are forced to the absurd conclusion that sales for which the customer pays promptly and takes the proffered discount are more "expensive" from the standpoint of the vendor than sales to customers who postpone payment and neglect the allowance. As a matter of fact the specific accounting costs tend to be about the same in both cases (aside from the greater collection costs in the case of slow accounts), but the long-run economic cost from the standpoint of the community is *greater* in the case of goods sold to slow customers because of the increased capital thereby required by the producer and the augmented risk attaching to such business. It is primarily because of these factors of increased capital and aggravated risk that the vendor requires a higher price when payment is slow.

All standard rebates and allowances on sales are closely allied to cash discounts. Such items are not expenses, but are deductions from nominal revenues; and their character is not altered by the fact that instead of being entered directly in the sales account as charges they are set up in special offset accounts.

The return of goods gives rise to a somewhat similar contra item. When a customer returns a shipment which is unsatisfactory for any reason, it is customary to charge a sales returns account and credit the customer. (Entries recognizing the value of the goods returned and the reduction in cost of goods sold arising thereby may also be made, of course.) The sales returns account then constitutes a valuation account, measuring the reduction in provisional revenue from this cause.

Where allowances are made for goods damaged in packing or in transit, or where goods are returned because of errors in selection or careless handling on the part of the vendor's employees, additional costs may, of course, be involved. But the sales returns account would not in any sense measure these costs. The added labor cost would be shown in the payroll, the additional transportation expenses in the freight account, the deterioration of merchandise through the inventories, etc. Ordinary accounting procedures, in fact, would not isolate the true direct or indirect costs of such happenings, however desirable such segregation might be. Certainly the sales returns and allowances accounts would in any case represent merely deductions from what would otherwise be overstated revenues.

A further item which may be most accurately conceived is an offset to the tentative gross sales is the estimated allowance for uncollectibles. Such a charge is more nearly a direct subtraction from ostensible revenue than a positive addition to expense or cost. True it is that from the standpoint of the community such losses tend to increase economic costs; unquestionably prices in general are higher because of the fact that not a few consumers do not pay for what they get. Nevertheless it should be recognized that from the standpoint of the specific enterprise customers' accounts are not assets like equipment, materials, or services which are used in production. Receivables do not contribute through use to the creation of revenue. The allowance for uncollectibles is a subtraction from provisional revenue rather than an addition to the cost of goods sold. The true expense for the accountant is made up of the value of materials, labor, advertising, etc., embodied in goods sold. The allowance for bad debts is more nearly a supposed revenue which one fails to collect than an addition to the value of structures, commodities, and services which have expired in the process of production; it is an offset to gross sales rather than an increase in cost.

This analysis is sound, it should be noted, only in the case of a normal allowance with respect to accounts which have arisen during the current period. That is, it holds only for the regular adjustment based upon experience and applied to current credit business. If an extraordinary collapse in the value of receivables occurs, or if an unforeseen loss arises in connection with accounts based upon the sales of an earlier period, it may be urged that true losses result and that the amounts thereof are properly chargeable to net income or undivided profits rather than to gross revenue. It is even more clear in these circumstances, however, that no proper addition to current *expense* is involved.

In closing the accounts and preparing statements at the end of the period it would evidently not be strictly accurate in the normal case to deduct from sales simply the discounts accepted by customers during the period. Some of the discounts accepted would naturally apply to sales made in the preceding period, and some of those offered in the period in question would be accepted after its close. Further, the total of discounts offered could not be taken as the proper deduction, as some might never be accepted. In other words, wherever credit sales are made which may be settled on either of two bases it is impossible to determine exactly the final effective sales figure until sometime after the end of the current period. In these circumstances the most rational procedure—in view of general accounting practice with respect to accruals and estimates—would be to estimate the percentage of the total of discounts offered on sales within the period which the customers will accept and use the amount thus determined as the offset to sales for the period. This procedure would be no more difficult and would give as reasonable results as the accepted practice of estimating the allowance for bad accounts as a certain percentage of the credit sales of the period.

An example may serve to make this more clear. Suppose that a particular company in its first period of operation sells goods—all on account—with a gross invoice value of $500,000 and a net of $490,000. During the period discounts amounting to $6,300 are accepted, discounts which are allowed to lapse total $700, and possible discounts are outstanding to the amount of $3,000. Assuming that the experience of the period is a fair indication of what can be expected with respect to outstanding possible discounts, it may be concluded that 90 per cent of the $3,000 reduction still available to customers will be taken advantage of. To give effect to this estimate in the accounts, sales discounts is charged with $2,700 and allowance for outstanding discounts is credited with the same amount. As a result of these entries the proper correction on account of discounts would be made in both income sheet and balance sheet. In the income sheet the total sales discount taken and to be taken ($9,000) would be deducted from gross revenue. In the balance sheet the allowance for outstanding discounts would constitute a special valuation account which should be treated as an offset to the face or gross amount of the outstanding customers' balances.

When the unpaid accounts were settled in the succeeding period the allowance for outstanding discounts would be charged with the difference between the gross of the accounts involved and the cash received from customers. If the estimate is proved to be correct no adjustment would be required. In practice such precision would of course be out of the question; but the necessary correction could be easily made. If the customers took advantage of more of the available discounts than had been anticipated the excess would be a charge to undivided profits or, if the amount were trifling, to current sales discounts. If less than the anticipated amount were accepted by customers the difference would be a credit to undivided profits or, as a matter of convenience, to current sales discounts. In case the error were very small the amount might be left in the allowance for possible discounts account.

If experience has shown in any case that the amount of discounts actually accepted in a given period is a reasonably accurate measure of the proper sales adjustment it would evidently be unnecessary, as far as the integrity of the income sheet is concerned, to carry out such an analysis. To neglect to set up an offset to gross customers' balances on account of outstanding discounts, on the other hand, would mean the showing of a somewhat questionable figure in the balance sheet. The extent of the error would depend upon the amount of the outstanding receivables and the percentage thereof made up of possible discounts. The adjustment illustrated above would be especially important wherever monthly statements, for example, were desired and sales fluctuated sharply from period to period. Under such circumstances discounts taken in the particular period would fail as a reasonable gauge of the deduction which should be made from sales on this account.

To sum up the suggestions made above an illustration of the way in which these valuation items should be handled in the income sheet may be given. According to our view the first section of this statement should exhibit an adjustment of the provisional gross revenue figure. Using the figures given in the example already offered and assuming in addition that customers are credited on account of returns with $1,500, that special rebates of $2,000 are allowed, and that the estimated amount of uncollectibles for the period is $7,500, the income statement of the hypothetical company should begin somewhat as follows:

Gross Sales..		$500,000
Less:		
Discounts Applicable (taken and to be taken).......	$9,000	
Returns	1,500	
Special Allowances	2,000	
Estimated Uncollectibles	7,500	20,000
Net Sales (or effective gross revenue)..................		$480,000

DISCOUNTS AND ALLOWANCES ON PURCHASES

Discounts on purchases—discounts from the standpoint of the vendee—are likewise current valuation accounts. This view, however, is seldom exemplified in practice. Even those who might be inclined to agree with the position taken above in regard to sales discounts would probably not admit the propriety of an analogous treatment of discounts on purchases. The concensus of professional opinion seems to favor the interpretation of allowances for prompt cash payment of bills as a financial gain, an item of income somewhat analogous to interest earned; and in conformity with this opinion such discounts are commonly handled in the income sheet as a miscellaneous earning.

Nevertheless it may be stated roundly that the position commonly taken is not correct. Purchases discounts are just as emphatically a deduction from nominal costs as sales discounts are a subtraction from what would otherwise be an overstated gross revenue. Cash discounts from the standpoint of the buyer are likewise in essentially the same category as rebates, allowances, and returns, whatever the reason therefor. From the viewpoint of accounting all such credits should be considered as current valuation items, offsetting provisional cost figures. It is true, of course, that it is distinctly to the advantage of a concern to have sufficient funds to be able to pay its bills promptly and secure thereby discounts ranging from 15 to 80 per cent per annum (a far cry from any reasonable interest rate, as has often been pointed out); but an advantageous operating condition should not be confused with a positive item of income.

At bottom the theory that a purchase discount is an earning is based upon a confusion of economic principles and practical accounting procedures. The use of capital funds in general involves an economic cost for the user and a gain for the capitalist who furnishes the funds. But, as has been emphasized repeatedly in this study, it is quite unreasonable for the accountant to recognize the significance of the available capital of the specific business enterprise except as it appears in the form of actual assets and equities. Estimated interest on the owner's capital is not a cost on his books; neither does the existence of funds with which goods can be purchased constitute an earning in itself. It is only as the assets are increased as a result of successful operation that income appears. Good buying does not immediately give rise to income; rather it brings about a lowering of costs. For the particular owner cost means the cost of *purchased* commodities and services; and earnings appear as a residuum when the amount which has expired is charged to gross revenue.

The charging of interest on investment to expense and similar practices—as was noted in Chapter XI—have received very little encouragement from accountants. Yet they treat discounts on purchases as an earning—a parallel error. To charge interest on the owner's capital to expense and credit income is consistent with the practice which permits goods purchased to pass into costs at an inflated price, while the credit which should have been closed against provisional cost is treated as a real earning.

A rather extreme illustration will serve to emphasize the impropriety of treating discounts on purchases as an item of income. Suppose that a new concern begins business on January 1 and buys raw materials during the first twenty days of the month to the amount of $500,000, gross invoice price. On all these purchases, it will be assumed, a 2 per cent discount is to be allowed by the vendors if payment is made within 10 days. Being in a strong cash position the company finds it convenient to pay all of these bills during January. In other words, it accepts all discounts offered and pays cash of but $490,000 to settle accounts with a gross of $500,000. During the month, however, the company makes no sales, although manufacturing operations are begun.

In these circumstances, it would seem clear, no income whatever has been realized during the month of January. At any rate the company, having made no sales, has realized no profit in so far as the sale is the proper criterion. But there would be a credit balance of $10,000 in the discounts on purchases account, and such discounts are said to constitute an earning! The absurdity of treating such contra items as income becomes apparent in this case. The truth of the matter is that the company has purchased goods at an actual cost of $490,000. The discount amount is merely a suspended credit to the purchases account, the purchases discounts being an adjunct of this account. The two accounts taken together show the correct cost figures. No income has as yet appeared. Efficient purchasing does not in itself offer a proper occasion for income entries.

If discounts on purchases are not income when there are no sales, it may be concluded that such discounts are in no case actual earnings.

A further argument may be drawn from the character of discounts in the case of the purchase of fixed assets. Suppose, for example, that a particular company buys a unit of equipment on account, the terms being $5,000, gross, with an allowance of 2 per cent offered (or a price of $4,900) if payment is made within 10 days. In this case no one would think of considering the amount of the discount, if taken, an earning. All would agree that it should be credited to the gross price of the unit to obtain the true cost of the asset. Then, if discounts allowed in the acquisition of fixed assets are subtractions from costs rather than positive items of income, it surely follows that similar discounts arising in connection with the purchases of current assets are likewise offsets to current gross costs.

As in the case of sales discounts the amount of discounts actually accepted during a given period would not usually be the correct figure for the purpose of adjusting the "cost of goods sold" in the income sheet. The proper credit to purchases would be the sum of the discounts which have been taken and those which will be taken. This could only be determined by estimating the percentage of possible discounts outstanding which will be later accepted. A simple illustration will serve to show how this might be worked out. Let us assume that a retailer buys goods during the first month of operation with a gross cost of $25,000. During this period he accepts discounts to the amount of $400. At the end of the month possible discounts outstanding total $100; and the dealer expects to make payment in time to take all these allowances. To recognize the additional offset to cost it would be necessary to debit a discounts to be taken account and credit purchases discounts. As a result of these entries the purchases discounts account would show the sum of discounts taken and to be taken applicable to purchases for the period; and this account would be closed into gross purchases in order to obtain a correct figure for the cost of goods acquired. The discounts to be taken account would constitute a special offset to the gross of accounts payable, and should be shown in the balance sheet as a provisional deduction from the face of the outstanding creditor's accounts. In this way the approximate effective liability would be exhibited. In the succeeding period, discounts taken which were outstanding at the end of this period would be credited to discounts to be taken. In the income sheet the cost of goods sold would be computed and exhibited as follows (assuming an inventory with a gross price of $10,000 and a net of $9,800):

Purchases—at gross prices		$25,000
Less: Discounts on Purchases Taken and to be Taken	500	
Net Purchases		$24,500
Inventory—at Gross prices	$10,000	
Less: Discounts Taken and to be Taken applicable thereto	200	
Net Inventory		9,800
Cost of Goods Sold		$14,700

In many cases it would doubtless not be feasible to carry out this analysis with respect to prospective discounts, particularly in connection with inventories. Certainly it would be quite inexpedient to attempt to make adjustments in detail merchandise or creditors' records and accounts. Further, in so far as it is more convenient to use gross rather than net prices in taking inventory there can be no serious objection to the practice; the approximately accurate adjustments may still be made in summary through the controlling accounts and in the statements. In many instances no serious distortions would result if the problem of outstanding discounts were even entirely ignored. The particular circumstances of each case should dictate the degree to which refinement in such matters can reasonably be carried.

In conclusion it should be emphasized that however the discounts applicable to a particular situation be computed the amount should always be handled as a reduction from gross costs and not as income.

DISCOUNTS ON CONTRACTUAL SECURITIES

It is a familiar fact that such terminable securities as notes and bonds are, like capital stock, often issued at a discount; that is, the amount received from the investor—the "price" of the security—is frequently less than the face or par sum which is to be repaid at maturity. Such a situation requires—if the view that face or maturity value should always be exhibited in the accounts be accepted—the use of a special type of valuation or contra account, an account somewhat analogous to discount on capital stock but differing therefrom in that it should be systematically extinguished or "accumulated" if the integrity of income statements and balance sheets prepared during the life of the security is to be preserved.

The correct treatment for such cases has been indicated many times, but current practice is nevertheless often highly unreasonable at this point. What is the essence of the discount balance? Is it an asset, a loss, an expense, or an offset to the nominal liability which should be gradually written off against the net earnings appearing throughout the period covered by the security involved in any case?

Unaccumulated discount is in practice very commonly labeled "prepaid interest" or "interest paid in advance" and is placed in the balance sheet as an asset, grouped with bona fide current assets such as unexpired insurance. In this connection the general caption "deferred charge to operation" is usually employed. This is surely an unreasonable usage. "Prepaid interest" in any proper sense of the term does not and in the very nature of the case cannot exist. The difference between the sum which will be paid at maturity and the amount received from the investor is in nowise an asset. If it were true that such discounts constituted actual assets this would mean that the funds and other properties secured by the borrower were in all circumstances at least equal to the face of the obligation issued. It would mean that the company issuing a note or bond at such a low rate of interest that the security sold below par, none the less received a sum of values equal to that obtained by another company which emitted a security with the same par amount at an interest rate sufficiently high to attract the capital of the investor at par. If discount is an asset, then the United States government actually received $5 of value for a war savings stamp in 1918, despite the fact that the investor supposed he was putting in a considerably smaller sum and the Treasury Department took into account only the net amount. But this, in a sense, denies the very existence of discount, and is palpably absurd.

An illustration will serve to emphasize the point. Let us assume that A is in need of funds and, expecting to be hampered by lack of cash for some time, offers his written promise to pay $10,000 two years from date, without explicit interest. B, an investor, agrees to furnish $8,900 for this note, and the transaction is consummated. On A's books the transaction might reasonably be recorded in either of two ways: (1) the notes payable account might be credited with the sum due at maturity, $10,000, and a discount account charged with the difference between this sum and the amount received from B; or (2) the actual amount received might be credited to notes payable, no subsidiary account being opened. The first procedure is the more conventional, and it will be assumed for the moment that the entries are made according to this plan. This gives, at the outset, a special debit balance of $1,100, the amount of the discount.

But this balance is not an asset. Initially it is purely an

offset to the gross amount shown in the notes payable account. The amount of discount measures the difference between the cash received and the amount to be paid to the investor at the end of the two-year period. Naturally the two sums are different because of the intervening period. Accumulation as a result of the passage of time (with or without a periodic retirement of such accumulation in whole or in part) is the very essence of any situation involving the deposit or investment of funds on a definite contractual basis. If the discount is an asset in this case this means that A has received altogether a total of $10,000 and that B, of necessity, must have loaned that sum. But such a conclusion is contrary to the facts. A has actually borrowed only $8,900. At the end of the period he will return this principal plus $1,100 in *interest,* or a total of $10,000. He advances nothing. He receives a certain sum and later returns this sum plus an increment for its use; but he does not forward a single dollar for interest. Nor would it have been possible for A to have prepaid any interest. Had A paid B anything when the loan was made—a peculiar procedure indeed—this would simply have altered the amount of true principal involved. Suppose, for example, that the instant the above loan were effected A had insisted on handing back $50. Such a transaction would not constitute a prepayment of interest. Instead the net amount actually received by A would have been reduced by $50, and whatever sum he later paid B in excess of this net amount received would represent interest on the true initial principal. To reiterate, prepaid interest—in the sense of advances like insurance premiums for services to be furnished in the future—cannot, in the very nature of the case, exist.

Further, it should be fairly obvious that the amount of the discount cannot be interpreted as a loss. The transaction is entirely voluntary and commonplace. As was stated above, it is quite to be expected that amounts borrowed or invested on a contractual basis should increase with the lapse of time.

The borrower does not expect to receive the use of capital for nothing, nor does the creditor willingly invest without the promise—explicit or implicit—of a return on his investment. Neither at the outset or finally can a moderate difference between initial principal and amount repaid be viewed as a loss to the debtor.

The correct interpretation is that mentioned last above. Unaccumulated discount is an offset to an equity balance—a liability—which is shown at its future rather than its present significance. It is not, of course, a fixed offset throughout the life of the security involved. It should be formally accumulated against earnings on a mathematical basis each accounting period. The discount—in the case given—measures the difference between initial principal and total future payments and thus represents the interest which will be paid (not which has been paid) during the entire life of the security. Thus if A closes his books one year after receiving the loan from B, for example, his net revenue account (or an interest subsidiary) should be charged with $534 (6 per cent—the approximate effective rate involved—of the initial principal, $8,900), and discount on notes payable should be credited with the same amount. This procedure would place the proper accrued burden on earnings and would correct the statement of liability. B loaned A $8,900 at the outset. Since A has not paid the year's interest implicit in the transaction B is in effect making an additional loan for the amount thereof. The credit to the discount account reduces the offset to $566, and hence the effective liability now stands at $9,434.

As was suggested above, it would not be unreasonable accounting to show the net liability in a single account, omitting the offset subsidiary. Thus, in the above case, the initial transaction might have been recorded on A's books by a charge to cash of $8,900 and a credit to notes payable for the same amount. In this event the recognition of the interest accrual would be accomplished by means of an appropriate credit directly in the notes payable account. This method would in fact show the realities of the case more clearly than the other.

It may be objected to the position taken in this discussion that the true liability in the illustrative case is $10,000, the amount which A has agreed to pay; and this is perhaps true in a sense. The legal liability is commonly considered to be the face or par sum, the amount to be paid at maturity. In the case of insolvency the face amount would usually be held to express the creditor's claim. But this is not the whole story and it is scarcely the controlling consideration. In the first place the creditor might not actually receive the full amount as a result of liquidation proceedings. The amount received in such an event would depend upon the amount of assets available and the amount and character of the other equities involved; and probably any court, in rating the various liabilities, would take into consideration whatever serious amount of unaccumulated discount there might be. Further, in general, accounting practices must not be based entirely or even largely upon the conditions of bankruptcy. The going concern is the typical case; and to such a going concern the face of a discounted security is not *immediately* the effective liability. A— to refer again to the example given—does not owe B $10,000 at the outset. This figure becomes the true liability *two years after* the date the loan is effectuated. If the assets received are valued on a current basis why should not the equities likewise be so treated? If, to satisfy legal and accounting prejudices, an equity is shown as an amount due in the future, there is clearly a need for an appropriate contra account.

That the true accounting liability to begin with equals simply the amount of funds received is true in more than a formal bookkeeping sense. A, for example, could doubtless shift his liability to a third party on essentially the basis of the net amount. That is, he could probably induce C, a banker, to assume the note by paying him the amount of its current value. Further, if such a note were made out as payable on or before the final due date, as would be quite possible, there would surely be a provision attached which permitted the payer to deduct the amount of any unaccumulated discount from the face in making such payment. The war savings stamps issued by the federal government are redeemable prior to the final maturity date but at a price less than par.[2]

In the case of a note or bond carrying an explicit "interest" rate but which is nevertheless issued at a discount the situation is more complex. The total interest in such a case is the difference between the amount originally invested and the sum of the "interest" payments plus the par sum returned at maturity. What is the true liability in such a case? Is it the total of all payments made to the investor, the lump sum returned at maturity, or the amount initially invested? According to the position taken here the true initial liability is the amount received; the final liability at maturity is the face or par sum. If the total of all payments, both as interest and principal, were set up in the principal equity account the discount charge would be the difference between this total and initial investment. If par or maturity value were treated as the gross liability the discount recognized would be the excess of par over the actual amount received from the investor. In either case the amount of the discount should be treated as an offset to the nominal liability and should be systematically accumulated, so that the difference between the two accounts may at all times express the true effective liability.

A graphic representation of the various possibilities applied to an actual case will perhaps serve to summarize the situation in the case of the discounted interest-bearing security. Suppose a 5-year, $100,000 note carrying a semiannual interest pay-

---

[2] In this case the rate of interest allowed the investor in the case of early redemption, it may be noted, is less than that which will be realized if the security is held until maturity.

ment of $3,000 were issued by a corporation at a price to yield 10 per cent, convertible semiannually. The initial investment, then, would be $84,556.53. In the following graph the line OX

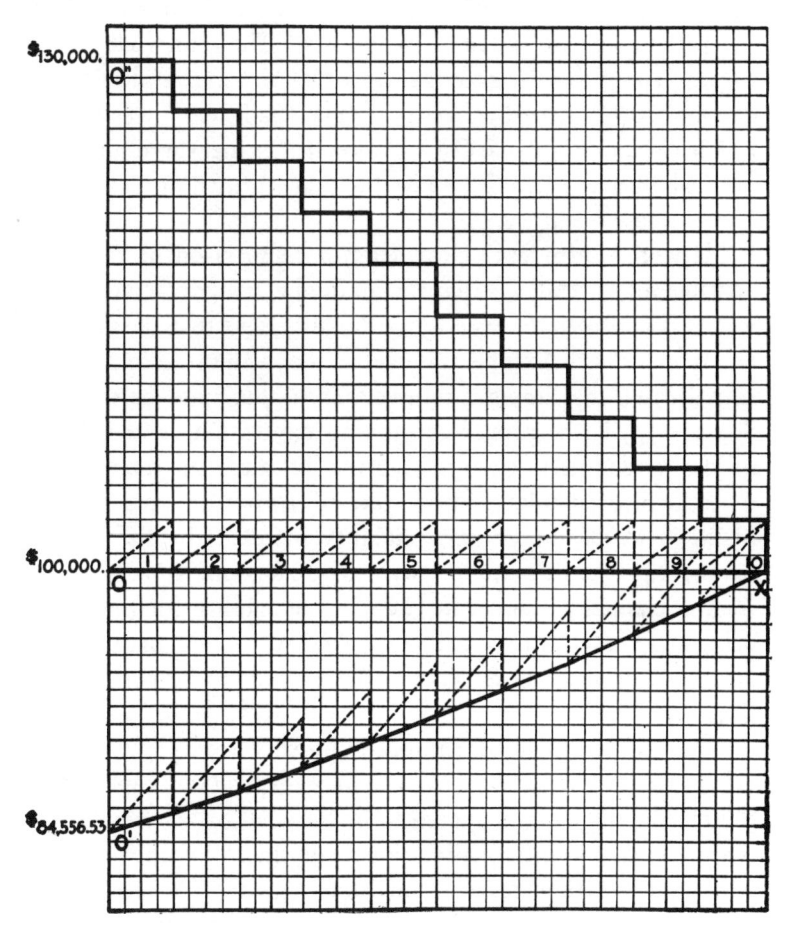

represents the par value; the line $O'X$ indicates the course of the net liability (including periodic accrued interest) on the company's books if par is shown in the main equity account and the difference between this sum and the effective liability in an offset account; and $O''X$ shows the course of the gross liability expressed in terms of the total payments, both principal and interest, which are due the bondholders. The serrated broken line attaching to OX indicates the accrual and liquidation of the several semiannual "interest" payments. The somewhat similar line attaching to $O'X$ shows the accrual and partial liquidation of the true interest charges. The half-year periods are numbered along the line OX. Amounts are measured along the vertical line at the left. The lines are drawn to scale with approximate accuracy.

It would seem very clear from a comparison of the three possible interpretations that the amount actually received or invested constitutes the true initial liability, and that the accountant should clearly exhibit this fact in the accounts. Thus, in the above case, the amount received from the note subscribers, $84,556.53, is the proper accounting expression, at the outset, of the noteholders' equity. During the first six months this investment accumulates at the rate of 10 per cent per annum; in other words the effective liability increases by the sum of $4,227.83. At this time a payment of $3,000 is made by the issuing company, the net increase in the liability for the period being thus reduced to $1,227.83. And so on. At maturity the liability will stand at $100,000, the amount to be paid at that time.

To accept either of the other possible interpretations involves thoroughly absurd conclusions, explicit or implied. If the true liability is considered to be the total of all payments to the noteholder—an interpretation really more logical than that which insists that merely the lump sum to be returned at maturity constitutes the liability—one is forced to accept the impossible position that a deficit of $45,443.47 (in the above case) has been in some manner incurred—unless he has the hardihood to maintain that this amount is in some mysterious way an asset charge. Further, this would involve the equally absurd position that this entire transaction lay outside of the periodic income account, that the payments made to the noteholders were entirely a retirement of an initial liability. To consider the par or face sum as the initial liability involves conclusions with respect to income and assets that are similarly unreasonable.

In conclusion a final consideration should be noted; viz., the effect of discount transactions on the books of the lender or investor. To return to the first illustration mentioned above, what is the note in this case worth, initially, to B? The answer seems clear. The cost of the note to B is $8,900, and, in the absence of unusual circumstances, this figure expresses the proper value for B's books, at the outset. B has as yet earned nothing. No interest in his favor has accrued. The note is not worth $10,000. If B were to assign or sell this asset immediately he would not receive—nor expect to receive—more than approximately the amount invested, $8,900. The correct procedure with respect to entries on B's books, accordingly, would be to charge notes receivable with only $8,900, the present value of A's note, or to charge notes receivable with $10,000 and credit a special offset account, unaccumulated discount on receivables, with the difference between this sum and the actual investment.

In this connection it may be noted that the practice of treating "unearned" discount as income is not correct, despite its adoption by many banks. Such a practice does not result in seriously improper conclusions, however, where the paper involved is short-term and the volume of loans does not fluctuate seriously between periods. Where, on the other hand, a bank attempts to draw conclusions with respect to net earnings and financial condition once a month or oftener, and the volume of paper discounted fluctuates sharply between periods, a careful distinction between earned interest and unaccumulated discount should be drawn.

CHAPTER XVIII

REVALUATION AND CAPITAL MAINTENANCE[1]

As was stated in the preface, it is not intended to discuss systematically in this book the problems of revaluation for purposes of accounting. Any such study would require one or more volumes in itself. There is one problem of valuation, however, which has a sufficient bearing upon the theory of accounts to warrant its consideration here; viz., the relation between the revaluation of fixed assets and the maintenance of physical capital. Especial attention has been attracted to this matter as a result of the wide fluctuations in prices in recent years. A number of writers and accountants have been insisting that the periodic charges to revenue to cover accrued depreciation of plant and equipment should be based upon the expected cost of replacement rather than original, actual cost. If only original cost less estimated salvage value is charged to operation, they urge, the physical extent and capacity of the plant and equipment is not maintained from revenues during a period of sharply rising prices. The integrity of the investment in a formal dollars-and-cents fashion may be preserved by the conventional policy, it may be admitted, but the volume of earnings retained in the business is likely to prove inadequate for replacement purposes. In order to insure the integrity of *physical* capital under these circumstances a management which has adhered to orthodox valuation and depreciation practices may find itself compelled, after a time, to draw in new funds in order to make the necessary replacements. On the other hand, if effective replacement costs are charged to gross earnings

---

[1] Adapted in part from "Depreciation, Appreciation and Productive Capacity," *Journal of Accountancy*, vol. XXX, pp. 1-11.

during the service life of a unit, it is contended that sufficient funds will be reserved in the business not only to make good the value expiration in dollars but to provide for actual replacement in kind.

There is undoubtedly much to be said in support of this position. It is clear that original cost is not an ideal expression of true value, or an ideal basis for depreciation charges, in a period of either rising or falling prices. Nevertheless some of the suggestions which have been made in this connection seem to indicate a failure to appreciate the inherent limitations of accounting, a lack of an understanding of the true relationship between the two fundamental classes of the balance sheet, and an uncertainty as to what properly constitutes income in the accounting sense. Further, they evidently involve an overemphasis upon the importance of the depreciation policy followed by the accountant with respect to its effect upon provision for replacements. It is particularly in these connections that the subject will be considered here.

BOOK VALUES, CAPITAL, AND PRICE MOVEMENTS

At the outset a general statement of the relation between price movements and accounting values should be made. As was pointed out in Chapter I, current conditions are emphasizing sharply the need for accounting devices which shall show as nearly as possible the actual economic situation in each case. It is coming to be clearly recognized that both the periodic statement of financial position and the report as to interim conditions of operation—with its resulting income figures—should consistently reflect true pictures of current business conditions and tendencies—as affecting the particular enterprise—if these statements are to form a basis for rational judgments on the part of the immediate management, the investor, and other parties concerned. It is coming to be recognized, in fact, that the entire accounting mechanism must become a more sensitive and accurate gauge of economic data—and certain long-standing theories and policies of accountants must accordingly undergo modification—if the purposes of the various interests in the business enterprise are to be adequately served.

But while improvement along these lines is much to be desired, the inherent limitations of accounting must not be overlooked in the advocacy of fundamental changes in established policies. Further, it must be remembered that new theories and plans for dealing with fluctuations in values on the books can only be adopted as technical methods are developed to express and control such schemes in a manner consistent with *all* the elements in the accounting structure. It may be a principle of good management, for example, to maintain the productive extent and capacity of the plant (the physical capital) out of earnings, but we cannot suffer this principle to be introduced into the accounts in such a way as to result in a distortion or misstatement of essential aspects of the balance sheet.

The complication which arises out of the change in the value of money should be first considered. Ideally, perhaps, the financial statements should show comparative economic conditions. An examination of successive balance sheets, it might be urged, should enable one to draw a reliable conclusion with respect to the relative financial position of the enterprise on each of the several dates involved. But such conclusions, it must be recognized, cannot be drawn directly from conventional accounting statements in a time of sweeping price changes. The significance of the money unit—the accountant's yardstick—is constantly changing. It is a commonplace, for example, that the present dollar is a quite different unit from that of pre-war days (despite some decline in prices); although it is doubtful if anyone—no matter how expert with index numbers—can state with precision the amount of this difference. "Dollar" is a term we attach to a varying economic significance.

The value of the dollar—its general purchasing power—is subject to serious change over a period of years, and the fluctuation in a single year is not always negligible. It is in this connection that one of the fundamental limitations of accounting arises. In some fields the units of measure employed are always the same; and this makes possible direct comparisons of situations and phenomena at different times. Accountants, however, deal with an unstable, variable unit; and comparisons of unadjusted accounting statements prepared at intervals are accordingly always more or less unsatisfactory and are often positively misleading.

An illustration may serve to emphasize the point. A real estate operator, it may be assumed, buys a tract of land in 1910 for $100,000. In 1920 he sells the same tract for $200,000. Ignoring interest, taxes, development costs, etc., and all other possible transactions, it now appears that he has made $100,000 —doubled his money; for he has twice as many dollars in 1920 as in 1910, and the dollar is the conventional unit employed by the accountant in assaying financial condition. But as a matter of fact the true financial position of the operator may be little if any improved as a result of this transaction. Indeed, it is generally admitted that the 1920 dollar had a value considerably under 50 per cent of that of the 1910 dollar; and to the extent that this was the case a transaction which showed an apparent profit of 100 per cent over the ten-year period actually resulted in a loss.

Many businesses and individuals have found themselves in a somewhat similar situation during the last few years. The ostensible economic gain measured in dollars has often been largely or entirely nominal because of the lessening value of the dollar as expressed by the general advance in prices. Many a taxpayer, under these circumstances, has felt the injustice of being obliged to pay large sums in income and profits taxes from his apparent net earnings, notwithstanding the fact that these were determined by orthodox accounting rules. When prices on all sides are climbing sharply it seems clear that mere increase in the number of dollars possessed is not a valid expression of true improvement in economic condition. The term "paper profits" might well be applied here. An appreciation with respect to unsold goods may indicate a genuine enhancement in financial strength, and is certainly less nominal in character than that part of the ostensible profit realized from sales which expresses the change in the value of money. It is probably true (as often claimed) that some wage-earners during the war period found all their apparent increase in compensation *more* than offset by the rise in the prices of the goods which they had been accustomed to purchase. It is probably also true that in some cases business men found that their buying prices advanced so rapidly as to require the use of all the nominal earnings of the business to maintain normal stocks of materials and other assets. These would be, of course, extreme cases. But the apparent improvement in the financial position of the typical enterprise during the war period was in no small degree merely a reflection of the change in the value of money. Thus the marked increase in corporate surplus accounts was not accompanied by—and did not express —a corresponding growth in physical capital.[2]

It would perhaps not be unreasonable to urge that the accountant should be held responsible for the preparation of supplementary statements at the end of each period designed to show—by making proper allowance for the change in the value of money—the true relation between the current statement and the one immediately preceding (or a series of earlier statements). Certainly all would agree that schedules of physical data and explanatory statements should accompany all comparative financial statements wherever there is serious

---

[2] In recent studies of corporate earnings and undivided profits during the war, this fact has not received sufficient attention.

danger of misinterpretation. It should be emphasized roundly, however, that comparative financial statements are not the chief concern of the accountant. It is not his task, primarily, to attempt to show in 1922, for example, underlying economic position in terms of a value unit of some earlier date. It is above all important that the accountant's statements present as accurately as possible a picture of *current* data in terms of the actual dollar as of the date of the statements. And this is not a matter of *general* price movements—which may be said to express the fluctuations in the significance of money—but of *specific* price and value changes. The particular business enterprise does not embrace goods in general but special classes of structures, commodities, services, and rights. It is thus the function of accounting to follow the investment of the specific business as it takes shape in various concrete items, and to register the effects brought about by changes in the values of these particular items.

Indeed, it would seem that any possible supplementary statements which might be prepared by the accountant should be couched in terms of individual price movements, with little or no reference to any precise calculation of the movement of prices in general. Thus, if the labor cost in a particular period showed a sharp increase over that of the preceding period, and the increase were due largely to higher wage rates instead of to an increase in the number of service units received, the accountant's explanation should consist in a statement of the specific physical and price facts rather than in a translation of current labor cost into terms of an earlier labor cost by means of an index number supposed to express the change in the value of money.

That is, the status of the particular business is affected directly by specific price movements and only indirectly by general trends. And, to apply this especially to the particular problem in hand, this means that the conservation of true economic capital is not purely a matter of the maintenance of the physical extent of plant, equipment, and inventories, or of productive capacity. The thesis that true capital is preserved if, and only if, the physical capital is kept intact cannot be maintained. Such a proposition would be true only if price movements were uniform and proportionate throughout all the ramifications of the economic structure, a condition which is not even approximated in the actual situation.

This can be shown emphatically by an illustration. Suppose that the Y Co. in 1910 installs an equipment of fifty units, each of which costs $1,000. Suppose further that in 1920 the Company finds it necessary to replace this property, and that the cost then is $4,000 per unit. This sharp advance in price, it may be assumed, is not due entirely to the change in the value of money but rather to the peculiar conditions affecting the cost of production of these machines (such, for example, as an unusual scarcity of the special manganese steel which, it may be supposed, is required in their construction) and to a sharp increase in the demand for the products thereof. For the same period the general price advance is, let us say, 150 per cent. This may be said to measure roughly the change in the value of money. The advance in the case of the Y Co.'s equipment, however, is 300 per cent, an increase double that of the advance in the general price level. If, now, the Company replaces the old equipment at a cost of $200,000 it may be said that it has a greater true capital invested than in 1910, whether gauged in terms of 1910 or 1920 dollars. The physical capital is unchanged but the true economic capital, due allowance being made for the change in the value of money, has been considerably increased. In general it takes two and one-half 1920 dollars to equal one 1910 dollar, but with respect to this particular equipment it takes *four* 1920 dollars to express a 1910 dollar. In terms of 1910 dollars, therefore, the new equipment represents a capital investment of $80,000 as compared with a former investment of $50,000. In other words, it requires an actual increase in capital—in terms of 1910 dollars—of 60 per cent to take care of replacements. In 1920 it takes more real capital (using the term, of course, in the sense of private capital) to carry on the company's operations; and if sufficient net earnings had not been retained in the business to take care of this genuine increase in capital costs, it would be necessary—and quite reasonable—for the management to raise the additional funds by issuing new securities.

The maintenance of true economic capital (from the standpoint of the private enterprise), then, does not insure the preservation of physical capital in the typical case, and the maintenance of physical capital would not in general guarantee the conservation of economic capital. Nevertheless it is clear that, from a managerial point of view, the extent and capacity of plant must be maintained if the volume of production is not to be curtailed, and sound management accordingly demands that adequate provision for replacements be made. Further, it is equally clear that in the long run the revenues of the successful business should furnish the required funds at least up to the amount of the initial true capital.[3] And if the raising of new capital is likely to prove difficult or undesirable for any reason, there can be no serious objection to the retention of additional earnings above this point, either for replacements or extensions as the case may be.

But the depreciation accounts must not be used to obscure a true increase in capital or the apparent increase which is necessary to reflect the change in the price level. That is, the depreciation charges should not be based upon the amount required to maintain the physical capital unless this can be done in such a way as to show at the same time the correct condition

---

[3] This does not mean, of course, that the particular unit may not be acquired through new financing, either temporary or long term. In many cases current revenues are drawn upon heavily for extensions, and replacements are later effected by raising additional capital. But nevertheless the general proposition holds, viz., that in amount if not literally in kind capital should be maintained from revenues.

of the capital accounts—the equities. An examination of the depreciation entries will emphasize this. To charge estimated costs of replacement to revenues instead of original cost, without further adjustments, would result in the building up of depreciation allowances or reserves in excess of the book value of the property retired. The accountant would then be confronted with an offset or valuation credit balance on the books although the property to which this credit was supposed to apply would have been replaced with new equipment which had suffered no depreciation. This balance in the reserve account would then evidently constitute a free surplus; and a belated recognition of an increase in capital equities (an increase which would, in the case of the above illustration at any rate, be in part a true increase in capital, as has been shown) would be forced.[4]

In other words, where assets are replaced by more costly units an increase in the equity accounts is inevitable unless the bookkeeping is definitely inaccurate and incomplete. The balance sheet consists of two fundamental classes of data, and a value change in one class must sooner or later be reflected in the other. The accountant cannot well apply a larger or smaller yardstick to one element in the accounting structure than is applied to all other elements. Thus fixed asset costs which have never appeared on the books as asset charges can scarcely be loaded into depreciation expense. Further, all elements of the accounting structure should be concurrently

---

[4] If the cost of the new units were charged to the reserve account (a reserve equivalent to an advanced replacement cost) the reserve would be canceled and the asset accounts would stand at the old figure. Such accounting, however, is quite unsound, despite its use and advocacy by many accountants. Abandonment is a distinct transaction; replacement constitutes another distinct happening. The two occurrences may be separated by many days in time. With respect to a particular unit discarded, indeed, replacement may never occur. At the time an asset item is scrapped or otherwise disposed of, accordingly, the property account should be credited and the reserve account should be charged for the amount therein which is applicable to the particular unit involved. When the new equipment is purchased the property account should be charged with its cost, and cash (or liabilities incurred) should be credited. This procedure, as has been indicated, would leave a balance in the reserve account (a balance which would evidently constitute a true surplus), provided the basis used to determine the reserve accumulation exceeded the book value of the asset involved. (See Chapter VII, p. 196.)

affected when price changes are introduced into the accounts. That is, it is not reasonable that an apparent depreciation reserve be converted to surplus in a lump at the time of replacement; the increase in capital should be exhibited systematically.

APPRECIATION AND DEPRECIATION

The solution of the matter lies in a revision of orthodox accounting policies with regard to closing valuations rather than with regard to depreciation methods. The maintenance of physical capital by means of depreciation charges can only be rationally accomplished as there is antecedent recognition of the advancing costs in terms of the book values of the assets. And there is in any event much to be said for the thesis that the values which the accountant uses in his periodic analysis should be based upon economic conditions as of the date on which the accounting period ends. At any rate it may be said that if plant and equipment assets were revalued at the close of each period on the basis of costs of replacement—effective current costs—depreciation charges would be automatically increased in a period of rising prices and the concomitant effect upon capital would be registered in a rational manner.

This can be best shown by an illustration. Suppose that the Y Co. buys a machine on January 1, 1915, at a cost of $10,000. This unit, it is estimated, has a service life of five years. Let us assume further that for the period 1915–1920 the replacement cost of this property advances 20 per cent (of original cost) each year. At the end of the first year, accordingly, the cost of replacement would be $12,000; and to recognize this situation in the accounts it would be necessary to charge the machine account $2,000 and credit surplus from appreciation for the same amount. If the straight-line method of apportionment is now used the depreciation for the year (ignoring salvage) would be $2,400; and this sum would be charged to revenue and credited to allowance for accrued depreciation.[5] At the end of 1916 there would again be a charge to property and a credit to appreciation account of $2,000. The depreciation for the year would then be $2,400 (20 per cent of book value at the end of the first year) plus 25 per cent (in view of the four-year life remaining) of the new cost increment of $2,000, or a total of $2,900. At the close of each of the remaining years appreciation and depreciation would be similarly recognized.

The depreciation charges for the years 1917-1919 would be $3,566.66, $4,566.67, and $6,566.67, respectively. (The third appreciation element would have a three-year life, the second a two-year life, and the last enhancement of $2,000 would be charged to depreciation expense in total the same year in which recognized.) This would result in total charges to depreciation expense during the life of the property of $20,000, the cost of replacement, instead of $10,000, the original cost. At the time of replacement the main property account would stand at $20,000 and its contra allowance would exhibit credits totaling a like sum. The surplus from appreciation account would show a credit balance of $10,000, the apparent increase in capital required to provide for the replacement of the machine. Somewhere among the assets—assuming that no dividends have been based upon depreciation—there would then be $20,000 (in cash, inventories, receivables, etc.) retained by the depreciation charges. When the old unit was discarded there would be a charge to the allowance account and a credit to property of $20,000. The acquisition of

---

[5] For simplicity it is assumed in this illustration that the advance in replacement cost has no effect upon service life. Of course, if such an advance induced the management to use the property for a longer period than was originally intended (either by making more extensive repairs or simply by using it beyond the period of its economical employment on the basis of original cost) the total depreciation would be apportioned over this longer life. The introduction of this complication, however, would not alter the illustration in any essential particular as far as the matter in hand is concerned.

a new unit would be recognized by a charge to assets of $20,000 and a credit to cash (assuming that cash is available and that payment is made immediately) of the same amount. This procedure would result in the maintenance of physical property through the recognition in the accounts each year of effective cost of replacement, in terms of both assets and capital, and the consequent increased expense charges. The net effect is the retention of new assets to the amount of $20,000 to replace the depreciated property which cost but $10,000, and the gradual restatement of the capital account (through surplus from appreciation) to correspond. From the point of view of the income sheet the result has been to increase sharply the depreciation cost of production, with a corresponding diminution of operating net revenue. In so far as it is admitted that cost of replacement constitutes effective managerial cost this procedure gives a more rational operating sheet.

To make the problem entirely clear it may be well to compare concretely, in terms of the special accounts involved, the results attained by the conventional method of valuation and depreciation with those of the heterodox plan just stated. Ignoring all other possible facts than those given, the accounts of the Y Co. on January 1, 1915, would appear as follows (in balance-sheet form):

Machine .... $10,000   Capital $10,000

Assuming that the orthodox valuation plan were followed, that all net earnings were withdrawn, and again ignoring all other possible transactions and circumstances, the accounts of the Y Co. on December 31, 1919, just prior to the moment of abandonment, could be represented as follows:

Machine	$10,000	Capital	$10,000
Sundry Assets (new).....	10,000	Allowance for Depreciation	10,000
	$20,000		$20,000

After the old unit is abandoned, we would have:

Sundry Assets (new)..... $10,000   Capital $10,000

To make the replacement at the new cost of $20,000 would now require a new investment of capital of $10,000; and, assuming that the additional funds were secured, that the sundry assets available were of such a character that they could be used in the purchase of the new equipment, and that the new property was acquired and installed, the accounts involved would stand as follows:

Machine (new)..........	$20,000	Capital (old).............	$10,000
		Capital (new)............	10,000
	$20,000		$20,000

If, on the other hand, replacement cost were used as a basis for valuation throughout, the first statement would appear as above but the second would stand as follows:

Machine	$20,000	Capital (original).........	$10,000
Sundry Assets (new).....	20,000	Capital (appreciation).....	10,000
		Allowance for Depreciation	20,000
	$40,000		$40,000

After the abandonment of the old unit we would have:

Sundry Assets (new).....	$20,000	Capital (original).........	$10,000
		Capital (appreciation).....	10,000
	$20,000		$20,000

Finally, after the new unit has been acquired (assuming that the sundry assets are in such form as to be capable of use for that purpose) the accounts would stand as follows:

Machine (new)..........	$20,000	Capital (original).........	$10,000
		Capital (appreciation).....	10,000
	$20,000		$20,000

In this event the company can evidently replace the discarded property without raising any additional capital, since the entire amount required has been obtained from earnings.

SPECIAL OBJECTIONS AND CONSIDERATIONS

Several more or less serious objections may be urged against the kind of accounting outlined above. In the first place it should be noted that the costs of replacing fixed assets do not usually rise or fall in any orderly fashion such as was assumed in the above illustration. These costs, like other prices, are subject to marked fluctuations; and it would ordinarily be impossible to forecast even the general trend for any considerable period with precision. Under these circumstances the use of estimated replacement costs in the valuation of assets for accounting purposes would appear to be a somewhat questionable procedure from the practical standpoint.

Further, if replacement costs should be used as a basis for valuation in a period of rising prices consistency demands their employment when prices are on the down grade. And this would lead to some rather unusual and objectionable results, as an examination of the procedures involved discloses. If replacement cost were less than original cost and this smaller sum were used as a basis for the determination of the depreciation charges and the concurrent credits to the allowance for depreciation, the resulting net income figures throughout the life of the property would evidently be somewhat higher than those which would be disclosed if the entire original cost were charged to operation. There would be a tendency, then, for the management to adopt a more liberal dividend policy. Sufficient assets would be retained from gross earnings to maintain capital in a physical sense, but the preservation of capital in terms of dollars would not be insured. And if the decline in the particular cost involved were more severe than the fall of prices in general true capital defined in terms of purchasing power might be impaired.

Evidently additional entries would be required under these circumstances. It would be necessary to credit the property account (or a special valuation account) with the difference between original cost and replacement cost, and charge the capital-equity accounts (or an appropriate offset account) with the same amount. To indicate the gradual shrinkage in dollar capital these entries should be made periodically; that is, the proportionate part (as indicated by the depreciation schedule) of the difference between actual cost and replacement cost should be extinguished each year. Otherwise the entire amount of this difference would of necessity be shown as a loss at the time of abandonment.

It would not be necessary, of course, actually to disburse in dividends this margin between original and replacement cost. But unless physical expansion were undertaken liquid funds would tend to accumulate if the return to the investors were not increased. As a matter of fact the law would in general view such a dividend as illegal. The law defines capital in money terms and does not consider the question of physical capacity in distinguishing between principal and income. Hence a "dividend" based upon the excess of actual cost over replacement cost would doubtless be treated by the courts as a disbursement of capital.

Further, most accountants would insist that the total depreciation expense involved in the operation of a fixed asset cannot legitimately be considered to be less than actual cost less salvage value. A calculation of expenses which does not include the total amount invested and consumed would seem to be definitely erroneous. If a machine costs $1,000, for example, and its value is completely consumed in operation, this entire amount must be charged to gross earnings if the actual facts of the case are to be shown. The depreciation policy is not merely a matter of retaining from revenues an amount which, on a new price level, will provide for replacements; it is also necessary to show the actual fixed asset costs.

This last point may be elaborated into a general criticism of the scheme suggested in the preceding section. Such a plan, it may be objected, is based upon an entirely improper conception of the purpose of accounting for accrued depreciation. There is at least some basis for the view that the essential purpose of recognizing accrued depreciation is to secure a rational apportionment of the actual cost of a long-term asset over the series of income sheets arising during its life.

And from this standpoint depreciation accounting does not involve provision for physical replacements or the maintenance of capital in any ultimate sense. Continuous and successful operation, of course, requires the preservation of physical capital; and this means that in a period of rising prices not all of the apparent net earnings can be safely disbursed to investors. It is the business of the directors in such circumstances to adopt a dividend policy which is consistent with replacement requirements. Thus there is a necessity for the accumulation of surplus not only to meet the demands for actual expansion, but also, in a period of sharply advancing replacement costs, to provide for the bare conservation of physical capital. In other words, the preservation and expansion of the physical capital of the enterprise depends upon the dividend policy rather than upon the method followed in booking accrued depreciation, especially in a period of rising prices.

On the other hand, it must not be denied that the depreciation policy has many implications and purposes. The effect of the recognition of accrued depreciation upon the net book values of the fixed assets for balance-sheet purposes must not be forgotten. Further, to insist that the depreciation plan should have a bearing upon the provision for replacements is not, in itself, unreasonable. It should be recognized that while good management may in itself demand that a conservative dividend policy be pursued it is the restriction of the net income figure by means of depreciation and other appropriate charges that above all indicates and enforces such conservatism. The charge to expense (for depreciation or other cost) reduces the figure for operating net revenue below what it would otherwise be by just the amount of the charge. This decreases the size of the gauge which constitutes the most fundamental criterion of dividend declarations. Every additional dollar charged to expense removes that sum of value beyond the realm of dividend possibilities. It is in this sense that it is proper to speak of the expense charge as "reserving" assets in the business. Indirectly, by reducing what would otherwise be the net income figure, the recognition of accrued depreciation undoubtedly tends to prevent the disbursement of capital as dividends.

As a further objection it might be urged that the alternatives discussed in the preceding section would lead to identical results for the entire period involved provided the income account were correctly exhibited. Income in the broadest sense may be conceived as including the entire net increase in the equity accounts after due allowance has been made for new investments and withdrawals. And from this point of view the credit of $10,000 to surplus from appreciation (see the illustration above) constitutes an income item, and exactly offsets the additional charge of $10,000 to expense. Thus the net effect upon the statement of income throughout the five years is nil if all income credits are taken into account. Is it not folly, then, to write assets up, crediting some surplus account for the amount of the appreciation, since this will mean merely that a like increase must be charged to depreciation expense and credited to assets (indirectly, through the allowance account) during the life of the property? If the entire net income in this broad sense were withdrawn from the business, is it not clear that the final status of both asset and capital accounts would be the same if cost of replacement were charged to expense as if only original cost were so charged? Admitting that revaluation and subsequent depreciation on a replacement-cost basis would bring about a somewhat different *apportionment* of net income over the life of the property involved, would not the resulting accounts and statements constitute a no more effective basis for sound administration than those prepared in accordance with orthodox rules?

This matter evidently hinges upon the definition of "net income" which should be accepted by the accountant and the management. Is the credit to surplus from appreciation (or other appropriate equity account), which should be made when a fixed asset is charged with the increment necessary to bring the book value up to the effective current cost, in any sense an index of income? This question is a difficult one. In so far as the price advance in the particular case were more acute than the general movement such a credit could be said to represent in part—as was pointed out in a preceding section—a genuine increase in capital. In the average case it would no doubt be true that such appreciation would for the most part express merely the application of a new measuring unit to the accounts. At any rate the appreciation credit would not in general measure an amount which could be conveniently or safely made the basis of cash dividend declarations. It is surely important from the standpoint of successful management that the physical capital be maintained, and, as a rule, from earnings. To revalue assets and base depreciation upon replacement costs would be an entirely futile policy unless the appreciation credit were excluded from the income account— at least as far as disposable income is concerned. If, however, this credit is considered to be essentially a capital item, a revision of initial equities or investments in terms of changing prices, the procedure outlined is highly pointed. Under these circumstances the increased charge to expense would actually tend to result in a more restricted dividend policy and the consequent retention of additional assets.

The method of accounting outlined in the preceding section involves the recognition of the appreciation of fixed assets; and to this many accountants would strenuously object on general grounds. What is the proper attitude to take on this question? While it is not intended to thresh over the pros and cons of this question here, one or two considerations may be noted. From the standpoint of management (which is essentially interested in current effective costs and not in the costs of five years ago) and from the standpoint of the creditors and others who would like to see the balance sheet really exhibit what it purports to show, viz., a correct statement of the assets and their equitable distribution as of a given date, there is much to be said in favor of such recognition. On the other hand may be urged the conjectural character of asset values at best and the consequent importance of conservatism, the difficulties in the way of determining reasonable replacement costs in the case of complex structures, the more or less continuous fluctuation in such costs, and the fact that having once made an investment the management is often thereby committed to a certain policy for a considerable period regardless of price movements.[6]

---

[6] A management, for example, cannot well scrap a plant which cost $3,000,000 in order to take advantage of an appreciation of $100,000 in the site on which it stands. The site in such circumstances is virtually removed from the market for a period of years at least.

As a matter of fact actual appreciation has been booked many times, and often with the authority of public accountants. Further, appreciation may be indirectly recognized by altering the rate of depreciation; for high replacement costs may induce a management to lengthen the service life of the fixed assets at its disposal.

The Treasury Department will not permit the recognition of appreciation as a basis for the depreciation of fixed assets for tax purposes except in so far as it has occurred prior to March 1, 1913.

CHAPTER XIX

CRITERIA OF REVENUE

In discussing the nature of the expense and revenue classifications and the general problem of the determination of net income in this book it has thus far been assumed for the most part that the ascertaining of periodic *gross* revenue is largely a matter of clerical routine. It has been assumed, in other words, that the assignment of revenue *credits* to the particular accounting period can be readily accomplished by means of ordinary bookkeeping, there being no serious questions of analysis involved. The difficulties in the way of expense determination and apportionment have been recognized at various points. It has been indicated that the calculation of periodic expense requires a complete revaluation of assets—an estimate of depreciation, a valuation of merchandise on hand, and so on. But in general it has been taken for granted that the basic revenue figure from which the total of the expense charges must be deducted is discovered by simply totaling the sales for the period.

It is intended in this chapter to show that this assumption cannot be accepted without important qualifications; that the difficulties involved in the determination of net revenue do not all come to a focus in the expense or debit side of the income account. The valuation of assets is a process which affects the amount of income directly as well as indirectly, through costs. Further, there are many important considerations of law and business expediency to be recognized in the computation of gross income. The ascertainment of the revenue figure is a problem in itself, a problem rendered particularly acute by the advent of heavy income tax levies. Indeed, the development of methods by which the amount of gross earnings may be determined on a rational basis is one of the most serious tasks facing the accountant.

For the accountant the problem of assigning income credits to a particular period simmers down to the question, what is the proper criterion of revenue? What is a satisfactory test or evidence of revenue? When is revenue realized? Or, putting the matter more specifically in terms of the accounts, what shall be the signal or occasion for credit entries in the revenue account? In the following sections this question will be considered.

THE RECEIPT OF CASH

The most conservative criterion of income is the receipt of cash. Cash—meaning thereby any generally recognized medium of exchange—can be used to purchase any desired commodity or service whatsoever, provided the same is available on the market, to retire obligations, to pay taxes, to pay dividends, to liquidate terminable proprietary investment, etc. Cash is the asset *excellent*. The receipt of cash for product, consequently, furnishes the ultimate test of revenue realization. From this standpoint the cash sale and the collection of cash following the so-called credit sale constitute the principal income transactions, the important occasions for entries in the revenue account.

Cash, of course, may be received in connection with many transactions which have nothing to do with revenue. An additional deposit of cash by investors, for example, evidently has no direct effect upon the income account. Further, it is not intended to imply that the amount of cash received as a result of sales could measure or express *net* revenue. Cash receipts from customers would simply represent gross revenue on a cash basis. Unless these receipts exceeded costs there would obviously be no net earnings.

In precisely what way would the accounting procedures be affected if the cash receipt were actually adopted by the business enterprise as the exclusive evidence of income? Essentially it would mean that the credit sale would not be recognized as a transaction affecting the financial status of the enterprise. That is, no formal accounting entries covering the sale would be made until collection were accomplished. When cash was received the transaction would be considered closed and the charge to cash and the concurrent credit to revenue would be entered. Periodically the cost of producing the goods for which payment had been made would be determined and charged against this gross revenue. The resulting balance would be net revenue on a cash basis.

It might be urged that if collection is to be the occasion for credits to income the expenditure should be the basis for income debits, expense. This, however, does not follow. Expense should always be defined as an adjunct of revenue, the controlling classification. It must be remembered that the accountant's expense is the cost of producing a particular volume of revenue. If revenue is represented by the receipts from a quantity of product sold expense becomes the cost value of this same product. That is, when a sale were finally closed on a cash basis (when collection had been effected) the gross revenue would appear. The expense of such a sale would be the cost, including marketing expenses, of the finished product involved. And current expenditures would be very unlikely even to approximate in amount the cost value of goods exchanged for cash. This would be especially true in connection with fixed asset costs, where expenditures are made considerably in advance of utilization and final expiration.

There would, however, be some force in the contention that if cash collection is the basis of revenue, cash expenditure is the proper evidence of *cost incurred*. That is, if a sale transaction is not closed until collection, neither is a purchase actually effected prior to expenditure. But cost incurred must be sharply distinguished from expense, as was pointed out in Chapter VI. Values coming into the possession of the enterprise and values finally disappearing embodied in finished product are entirely distinct in principle, and only in the simplest trading situations are the two likely to approach identity in amount in a given period. This would be true whether the cash evidence of revenue were adopted or not.

Numerous objections to such accounting for income at once present themselves. The account receivable, it may be contended, is a bona fide asset.[1] Further, it can be pointed out that title to the goods involved may, under certain circumstances, pass to the buyer before payment is made. In this event the selling company must either consider the goods which have been shipped as still an asset on its books, an actual misstatement from the legal point of view, or view the transaction as one which involves a temporary loss, a loss which will be recouped as soon as cash is received. If the seller treated finished stock as an asset until the date of collection, and the buyer recognized purchases prior to payment therefor, this would mean that the same merchandise were being considered an asset simultaneously on the books of vendor and vendee—a highly anomalous situation. As was stated above, the view that collection is the proper signal for income entries is consistent with the theory that payment is the accounting evidence of purchase. Evidently if this theory were actually adopted with respect to the recognition of cost incurred it would mean, in extreme cases, that materials would be acquired, manufactured, and sold for cash prior to their acquisition from an accounting standpoint. In other words, the appearance of cash revenue might antedate the recognition of some of the actual costs of this revenue, an obviously ridiculous state of affairs.

---

[1] This matter will be further discussed in the next section.

This would be an unusual situation, however, at any rate in manufacturing. In general the manufacturer would make payment for his principal current costs as well as for his fixed asset costs before receiving cash from the sales of goods in which these costs were embodied.

It is not intended to argue in support of the cash standard of gauging revenue, but simply to suggest what would be involved if any such criterion were actually adopted. It should be emphasized that accounting for revenue on a cash basis by no means involves merely a comparison of the cash balance at the beginning of the period with that at the end. Such a crude device for measuring income, although still employed in a surprising number of cases, is without a shred of justification, of course, as applied to the conditions of the ordinary business enterprise. Cash transactions which relate to capital equities and fixed assets are wholly outside the current income account. The procedure suggested above is the most satisfactory method by which the cash criterion can be applied to the income account. To credit revenue with the amount of closed, i.e., cash sales, allocating thereto the cost of these sales and considering net income to be disclosed by the balance, is an accounting scheme not wholly devoid of reasonableness. Memoranda covering credit sales would of course be necessary. Journal entries in suspense accounts might even be made, the registering of effect upon income, however, being postponed until payment is received.

In individual affairs as opposed to the business enterprise cash accounting for income is common. Probably a majority of individuals are not satisfied that income is actually realized on any but a cash basis; conversion to cash is here usually accepted as the proper evidence of revenue. This state of affairs is definitely recognized by the federal government in the administration of its income tax program. The individual may prepare his return on a cash basis provided he elects to do so consistently; and a great majority of the individual returns filed are actually prepared according to this plan.

In business the principal case where cash income accounting is recognized as a satisfactory procedure arises in connection with so-called instalment sales. Here it is considered good practice to make collection the occasion for the recognition of income. When goods are "sold" on this plan collection is not always a mere routine incident, following sale as a matter of course. The collection department may be of the utmost importance; the cost of collection may be a significant fraction of total expenses; the collection of instalments may constitute, in a sense, the last important stage in the process of production. In extreme cases the cost of collection overshadows all the other costs. Certainly in such instances it is not unreasonable to await the receipt of cash before recognizing revenue.

The Treasury Department, to refer to income tax procedure again, permits the taxpayer to report income arising from instalment business on the basis of cash receipts, instalments paid. The taxpayer may, however, if he chooses to do so consistently, treat the total of the obligations of his customers as the equivalent of cash. If a considerable percentage (more than 25 per cent, for example) of the gross contract price is immediately paid in cash the vendor must consider the transaction as closed for income tax purposes. In general the accounting profession approves these rulings, it being recognized that the typical instalment sale is a rather flimsy evidence on which to require a showing of income.

When credit relationships are soundly established receipt of cash may be a fact of minor importance, an incident occurring more or less automatically. In other cases, even outside of instalment sales, when the relation of seller and customer is not solidly grounded in business practice, collection is a serious matter. It is a well-known fact that in many lines of business a considerable percentage of the total of sales is never collected. This matter will be further discussed a little later.

As was pointed out earlier in the book, the idea that effective net income for a period is actually present in the cash account is common. This conception, it may be reiterated in this connection, is quite erroneous. Even if the cash sale were taken as the sole evidence of revenue the net income for a period would not, usually, measure the cash balance or the change in that balance. It should be emphasized that net revenue, determined on any reasonable basis, does not commonly measure any specific asset. All that may be said of the credit balance of the income account in terms of the assets is that this balance, from the standpoint of ownership, expresses the recognized increase in the *total* of assets, due allowance having been made for additional investments, borrowings, and payments of principal or income to the creditors and proprietors. This increase is likely to be represented in various asset accounts—merchandise, receivables, cash, equipment, etc. Only in the event that there were no cash investments or retirements whatever, that there were no fixed asset costs, that all current items were acquired, paid for, and consumed within the accounting period in question, and that all sales were for cash, would the net income balance for a period precisely measure the change in the cash balance. Even if the cash collection is taken as the exclusive token of revenue throughout the period, this simply means that gross revenue, from the asset standpoint, passes through the cash stage. If the increase in the cash balance corresponded to the net revenue, it would be purely a coincidence in the typical case.

THE CREDIT SALE

The evidence of income most widely adopted by the accountant, of course, is the sale transaction, the credit sale and the cash sale being treated as of equal importance with respect to effect upon revenue. That is, the conventional sale, whether payment is made immediately or is postponed, is considered as the proper occasion for credits to the revenue account. Since, in many lines, from 80 to 95 per cent of all sales are on a credit basis, this means that the credit sale is often the typical revenue transaction.

What is the credit sale? Only a brief statement of the nature of this transaction will be attempted here. The passage of title is probably the test most commonly applied to distinguish the genuine sale from the order or contract. As a matter of fact little attention is usually paid to the technical matter of title passing in the routine work of entering gross revenue. The order is received and acknowledged; the goods are manufactured or, if in stock, are prepared for shipment; the goods are consigned; receipt of shipment is acknowledged by consignee; the buyer accepts goods and pays transportation charges; a check on account is received by the vendor. At what step in such a chain of circumstances is the sale completed? When does title pass? The accountant, without attempting to thresh out the legal niceties of each cash usually seizes upon the act of consignment as the evidence of the completed transaction. That is, shipment is taken as the occasion for the credit to revenue. Some orderly plan for establishing sequence of book entries is necessary; and the conventional procedure seems fairly satisfactory. In many cases title doubtless actually passes at this point; but this is certainly not always the case.

To consider the credit sale as an indicium of revenue involves the recognition of accounts receivable, claims against customers, as an asset. The accountant views the credit sale as an exchange of product, valued on a cost basis, for an amount of current claims exceeding these costs, supposedly, by the income margin. The sales account is of course commonly credited with the gross amount of these claims and the costs are periodically deducted, in total. The question arises, just how valid an asset is the account receivable?

An account receivable constitutes precisely what it has already been labeled, a *claim* against the customer. It is commonly supported by some formal documentary evidence, such as the order, shipping-room records, bill of lading, etc. It is, in general, an enforceable claim; i.e., if the seller can demonstrate that valuable commodities have been shipped on account to the buyer he can take definite legal steps to require payment or, in some cases, force a recovery of the goods. The trade creditor has a solidly established legal status.

On the other hand, if attention is directed to the specific transaction it becomes apparent that the credit sale is really but a kind of "gentleman's agreement." The customer has merely promised payment in the event goods are delivered as ordered; and in many cases the promise is tacit rather than explicit. Frequently no definite date for payment is set and the terms are in some other respects vague. The situation often lacks finality. The consignor expects payment, but there may be many a slip between shipment and collection. In general the buyer is conceded the right to return the whole consignment if the goods are unsatisfactory. At least this is widely true in the trading field and to a considerable degree elsewhere. If the vendee were to insist on returning the shipment, whether or not the excuse given therefor were reasonable or convincing, the seller would very seldom attempt to enforce settlement. If the goods are reconsigned to him about all he can do is make the best of it. In other words, while collection follows more or less automatically in many instances, there is a sense in which the specific credit sale is only a tentative transaction. Settlement will probably follow in due course, but this is not certain to be the case.

Even if the goods are accepted by the buyer collection may be a long and costly process. This is especially true of instalment business, as was pointed out above; and it is true to a most unfortunate degree in many other cases.

It appears, then, that the account receivable is a bona fide asset, and the credit sale, hence, a valid evidence of revenue, to the extent that such a claim may be reasonably said to be enforceable, sure of collection. Obviously this depends upon the actual circumstances of each case. The accountant's assumption that these claims are assets is, in general, not unreasonable. Accounts receivable are almost universally recognized as an important current asset, but one degree removed from cash. Cash may be borrowed on the basis of this asset; and the accounts may be actually sold for cash in some cases, although commonly at a ruinous rate of discount.

It may be pointed out that, if sales and collections happen to coincide in amount in a particular period, the gross revenue figure is the same whether the cash or the combined cash and credit basis be followed. However, any precise correspondence or consistency between sales and collection curves is in general very unlikely. In principle the two criteria, the cash receipt and the credit sale, are quite distinct. The conventional plan of accounting for income involves taking the credit transaction as the typical occasion for the revenue entry. Conversion to cash is not awaited, and hence the cash receipt is not insisted upon as the evidence of income. In view of popular misconceptions in this connection, this fact needs emphasis. Conventional accounting income is not exclusively cash income. In a particular case collections may be very slow and the cash condition quite unsatisfactory; yet the showing of income may be highly favorable. Evidently a part of the income in such a case has not been realized in cash.

It is important to notice that if the sale is to be used as the exclusive evidence of income all unsold product must be revalued, consistently, on a cost basis. To take any such asset into the inventory at a figure above cost would involve the recognition of value enhancement (income in the broadest sense) without sale. Similarly, to value product at less than cost results in a reduction of income below what it would be on the basis of sale transactions. Further, the widely advertised rule for pricing current stock, "cost or market whichever is lower," is really inconsistent with the view that the revenue account depends entirely upon sales. If the sale is the proper criterion of income then it follows that all merchandise assets should be valued at cost. The accountant who in one breath insists on the importance of the sale as the only trustworthy evidence of income, and in the next contends that current assets should be priced at cost or market, whichever is lower, is throwing reason to the winds.

One further question may be raised in this connection. If the customer's order or contract is binding, why have we not therein a satisfactory evidence of income? In other words, if the buyer obligates himself to purchase a definite quantity and value of goods why cannot the effectuation of this arrangement, the securing of the order, be taken as a determinant of revenue?

It is true that the booking of the order is sometimes the most significant occurrence in the whole chain of circumstances surrounding the sale, shipment and collection being routine matters. It is not hard to find cases in which the sales management considers the securing of the contract as more than half the battle. The order may be a very "valuable" consideration. In fact money may, in some cases, be borrowed upon a showing of orders as well as upon a showing of accounts receivable. The intrinsic financial status of the enterprise may be decidedly affected by orders. Why, then, is not the binding order as fair an evidence of income as the enforceable customer's account?

In the first place it is evident that unless the goods ordered are produced and in stock, it would seem rather unreasonable to recognize the order as a valid asset, and thus accrue income in advance of both production and delivery. Revenue can hardly arise prior to the incurring of the expense of production. Contracts and orders have sometimes been included in the balance sheet as an asset, even though the goods involved were not produced; but accountants have wisely frowned upon such practices. Certainly orders are not receivables. On the other hand if the goods ordered are already in stock, and the sales agreement is binding, there is some force in the contention that the consummation of the agreement is a significant evidence of income. The accounting for such income would be somewhat troublesome, however. As long as the goods ordered were viewed as included in the seller's assets the order itself could hardly be considered an asset, at least in gross. The realized additional value would be, at the most, the amount of net revenue involved. This enhancement could be conceived as inhering either in finished stock or in the sales agreement itself. If the finished stock account were charged with the estimated net income on orders received, the income account being concurrently credited, the balance of transaction would naturally be viewed as: (1) an exchange of finished stock, plus shipping costs, for accounts receivable of the same amount, and (2) an exchange of receivables for cash. This amounts to valuation at the contract price less estimated costs yet to be incurred. The propriety of this method of valuation is sometimes recognized in practice. In such cases it appears that the contract, the binding sales agreement, is recognized as having some force in determining the incidence of income.[2]

Finally, it must be remembered that the binding order is not as typical of business as the enforceable account receivable. Wholesale cancellation of contracts and agreements is common

---

[2] It is doubtful if such procedure would really mean that the order was being taken as the basis of income. This will become apparent in the next section.

in a period of price recessions. In general the delivery of goods constitutes a sounder basis for legal action than the booking of an order.

PHYSICAL COMPLETION

Another possible accounting evidence of revenue of considerable theoretic importance, and having a limited application in practice, is physical completion. In some fields of industry, it has been urged, physical completion rather than final sale and disposal, on either a cash or a credit basis, is the significant test of revenue realization. Let us briefly examine this proposition.

The validity of this criterion in a particular case depends essentially upon the conditions actually obtaining. The allocation of revenue to accounting periods in terms of *production* rather than *sale* is not an entirely unreasonable procedure if production is the main end of the enterprise, subsequent sale being merely a routine incident, to be taken for granted. If the efforts of the management and the costs incurred relate almost entirely to physical production, the piling up of finished stock is the significant goal of the enterprise. In other words, if the operating staff is large, the equipment elaborate, and the technical processes long and costly, while the sales department is small, engaged in routine work, and with insignificant costs, there is some justification for considering the transfer of the completed article to the stockrooms, rather than consignment, as the most reasonable occasion for the income entry. In such a case it may fairly be argued that technical completion, not the sale, is the significant financial event.

Where, if at all, do we find such conditions? Evidently only where there is an assured demand for all output. This is approximately the case in the production of certain staples. Agricultural products furnish perhaps the best examples.

The farmer is virtually assured of a market under almost any set of industrial conditions, although not, however, at any particular price. Getting the wheat to the bin is for him the long and expensive task. Sale and delivery are thereafter largely routine matters, although delivery cost is by no means always negligible. Thus the farmer frequently hauls produce some distance to market without having made in advance any specific provision for sale; he knows that sale is assured at the going price.

Coal mining furnishes, perhaps, another illustration. Coal is a staple raw material throughout industry, and the principal household fuel. The coal producer, consequently, can market his output without special selling effort, his deliveries being conditioned primarily by the availability of transportation facilities. Sale of a reasonable output is practically assured. The production of lumber, copper, petroleum—in fact almost any fundamental raw material—presents these conditions to some degree. Gold mining is, of course, a clear case.

The Treasury Department, in allowing farmers the privilege of pricing unsold product at the end of the period at current selling price less estimated marketing costs, is recognizing the validity of this principle as a basis for reporting income in a special case. If a farmer adopts this rule it means, essentially, that he "takes his profit" in the year in which his wheat, for example, is raised, rather than the year in which it happens to be marketed, provided the two are different. In other words, he recognizes physical completion as an evidence of revenue realization. This heterodox ruling of the Department is having a considerable influence on accounting opinion with respect to rules for valuation and income-reporting. It would not be very surprising if the plan were extended to other branches of the extractive industries.

In manufacturing, selling costs are likely to be high and sale can seldom be taken as a matter of course. Specialized goods do not usually have an assured market for any considerable period. Sale thus becomes a financial fact of the first importance and a more reasonable evidence of revenue than mere physical completion. On the other hand, wherever sale does follow manufacture more or less automatically, without heavy additional costs, there is something to be said for the other principle. Certainly this is true in the case of binding orders, contract sales. While the occasion of securing an agreement in advance of production hardly furnishes a reasonable basis for the recognition of income, as was explained above, the completion of the article under such an agreement virtually settles the question of income. The profit is realized; shipment and collection follow as routine incidents in the conversion of product to cash. The accountant is indeed usually willing to admit the propriety of this principle under such conditions. Title, strictly speaking, may not have passed; but all essential steps in production have been taken.

As was stated above, booking income on completed but unsold goods involves the valuation of stock at selling price less estimated marketing costs to be incurred. In general accountants are agreed that such a rule of valuation is vicious. It involves, they say, the recognition of an "unrealized" profit; if sale is not finally made the supposed profit will disappear. As a matter of conservatism this position is reasonable enough; although its logic is weak as is the case with all accounting views based largely on conservatism. The same thing may be said of the credit sale: unless collection follows the supposed profit evaporates. Sale is only one test of realization; there may be others having some validity. It is not intended here to defend strongly any heterodox principle of valuation; but it may not be unreasonable to raise a question as to the legitimacy of this wholesale condemnation of selling prices, properly adjusted, as a basis for pricing finished goods. Conditions in the business world are highly varied, and probably no one principle of valuation and no single evidence of income, should be universally and rigidly applied. The instances mentioned above (inventories of farm products and goods produced on binding contract) of the acceptance, in practice, of technical completion as a basis for income entry, make it necessary to treat this principle seriously.

Doubtless the accountant's position in this matter is justified in the majority of cases. Certainly in the trading field and in most manufacturing lines the sale is not an event to be taken for granted; it is rather a most significant circumstance in the chain of operating and financial happenings. Sale, rather than completion, is probably much the better evidence of revenue in such cases. Viewing production broadly the selling activity here becomes a part of operation, the capstone of the whole process; and, hence, to consider income as realized prior to sale involves the recognition of revenue prior to completion itself, in the economic sense.

PERCENTAGE OF COMPLETION

Percentage of completion as a criterion of revenue is a modification of the principle we have been discussing which should receive some consideration. "Completion" here may mean mere physical production or, better, economic production in the broad sense just mentioned. The argument in favor of this basis for measuring income may be put somewhat as follows. Why take a specific occasion such as completion or shipment as an evidence of income realization? Is it not unreasonable to assume that income suddenly appears, on the instant, *in toto?* Business operation is a continuous process, not a succession of completions and consignments. Why, then, should not the acquisition of income be viewed as an orderly, gradual accrual arising throughout the entire period of production? In other words, why should not income be accumulated on the books in terms of some reasonable scheme of completion percentages?

From a broad economic standpoint this idea has much to commend it; and it would seem to be consistent, in a sense, with one of the fundamental assumptions of accounting. As has been noted several times in preceding chapters, the accountant always takes it for granted that the costs of all commodities and services expended toward a certain end in some way come to pass over into and inhere in the object for which they were expended. Cost accounting is based on this assumption throughout. If, then, the values of the purchased commodities and services flow into work in process and, finally, into finished goods, why can we not assume that the values of the peculiar services and conditions furnished by the business itself also gradually accumulate in these goods? From the standpoint of economic theory one idea is quite as sound as the other. The consumer pays a price which covers the enterpriser's costs and his income as well.[3] As far as the purchaser is concerned the entire sum is economic cost, and the item would be charged on his books at this total figure. And if this cost may be gradually accumulated on the producer's books with respect to certain essential commodities and services, why can we not say that all costs so accumulate?

As a matter of price determination both assumptions are unsound. That is, the fact that a particular business establishment has certain costs, and desires a satisfactory rate of payment for its own services, will have little or no effect upon selling prices in the long run. The commonly accepted idea that the specific business management can literally set its own prices, does not at all square with the facts except in special and usually temporary situations.

But the accountant depends upon the Marxian doctrine

---

[3] The income of a particular enterprise may, of course, include pure differentials as well as a payment for necessary, price-determining services.

that costs expended upon an object in some mysterious way pass over into that object and constitute its value. It might seem, then, that he could consistently go a step further and assume that the values of the services of the enterprise itself flow steadily into production and do not instantaneously appear, full-fledged, on the occasion of shipment or other specific event.

Just what would be the procedure involved if percentage of completion in either of the senses mentioned above were used as the basis for income recognition? How, specifically, could percentage of completion be gauged? Should time, physical quantity, or cost be used as a test? As was implied above, the most reasonable plan would be to recognize income (in part, at least, in itself an element of true economic cost) as accruing in proportion to costs incurred. For example, if an article cost $100 from the standpoint of the producer and sold for $120, every dollar of cost incurred might be said to give rise to 20 cents of income. The value of the finished article could be gradually built up on this plan to $120. The charges to the product in excess of cost incurred would be concurrently credited to income. The final disposition of the article would then constitute merely the exchange of product valued at $120 for new assets of equivalent amount. The entire profit, therefore, would have been gradually recognized prior to sale.

Even if such a scheme were adopted it would of course be inexpedient to attempt to organize the accounting procedures in such a way as to bring about a steady flow of entries in the income account. Periodic recognition of the accrued income would be all that could be accomplished. Thus, in the above illustration, if production consisted of four important stages, each of which required the incurring of $25 in costs, the goods account might be charged with the accrued income in four successive increments of $5 each, the income account being concurrently credited. Or, such analysis might even be neglected entirely until the close of the fiscal period, at which time goods produced in the current period and still on hand might be written up and income recognized for the proportion of the income margin applicable to goods on hand which the costs incurred to date bore to the total of costs to be incurred thereon (including those to date) prior to completion. This last procedure would mean that percentage of completion was being used merely as a supplementary evidence of income. The income which would result for the period, however, would be the same in each case.

In practice about the only important case in which such a scheme of valuation and income accounting is conceded to be valid arises in connection with long-term processes. The process of fabricating a vessel, for example, may cover several accounting periods. It is recognized that if final completion and disposition were used as the evidence of income in such situations very irrational income statements would result. Thus a shipbuilding company might begin several jobs in a particular period and complete none till a later period. In such a case it is evident that the conventional scheme of income accounting is somewhat unreasonable; all of the income can hardly be said to arise in the single period in which the several vessels are finished and turned over to the buyers. In general, accountants have long admitted the propriety, in such instances, of the recognition of income in terms of completion percentages.[4]

Has this criterion of income any wider application, however, in the field of practical accounting? Probably not. While it is true that from the standpoint of economics there is as much force in the assumption that business income accrues as surely as do the actual costs incurred by the buyer, there are fundamental objections to the general adoption of such a con-

---

[4] The same principle is approved by the Treasury Department in Article 36 of Regulations 62 (issued in connection with the Revenue Act of 1921).

ception by the accountant. Accounting, it must be remembered, deals with specific enterprises; and hence the accountant must adopt essentially the viewpoint of the owners and managers of the particular business entity. And from the standpoint of the owners, costs incurred—purchased commodities and services—constitute a very different classification as compared with the peculiar services and conditions implicitly furnished by the business itself. The business does not buy or incur its own services; hence their value should not be entered as if they had been actually acquired. It is the buyer of the completed article who purchases the services of the producing enterprise. The expense of doing business and the net return are quite distinct from the standpoint of the owners. Expenses are actually incurred; there is no assurance that income is thereby accruing. One process is a definite matter of record; the accrual of income would be based purely on assumption. The whole scheme of modern income accounting is organized in such a way as to show net return as a residuum, a difference between selling value and expenses. To accrue profit in general on the basis of completion percentages would be entirely unsound. Only where sale is assured, and the process long, should any such accounting be attempted.

In concluding this section a graphic comparison of the percentage of completion basis for reporting revenue with the other principal plans which we have been considering may be of value. In the accompanying figure the line OC represents the gradual accumulation of cost values above the base line OX from zero to the amount CX, the cost at the instant of technical completion. During the interval the finished stock is held in the storeroom awaiting shipment, the accountant commonly assumes that this value remains unchanged; and thus we have, just at the instant of consignment, the equivalent amount, $C'X'$. To the extent that storage and marketing costs are being incurred such an assumption, of course, would not be strictly correct. Actual consignment, however, the signal for income recognition, involves an instantaneous increase in values (the total being booked as cash or receivables) by the amount of the income margin, $C'S$ (ignoring storing, shipping, and collection charges). The solid line $OCC'S$, then,

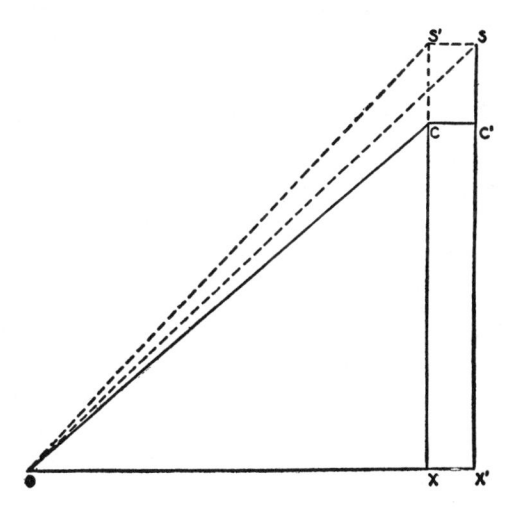

represents the course of value accumulation on the books when the sale is taken as the evidence of revenue. Similarly, if physical completion is adopted as the criterion of income, the course of value accumulation is represented by the line $OCS'S$. In this case also the period during which stock lies in the warehouse is considered to bring about no change in value, the essential difference between this plan and the more conventional procedure evidently lying in the choice of the occasion for the income entries.

If, now, income as well as cost be considered to accrue uniformly during the period from initiation to physical completion, the dotted line $OS'S$ represents the accumulation of values. Again the value is assumed to be constant in the interval between completion and disposition; but the whole process of manufacture, not the specific occasion of completion or shipment, is considered to give rise to income. The dotted line *OS* represents the course of value enhancement if income and cost are assured to accumulate steadily during the entire period from initiation to actual sale. This variation would be the more reasonable if storage and marketing costs, and the interval between completion and sale, are assumed to be of importance; for surely if income can be said to accrue in terms of costs and time one class of costs and one section of the period is as valid an evidence as any other.

The dotted lines are used in the figure to indicate the unorthodox character of the schemes of valuation involved. For convenience *OC* is made a straight line, although of course cost is seldom if ever incurred in any uniform progression.

APPRECIATION AND REVENUE

In none of the evidences or criteria of revenue thus far considered has the matter of price movements been recognized. Because, however, of the fact that serious changes in prices may occur while particular assets are held by the business enterprise it must be admitted that the financial position of the enterprise becomes affected thereby. The question arises, should specific recognition be given to changing costs as applied to units on hand in determining business income? Or, more specifically, is mere enhancement in the value of unsold goods a valid evidence of income? Should credits be made in the current income account to cover appreciation?

It is entirely beyond the scope of this book to discuss this question fully. It is desired, however, to call attention to a few considerations in this connection. In the first place it should be emphasized that the broad definition of net income as measuring the difference between the true economic position of a business at the beginning of a given period and its position at the end of the period (allowance being made for investments and withdrawals) has considerable force. In the individual's economy some such calculation is common even if his accounts are not prepared strictly in accordance therewith. And the accountant or business manager is likely to agree that this conception of income is a fairly valid one, at least as a starting point. But what measures true financial condition, the literal original cost of unsold assets or the current cost or cost of replacement?

There is at least some reason for the opinion that, in the case of the current asset at any rate, the true economic significance of an asset to a business is in general measured most accurately by what it would cost, currently, to acquire the item. As was pointed out in the preceding chapter, costs of replacement are certainly of more importance in price determination than original costs. *Cost of replacement is effective actual cost* in most cases. Any business man who ignores this principle is taking a step in the direction of business failure. The manufacturer of munitions who acquired plant and materials on the basis of low prices, for example, could not thereby have afforded to undersell his representative competitor who had constructed plant and equipment at war prices. Further, representations of values in terms of reliable current conditions are more satisfactory evidences of true worth as a basis for credit, or for most other purposes, than figures prepared on any other basis—this despite the protestations of some accountants to the contrary.

There is no question, of course, about the fact of appreciation. Thousands of land owners have become well-to-do through the enhancement in the values of their holdings. The same may be said of the holders of securities. The individual or the business that owns securities actually worth a million dollars on the market has one million dollars in effective property, regardless of the cost. Later the amount may be more or less than this sum, but present worth is unquestionably the one million. To argue that the owner of property which has doubled in value has no more wealth than before is folly. If the value measured on the same basis that was used when the property was originally acquired has doubled, his wealth has doubled. Wealth can surely be acquired through appreciation without transfer.

The typical extracting, manufacturing, trading, or financial enterprise, however, is not in the business of holding property for an appreciation. It is rather acquiring materials and services so as to carry on certain operations which will result, presumably, in salable commodities or services. Despite the truth of what has been said above, it does not therefore follow that mere enhancement is, in general, a satisfactory criterion of income to apply to the conditions of the business enterprise. The recognition of revenue in terms of sales is a policy conforming to the actual business process; and a convenient accounting procedure consistent with this plan can be readily worked out. Enhancement in value due to an advancing cost of replacement is, at the most, an incidental and supplementary kind of income. In so far as the enhanced goods are sold the appreciation becomes a part of sales revenue. Evidently, then, the recognition of appreciation *per se* involves merely the valuation of goods on hand at cost of replacement.

In this limited sense there is something to be said for the booking of enhancement, particularly in connection with certain types of assets. The consistent valuation of standard materials and marketable securities on the basis of replacement costs is a thoroughly sound procedure. Further, it is generally agreed among accountants that the most reasonable substitute for the cost of goods on hand, where it is not expedient to attempt to discover actual, literal cost, is the cost of the most recent purchases up to the amount of the physical inventory; and the use of this plan, it should be emphasized, would approach in many cases the adoption of current cost as a basis for valuation.

It should be clear from the preceding discussion that, so far as realization is concerned, actual enhancement represents effective income about as fully as do accounts receivable or new merchandise acquired following the conversion of customers' accounts to legal tender.[5] Further, a merchandise value based on cost of replacement is no more likely to disappear than any other asset value in the business. There is no assurance that original cost values will be maintained. Again, it should be clear that the recognition of the enhancement which simply measures the change in effective current cost would not in general involve the anticipation of income, the accruing of the normal income margin. Of course selling prices follow changing costs of replacement more or less imperfectly in specific cases, and where this is true the pricing of stock on hand at current cost may mean the recognition of a fraction of the normal income margin in advance of sale. It should be emphasized, however, that, in principle, pricing stock on the basis of selling price and pricing on the basis of cost of replacement are entirely distinct procedures.

Income consisting solely in appreciation is evidently a particular kind of income from the accounting standpoint. It would usually be thought of as a non-operating income. Its recognition, however, would not mean that the accountant should abandon all effort to distinguish between operating and incidental or speculative income. Income arising in connection with the main purposes of the business may well be segre-

---

[5] That this is true in the case of readily marketable securities can be shown effectively by a rather extreme illustration. On January 1, A and B each buy ten shares of Merry Steel at 100. Later B sells at 110 and buys Locomotor at the same price. On December 31 he sells Locomotor at 125 and buys Merry Steel at 125. A "sits tight" throughout the year. A and B begin the year in identical positions. At the end of the year the identity persists; yet B, according to conventional accounting methods, would have realized an income of $250, while A's books would show no income. As a matter of fact A has clearly made the same income as B.

gated, as far as possible, from ancillary or accidental revenue. But it should be emphasized in this connection that operating income as conventionally determined by the accountant is by no means the result of a purely physical process. In any business the current of technical operation and that of economic movement and accident are more or less inextricably tied together. In other words, it is exceedingly difficult for the accountant to trace separately, on the one hand the precise effect of the efforts of the management and on the other the effect of price movements and other influences over which the management has little or no control. Business operation, for the accountant, is more of an economic process than of an engineering process. From the operating standpoint also net revenue is a conglomerate. The inclusion of an item of enhancement, then, need not be viewed as an accounting catastrophe.

Readily marketable securities, as has been indicated, are an asset with respect to which current price is a particularly valid basis for inventory. Buying price and selling price are here approximately identical. Standard raw materials and merchandise may also, with reason, be valued at cost of replacement. Goods in process and finished stock furnish a more dubious case. With respect to plant and equipment and other classes of fixed assets the propriety of the cost-of-replacement valuations is still more questionable, as was shown in the preceding chapter.

In this section it has been intended merely to indicate that appreciation is one evidence of income, an evidence which has some validity in certain connections.

In concluding this chapter a few general considerations should be emphasized. First, the determination of a satisfactory evidence or test of revenue is essentially one aspect of the problem of valuation. Thus if the sale is to be used as the exclusive criterion this means that all stock on hand must be priced at cost. Assuming technical completion to be the gauge of realization involves valuation at current selling price less estimated marketing costs. Percentage of completion as a basis for revenue recognition implies inventories calculated by applying completion percentages to prospective selling figures. The recognition of appreciation as income results from the taking of inventories on the basis of costs of replacement.

In the second place it should be emphasized that that accounting procedure or principle is best which most nearly preserves the integrity of the statements for each fiscal period. It is true that the effect upon the income sheet of the adoption of one particular scheme of recognizing revenue as compared with another is virtually nil over a long period. That is, one criterion of revenue—with its concomitant principle of inventory valuation—will give approximately the same total revenue figure for a period of, let us say, ten years, as will any other. But with respect to the allocation of gross revenue to each year (or other accounting period), and the amount of the periodic net revenue, each method varies. And these are important matters. The familiar view that a mistake or a misjudgment in the accounts of one year will be automatically offset or rectified in the succeeding period, while sound to a degree, cannot be recognized by the accountant as a controlling consideration. Accounting, as has been emphasized before in this study, might almost be defined as the art which attempts to break up the financial history of a business into specific units, a year or less in length. In other words, it is the business of the accountant to prepare valid statements of income and financial condition in terms of specific periods of time; and the propriety of a particular procedure cannot be judged fairly except in terms of its effect upon the integrity of the particular statement. A mere record of purchases and sales would doubtless give an essentially correct picture of the business for a twenty-year period. It is the emphasis upon the integrity of the particular year which makes real accounting important. If there were no such emphasis accounting practice would degenerate to the level of a presentation of a bare diary of business events.

Finally it should be remembered that the problem of measuring business income is a very difficult one even under the most favorable circumstances. Absolute standardization in method for all businesses cannot be hoped for, nor, in the main, would such uniformity be desirable. The accountant, manager, or owner, on whom rests the responsibility for the adoption of a plan for calculating gross revenue and determining net income, should make his decision with a full knowledge of what any given base involves or implies, and should adopt that device which, all things considered, gives the most reasonable results.

CHAPTER XX

THE POSTULATES OF ACCOUNTING

Impressed by the neatly ruled lines and the array of equal footings exhibited by the typical system of accounts and financial statements, the layman is likely to conclude that accounting deals with certainties, with data capable of exact and precise statement; that accounts are either accurate or inaccurate; that the principles and procedures of double entry, if applied without clerical error, will always lead to correct conclusions. Indeed, the accountant at times may be found slipping, somewhat unconsciously, into the same misapprehension. This is evidenced by the attitude of the auditor who spends perhaps several hours of time trying to locate the source of an error of a few cents in the purchases account, and then passes lightly over the question of the method of pricing adopted by the management in taking inventory.

Praiseworthy as is an effort to locate and correct clerical mistakes, great emphasis on this side of accounting indicates a lack of an appreciation of its more important purposes and of the inherent weaknesses of the art from the standpoint of literal accuracy. As a matter of fact, the accountant is being constantly faced with the necessity for judgment. Accounting is full of estimate, assumption. At times, unfortunately, the conclusions of the accountant must be well-nigh conjectural. The accountant, it must be remembered, is dealing primarily with economic data, with values, not with physical certainties; and values are highly uncertain and unstable aspects of structures, commodities, rights, services, and situations.

Not only does modern accounting involve estimate and judgment at many points, but the entire structure is based upon a series of general assumptions. In other words, underlying the specific conclusions of the accountant with respect to present values, costs, incomes, etc., are certain fundamental premises and postulates, few if any of which are capable of complete demonstration. It is intended in this final chapter to state and examine briefly the more important of these basic assumptions. In particular, stress will be laid upon their limitations. This does not mean that an attempt will be made to show that some of these postulates should be discarded. Accounting is a highly purposive field and any assumption, principle, or procedure is accordingly justified if it adequately serves the end in view—assuming that end to be reasonable, all things considered. Without certain assumptions, indeed, it would be impossible to proceed very far in accounting practice. On the other hand it is believed that accountants are sometimes in danger of forgetting their own premises and, therefore, the limitations of their work. If the accountant sees clearly the foundation upon which he is standing, with all its implications, he is less likely to fall into the mire of improper applications and erroneous general conclusions.

Several of these underlying propositions upon which accounting is based have been referred to from time to time in the preceding chapters. The present chapter will accordingly involve repetition to some extent. It is believed that it is desirable, however, in concluding this study, to attempt a systematic statement of all the important postulates of accounting. Such a statement will serve in a measure as a recapitulation, and should also aid in indicating the main relationships between the various problems which have been considered.

THE BUSINESS ENTITY

To start with, *the existence of a distinct business entity* is something which the accountant almost universally assumes. The unit of organization with which he is chiefly concerned, as was pointed out in Chapter I, is the specific business enterprise. Accordingly, it is convenient for him to assume that this enterprise or business situation has a distinct existence, that it constitutes a real institution through which flows a stream of values and in the operation of which several, perhaps many individuals have a part. It is "the business" whose financial history the bookkeeper and accountant are trying to record and analyze; the books and accounts are the records of "the business"; the periodic statements of operation and financial condition are the reports of "the business"; the assets are the properties of "the business," and the equities are its ownership and obligations.

The assumption of a business entity somewhat apart and distinct from the actual persons conducting its operations, is a conception which has been greatly deplored by some writers and staunchly defended by others. Is it a valid premise for the accountant? Is there any such thing as "the business," a something having an independent and real existence? Or is this postulate unsupported by the facts of the business world?

The business enterprise of course is not a person. Hence to speak of it as a person or to endow it with personal attributes is to make use of a figure of speech. But this does not mean that the particular business enterprise has no real and measurably distinct existence. A particular enterprise is an institution, not a person; but an institution may be a very real thing. We are all living in the midst of a complex system of institutions. The federal government is not a person, but there are few things more real, as most of us have come to appreciate these last few years. A great university is an institution, not a person, but has none the less a distinct existence. Destroy all its current properties, scatter its staff, and the institution would doubtless still persist in some fashion. Similarly the business enterprise may have its reality. It is not always a mere figment of the imagination. It may be a living organism, in some cases huge, powerful, overshadowing, exerting a tremendous influence in the industrial community. The accountant's assumption is based at least in part on fact. There is, in many cases, a genuine business entity.

In the case of the corporation this postulate is validated from the legal standpoint. The corporation is a real entity, endowed by the state with all the privileges of any business person. It may acquire title to property, borrow money, engage in virtually any recognized business operation, hire labor, buy and sell merchandise and other property, etc. In this case the accountant's assumption is given flesh and blood by governmental authority. In general it may be said that the corporation, not its human members, owns the assets, directs the business, borrows funds, establishes dividend policies, and so on. From the legal point of view, evidently, the accounts and statements in this case exhibit nothing more nor less than the affairs of the corporation.

In the case of the sole-proprietorship, so-called, and the partnership, it must be admitted that, in general, the law does not acknowledge the existence of any business entity. The Revenue Act of 1917,[1] it is true, provided for an excess-profits tax upon the income of the unincorporated business, thus recognizing a taxable business entity in this case as well as in that of the corporation; but the view established in this act may be said to be exceptional in American law. For the most part there is no sharp distinction from the legal standpoint between the business affairs of the sole-proprietor or partner and his other interests, as was pointed out in Chapter III. There is here no segregation of business assets as in the case of the corporation. The residence of Smith, the grocer, for example, from the standpoint of the satisfaction of creditors in the case of insolvency, is in essentially the same position as is his store building.

---

[1] That is, the act passed in 1916 as amended in 1917.

But the legal point of view does not furnish the sole criterion. The law may look upon the partnership as merely a contractual relationship between two or more persons, yet there may be a business entity involved from other standpoints. A business need not be incorporated to become a distinct institution. Many an important business has been built upon the sole-proprietorship or partnership plan. Acquiring clientele and business standing, developing characteristic methods, exercising a powerful influence in the business community, swallowing up a succession of owners and managers with scarcely a ripple as affairs changed hands—such a business often has gone on for many decades. The great private banking houses of England and this country are good examples. There is nothing imaginary about the reality and continuity of existence of some of these venerable institutions.

The general proposition requires little argument for its justification. The concept of the business entity is constantly used outside the corporate form of organization by economists and others interested in the business process. The same view is solidly established in the business man's thinking as is evidenced by the fact that the expressions "house," "concern," "company," etc., are applied freely to the unincorporated enterprise.

As was explained in Chapter I, there are, of course, many situations requiring the use of accounts and other statistical records which are in no strict sense business enterprises. Something in the way of accounts may be needed in connection with the record of an individual's investments and personal property. One meets an occasional enthusiast who is obsessed by the fascinations of household accounting. Clubs, societies, and other organizations outside the business field need a systematic record of their financial transactions. In some of these situations a distinct entity may be involved, but, evidently, they do not constitute business institutions.

Even in the business field, situations so simple and temporary arise that there is little excuse for the conception of a business entity. To conceive of the business of the pop vender at a football game as having any distinct existence, to take an extreme example, would obviously be quite fantastic. The importance of the entity depends upon the circumstances of each case. Enough has been said, however, to justify the statement that the assumption of a business existence is based to an important degree on the actual facts of the business world.

On the other hand, there is a danger that this assumption may be carried too far. The fact of the independent existence of the business entity must not be overstressed. No institution, however real, has any absolute existence. The accountant must remember that human beings are the immediate means by which the affairs of a business institution are conducted and that, in particular cases, it may be necessary to focus attention directly and exclusively upon the individual owners and managers and their acts. As was stated in Chapter XV, the courts have long recognized that the apparent act of the business must sometimes be construed to be the act of an individual owner, and that, in other cases, the apparent act of the individual may be virtually the act of the institution. In order to get at the realities of the situation it is accordingly sometimes necessary to brush aside formal evidences and transactions.

Several illustrations were given in Chapter XV of situations in which the business entity must be ignored by the accountant. In general it may be said that the relations between the "business" and its individual owners and managers must be considered as being on a different level from those between the business and outside persons or entities. Directors' borrowings, officers' salaries, partners' drawings, purchases by a corporation of its outstanding securities, are cases in point.

A blind insistence on the independence of the business entity in such situations is bound to lead to unreasonable conclusions.

Some might contend that the practicing accountant makes no such universal use of this assumption as has been claimed above. The accountant, it might be urged, adopts the viewpoint of the proprietor, the individual or individuals who largely control the business, and constructs his system of accounts and statements on the basis of the relation of the business transactions to this specific person or persons. Now while it is true that many statements of accounting theory have been couched in terms of proprietorship, the writer does not believe that the professional man has ever abandoned the business-entity conception. Consciously or unconsciously he adopts this assumption as a basis for his work. He prepares the balance sheet of the *X* Co., not of the stockholders of that enterprise. Even the partnership or sole-proprietorship balance sheet is headed with the firm or house name, if there is one, rather than with the names of the individual proprietors. No one would think, for example, of listing at the top of the balance sheet of a certain large publishing concern the names of the more than a score of partners making up its proprietorship. It is the balance sheet of the business, not of its various owners, in which all are interested.

Accounting theory is much less rational than practice at this point, as was pointed out in the preface. In spite of the tremendous development of the corporation in the last few decades, most writers, unfortunately, persist in attempting to state the philosophy of accounts in terms of the conditions of the small sole-proprietorship. The result is a system of concepts and principles highly inapplicable to the facts of modern business organization. This is the day of the *business enterprise* and the accounting theorist must thoroughly realize this fact. It is especially important in view of the emphasis placed nowadays upon the uses to which accounts may be put for managerial purposes. The conception of the manager must be exactly that of the business entity as an economic unit; and if, as is repeatedly said, the most important purpose which modern accounting can serve lies in the rationalizing of business administration, the accountant must of necessity adopt the viewpoint of the manager in large measure.

THE "GOING CONCERN"

Not only does the accountant assume the existence of a business entity, but he also, as a corollary, takes for granted *the continuity of this entity,* i.e., he assumes that the business with which he is dealing is a "going concern." This second assumption, it need hardly be said, is largely one of convenience. No one is in a position to predict, with certainty, the future of a specific business. Business in general is reasonably sure to go on in some fashion; but assurance of success in the particular case is not found in this fact. All business involves the speculative element, although in some cases it is much more pronounced than in others.

On the other hand the going-concern assumption is entirely reasonable. In the absence of evidence which gives a definite presumption to the contrary, it is surely fair to assume that the particular business is going to continue, at least for the near future. In the case of large and strongly intrenched enterprises the assumption approaches practical assurance. Further, when the number of business enterprises in the United States is taken into account it is clear that the percentage of failures in a particular year is very small. The accountant accordingly has the right to take it for granted that the specific concern in which he is interested will continue to operate for some time. Conceivably bankruptcy may occur, but it need not be anticipated in the accounts.

The going concern rather than the seriously embarrassed or insolvent business is the normal case. Accordingly, in developing accounting principles and procedures the accountant must keep this in mind. It would certainly be unreasonable to set up the conditions of insolvency as a background in determining present values, effective liabilities, etc. Thus we have the principle that the assets of a business should be revalued for balance-sheet purposes on the basis of their value to the going concern. This rule or standard of measurement is, of course, especially important in the valuation of the fixed properties. The immediate market value of the highly specialized machine bolted to the factory floor is likely to be very much below its cost less conventional depreciation. The liquidation value of a factory building may be even less. A railway roadbed and track furnish a still more extreme case of the discrepancy between use value and immediate selling price. In general, costs less systematic depreciation are considerably higher than immediate selling values in the case of plant and equipment assets.

Similarly the legal liability in the case of insolvency may differ from the effective accounting liability from the standpoint of the going concern. The face or par value, i.e., the amount to be paid at maturity, is usually conceded to be the legal liability and the amount which would become effective—as a base figure at least—in the case of reorganization or complete liquidation. But in the case of a heavily discounted bond issue running for, let us say, twenty years, the true accounting liability at the end of the first period, for example, would be simply the original principal or actual investment plus any accumulated discount (true interest accrued and unpaid). By the date of maturity the accountant would have accumulated out of earnings the difference between original principal and the face or par sum; and the accounting liability and the lump sum payable would then be identical. Certain aspects of this question were considered in some detail in Chapter XVII.

The accountant need scarcely be reminded of the profound influence of the conception of the going concern upon accounting principles and practices, especially in connection with valuations. Accounting practice is saturated with evidence of a dependence upon this assumption. It has an especial importance in the two connections already mentioned, but has many other applications as well.

As was implied above, this assumption, although incapable of demonstration in the particular case, is thoroughly reasonable and needs little qualification. The accountant should, of course, keep the possibility of financial embarrassment and insolvency in the background of his consciousness. If the trend of events points toward bankruptcy in a particular case the financial reports should be so constructed that all interested are apprised of the real situation. The chief reason why the accountant and business man should clearly recognize the use of such an assumption is the emphasis thereby given to the provisional character of the balance-sheet statement, even under the most favorable circumstances. A balance sheet is not an absolute statement of fact. The financial history of a business enterprise is a continuous stream, not a succession of mutually independent segments. The accountant, accordingly, in attempting to break up this history into definite periods, setting a balance sheet at either end, must sever many real connections, hazard many judgments. The future is uncertain; and yet the validity of the statement of asset values as of December 31, 1921, for example, depends in a large measure upon the future course of events. In presenting a balance sheet what the accountant says, in effect, is this: "Here, managers, directors, stockholders, creditors, bankers, and others interested, is a balance sheet of the X Co. as of the close of the last fiscal period. Assuming that the company is going to continue operations successfully, I adjudge the statement of the assets and liabilities presented herein to be reasonable."

THE BALANCE-SHEET EQUATION

We may now turn to certain more specific and technical postulates of the accountant. First among these will be considered the assumption that in every business enterprise an equation exists between the total of the properties and the total of the representations of ownership, proprietary and other elements combined—the assumption, in other words, that the total of the assets of every business is equal to the total of the equities.

This proposition is probably the most nearly capable of a superficial demonstration of any of the accountant's premises. It will be convenient, in this connection, to reiterate some of the discussion of Chapter II. As was stated there the two classes of the balance sheet, in a sense, are merely different aspects of the same situation. The assets represent a *direct* statement of the value of the properties of the enterprise; the liabilities represent an *indirect* statement of the same values. In one case the accountant is listing the objective properties; in the other he is recording the proper distribution of the asset total among the various individuals and interests having claims therein. In one case attention is being focused upon the objects for which funds have been expended; in the other, upon the sources of these funds. The total of the properties constitutes the total of the wealth or capital of the enterprise; the equities express the dispersion of this capital among the various investors involved. And since the same measuring unit, the dollar, is used in stating both classes of data, the totals are inevitably equal.

Yet this equation is far from being an absolute statement of fact; it is easy to exaggerate its intrinsic validity. It, too, savors of a proposition of convenience. What the accountant is saying in starting with this premise is simply this: "I find the total of the assets of a business situation to be such and such an amount. Next I divide this amount among the various investors in accordance with what seem to be the legal rights and privileges of each. My two lists now constitute a balance sheet."

Evidently the determination of the equities, at least as far as the total is concerned, is a secondary process which is based directly upon the amount ascertained to be the total of the assets. A serious assumption, incapable of any complete validation, is here involved. Why should the legal and economic rights in a particular business situation be considered to equal precisely the sum of a list of asset values arrived at by divers and complex processes of valuation? As a matter of fact they do not, in the absence of immediate and complete liquidation.[2] The equity of the common stockholder, for example, is expressed in the corporate balance sheet by what is left over, the residuum of the asset total after all prior equities have been deducted, as was indicated in Chapter III. Does this represent the true equity of the common stockholder in any fundamental sense? Is not this arrangement largely a matter of convenience? To what, precisely, is the common stockholder entitled? Not to what he originally invested nor to this balance-sheet residuum. As far as the assets are concerned, he is entitled in the case of liquidation to any balance available after all other claims are met. In the case of forced insolvency this amount is likely to be nil or negligible and to bear little relation to any previous balance-sheet figures. In addition, he has a right to a share in all the excess future earnings of the company, a right the realization of which, however, is more or less contingent on the specific policy of the board of directors. Is it not evident, under these circumstances, that the usual balance-sheet representation of the residual equity is a very imperfect statement of the situation?

---

[2] And even in the case of liquidation asset values based upon the going-concern conception would probably not be realized, and hence would not express accurately the various equities in the situation from this standpoint.

The "book value" of the stockholders' interest in the corporation is a highly conventional thing. It can be explained only as the process of asset valuation is explained, a process which is itself based upon numerous assumptions. No wonder that the market price per share seldom approaches book value and often does not even follow its trends! Because of the control of management vested in the common stockholder and the possibility of future returns, common shares sometimes have a market value when, according to orthodox principles and rules of valuation, there is no book value whatsoever.

In the case of the liabilities the amounts attached by the accountant are likely to be somewhat more reasonable. In general—ignoring unaccumulated discounts, unamortized premiums, etc.—it may be said that the accountant regards the sum due at maturity as the true liability. In the absence of insolvency this is the amount which will finally be realized by the contractual investor; it is likely to approximate the original principal; if the company becomes bankrupt, there is yet some possibility of the creditors receiving the full amount. Consequently, there is a large element of precise fact in the balance-sheet figures which are attached to the contractual equities. Even here, of course, the market value of a particular bond or other similar security may vary noticeably from the amount appearing in the issuing company's financial statement.

It should be emphasized, however, that even if all the liabilities were stated with absolute precision and were shown at figures representing real significance in every case, but the residual equity were shown for convenience as the difference between the asset total and all other equities, the equality of footings of balance-sheet classes would still, to a degree, be a matter of assumption.[3]

---

[3] The footings as given are, of course, equal. But the question is, are the two classes of data really equal? The accountant assumes an affirmative answer to be correct.

In view of the fact that the statement of the stockholder's equity in the balance sheet, as has just been indicated, is likely to be the most questionable of any balance-sheet item, the stress placed upon the "net worth" figure in current statements of the theory of accounts is perhaps not entirely justified. As was indicated in Chapter III, the implication seems to be that there is something peculiarly valid about this concluding figure. While it is true that this residual figure is of especial consequence to the accountant, its importance, in the case of a corporation at any rate, does not lie in its accuracy or precise validity as an expression of the equity of the buffer interest. To reiterate some of the statements in Chapter III, it is rather of especial significance to the accountant because it is his doubtful territory. It is the place where all his peculiar estimates, hazards, adjustments, etc., "come home to roost." Its trend is of much more importance than its exact amount on any particular occasion, for, if consistent methods of valuation are followed, its increase is a fairly reliable evidence of operating success and growing financial strength, while its diminution indicates just the reverse situation.

It is not intended to attempt to show by the foregoing that the equation postulate of the accountant is unreasonable or improper. It is instead a thoroughly rational and essential premise, upon which depends, in a sense, the entire technical structure of the accounts. The equation of assets and equities, as has been shown in this study, is the foundation of the double-entry system. And, as was stated at the outset, the equation holds, in the limited sense indicated, for every business enterprise. In the nature of the case the asset total, dispersed among the equities, gives another equal class. The assets are the only objective residence of value. At a certain date they are found to total up to a particular sum. It is then entirely reasonable, indeed unavoidable, to state the evidences of ownership and claims against the business in these terms.

There is no alternative. Future earnings are indeterminate; the amounts which will finally be withdrawn are unknown (as far as the residual interest is concerned); a stating of equities in terms of property values is then the only feasible procedure.

It is desired, however, to suggest that the accountant should not take this balancing equity figure too seriously. It behooves him to be fully cognizant of the underlying process by which this figure is ascertained, and thus to realize that it is not an independent and directly determined fact.

Finally, it may be reiterated that there are certain situations outside the business enterprise proper which do not present an equation of assets and equities in the ordinary sense. Perhaps the most important case is the governmental unit, federal, state, or local. A government may owe huge sums far in excess of the value of the assets to which it has specific title, as was pointed out in Chapter II, and yet ultimately pay 100 cents on the dollar. The state, of course, has the power to tax, and thus ordinarily possesses potential control over sufficient assets to liquidate all its obligations. But since the tax power in itself is not an asset that can be evaluated by ordinary means, it is not ordinarily possible to prepare a conventional balance sheet for the governmental unit.

Similarly, the individual sometimes "mortgages his future" and borrows sums for consumption purposes. A college student, for example, may have liabilities galore but no assets in the usual sense. Yet his creditors may consider him "perfectly good." The liabilities are capable of definite statistical expression in terms of sums due in the future, but there is no way of assaying the future assets. The student has a one-sided balance sheet. No equational statement is possible.

FINANCIAL CONDITION AND THE BALANCE SHEET

This brings us to another, somewhat related, balance-sheet postulate. The accountant commonly assumes that all facts expressing the financial status of an enterprise can be presented in the two classes, assets and liabilities, measured in terms of the dollar. That is, he assumes that *a statement of assets and liabilities in dollars and cents is a complete representation of the financial condition of the enterprise* on the date of the statement.

This proposition not only cannot be demonstrated but it can be pretty thoroughly disproved, as was shown in Chapter II. The balance sheet, as a true statement of financial condition, should not be taken too seriously; it has very definite limitations under the most favorable circumstances. In the first place, as has just been indicated, the future costs, earnings, and losses of a business enterprise are largely indeterminate; and yet the reality of the present value depends essentially upon the assumption that the business will be at least moderately successful. A balance-sheet statement of asset values is really only provisional; it depends upon the future for its validation.

In the second place, there are many vital considerations and conditions involved in every business enterprise of such a character as completely to escape classification as assets and equities and measurement by the dollar. In the individual's economy, for example, health, energy, resourcefulness, skill, and similar qualifications and endowments, may be of much greater ultimate consequence, even from a strictly economic point of view, than a disposal over a considerable sum of present wealth. These and other "imponderables" are also of the utmost consequence in business. The note of a man of unquestioned integrity, for example, may be better security than a lien upon specific assets. Our college student, as was stated above, may be a "good risk." In the business enterprise a well-organized and loyal personnel may be a much more important "asset" than a stock of merchandise. In other words, the loss by fire, for example, of the goods on hand might not be as serious a matter as the disruption of the staff. Location, trade-name, clientele, and similar considerations are likewise of extreme importance. Such conditions come to definite expression as assets if they are paid for; otherwise they find no place in the ordinary balance sheet.

Until some scheme is found by which these imponderables of the business enterprise may be assayed and given definite statistical expression, the accountant must continue to prepare the balance sheet as he has been doing. At present there seems to be no way of measuring such factors in terms of the dollar; hence, they cannot be recognized as specific economic assets. But let us, accordingly, admit the serious limitations of the conventional balance sheet as a statement of financial condition. How frequently do we note a business which shows a highly favorable "statement of financial condition" and then, within two or three years, because of a change in management, a lapse of demand, the advent of new methods, a decline in labor efficiency, or other reason, we find that the supposed values have evaporated and that the business is insolvent or financially embarrassed! The stockholders and others interested should realize that the balance sheet, even if the underlying accounting is thoroughly sound, is an imperfect representation of the current indication of the enterprise and only an indication of its probable position in the near future.[4]

The accountant, of course, commonly recognizes the fact that the balance sheet has serious limitations. In some instances he even tries to allow for the future by appending statements of "contingent" assets and liabilities. That is, if there are potential assets or potential liabilities in the situation, which are sufficiently in sight to be more than bare possibilities, it is considered good practice to indicate these elements, in

---
[4] The balance sheet of the large and complex enterprise is, of course, also likely to be imperfect for various technical reasons. The taking of inventory, for example, may consume several weeks, and the final figure placed in the balance sheet will accordingly be no more than an approximation of the value of goods on hand at the precise date of the statement.

some supplementary fashion, in connection with the balance sheet.

There is still a further assumption made by the accountant which is of especial importance in this connection. Not only does he commonly take it for granted that the entire financial status of an enterprise can be set up as assets and liabilities measured in terms of the dollar, but in general he assumes that *the value or significance of the measuring unit remains unchanged.* This postulate is, of course, not sound. As was pointed out in Chapter XVIII, the value of the money unit, the accountant's standard of measure, is constantly fluctuating. One of the fundamental limitations of accounting arises here. Since the measuring unit is unstable, comparisons of successive financial statements are likely to lead to erroneous conclusions, unless great care is exercised in making such comparisons. The increase in asset dollars and cents during a particular period, for example, may be unreliable as evidence of increase in the actual stock of structures, commodities, etc.; instead it may largely reflect simply the application of a less significant measuring unit to an amount of physical goods no greater than the supply at the beginning of the period. Similarly, the net income balance may be a very imperfect indication of genuine improvement in economic well-being; and an enterprise may build up a huge surplus account in a period of rising prices without increasing its stock of goods or enlarging plant proportionately.

It would not be fair to imply that the accountant does not realize that his measuring unit is unstable. But, nevertheless, he sets up comparative statements of income, surplus, assets, etc.; he values fixed assets on the basis of cost less depreciation; and in many other ways he makes use of the assumption that the dollar has a constant value. Various schemes have been discussed by means of which the accountant might take closer cognizance of the fluctuations in the value of money, but as yet there have been no developments of consequence in this direction.

COST AND BOOK VALUE

The accountant makes certain important assumptions in connection with costing and valuation. In the first place, he assumes that *cost gives actual value for purposes of initial statement*. This assumption (referred to repeatedly in the preceding chapters) is one of the most important premises underlying technical accounting. Its necessity is plain. Cost is the only definite fact available when a property is purchased, constructed, or otherwise acquired. It is accordingly entirely reasonable to charge the appropriate asset account with the amount of this cost in any case. It is a part of the accountant's business to record what has actually happened, to set down a systematic statement of all explicit transactions. It follows as a matter of course that he will assume the original value of an asset in the hands of a particular enterprise to equal its cost.

To put the matter in other words, the accountant, like the economist, postulates a world full of rational business men. He assumes that every exchange is fair, that buyer and seller are in every case equally informed and equally gifted in ability to trade. If a manufacturer pays $500 for a unit of equipment, for example, this means that the true value of the unit to him is $500, and that this amount, therefore, should be entered on the books as an asset. Under all circumstances, business men are deemed to proceed rationally. Coercion, fraud, bad judgment, carelessness—all these factors are in general assumed to be entirely absent from business transactions.

This is, of course, not literally the case. Business transactions are not actually equal exchanges; for the parties involved are not always equally strong or fortunate. Losses occur in actual purchases as well as in other connections. No one is infallible. How often the individual, in his personal economy, comes to feel that he has dismally failed to get full value for his expenditures! Similarly, the business man proceeds unwisely in many of his commitments.

But, as was just stated, in the absence of definite evidence to the contrary the accountant has every right to treat initial value as equivalent to cost. It is difficult to see how he could proceed otherwise. He cannot set himself up as an absolute judge of values. If the transaction is entirely voluntary, and both parties thereto appear satisfied, he is justified in treating the figures that appear in the exchange as bona fide values. Later, if substantial evidence of depreciation or original loss is adduced, it will be time enough to revise the initial figures.

An initial record of total cost would, of course, be necessary even if cost and original value were not identical. However, if it immediately became evident in any case that real value were greater or less than cost, the profit or loss could be recognized at once. But seldom, indeed, does the accountant attempt to pass judgment upon the validity of bona fide purchase price as a determinant of initial asset value.

An asset may occasionally be acquired by gift, accident, "strategy," etc. In such a case the accountant would usually admit that, if the asset were one which had a determinate purchase and sale value, the fair market value of the asset so acquired should be set up in the accounts; for otherwise the existence of a definite property would be concealed so far as the accounts were concerned. On the other hand most accountants would probably agree that cases may arise in practice where cost greatly exceeds initial value. In general, however, the cost-gives-value assumption is rigidly adhered to.

In the second place, the accountant makes the closely related assumption (also referred to at various times in this study) that the value of any commodity, service, or condition, utilized in production, *passes over into* the object or product for which

THE POSTULATES OF ACCOUNTING 491

the original item was expended and *attaches to* the result, giving it its value. This postulate is the essential basis for the work of the cost accountant; without it, there could be no costing.

Just how valid is this assumption? In attempting to answer this question it may be noted first that the physical essence of assets utilized in production does not always literally pass into the product. Even in the case of raw materials there is much waste. The fixed assets, of course, contribute nothing to the product but certain essential conditions. Similarly, supervision and many other services do not attach directly to the physical output. Evidently, then, there is no complete and clear-cut physical connection between cost items and product on which the accountant can base his premise. Further, even if the product were simply an amalgam, physically, of the commodities used in production, this would not mean that the original values had literally passed into the result. A dollar's worth of gold in a watch case may be worth intrinsically somewhere near a dollar. But the value of the recoverable steel from even a new automobile would be much less than the value to the manufacturer of the steel materials used in fabricating the car. In general there is no guarantee that converted materials, in product, will have the same values as when in the raw state.

To the economist this is perhaps the most interesting of all the accountant's assumptions. It constitutes a kind of cost theory of value. The accountant in general assumes that work in process—in all its various stages—and finished stock are worth for balance-sheet purposes the sum of the labor, material, and other costs expended in getting these results. He assumes that in some mysterious manner the values of these original commodities and services, which are worth cost for purposes of initial statement, pass over into and inhere in the object for which they were utilized. This is clearly an application of a cost theory of value to the internal conditions of the specific enterprise. Values are acquired in various original forms;

then they are converted into inchoate and, finally, finished goods.

So far as price determination is concerned this is, of course, unsound in most cases. Costs, a partial explanation of supply limitation, undoubtedly influence prices. But in general the influential cost is not the specific cost to the business enterprise in which the accountant is concerned, but rather the cost to the marginal producer (or, in certain cases, the representative producer), whoever and wherever he may be. The specific cost has, in the production of standard goods, little or no influence on selling price.[5] If a particular producer's cost is high, due to labor inefficiency, mismanagement, accident, or other cause, this will not make the product worth any more to the consumer nor enable the producer, who must compete with others in the same field, to advance the price to a point which will cover the unusual expense of production. Further, unless production is directed toward effective demand, output may be of little or no value, regardless of its cost. Or, if demand suddenly lapses the fact that costs are such and such a figure will not in itself hold up price.

The accountant, however, is not trying to determine selling value but cost value. He is asking the question, what are the costs of this particular enterprise? Evidently this is a matter of fact (although it may be very difficult to get the correct data). It is the accountant's business to report the actual costs, whatever the figure. If he finds at the end of a particular period that a certain fraction of the total costs incurred are still within the business, or at least have had nothing to do with current sales, it is entirely natural, then, for him to conclude that these values attach to work in process and finished stock to the extent that they have entered into production. Since

---

[5] Many would disagree with this statement, but the writer believes it is essentially sound. On the other hand, in the case of specialized goods and equipment produced to order, specific estimated cost undoubtedly plays an important part in determining selling price.

these costs bear no relation to current business, they must be held back; later they will be passed on as expense, conceived to be embodied in finished product sold. To place the deferred amount in the balance sheet as an asset involves, of course, precisely the assumption that we are considering. But since these values are not an expense, or cost of current sales, they must represent either an asset or a loss. If the continued production of the commodity or service in question is in prospect it is accordingly entirely reasonable to place these values in the balance sheet.

The work in process and finished stock of the manufacturer as well as the stock of the trader are sometimes inventoried at "cost or market, whichever is lower." To the extent that this rule is followed by the accountant he is evidently not adhering literally to the assumption we have been discussing. Nevertheless, it constitutes, in general, one of the most important premises of accounting.

COST ACCRUAL AND INCOME

The accountant assumes, as has just been indicated, that costs *accrue*, that is, that the values of structures and commodities utilized in production gradually expire and attach to work in progress. In general he limits this assumption, however, to costs from the point of view of the particular enterprise, disregarding the margin between this figure and cost to the purchaser, or selling price. In other words, he assumes that expense accrues but that net revenue or profit suddenly appears, full-blown, on some specific occasion, commonly that of the sale. This premise has been used repeatedly in this study, and was discussed from one standpoint in Chapter XIX. The significance of this postulate may be reiterated here. It means that the accountant's "expense" for the particular business and the economist's "cost of production" are two quite different things. The economist is talking about price-determining cost, the cost to the purchaser. From this standpoint cost and selling price, at least in the marginal instance, are essentially equal. Cost in this sense includes not only the marginal producer's outlays but his net return as well. Thus, the economist assumes that business net revenue, in part at least, is an essential cost of production, an element which price must cover if production is to continue in satisfactory volume.

On the other hand, the whole scheme of accounting is based upon the plan of showing as costs or expense only the expirations of purchased commodities and services, not the economic value of the services contributed by the business itself in furnishing capital and management. The accounts are organized so as to disclose the difference between expense and revenue as a residuum, a balance. And this margin of value, the net revenue, is assumed to appear with respect to the particular transaction, *in toto,* not to accrue. Purchased commodities and services are assumed to expire steadily and pass into the expense category; services furnished by the business and its owners are assumed to accrue only as sales of finished product are made.

This is, of course, poor logic, as was pointed out in the preceding chapter. If the value of work in process accrues because of purchased commodities and services utilized, it would seem to be reasonable to assume that the values contributed by the enterprise are likewise accumulating. To admit this, however, would involve the recognition of profit prior to completion and sale; and this the accountant, in general, steadfastly refuses to do.[6]

In the case of rent, insurance, and other costs, where payment is made for the service involved on a time basis, the accountant commonly takes it for granted that the cost accrues with precise uniformity.

---

[6] Some exceptions were noted in Chapter XIX.

That the depreciation of fixed assets is uniformly continuous is an interesting and important subsidiary assumption in this connection. The only method of apportioning depreciation widely used in practice involves the assumption that the values of fixed properties expire continuously and at a uniform rate. In the nature of the case, the accountant must apportion depreciation on the basis of premises of convenience. The whole depreciation analysis must be based upon a series of estimates. In the entire life of a fixed asset but two explicit transactions arise, purchase and abandonment. The situation between is entirely obscure. A machine, for example, is purchased and installed at a cost of $1,000. It is estimated that the service life is ten years. This is the first assumption. Second, it is estimated that the salvage value less demolition expense is $100—another assumption. On the basis of these assumptions, then, the total depreciation during the life of the unit is $900. The accountant is now faced with the problem of apportionment. He has two figures: cost, a known fact; and net salvage, an estimate. It is his problem to bridge the gap in time, estimated at ten years. How shall this total depreciation be spread as a cost of product throughout the period? Evidently his decision will again be based on assumption.

Three or four principal courses at once present themselves. First, shall the depreciation be assumed to be a function of physical product? That is, shall each item, pound, or other unit of product be charged with so much fixed asset cost? Evidently no definite physical connection could be traced on this basis. It might also be pointed out that deterioration is going on steadily in most cases regardless of the number of units of output. In fact, in some instances inactivity accelerates the process of disintegration and decay. Yet this assumption would not be wholly unreasonable. The assets are acquired because their services are deemed to be necessary in turning out product. Why then should not each unit of product bear a proportionate part of this total cost? As a matter of fact the depletion of natural resources is commonly computed and charged in terms of some convenient unit of output.

Or shall depreciation be assumed to accrue in terms of the value of gross revenue rather than its physical volume? This idea again has much to commend it from the standpoint of expediency. And it has been adhered to in business practice to an important degree. Formerly some business managements followed the policy of making heavy depreciation allowances in years of large gross revenues and smaller or even no depreciation charges in lean years. The current practice of incurring heavy maintenance costs in boom years, and of postponing repairs in dull periods, results similarly.

In general, as was stated above, modern practice assumes depreciation of plant and equipment assets to be continuous and uniform. The straight-line method of apportionment is the technical expression for this assumption. Thus, in the above illustration, the depreciation according to this plan would be 10 per cent each year of the total depreciable amount, or $90. This is the scheme now almost universally followed. Yet, obviously, there is no way of demonstrating its validity. True, as already noted, there is evidence that the processes of deterioration are more or less steady and uniform, though not perfectly so. And no doubt these inevitable processes are the important physical expression of value depreciation. But depreciation is lapse in value. It is a value problem and it can never be shown that this value expiration is a direct function of physical processes. If value were a physical essence it would be possible, no doubt, to attach some sort of gauge which would exactly measure its flow. There are still some who believe that valuation will sometime be reduced to an exact physical process. But an appreciation of the true nature of value should make it clear that this is out of the question. Valuation will always involve specific judgments and general assumptions.

SEQUENCES

One further class of assumptions will be discussed. At various points the accountant finds it necessary to adopt certain premises with respect to sequences of data and relationships between series of facts. For example, he commonly takes it for granted that a loss in asset value falls upon or extinguishes the most recently accumulated proprietorship. Thus, expirations are commonly charged first against gross earnings or the otherwise net earnings for the period; in the second place they are deducted from accumulated profits; and they are charged to the accounts showing original investment only as a last resort. In other words, losses are in general assumed not to have any effect upon original investment or capital until the entire amount of accumulated profit is absorbed.

This is evidently purely an assumption. It has been repeatedly pointed out in this study that no particular asset has any direct connection with a particular section of proprietorship. The residual equity simply represents an element in the asset total, it does not represent particular items. Consequently, when an asset disappears it would be just as reasonable, theoretically, to charge the amount against one proprietary account as another. In fact, as it is often the older assets which first expire or are lost, it might be argued that the accounts showing original investments should be used first in the recognition of losses.

This assumption appears entirely proper, however, when attention is focused upon the purposes which the accounts are designed to serve. The investors are interested in seeing the margin by which their original equity is increased. It is accordingly quite rational to retain the original figure unchanged, and show all variations, as far as possible, in supplementary accounts. Even in the case of loss in connection with an original asset—such, for example, as a loss on the sale of the securities of a subsidiary company which were purchased with the stockholders' initial funds—it would be more reasonable, for purposes of financial statements, to charge surplus rather than capital account.

The assumption that all disbursements to shareholders absorb earnings before tapping investment is a closely related postulate. A formal statement of this premise is found in the Revenue Act of 1921. In section 201 (b) it is held that every corporate distribution is made out of earnings and from the most recently accumulated earnings until the entire amount of the undivided profit has been extinguished. Numerous similar assumptions might be cited from this act and its supporting regulations.

Another assumption of this type which is widely adopted by the accountant is that units of raw materials or merchandise consumed or sold are always taken from the oldest in stock, or, to put it differently, that the inventory is always composed of the units most recently acquired. Here we have an assumption which is, quite obviously, not based on literal fact. It is perhaps true to some extent that the trader attempts to dispose of his oldest stock first, especially in the case of perishables; but in other cases quite the opposite holds. The oldest shipment of coal, brass castings, or of other raw materials is quite likely to be at the bottom of the bin.

A justification for this assumption may be found, however, in the fact that the accounts are thereby kept more nearly up to date from the standpoint of sound economics. One of the basic principles of economic reasoning is the law of single price. Another principle is that, in general, cost of replacement is the only cost which has any influence on the determination of price. In view of these laws the most reasonable interpretation of the "cost of goods on hand" is the cost of the most recently acquired lots up to the amount of the physical inventory.

The Bureau of Internal Revenue, it may be noted, has

adopted a similar rule of procedure in connection with the determination of taxable income from the sale of securities. The taxpayer who buys and sells securities, unless he can indentify specific lots sold, is obliged to treat blocks sold as arising from the earliest purchases.

The accountant makes use of many other assumptions of this type, but the foregoing illustrations will be sufficient to indicate the character of this class of premises.

In conclusion it may be reiterated that many of these fundamental propositions are incapable of any complete proof or demonstration. Indeed, some of them can be disproved from the standpoint of literal accuracy. Yet, in view of the conditions and purposes of accounting practice, they are, for the most part, entirely reasonable. They are largely assumptions of expediency, without which it would be impossible for the accountant to proceed.

The accountant should be thoroughly aware of his assumptions, however, else he is likely to forget the inherent limitations attaching to his exhibits and conclusions. Not only is accounting practice fraught with all kinds of serious technical perils but the entire structure of accounts and the recognized system of procedures is based upon assumptions. In view of this situation, a mild skepticism as to the reliability of accounting data and interpretations, still apparent on the part of some business men, may perhaps be pardoned. Accounting has taken long strides in recent years; the present interest in the subject is unparalleled. It is highly desirable, in the course of this rapid development, that the pillars of theory and practice be occasionally scrutinized and assayed, with a view to discovering precisely how firmly they are grounded.

INDEX

A

Abandonment,
 contrasted with replacement, 196
Account,
 advantages of parallel-column form, 105
 arrangement of columns in, 102
 balance sheet, 96–98
 divisions under each, 99–100
 fuel, closing the, 219
 fundamental requirements of, 96–101
 labor, closing the, 222
 net revenue, need for, 172
 parallel-column, 101–105
 relation of balance sheet to individual, 102–103
Accountant,
 his relation to valuation, 5
Accounting,
 and business cycle, 12
 and business enterprise, 16–21
 and management, 12–15
 and price fluctuations, 11
 constructive, 4
 cost, 13
 definition of, 3–6
 effect of income taxes upon, 14
 for socialistic unit, 26–27
 from social standpoint, 6–10
 from standpoint of student, 6
 governmental influence upon, 14–15
 present emphasis upon, 10–15
 relation of,
  to price system, 7–8
  to valuation, 5

Accounting—*Continued*
 rôle of, 6–10
Accounts,
 classification of, 205–217
 closing, 219–233
 current asset, 219–222
 expense and revenue, 142–170
 first step in construction of, 99
 functional classification of, 210–213
 importance of separating pluses and minuses in, 100–101
 mixed, 208–209
 overlapping of asset and expense, 206–210
 payable, as an equity, 112
 periodic analysis of, 218
 receivable,
  as an asset, 34
  as a current asset, 111
  validity of, as income determinant, 450–452
 statement classification of, 213–217
 supplementary, need for, 142–146
 valuation, 191–200, 400–423
 with current assets, 105–111
 with current liabilities, 111–112
Adams, H. C., 375
Advertising reserve, 237–239
Allowance,
 for depreciation, 191–196
  final allocation of, 195
  need for special account in connection with, 194
  recognition of, 192
 for uncollectibles, 197–198, 406–407
Annuity, analysis of, 236

501

INDEX

Appreciation, and revenue, 464–470
  in relation to,
    depreciation policy, 433–437
    surplus, 187
Appropriation of surplus, 184–186
Asset, account, arrangement of columns in, 102
  definition of, 30
  transactions, 116–123
Assets,
  changes in, accounting for, 143
  classification of, 31
  current,
    contrasted with fixed, 108–109, 214–216
    necessity for, 105–106
  deferred charges as, 216
  effects of operation upon, 99
  intangible, 35, 307–312
  kinds of, 30–31
  liquid, 216
  relation of,
    to capital, 35–36
    to equities of changes in, 94–96
    to wealth, 33–35
  tangible and intangible, 213–214
  types of changes, 92–93, 159–160
  working, 216
Auditing,
  as a branch of accounting, 5

B

Bad debts (See "Allowance, for uncollectibles")
Balance sheet,
  as conclusion of the double-entry system, 204
  as sole accounting device, 96–98
  as statement of financial condition, 485–489
  character of governmental, 49
  definition of, 44
  equation of, 43–49, 481–485
  headings on European, 83–84

Balance sheet—*Continued*
  relation of individual accounts to, 101–102
Belding, G., 44
Bondholder,
  as an owner, 77
  control of, 81
Bonds,
  contrasted with stocks, 79–80
  coupon, 71–72
  debenture, 72
  kinds of, 71
  mortgage, 72
  refunding of, 78
  registered, 72
  terminability of, 78
Bookkeeping,
  as a branch of accounting, 4–5
Borrowings, of owners, 355–360
Business enterprise,
  and accounting, 16–21, 472–477

C

Capital,
  maintenance of, 424–442
  relation of,
    to assets, 35–36
    to change in the value of money, 425–433
  stock (See also "Stock" and "Stocks")
  phases of, 372–399
Cash, 214
  as a criterion of revenue, 444–449
Collection, as a criterion of revenue, 444–449
Commissions on securities, 350–353
Completion,
  percentage of, as a criterion of revenue, 458–464
  physical, as a criterion of revenue, 455–458
Consumers' goods,
  as assets, 36
  relation of, to accounting, 21

INDEX

Contingent assets, 36
Contingent liabilities, 39
Contra accounts, 191–200
Contracts,
  as criterion of income, 453–454
Copeland, M. A., 95
Corporation,
  as an enterprise, 17–18, 68
  equities in case of, 68–75
Cost,
  accounting, development of, in relation to accounting, 13
  and income, 493–496
  as a basis for value, 293–295, 489–493
  economic, contrasted with expense, 255–256
Credit,
  definition of, 240
  transactions, 130–131
Creditor,
  corporate, 75–82
  significance of term in double-entry system, 241–243
Current assets (See "Assets")

D

Debit,
  meaning of term, 240
Debit and credit,
  and proprietorship, 245–247
  in terms of assets and equities, 247–248
  relation of, to debtor and creditor, 241–243
  rules for, 241–249
Debtor,
  use of term, in double entry, 241–243
Deficit, 179
Depreciation (see also "Allowance for depreciation")
  during construction, 340–344
  in relation to,
    appreciation, 433–437
    capital maintenance, 439–440

Dewing, A. S., 75, 80, 82
Discounts,
  on contractual securities, 415–423
  purchases, 410–415
    accrual of, 414
  sales, 402–410
  stock, 373–380
Dividends,
  in relation to interest, 267
  prior to operation, 297–301
  scrip, 398
  stock, 188–189, 389–399
    contrasted with cash dividend, 395–396
    reasons for, 391–393
    significance of, to shareholder, 393–394
Donations,
  of property, 129
  of stock, 386–389
Double entry,
  definition of, 139

E

Eisner V. Macomber, 76
Equation of assets and equities, 43–49, 481–485
  exceptions to, 47–49
Equities, 37–43
  corporate, 68–75
  effects of operation upon, 99
  importance of, 42–43
  in sole-proprietorships and partnerships, 61–68
  measurement of, 41
  of employees, 40–41
  of state, 39–40
  relation of, to type of organization, 42
  relation to assets of changes in, 93–95
Equity,
  account, arrangement of columns in, 102

Equity—*Continued*
  transactions, 123–126
Expenditure,
  relation of, to expense, 163, 445–446
Expense, 153–159
  as a one-column classification, 155
  charging of proprietary salaries to, 273–279
  contrasted with economic cost, 255–256
  definition of, 154
  determination of, in manufacturing, 156–157
  relation of,
    to cost incurred, 160–163
    to revenue, 154
  significance of, 155, 159
  subdivision of, 156
Expense and revenue,
  relation of to proprietorship, 167–170

F

Farm inventories,
  valuation of, 456
Fixed assets (See "Assets")
Floating debt,
  as a corporate equity, 74

G

Gain (See also "Revenue" and "Income")
  net, 175–176
Going concern, 478–480
Going value, 326–332
Goodwill,
  an analysis of, 313–317
  appreciation of, 325
  definition of, 313–314
  determination of, 324
  factors creating, 315
  in relation to,
    "producers' surpluses," 315

Goodwill—*Continued*
  in relation to—*Continued*
    security prices, 325–326
  treatment of,
    later, 324–325
    when not purchased, 317–321
    when purchased, 321–326
Governmental accounting, 25–26

H

Hardy, C. O., 80
Hatfield, H. R., 20, 51, 52, 167
Hepburn Act, 15
Household accounting, 22–23

I

Income (See also "Revenue" and "Net revenue")
  and cost accrual, 493–496
  as affected by appreciation, 441
  criteria of, 443–470
  prior to operation, 283–306
  sheet, net revenue division of, 269–270
Insolvency,
  relation of stockholders and bondholders to, 79–80
Instalment sales, 448
Intangibles, 307–312
Interest (See also "Discounts")
  adjustments, in case of proprietary loans, 360–364
  and dividends, 267
  as a cost, 270–271
  as net revenue, 174, 266–269, 306
  during construction, 285
    in case of public utility, 303–306
  on proprietary investment, 279–281
Inventories (See "Valuation" and "Income, criteria of")

INDEX

K

Keister, A. S., 71
Kester, R. B., 52

L

Labor,
  as an asset, 120
  purchased on account, 131–132
Liabilities (See also "Equities")
  accrued, 217
  and control, 57–58
  and title, 59
  current,
    in case of corporation, 74–75
    relation of, to net revenue, 260–264
Liquidity, 215
Loss,
  contrasted with asset, 178
  contrasted with expense, 177
Losses,
  capitalization of, 327–330
  effect of, upon proprietorship, 497
  preliminary, 344–348

M

Maintenance,
  of capital, 424–442
Merchandise account, 225–229
Money,
  change in value of, in relation to accounting values, 425–433
Mortgages,
  relation of, to situs of title, 58–59

N

Net revenue, 171–175, 253–281
  and current creditors, 263
  and current liabilities, 260–264
  and economic income, 258–259
  and interest, 266–269

Net revenue—*Continued*
  and labor services, 260–262
  and proprietary profit, 264–272
  and proprietary salaries, 273–279
  and rent, 263–264
  apportionment of, into economic elements, 276
  definition of, 88, 171–172, 253–254
  from managerial point of view, 259
  in a socialistic unit, 258
  in terms of assets, 254
  operating, 253–259
  point of view from which it should be defined, 169
  statement, 269–270
  transactions, 173
Net worth,
  as invested capital for tax purposes, 87
  statement, use of, 86

O

Obsolescence, reserve for, 183–184
Operation,
  fundamental effects of, 90–96
Organization costs, 333–340
Ownership (See also "Equities")
  and control, 55–57
  and possession, 55
  and title, 58–59
  in case of corporation, 69
  significance of, 54–61

P

Partners,
  loans to, 356–360
Partnership,
  as an enterprise, 18, 62
  equities in, 61–67
  legal aspects of, 62
  liabilities in, 65–66
Patents,
  valuation of, 320–321

Payroll (See also "Labor")
  accrued, 224
Percentage of completion,
  as an income determinant, 458–464
Perpetuities, 78
Postulates, 471–499
Premium,
  bond, 234–235
  stock, 189, 379 (See also "Stock, donated")
Prepaid interest (See "Discounts, on contractual securities")
Price movements,
  in relation to book values, 425–433
Profit (See also "Income," "Net revenue," and "Revenue")
  proprietary, in relation to net revenue, 264–272
Properties, 33–37 (See also "Assets")
Proprietary interest, 279–281
Proprietor,
  as owner, 57, 67
  as entrepreneur, 60
  in case of corporation, 75–82
Proprietorship (See also "Equities")
  and control, 57–58
  and economic distinctions, 60
  and liabilities, 50–89
  and title, 59
  as difference between assets and liabilities, 51
  as residual interest, 84–87
  in the balance-sheet equation, 50–54
  relation of, to debit and credit, 240–247
Public utility,
  interest during construction in case of, 303–306
  valuation in case of, 330–331
Purchases discounts 410–415

R

Rent,
  account, closing the, 229–233

Rent—*Continued*
  allowance for, on proprietary assets, 280–281
  in relation to net revenue, 263–264
Reorganization,
  exchanges of securities in, 152
Replacement,
  contrasted with abandonment, 196
Reserve,
  for depreciation, 191–196
  for fire loss, 189
  for sinking fund, 185–186
Reserves, 184
Responsibility,
  rules for debit and credit based on, 243–245
Revenue, 146–153
  analysis of, 152
  character of,
    criteria of, 443–470
    when gross, 149
    when net, 147–148
  deferred, 235
  gross, recording of, 151
  recording of, in balance sheet accounts, 150
  relation of, to equities, 152
Rindler, Milton, 72
Rules,
  for debit and credit, 241–249

S

Salaries,
  proprietary,
    in case of corporation, 278–279
    relation of, to income taxes, 369–370
Sale,
  and valuation at cost, 452–453
  credit, as a criterion of income, 449–455
  transaction,
    in terms of balance sheet, 133–136

INDEX

Sales,
  cost of, 144
  discounts, 402–410
    accrual of, 409–411
    as offsets to nominal revenue, 405
  instalment, 448
Securities, (See also "Equities")
  as an asset, 34–35
Services of owners,
  economic elements in, 272–273
Single entry, 46–47, 140
Sinking fund,
  entries establishing, 119
  reserve, 185–186
Sole-proprietorship,
  as an enterprise, 17–18
  equities in, 61–68
  liabilities in, 65–66
  viewpoints from which accounts may be organized in case of, 65–66
Sprague, C. E., 44, 47, 51, 88
Stock,
  common, as representing residual interest, 85–86
  discounts, 373–380
    elimination of, 375–379
  dividends, 188–189, 389–399
  donated, 386–389
  no-par, relation of, to property values, 349
  premium, 189–190
  treasury, 380–389
Stockholder,
  as creditor, 77–78
  as proprietor, 76
Stocks,
  and net worth, 86
  as a type of corporate equity, 69–71
  common, compared with preferred, 69–71
  contrasted with bonds, with respect to insolvency, 79–80
  exchanged for bonds, 125

Stocks—*Continued*
  in terminable enterprises, 79
  kinds of preferred, 70
  recent developments of preferred, 70–71
Surplus, 181–189
  donated, 190
  from appreciation, 187
  relation of, to assets, 186–187
  relation of, to cash, 185–186
  transactions, 183–184

T

Taylor, F. M., 60
Taxes,
  nature of, in accounting system, 179–181
Title,
  and mortgages, 58
  passage of, in merchandising, 59
  relation of, to ownership, 58–59
Transaction,
  definition of, 114
  the sale, analyzed, 133–136
Transactions,
  combination, 133–137
  credit, 130–131
  equity, 123–126
  explicit, 114
  formal, 115–116
  implicit, 115
  mixed, 137
  property, 116–123
  property-equity, 127–133

V

Valuation,
  accounts, 191–200, 400–423
    definition of, 191
    confusion of, with assets, 199
  and capital maintenance, 424–442
  and new investment, 364–368
  and securities, 348–353

Valuation—*Continued*
  at cost, in relation to income recognition, 452–453
  during preliminary period, 333–353
  in extractive industries, 455–457
  in public utilities, 330–331
  of property, at selling price, 289
  on a cost basis, 489–493
  relation of, to accounting, 5

Values, book,
  and price movements, 425–433
Van Cleave, C. M., 246

W

Wealth,
  relation of, to assets, 33–35
Working assets, 216
Work in process,
  recognition of, 119